H. G. Wells

PROPHET OF OUR DAY

BOOKS BY ANTONINA VALLENTIN

STRESEMANN

POET IN EXILE
The Life of Heinrich Heine

LEONARDO DA VINCI

MIRABEAU

THIS I SAW
The Life and Times of Goya

H. G. WELLS
Prophet of Our Day

H. G. Wells

H. G. Wells

PROPHET OF OUR DAY

by Antonina Vallentin

TRANSLATED BY DAPHNE WOODWARD

The John Day Company, New York

COPYRIGHT, 1950, BY THE JOHN DAY COMPANY

This book is published by The John Day Company, 62 West 45th Street, New York 19, N. Y., and on the same day in Canada by Longmans, Green & Company, Toronto

TRANSLATED FROM THE FRENCH

Manufactured in the United States of America

*To my dear friend Katherine Woods,
without whose help and encouragement
this book might not have appeared*

CONTENTS

IN JUSTIFICATION

SOME PEOPLE MAY object that it is too soon to bring out a book about H. G. Wells as writer, with an impartial appreciation of his work and influence, and too late to pay a tribute of friendship to his memory. Indeed, I had first intended only to tell, in a long essay, what manner of man he was. But as the work went on, I perceived that through Wells there flowed all those currents of thought upon which our century has been tossed. He was so infinitely sensitive to the changes taking place around us, so far ahead of our time and yet so closely, so intensely present in it, that he sums up its whole content. He *is* the history of our day. To study his personality from every side and to delve again into his writings is to bring more than half a century back to life without seeking further. That is the purpose of this book.

Wells himself realized that he was placed at a viewpoint from which he could embrace the widest possible stretch of horizon. In one of his last works, *The Outlook for Homo Sapiens,* he said that his role in life had been to assemble such facts and interpretations of facts as had influenced man's power to control the future, so that he felt no need to apologize for having charted the course of the thoughts that had passed through his mind during his last fifty years. He was, indeed, the turntable of our fast-and-faster spinning epoch.

But he was something more than a particularly clear cross section of humanity, more than a mere summary of trends of thought. He was the leaven of our day. The lesson that emerges from his achievements and his failures can be applied to every instance of creative impatience and to all the aspirations of men of good will.

When he was outstripped by events, it was only because they

crowded forward too rapidly, dwindling from anticipations into things of the past. Real life, with its whirlwind pace, often caught up with him—usually to the misfortune of mankind. The currents of thought that had been fed by his intrepid mind flowed on, sometimes, to leave him behind; his influence was exerted secretly, in great measure, over generations of young people who were so impatient that they never perceived what stimulus he had given them. He scattered seed by the handful; it often sank so deep into fertile ground that the succeeding harvest had no heed of him.

He was more, however, than a great influence, a stimulus to intellectual progress. And today he is by no means a figure of the past. His words have not yet exhausted their meaning. Death has not been able to silence the urgency of his falsetto voice, the mighty rage of his warnings and his angry compassion. The aim of this book is, in the first place, to seek out the meaning of his insistent message to mankind.

His eventful life and his very marked personality lie beyond the bounds of his work. No mere tribute of friendship could have done justice to what was most individual in him. But no detached observer could have followed him up in all his contradictory ramifications. To those who met him only in passing, he often showed little but his defects. To have known him for years was not enough, perhaps, to bring understanding of him; real affection was needed too, not in order to take the best possible view of him, but in order to look into the background of his personality and see him stand out in the round.

While writing this book I never felt that I was speaking of a man who was dead and gone. From beyond death, H. G. Wells was once again transmitting to me the impatient thrill of his vitality. I do not in the least believe that I have been laying wreaths on a tomb. The thought that he had ceased to live seemed so ridiculous that I just dismissed it from my mind. Humanity's terrible neck-and-neck race against destruction is still going on. H. G. Wells is still scanning the peril-clouded horizon.

H. G. Wells

PROPHET OF OUR DAY

I

THE BACK STAIRS

"I CAME UP from the poor in a state of flaming rebellion, most blasphemous and unsaintly," H. G. Wells wrote in one of his last books. He never quite got over this early rebelliousness. He never forgot anything that poverty had taught him. He never drew a veil of false sentimentality across the difficult years of his childhood, as the self-made man is apt to do. He describes them with all their sordid penury in his *Experiment in Autobiography,* and several of his novels—*Tono-Bungay* in particular—draw freely upon personal memories.

He was the son of a housemaid and a gardener, who had gone into a precarious business as small shopkeepers, not through any urge for independence but because they had lost the employment in which they had been perfectly happy. His mother looked upon "service," dependency, as heaven, a haven of security; it represented all she had known of kindness and beauty, the romantic element in her life, the light that still shone through the gloom of her poverty-stricken days.

It was a freak of heredity that this woman, cast in the mold of servitude, should give birth to a son whose spirit was remarkably impatient of constraint. Wells describes her in his autobiography with a gruff tenderness all his own, and with boundless pity. But she also served to some extent as a model for George Ponderevo's mother in *Tono-Bungay,* the novel through which he vented much of his youthful defiance. He shows her as helpless in the face of real life, from the moment she lost the guidance of higher authority to which she had always given implicit obedience. Used to working among many other servants at certain limited tasks, she was quite overwhelmed by the responsibilities of running her own house, for, as her son says, people of that kind do not possess the slightest initiative or power of learning.

Having often gone hungry in his childhood, Wells had an abiding dislike of bustling housewives such as Mr. Polly's wife, Miriam, who combine "earnestness of spirit with great practical incapacity." Sarah Wells, like Miriam, displayed that indifference toward food so general among the lower classes in England, which amounts to an unconscious mortification of the flesh. Like Mr. Polly, the little boy was driven into a state of bad temper by the battle that his stomach had to wage against a diet both insufficient and indigestible, tasteless and lacking in nourishment. Also, though he remembered how his mother wore her fingers to the bone in mending the family's clothes, he could not forget that the stitches she put into the knees and heels of his garments were huge and clumsy. Childish humiliations are slow to fade, and his memory kept a vivid record of the day when he and his brothers first protested against the suits she always tailored for them with her own hands, and which made them, the laughingstock of their young neighbors.

It was these apparently insurmountable difficulties, thrusting themselves into his daily life, that set Wells dreaming about a future that should be free of domestic slavery, about big, bright, bare rooms with no corners to collect dust. The cracked linoleum that his mother, on her knees, toiled in vain to polish was to give him the idea of that unknown substance, smooth and shining, which in centuries to come would be spread over the floors and walls of every house. The ungainly patches of which he was so ashamed, and the pathetic sight of his mother as she bent mournfully over a heap of threadbare garments, suggested to him the figure of the tailor equipped with instruments that enable him to produce, in the twinkling of an eye, a fine suit of clothes for the Awakened Sleeper.

Owing to her grim energy, Sarah Wells, despite her limitations, was the chief figure in the home, the decisive influence in young Herbert's life. The father, Joseph Wells, several years his wife's junior, was even more bewildered than she by their enforced independence. As a gardener or undergardener, he was naturally fond of open-air life, flowers, and fruit; fond of sport, too, particularly swimming and, above all, cricket—the red-letter days in his calendar were those on which his team had won a match. He must have felt some stirrings of unrest, some vague ambition, for at times he talked of emigrating

to America or Australia. But he was one of those vacillating creatures
who never get further than making plans. As to the sorry commercial
venture into which he had launched himself, he was utterly unsuited
for it. With no instinct or liking for business, he went downhill, un-
resisting, as though unconscious of his family's straits; his incompetence
protected him, as it were, against any feeling of remorse. He played
only a small part in the lives of his children, who were given over to
their mother's muddleheaded tyranny. But though Joseph Wells seems
to have looked forward to bankruptcy with the same resignation as
Mr. Polly, he never admitted himself to be a failure. He simply avoided
unpleasant arguments. He seized every chance of escaping from his
cheerless home and his querulous wife. He never thought twice about
leaving the shop unattended, and one day it was invaded by a flock
of sheep, which trampled his stock of china to smithereens. But his
happy-go-lucky nature made him proof against such mishaps, and he
continued to lounge in doorways, arguing loudly with the neighbors
and guffawing with laughter.

Still, it must have been from this noisy, jovial, and shiftless father
that H. G. Wells inherited a gift for dreaming. Joseph Wells was inarticulate; he never told his sons about his own particular method of
escape. But one day, many years later, he happened to take a country
walk with H. G., and he pointed out to him a certain hill where
he used to go as a lad to look at the stars. His youngest son carried
in his mind from that day the picture thus tardily imprinted there—
the picture of a man lying, the long night through, stretched out on the
grass, gazing up at the stars, and dreaming of vague and wonderful
things. It was his happiest memory of his father.

The gloomiest factor in Wells's childhood was the house where,
on September 21, 1866, he was born, in a narrow lane off the High
Street of Bromley, in Kent, now a suburb of London. A tall, thin
building, it too seemed to be straining up toward an independence that
it could never achieve. There were only two small rooms, one front,
one back, on each of its three floors, which were linked by a dangerously steep and narrow staircase. The real life of the house went
on in the basement-kitchen, whose only light, filtering through a barred
window level with the sidewalk, was streaked by the shadows of feet
passing outside. The only warmth the little boy ever felt came from
the kitchen stove. Coal was a luxury in that needy household; and he
remembered his mother struggling to lift the heavy black buckets.

The sense of the value of fuel was to remain with Wells all his life. He used to confess, with a wry smile, that in one or another of the many well-staffed houses that he owned later on, he would sometimes get up in the middle of the night to throw ashes on the fire—an absurd reflex of economy left over from his childhood.

He never lost his memories of filth, memories of crushed bugs (the house was infested with them), cockroaches, and the smell of the disinfectants used in the hopeless struggle against these and other vermin. His playground was a narrow, fetid yard reeking of latrines and garbage. But at one side of this yard, in a crack between two of the bricks that paved it, beneath withered cabbage leaves, dirty water, and cinders, Joseph Wells had planted a creeper, which he tended with all the obstinacy of a countryman cut off from nature. The creeper was absurdly energetic; it climbed up the crumbling wall and even tried to break into flower—symbol of a fond dream, a strange kinship with the round-faced, towheaded little boy below, exploring the ash cans for some shining treasure of battered tin.

The house was nicknamed Atlas House, from a small figure of Atlas that stood among the crockery in the shopwindow. And Atlas House cast its shadow across the whole of Wells's existence; the nightmare is even recalled in the huge statue of Atlas that dominates the council chamber in *When the Sleeper Wakes*. The wretchedness of life in that house was not only due to privation, to cold, and to hunger. It was made far worse by constraint and humiliation, by the effort to adapt oneself to an unnatural state of things. Sarah Wells wore herself out in trying to keep up appearances. Behind the chinashop was a parlor which she looked upon as the symbol of middle-class respectability; the furniture was ill matched and the carpet threadbare, but still it was a parlor, reserved for the leisure hours that she never indulged in. It was a deserted parlor, for Sarah Wells kept to herself. She would not let her boys play with the children of their working-class or shopkeeping neighbors who, she said, were rowdy and badly brought up. She also gave it to be understood that she had a servant, another middle-class convention, and the children were strictly forbidden to tell anybody that she herself did all the housework. They were also forbidden to take off their jackets and reveal their patched shirts.

With fanatical insistence she made her family obey all the unwritten rules of Victorian society, as seen from the viewpoint of a domestic servant, rules which were very often beyond her own understanding.

Herbert George, the youngest son, came in for the chief share of this sort of thing. Two years before he was born Sarah had lost a nine-year-old daughter, her eldest child, the only reminder of those bright hopes with which she and her husband had begun their life together. The tears she shed for the quiet, sweet-natured little girl were made more bitter by all that fate had denied her, by the misfortunes of her marriage, by hardship in the present, and by fears for the future. She let herself sink into grief, as though welcoming the excuse to turn her back on a world she had found too difficult.

When her youngest son was born, she accepted him as a consolation prize from heaven. Her awkward tenderness and disappointed hopes were now concentrated on him. Herbert George, Bertie, grew up in an atmosphere of vague ambition that seemed out of keeping with his squalid surroundings. A false light was shed upon his sad, childish universe by the reflected conventions, the confusing taboos, the futile pretenses that followed each other, at his mother's will, across the back-cloth of their dreary existence.

He declared later that the prejudices of that period were strengthened in him by his backstairs upbringing. But though at first he was infected by these prejudices, his exceptional temperament led him into early revolt against them. Sarah Wells tried to pass on to her sons her own simple faith in an all-powerful God—a faith that had been shaken by her little girl's death, but had later reasserted itself all the more strongly. H. G. describes the effect her teaching produced upon him. At first he had no doubts, but was filled with indignation against a God who watched out for human weakness and punished backsliders with hell-fire. This struck him as unfair and his sense of justice was outraged. Soon his hatred for what he called the "Old Sneak" led him to a conviction that the whole thing was simply a fake, "a trick of sham self-immolation."

He horrified his mother by assailing the articles of faith with that mockery which, though he did not yet know it, was his strongest weapon. This childish attack on religion was his first attempt to breach the walls that hemmed him in.

During this period, he says, he was "a prodigy of Early Impiety."

His mother's respect for the nobility and gentry reached its highest point in that natural reverence for royalty which, among the English public, takes the form of a lively curiosity about everything connected with the reigning house.

Wells was that very rare phenomenon, an English republican. It is hard to understand why he supported such a hopeless cause, except by remembering that he was ridding himself of a complex engendered in his childhood by his mother's tedious and unbounded admiration for Queen Victoria.

Bertie Wells was fourteen years old when he first came into contact with the world in which his mother used to earn her living. There had been a disaster in the family. His father, while pruning the creeper in the yard, had fallen and broken his leg. Thereupon, poverty had become still deeper and hunger still sharper at Atlas House. It was only when Frank, the eldest brother, brought home his first meager earnings that little Bertie was able to have a new pair of shoes.

But not long after this, the gates of her lost paradise reopened for Sarah Wells. She went back, as housekeeper, to Up Park, a big country place where she had formerly been housemaid. During the school holidays, or when they were out of work, her sons descended upon the estate. The back stairs became an impressive reality for the youngest boy, to whom Up Park was a complete and authentic universe, a small-scale model of the outside world. It was the original of Bladesover in *Tono-Bungay,* where Wells describes life as it was led in the housekeeper's room, and echoes the talk he used to overhear in his childhood.

In the Up Park–Bladesover universe, which a deaf and aged spinster governed as though by divine right, each human being had his place allotted to him at birth, to be his unchangingly and forever, like the color of his eyes. The staff had their own social system, which they carried to the point of absurdity. The servants' hall was a reflection, seen in a distorting mirror, of the world abovestairs; its inhabitants had their different ranks, and these were respected with fanatical exactitude. The butlers and lady's maids of the big houses knew quite as much as their employers about family connections, changes of title, and rights of succession. Toward social climbers they were even less indulgent than their masters. And the whole lower middle class, the villagers, the local shopkeepers, were zealous in helping them to preserve this almost feudal state of things, unaltered since the seventeenth century.

"The ideas of democracy, of equality, and above all of promiscuous fraternity have certainly never really entered into the English mind," writes Wells in *Tono-Bungay*. The book was published in 1909, and for a long time after its appearance the social framework still remained unshaken. In the course of the last twenty years the long-delayed changes have come with the rush of a landslide, for the ground was already undermined.

"I have written of England," says Wells again, "as a feudal scheme overtaken by fatty degeneration and stupendous accidents of hypertrophy." The symbol of that scheme—the country mansion where the little boy must keep to the back stairs—decided his future development. "In a sense," admits his double, George Ponderevo, "Bladesover has never left me: it is . . . one of those dominant explanatory impressions that make the framework of my mind."

Trotsky tells in his memoirs of a talk that Lenin had with Wells, whom he declared afterward to be hopelessly bourgeois. But if Wells was a bourgeois, it was not in the sense in which Lenin used the word, but in the eighteenth-century sense: a member of the Third Estate, out to destroy the feudal system. In that respect, he had lagged behind the social evolution of the day.

Like so many of the foreigners who at various times took refuge in England, Lenin did not understand that the average Englishman had a long way to go before catching up with twentieth-century ideas. Wells himself had passed through a stage corresponding to the French Revolution, and had lingered there in the uncompromising, stubborn manner that was usual with him. He never quite came to terms with what the English call Society.

His success led to his mingling with the sort of people he had glimpsed through half-open doors at Up Park, or peered at from behind the bushes in the grounds; but perhaps he could not forgive them for having seemed so godlike in those days. His mutinous attitude had something childishly ostentatious about it. He remained incurably distrustful of those who claimed to judge the world from the heights of their own well-established position. Very early memories were always at hand to remind him how narrow was their universe, how sheltered from the sordid realities of life.

In a dispute with Winston Churchill about Russia, which took place early in 1921, Wells, not content with fighting his opponent's arguments, attacked "his naïve belief that he belongs to a class of particularly gifted and privileged human beings" to whom the lives and affairs of ordinary men were simply the raw material of a brilliant career. Wells also had something of that touchiness which constantly leads the self-made man to suspect allusions to his origin. He alleged, elsewhere in their dispute, that Churchill looked upon it as insolence for an ordinary man like him to express opinions about matters of state.

He was easily annoyed by those scions of the aristocracy who believed they had a natural right to govern a world of which they knew only the easy and pleasant side. He was sometimes unjust to them, in a way that puzzled those who could not guess the cause of his irritation. He was particularly exasperated by the so-called Oxford accent. His own speech, especially in moments of ill temper, had a touch of the cockney, though so slight as to be unnoticeable except to English ears; and his falsetto voice sometimes took on tones that made an uncouth contrast to the quiet restraint of English conversation.

One day at a party, he made a fierce attack on someone who was perfectly sincere and well intentioned—misinterpreting him deliberately, as it seemed, and contradicting his statements with calculated malevolence.

"But why do you dislike me so much, Mr. Wells?" his victim suddenly asked, blushing as grown men blush only in England. For a moment Wells stared at him, dumfounded. Then he launched into an impassioned diatribe against the dim-wittedness of diplomats in general and hereditary diplomats in particular. The man who had thus enraged him was a member of the Foreign Office and the son of an ambassador, and it was his voice, with its Balliol accent, that had jarred on Wells's nerves. As his opponent listened to the onslaught, pity mingled with his growing surprise and contempt. How, he wondered, could such a famous man show such ill breeding?

In fact, English society, of which Wells disapproved, never really accepted him. This had nothing to do with his humble birth. For instance, though Ramsay MacDonald was the son of a washerwoman, society found him perfectly eligible. His outward appearance was of a familiar type, and his mind was ready to submit without argument to all the proper taboos and rules of behavior. Wells, on the contrary, made a point of displaying his plebeian manners, struck at deep-seated prejudices, talked freely about subjects that it was "not done" to mention, and, in general, smilingly laid himself out to shock his hearers.

His backstairs upbringing seems to have bred a kind of inverted snobbery in him. Not content with refusing all the honors that were offered to him at various times, he used to break the most harmless rules of the social game, often without any provocation. "If only your father had been a gentleman," Sarah Wells would lament, but in vain; despite his remarkable career, her youngest son never became the gentleman she would have liked to make of him. Toward the end of his life he said of himself, "I am a scientific aristocrat, but I am no gentleman." The chief obstacle to his becoming one was the fact that he had no *bosse du respect* (bump of respect), a French expression that always made him laugh. He used to declare that no typical cockney, such as himself, could be a respecter of persons, or could sincerely entertain the notion that he might be inferior to any human being whatever.

By thus flinging a challenge to the world at the top of his high-pitched voice, Wells avenged the humiliations of his childhood.

II

THE BATTLE FOR EDUCATION

H. G. WELLS never tired of declaring that immense changes had taken place in the English educational system during the past century.

Little Bertie Wells was a pale, underfed boy, about seven years old, when he went to school for the first time. His small face, with its indecisive features—the narrowed, lively eyes, the button of a nose perched high above the mouth with its straight, mobile upper lip— was polished for the occasion until it shone like a new penny. He was to find at Bromley the same educational conditions and the same spirit from which Charles Dickens had suffered more than thirty years earlier.

There were indeed, by that time, some state schools in England. They had been hastily set up after the passing of the Elementary Education Act of 1871, but the little town of Bromley had nothing but one old-fashioned private school. While the state schools were inspired by the nineteenth-century spirit, this particular private school was a survival from the eighteenth century. It was exactly suited to the ideas of Sarah Wells and the order of things at Up Park, which flung its shadow over the inhabitants of Atlas House. It called itself an academy, the better to impress the lower middle-class parents whose sons attended it. It was run, in complete freedom, by a man with no university training and, in fact, nothing whatever to qualify him as a teacher. He had previously been usher in another school, and the only point on which he was clear was that discipline must be maintained among his pupils, of whom there were about thirty. His ignorance had no doubt prevented him from taking up any work for which special training was needed. But he was careful to display the outward signs of his profession—top hat, frock coat, and white tie.

Looking back at those days, Wells is unusually indulgent toward his first schoolmaster. He credits him with some degree of intellectual curiosity, which had grown on him as he taught his pupils, and with a taste for "certain mental exercises." But despite this tolerant attitude Thomas Morley still remains the fantastic figure of a medieval domi-nie, who considered the thirty young minds entrusted to his care as his private property, with which he could do as he chose.

No public health officer ever came to inspect and protest against this makeshift school, with its one big, dark, dusty classroom where the windows were never opened. To the pale-faced urchin it made no change from his drab, airless home, while the master's bad manners were those to which he was accustomed in his own circle. And after all, this vulgar, uneducated man held the key to a world of wonders.

Before being sent to school, the boy had discovered, thanks to a broken leg, the blessing of books, chosen at random and read greedily. This, the easiest way of escape known to mankind, was the miracle of his childhood. In later years he admitted that if that accident had never happened, he might have left behind him nothing more than the memory of a weary shop assistant, dismissed from his job and fi-nally buried.

A world he had never dreamed of was now thrown open to him. Distant landscapes passed before his eyes, colored men and strange animals became familiar sights, his eager gaze was lifted toward the stars, and certain great figures stood out from past epochs. The grimy walls of Atlas House no longer bounded his universe. He felt a great hunger now, a hunger for knowledge which was never to be satisfied. But he fed his mind haphazardly, to the point of indigestion, under the guidance of Thomas Morley.

Wells later summed up the intellectual equipment of a thirteen-year-old boy, considered to have finished his education and to be ready to take his place in the world. A boy who was no precocious genius, whose only unusual feature was a passionate curiosity. This curiosity remained with Wells all his life as a sign of perpetual youth.

His childish universe was based on the conviction that it was "a matter of general congratulation" to have been born English. His spiritual development, the rapid widening of his horizon, and perhaps an unconscious reaction against this first belief prompted him in later years to declare his faith in internationalism, which took the place of a religion for him. But in fact, within Wells, the most earnest and uncompromising cosmopolitan of our day, there always lurked something of the little boy who believed in the superiority of his race. Though he made himself the prophet of a world religion, he remained a typical Englishman. He was sharply attacked by English nationalists and Conservatives because of his international outlook. One of his harshest detractors accused him of hating England, of being "one of those thinkers who think against their own country." Yet Wells's satire has none of the fierce bitterness of Swift, with its underlying strain of despair. Through his criticism peeps affection, or at any rate a secret amusement. He has the indulgent outlook of a close relation, a kind of tacit fraternity. He was so familiar with the state of mind he criticized that his attacks have a slight air of complicity, or even of compassion. He knew that he himself might easily have remained one of those middle-class Englishmen, obstinately enclosed in the narrow circle of their traditional notions. If his progress had been stopped at any point, he too might have frozen into one of the ridiculous attitudes that he was making fun of. Many of Wells's comic figures are drawn from among the enemy ranks; but many others embody outgrown stages in his own development, skins grown too tight and that he had been able to cast off. His path is strewn with the corpses of former prejudices and the fragments of shattered beliefs. As he went on his way he gave them an angry glance, and a knowing wink.

While calling up visions of a world where frontiers would no longer exist, he carried around with him the frontiers of his own country, and all the limitations and virtues that they encircled. Perhaps that was the secret of his strength. Perhaps it was just because his roots went so deep into the ground that he was able to travel so far and rise to such heights. Though in his own country he passed for a hotheaded rebel, he was attached to it by the strongest of bonds, and to this was due an underlying stability that nothing could destroy.

Even in appearance he was a typical Englishman. Looking at the early photographs which show him as a solemn little boy in a Sunday suit of rough serge, his rather short arms folded on the table in front of him, whereon lies an open book, we feel at once, without quite knowing why, that he must be English. Is it because of the exaggeratedly long space between the nose and the upper lip, or is it the deliberately blank expression on the round, fair-skinned face?

The sturdiness that his little body inherited from a line of ancestors who were in the habit of living to a hale and hearty old age had overcome the privations of Atlas House. Sarah Wells had guarded him against rickets, from which her elder children had suffered, by copious doses of cod-liver oil.

Like all lively boys the world over, Bertie Wells was thrilled at the thought of warfare and heroic deeds. He saw himself as Napoleon or Cromwell. Plots of waste ground in the town were the scenes of imaginary but bloodthirsty battles. He was often cold, and still more often hungry; but he whistled cheerily as he went on his way, because he was riding in triumph through some captured city, with his gallant dragoons clattering behind him.

As a grown man, he still remembered the lurid glories of this make-believe warfare. He bought his children quantities of lead soldiers, just like those in the shopwindows at which little Bertie used to gaze so longingly. He played with them too, now, to make up for having missed them before. Marshalling the troops that a towheaded little boy had commanded, fighting pitched battles with cannon, he enjoyed himself hugely under cover of amusing the youngsters. As he never did anything by halves, and always intermingled his work and his dreams, he gradually developed this game into a kind of model warfare. For the benefit of the many children whose warlike imaginings were apt to fade vaguely away, he set out the rules in a booklet dedicated to "boys and girls of all ages" and entitled *Little Wars*. It was published just before the outbreak of World War I, which was to put a stop forever to his childish dreams of strategy and his games with toy soldiers.

As a lad of thirteen Wells was, as it were, borne along on the crest of the waves over which Britannia ruled. Not a single doubt had as yet come to trouble the stability of the empire on which the sun never set. Though the boy might be roused to defiance by fulsome admiration of Queen Victoria, he could not escape the atmosphere of complacency that prevailed everywhere during her reign. The immense self-satisfaction of Victorian England had perhaps more Germanic than Anglo-Saxon elements about it. The influence of the Prince Consort, perhaps never fully realized, made itself felt in the most subtle ways. He seems to have taught the English to respect the splendid minor virtues of his own countrymen—their placid solemnity, unalloyed by any trace of humor, their passion for hard work, their self-righteous belief that success would come to them by the will of heaven and the strength of their own merits, and their insidious conviction that any race with Germanic affinities was of the salt of the earth. There was nothing in the formation of the British character that could counterbalance this German element.

During their two centuries of aggressive Protestantism, the English had become deeply distrustful of popery; their spiritual universe had been swept clear of all mystical dreams, all tendency toward self-effacement or self-surrender. The defeat of France in 1870 was dimly connected with this spiritual weakening, it was a sign of Latin decadence. "England was consciously Teutonic at that time," notes Wells. (It should not be forgotten that the whole of his generation was brought up in this more or less conscious admiration of Germany, and that Heidelberg was to the English intellectuals of those days what the Sorbonne had been to their forerunners in the Middle Ages.) Another phenomenon which comes into the same category, and has been too quickly forgotten, was the concept of Aryanism, which spread so widely in England that it even entered the heads of the lower-class boys who attended Thomas Morley's academy.

The fact that the English were at first inclined to be indulgent toward Hitler's doctrines is due, as in the case of Wells, to certain amused remembrances of their childhood. Recalling these toward the end of 1933, Wells admitted to having held, in his early days, ideas about Aryans which were "extraordinarily like Mr. Hitler's." The more he inquired into the matter, he declared, the more convinced he became that the Führer's mentality was almost the twin of what his own had been at the age of thirteeen, around 1879; but expressing itself through a megaphone and organized for practical ends.

Owing to a sense of proportion which is the very basis of English humor, Wells refused for a long time to pay any serious heed to the childish ranting that went on in the totalitarian countries. He believed that Hitler and Mussolini were only pimples on the adolescent face of humanity, and would vanish as humanity grew up.

But what else helped to fill the world of a lad whose school days, in the then state of things, were to all intents and purposes at an end? Wells says that Mr. Polly's mind, when he left his private school at fourteen, was in a state of inextricable confusion, and that he had "lost much of his natural confidence, so far as figures and sciences and languages and the possibilities of learning things were concerned." It was of his eldest brother that Wells was thinking when he described Mr. Polly, but his own memories of Thomas Morley's school were drawn upon too.

So Wells's "blasphemous and unsaintly" rebelliousness was directed in the first place against the defective educational system. Over and over again in his books we come across victims of that intellectual starvation from which he himself had suffered so terribly. Those whom the schools sent away with their minds hungry or crippled are favorite subjects with him. He pours out over them the full flood of his righteous anger and his immense pity. Within the prosperous author of later days, the floundering schoolboy lived on just as vividly as the unhappy little fellow of the preschool years.

At the age of thirteen he was thirsting for knowledge, and when the school doors closed behind him, forever, as it seemed, his fury was as great as his perplexity. Wells's various pictures of an ideal social state all have one thing in common: as well as a long period of schooling for children, they all offer the chance of further study to those grownups who, like himself, wish to keep on learning throughout their lives. With the fervor of the self-educated, Wells gave to education the foremost place in social life. He believed that the evils of his own time all had their roots in the educational system, which he considered to be still fitted to the period when people traveled on foot or horseback and everything was made by hand. The world was expanding rapidly, but at thirteen years old he had only gained the same sketchy notion of it that schools had been providing for the past half century.

He never forgot the rages and frustrations of his childhood. He never gave up his fight to improve the educational system. Among all the responsibilities that he felt called upon to assume in the course of his life, this was the chief, the sacred mission. In *The Undying Fire* he proclaims the task of the educator to be the greatest of all human tasks. That is the guiding principle of his work. His realistic novels, the tragicomedies in which he shows us men and women whose brains have been stunted by faulty schooling, his pictures of future Utopian states, and his popular scientific works, all help to put forward the same urgent plea. It was impossible, he pointed out, to build up a new civilization with millions of minds formed in the ancient mold, a material as dangerous, in its utter, disastrous inertia, as the sand that slides down to bury a newly cut, hollow road.

Like the eighteenth-century thinkers, he believed that the spread of enlightenment would put everything right. And in spite of numberless disappointments, his ardor never diminished. He never ceased to wage this primordial battle of his life, he never ceased to wish that his fellow men would become as engrossed with education as he was himself.

III

THE TADPOLE LEAVES THE WATER

WHEN SARAH WELLS made plans for her youngest son to mount the social ladder, she never even gave a thought to its lowest rungs—domestic servants, farm laborers, workingmen. Halfway between these and the gentry stood the clerk or shop assistant, whose black jacket and white collar were the emblems of his higher rank. Individual talent or lack of talent for this kind of work was not to be taken into account.

Joseph Wells still hobbled listlessly around his shop, but he was on the verge of bankruptcy. Soon he would give up his attempt at independence and settle down to live near Up Park, on money that his wife put aside for him out of her wages. So the helpless little woman was left with the entire responsibility for a husband and three sons. For the time being she herself was safe. But her strength had been worn down by years of sordid toil. Honest and well-meaning, she had shown herself to be quite a good housemaid, but she was hardly fitted to rule as housekeeper over a large staff. She was confused by the need to organize things here, just as she had been overwhelmed by the simple task of running her own home. Her sums would never come out right, and when her youngest son visited her he always had to straighten her accounts.

But pride in the dignity of her new situation made her blind to the fact that it was really too much for her. Owing to the complicated mechanism of a big place like Up Park, her employer took some time to become aware of the old housekeeper's defects. And in any case she was absolutely loyal. Thanks to this quality, she kept her situation for thirteen years, even after she had become deaf and was obviously failing.

A boy who had turned thirteen could not possibly go on living at his mother's expense. It was high time for him to make his own way in the world. But little Bertie did not seem to have a proper understanding of that harsh law. He had no say as to what work he should take up, neither had his brothers been given any choice when their turn came. They were like all the children of the poorer classes, "three tadpoles taken out of the water before their legs and lungs would act properly."

Human society was neither so patient nor so resourceful as mother nature. The human tadpole must fend for himself, or die. Bertie as yet knew nothing about social injustice. He had too much vitality to sink into resignation as his elder brothers had done, but he did not fling himself into a hopeless struggle. Joseph Wells had passed on to his sons his own lack of fighting spirit. They had inherited his faculty for bowing, silently and good-humoredly, before the inevitable. But he had also gifted them with his capacity for spiritual escape. His youngest son seems to have been granted an especially large share of this.

The day came when the pale, pasty-faced lad, wearing a threadbare suit and a black velvet cap, found himself suddenly installed as apprentice in a draper's shop at Windsor. He spent his time sweeping out the shop; cleaning the windows; or, perched on a high stool at the cash desk, taking money, giving change, and keeping account of it all. Ten hours' work a day. At night, he shared a dormitory with other apprentices and with the senior shop assistants. His scanty meals were eaten in the same company. A merciless, hopeless grind, with no possible end in sight. He felt he would never get used to the monotony of this existence. He made no protest, he just let his thoughts wander. He refused to make the slightest effort. His awakened mind closed up like an oyster when confronted with these horrible surroundings and unpleasant tasks. (All through his life Wells retained this ability to step aside from disagreeable contacts with reality; he had a genius for withdrawing himself when too many difficulties were closing in upon him.)

He now took refuge in vague, aimless dreaming. His whole fortune consisted of sixpence a week pocket money. But he handled the sums paid over to him at the cash desk with complete indifference. He took it as a matter of course that the amount found in the till at closing time never corresponded, "not even accidentally," to the total of his entries in the register. He was to endow many of the characters in his novels with this absent-mindedness, which he liked to describe by the French word, *rêverie*.

But it was his inattentiveness that rescued little Bertie from the slavery to which his brothers succumbed. He was fired; and he left the draper's shop, with no regret, but with no pleasure either, because he knew that much the same thing would be waiting for him somewhere else.

Then came a brief pause—brief, but with a decisive effect on his future. A friend of Sarah's, vaguely related by marriage to one of her cousins, was moved by Sarah's dismay at finding Bertie on her hands again, and offered to take charge of him for the time being. This "uncle" had been through many adventures, one of which had cost him an arm. He had traveled in foreign parts; taught school, without any qualifications whatever, in the West Indies; and when he came back to settle down in England, had opened a factory, but soon lost every penny he had put into it. For a long time the teaching profession had been the refuge of the unsuccessful, and after the failure of his plans for getting rich quick, Uncle Williams took up schoolmastering again.

But as ill luck would have it, the Education Department was beginning to show curiosity about the standard of learning of its elementary schoolteachers, and Uncle Williams was turned out of his post after a few months. Still, they were months that taught some useful lessons to the bewildered and unemployed Bertie. H. G. Wells had a natural urge to share with others any knowledge that came his way. A piece of experience, a fresh notion, a wider view of some particular subject never seemed really to belong to him until he had passed it on and given someone else the benefit of it. It was by trying to spread his ideas around him that he himself made progress. The pedagogic virus was in his blood.

He realized this for the first time while acting as pupil-teacher in support of that self-appointed headmaster, his uncle. He took the job very seriously, and carried it out with youthful severity and precision. The gates of the paradise of learning, which had closed behind him forever as it seemed, were slowly opening again.

Filled with relief at having escaped from a prison of boredom, he began to become aware of himself. He was gaining something more than just the satisfaction of doing work for which he had a natural talent. The adventurous Uncle Williams gave him his first feeling of release from the narrow world of Sarah Wells. Stories of travel, of adventures in far-off countries, descriptions of strange, outlandish ways of life revealed a new universe to a lad who until then had been content to maneuver imaginary armies on stretches of waste ground.

But his rescuer did more for him than open a window in the wall of a stifling London suburb. Like Joseph Wells and, later, his eldest son Frank, Uncle Williams was a failure. But he failed in a big way, not hiding his light under a bushel as they did. He had all the savor of a character from Dickens. Though defeated by the realities of life, he rose above them, thanks to his gift of humor. He looked at familiar things with the same fresh eyes that he had turned upon the sights he met with in his travels. This changed the whole outlook of the boy from Atlas House, making him see things from a new angle, showing him the world as something fundamentally ridiculous, fit only to be laughed at.

Wells was born with a strong sense of humor. His father must have had it too. But according to the Atlas House code, flippancy was a defect, a sign of ill breeding. The constraint that ruled there made laughter afraid to let itself be heard.

The future trend of the lad's mind was decided by these few months spent in Somerset with Uncle Williams. The chief lesson Wells learned during this short period proved to be the lesson that guided his whole career. It was his salvation. Thanks to Uncle Williams, the fourteen-year-old boy had discovered that it was better to face real life with a laugh, than to shrink away from it into dreamland.

In *Tono-Bungay* Wells gives one of his fragments of autobiography, the story of his apprenticeship to a chemist in the little town of Midhurst. This episode, in reality, lasted only for a month. In his books he dwells upon it at some length, because it was a comparatively bright spot in the gloom of his early years. He found it easier to deal with memories less distressing than those of his childhood. Indeed, not one of his novels draws the picture of Atlas House. Until he came to write his autobiography he never stirred those earliest recollections; it was as though they had left a wound that he could not bear to touch.

Bertie's short stay with the chemist (he and his wife served later as models for the Ponderevo couple) came to a sudden end when it was discovered to be based on certain misunderstandings. The training of a future chemist had to be paid for by sums far too large for Sarah Wells's purse. Also Thomas Morley's teaching had not included Latin, which was absolutely necessary. Before it became clear that the money question would settle the matter, Wells took some Latin lessons with the headmaster of the local grammar school.

"What, me learn Latin!" exclaims George Ponderevo in wonder and delight. "I had long been obsessed by the idea that having no Latin was a disadvantage in the world . . . Latin had had a quality of emancipation for me that I find it difficult to convey." This was Wells's own state of mind when, at the age of fourteen, he took his first Latin lesson.

He knew he had brains. He was particularly good at mathematics and drawing, and could express himself with great fluency. But his best friend at Morley's school, the son of a Jewish innkeeper in London, had a still livelier mind, a better memory, and was quicker and more accurate at his sums. Wells by no means looked upon himself as a budding genius, though he thought that both he and his friend had more than average intelligence. (Never, even amid the brilliant successes of his later career, did Wells claim to have anything unique about him. He gave to his autobiography the subtitle, *Discoveries and Conclusions of a Very Ordinary Brain*. This was not out of false modesty, his superiority lay on a different plane.)

The would-be chemist astonished his teacher, who was used to the slow brains of Sussex tradesmen and farmers. The boy absorbed the long-desired language with amazing speed. He must have had a natural feeling for it, or else his longing to be educated had sharpened his ability. In four or five lessons he learned more than the other pupils could master in a year. Latin could be of no help in the trials that lay before him; but his self-esteem, thus nourished, gave him confidence, supported him against the humiliations of poverty.

Wells shows the importance of this sense of balance when describing Billy Prothero in *The Research Magnificent*. Billy is the son of a poor seamstress. The snobbish mother of one of his school friends makes him so much ashamed of his rough hands, his shabby clothes and battered valise, that in order not to break out in pitiful rebellion or fall into self-disgust, he takes refuge in a feeling of intellectual confidence.

The Latin lessons turned out to be more useful than young Bertie had expected after he failed in the immediate aim toward which they were to have helped him, that of gaining a foothold in the chemist's shop. For in them lay the seed of a still unsuspected future.

The boy was now left for a short time in suspense. No fresh servitude was as yet in sight. But Up Park could not be used as a permanent refuge for stray members of Sarah Wells's family. In sheer despair, she sent her youngest son to spend two months as a boarder with his Latin teacher, the headmaster of the Midhurst grammar school.

This was another respite, another open door for the tadpole. More scraps of knowledge were to be picked up. The tadpole's legs and lungs were steadily developing. Wells benefited greatly from the evening continuation classes which were a new thing at that time, and chiefly devoted to scientific subjects. The schoolmaster was paid a fee of a few pounds for every pupil who passed the examination with which the course ended. He insisted that the fourteen-year-old boy, whose progress in Latin had astonished him, should enter for this test. So for the time being young Wells put aside his Latin grammar and turned to books on physiology. Destiny was knocking at his door, under the disguise of a country schoolmaster, eager to add to his income by pushing as many pupils as possible through their exams. Circumstances had put Wells in a specially receptive frame of mind. He was discovering the joys, unknown to him before, of living in a comfortable house and getting enough to eat. His lungs were breathing fresh air. His eyes, so long accustomed to the semidarkness of Atlas House or the draper's shop, were turned eagerly toward full daylight.

He began to suspect that life had other and better things to offer than any he had known so far, better things that were within his reach and not confined to a higher, inaccessible sphere, such as Up Park.

During this period he developed suddenly and rapidly, along lines that helped him to make full use of the gift he had so recently received from Uncle Williams, an eye for the ridiculous. The blank spaces in his own schoolbooks and those of his classmates (not always to their pleasure) gradually became filled with drawings which were mostly caricatures, human faces with animal-like features. And he made up stories as captions to his drawings, or drawings to illustrate his stories.

He got into the habit of noting down everyday happenings in dual form, by means of words and sketches. The first of his excursions into comedy tells the tale of an escaped bull being chased through the village. It is no more than a piece of childish fun. But, thus early, it bears a truly Wellsian title, "The Battle of Bungeldum." The headmaster had a sense of humor, and of quality too, perhaps, and he encouraged this new hobby. The Bungeldum drawing was enlarged and given a place of honor in the classroom. It was probably no better and no worse than the average schoolboy efforts of the kind. But in this new mirthfulness we get our first glimpse of Wells, the humorist, a figure who was not to emerge clearly until much later.

When he was fifteen, Bertie Wells went into another draper's shop at Southsea. The new job was the best he had been able to find after his one year of freedom. Constraint was not made any less irksome by the fact that this time his newly awakened mind had consciously accepted it. He felt that his last chance was gone. He looked around his dormitory with the eyes of a prisoner condemned to a life sentence. Every nerve in his young body was alert for some possible chance of escape; he felt caught, he says, like a rat in a trap.

In the course of time, comparing his own memories with those of others, he realized that the worst features of a shop assistant's life had been spared him. Conditions at Southsea were far better than those of the Windsor shop where he had had his first experience. The new boss, he realized later, was exceptionally kind. So he never knew the paralyzing dread of sudden dismissal. He never knew the horror of unemployment, the desperate search for another job, the hunger that lay in wait for the unsuccessful.

Yet when he came to strike the balance of his past joys and sorrows, he still remembered those years of imprisonment as the most hopeless of his life. He never forgot the endless hours spent on work that was without the slightest interest. He never forgot the choking sensation of being doomed forever to this flat and dreary existence. He was clumsy and absent-minded. When a badly wrapped parcel came to pieces in his hands and the head of the department heaped reproaches on him, there was only one secret consolation for his boyish dignity, the satisfaction of having quickly mastered the principles of Euclid and of having learned Latin with such brilliant ease.

A sullen, mutinous feeling was growing within him, but as yet it had not found its object. Could he rebel against his poor mother, clinging so desperately to her own insecure position? Against social injustice? As yet he knew too little about social problems to be able to lay his wrongs at that door, and the influence of Up Park was still strong upon him. Against fate? But one's fate was governed by unintelligible forces. Very early in life he had shaken off the yoke of Sarah Wells's personal and jealous God. But he still believed in Providence, the first cause of all things human. He had rejected the cruel concept of hell-fire. But he believed in an afterlife of the soul. The discontentment that seethed within him must soon find an outlet.

It was as a result of visiting a Roman Catholic church that the chaos in his mind took definite shape for perhaps the first time. Though the effects of his Protestant upbringing had almost entirely worn off, prejudice, being harder to kill than positive faith, had left him with an instinctive distrust of Catholicism.

During a chance visit to the Roman Catholic cathedral at Portsmouth, he heard a sermon that at first impressed him. Soon, however, he realized that its eloquence was quite artificial. There before him was an actor, making a studied speech, with the help of flowing gestures and twinkling candles. He himself was a young man of few words, this being another of his typically British qualities, and he disapproved of sentences that were too well turned and tones that were too mellow. This suspicious attitude toward eloquence remained with him for the rest of his life; it always cost him a visible effort to accept even well-founded arguments if they were put forward with Latin volubility. The Portsmouth cathedral experience shocked his deep-seated reserve and made an impression which was strengthened by the doubts that almost unawaredly had been growing in him. The first result was to awaken the distrust of popery that had been slumbering at the back of his mind. He never relaxed the hostile attitude toward Roman Catholicism which grew out of this distrust. He fed it privately with arguments and collected facts to back it up until, toward the end of his life, he launched an open attack.

But the violence with which, at the age of fifteen, he reacted to the honeyed tones and consciously graceful gestures of a preacher describing the torments reserved in hell for unbelievers, was based on something more than accumulated resentment. It expressed something deeper than a surge of indignation directed against the first available object.

One of Wells's most deeply rooted characteristics was his horror of cruelty. This horror was no mere gush of pity for all living creatures. He was not naturally tenderhearted, or easily moved to pity. On the contrary, a secret austerity, an inward sense of discipline, made him refuse to sentimentalize either about himself or about others. Neither had he any of that domineering largeheartedness which longs to embrace the whole world, that unconscious Messianic spirit which soaks up all human misery like a sponge. He would not have understood Karamazov's rejection of a paradise paid for by the tears of a child. Any piece of cruelty "made him sick," as he said, and this was the reaction of his vital instinct. He looked upon cruelty as the negation of all human dignity, of man's most essential quality.

Toward the end of his life, amid the nightmare of war and of Nazi occupation of Europe, he devoted a chapter in the second part of his autobiography to a sociological study of cruelty. He tried to answer the question as to whether cruelty is a part of man's nature, or whether it is due to the intolerable pressure of social conditions. But long before he was capable of discussing cruelty in the abstract, his horror of it had drawn him toward one of the paths of his future development.

Hearing hell described by a Catholic priest with a certain smug relish that struck him as excessive, the fifteen-year-old boy had felt a dim sense of peril. He realized for the first time, he says, the danger represented by these foreign men, with their clean-shaven faces, their skirts and lace, their chants and ritual gestures, and "enthronement of cruelty."

But to fight the Roman Catholic Church was not enough for him. For a mind in the throes of doubt, there was but a short step from disapproval of this ancient form of worship to rejection of Christianity as a whole. In a book he wrote during one of his periods of belief, *The Undying Fire,* the hero wrestles fiercely with his faith, in a desperate hand-to-hand struggle. It is cruelty that has given rise to his doubts. Cruelty is the nightmare of the universe. This modern Job goes for a country walk on a sunny day when a gentle breeze is blowing. He walks with bent head, his gloomy eyes scanning the hedgerows. He catches sight of a baby rabbit, torn by the powerful fangs of some enemy, its tiny body coated with blood, flies swarming over its wounds. A little farther on a cat rushes across the path and, taken by surprise, drops at his feet a beautiful little bird whose blood-bespattered wings flutter pathetically. He tries to put the bird out of its pain, but the life instinct is still strong in its little mangled body, and it pecks furiously at his merciful hand.

This, cries Wells's hero, this revelation of hell, is God's handiwork!

He thinks of the pitiless, never ending struggle of nature. He thinks of the cruelty with which man exterminates living creatures. He thinks of the way in which man himself is attacked by parasites, of the terrible suffering caused by invisible larvae and bacteria. He decides that the creator of the universe must be either unimaginably malicious or else completely negligent and indifferent, with an absolute contempt for justice.

The young Wells of the Southsea days had not yet begun to wrestle with his God. He did not yet feel that burning need of faith which was later to bring him back to religion. He had been fond of talking with the Vicar of the Anglican church about original sin and the moment at which it could have taken place. But suddenly, after the shock he received in Portsmouth cathedral, he left off these discussions. His mind was still unsettled and foggy, his arguments were drawn from a weekly paper, *The Freethinker,* taken over lock, stock and barrel, and scarcely half digested. He was still under the powerful influences of the world of his childhood, which he had only just left behind. But stronger even than these was the urge to rebel. He felt "small, frightened, but obstinate."

Because he was frightened, he forced himself to be brave. His defense against the hardships of his daily life took the form of a fierce atheism. His uncertainties heightened the excitement by conjuring up the danger that would threaten him if by any chance there really were an avenging God.

In the dormitory above a draper's shop, a young fellow in his teens carried on arguments with several lads older than himself. He struck terror into them. The hero of *The Research Magnificent* brings out bold blasphemies of the same kind in his school dormitory, while his roommates put their fingers into their dismayed ears. A thunderstorm is raging outside, and forked tongues of lightning split the darkness of the room. The boy sits up in bed and, while the thunder crashes, declares that there is no God. In his voice is a note of despairing rage. He is terribly afraid.

But not even the excitement of open rebellion, the inner shudder at his own boldness, could free young Wells from his crushing sense of bondage. His boyish appetite was left unsatisfied by meals that consisted chiefly of bread and margarine, washed down either with a brew made from tea dust or with a black liquid which would never pass as coffee in any country except England, a little imported meat and a lot of potatoes and a small beer. In winter he shivered in his icy dormitory and eked out the niggardly supply of blankets with several layers of newspaper.

He was standing up all day, running errands or just waiting about; his ankles were swollen and stabbing pains ran through the soles of his feet. Every muscle in his undernourished body was ready to give way with fatigue.

Many years later, addressing a conference of shop assistants, he spoke with wonder and admiration of the way in which his former colleagues managed to keep on their feet for so long at a time, of their unfailing good humor, and their amazing patience. Like Kipps, to whom he lent some of his experiences as a little errand boy, he used to lie awake far into the night, despite his weariness, and think about what had happened to him, about the ridiculous mechanism in whose cogs he was entangled, its tremendous, irresistible power, a power from which he had neither the means nor the strength of will to escape. And this would be his life to the end of his days. . . .

How could Sarah Wells's son possibly hope to scrape together a little money and have a corner to himself, where he would be his own master? Even if his dream of independence should come true, what then? The remembrance of Atlas House was a grim warning to him.

Two years went by, but neither training nor force of habit could lessen the disgust that young Bertie felt for this kind of existence. During these two years it became quite clear that he would never make a good shop assistant. He could not get the better of inanimate objects and their malicious tricks. The crafty lengths of material refused to fold up neatly, the paper crumpled itself, the string twisted into hopeless tangles. His quick mind was served by fingers that were all thumbs. He found it easy enough to pursue an idea to its logical conclusion, or to line up convincing arguments; but he lost his head when expected to deal with any quantity of tangible objects, and he would gaze helplessly at the untidy mess that his well-meant efforts always seemed to create. He used to say that it was to sheer incapacity that he owed his escape from that kind of work.

Later on he was haunted by the thought of the immense numbers of people belonging to his own generation who must have dropped, without training, without inclination, and regardless of their natural talents, into jobs where they were tied down for the rest of their days. The ever growing social unrest that he saw around him, the discontent, the passive resistance to monotonous work, absenteeism, factory accidents, unintentional sabotage, clock watching—all these he looked upon as the direct result of the overhastiness and lack of professional guidance with which boys and girls were flung onto the labor market.

Young Bertie Wells, however, had not yet begun to see himself as a tiny cog in a warped machine. He talked to his eldest brother about his longing to get away from the draper's shop; but Frank, who in due course was also to escape from servitude, had not yet shaken off the cautious resignation proper to a penniless youth. "But what else can you do?" he asked his junior. Bertie could find no reply.

What else could he do, indeed? The thin lad, his white face set and expressionless, repeated the question to himself one summer night, as he paced up and down beside the sea whose vast surface stretched out to mingle imperceptibly with the soft darkness of the sky. The lapping water, black and cool, had a certain dreadful fascination. Suicide as a way of escape is more often chosen by vital natures than by those whose weaker temperament does not bind them as passionately to life. Something whispered to Bertie Wells that this way out was too easy and, like all easy things, unworthy. But the life he was leading seemed even more degrading, and there were no religious scruples, no thoughts of an afterlife, to hold him back.

One of his books, *The Anatomy of Frustration,* has a chapter on suicide, where he speaks of those unbearable moments when the thought of going on until the end becomes a torture that can no longer be endured. Suicide, he says, is a confession and acceptance of final frustration. But one does not experience one's own death. Your death never takes place in your own consciousness; it takes place for those around you.

We die for others, not for ourselves. But with the selfishness of youth, Bertie Wells was not thinking very much about his mother's grief. Besides, any concern he might have felt for his family was probably counterbalanced by a grudge against those who had put him in such an intolerable situation. He pondered the question of his death with all the solemnity of the seventeen-year-old for whom suicide is both very close at hand and very far off; and he decided that the sea could wait. That way out would always be available, but suppose there really were some other, less drastic?

He wrote to Horace Byatt, his Midhurst headmaster. Couldn't he come to work at the school, make himself useful in some way?

"He answered that he thought I might be quite useful," relates Wells. Rescue had come!

There was still one battle to be fought. Sarah Wells had signed up her son for four years' training, and had already paid forty of the fifty pounds premium. She would never agree to forfeit so much money and let him take this mad step. But the mutinous feelings that were simmering in Bertie Wells now found expression in an idea that was to guide him for years to come. He said to himself, in plain and simple words, "If you want something sufficiently, take it and damn the consequences." If the worst came to the worst, there was always the sea, lapping patiently along Southsea beach.

At the moment when he decided to make his leap into the unknown, it had ceased to be an entirely rash step. Byatt had promised to pay him twenty pounds for his first year, and double that amount the year after.

Matters were brought to a head by an unpleasant scene with the floorwalker, on whom Bertie had long ago concentrated his very considerable power of hatred. Next day at dawn, the boy slipped quietly out of the horrible shop and started to walk to Up Park. It was seventeen miles away, but he felt he could go on foot to the world's end to escape from the bales of cloth and the contemptuous voice of the supervisor.

A breeze swept away the dawn mists and the sun was soon shining in a clear sky. One of his shoes was too tight and hurt his foot. He was walking on an empty stomach too. Hunger and weariness grew to a torment. Thirty years later, that walk was still very clear in his memory. The farther he went, the more he doubted the wisdom of his plan. The courage began to ooze out of him. He felt like a criminal.

He tells in *Tono-Bungay* of his return to Up Park. Tortured by his uneasy conscience, he resolved not to let anyone see him until he had spoken to his mother. It was a Sunday. The peaceful inhabitants of Up Park had been out in search of religious consolation. They were now coming back, with a good conscience, at peace with God and creation. The lady of the house drove home in her carriage. The servants walked across the park, in a procession whose order had been unchanged for centuries. The gardener, the undergardeners, the laundrymaids, the footman, the butler's family, the head housemaid, the cook, and, last of all, walking between two very old women, the little housekeeper, dressed in solemn black. Bertie peered at her from behind the bushes, with "a queer feeling of brigandage," as though he were an interloper in this orderly world, as though there were no real place for him and he must wedge his way in.

Deep down within the young rebel there was still a child—a very scared child. He emerged from the bushes with a forced smile on his drawn, dirty little face, and called out with pathetic playfulness, "Coo-ee, Mother! Coo-ee!"

Sarah Wells turned her worn face in his direction, went very white and put her hand to her heart. "The bad shilling back again!" remarks H. G.

Being firmly convinced that even the knottiest problems always solved themselves sooner or later with the help of prayer, Sarah Wells had not so far taken Bertie's restlessness very seriously. But now the skies of her obedient world were falling. Her reproaches, tears, scoldings, were of no avail against her son's desperate obstinacy. She did not see how frightened he was himself, how much of his stubbornness was mere bravado. The dark water was still waiting to swallow him. Truth to tell, by the time he began to speak to his mother of suicide, the idea had lost most of its charm. But the threat worked wonders. It put an end to slavery, once and for all. Soon afterward he took the train back to Midhurst, his doubts forgotten and his mind at rest. In the joy of his new freedom he stood up and danced a war dance. The train wheels jogged an accompaniment to his triumphant whoops of liberation.

The basic and dominant feature of H. G.'s character was his unfailing optimism. Together with his belief that all things were moving toward ultimate harmony and all humanity striving toward enlightenment went a conviction that nothing in life was ever wasted, that a secret meaning lay hidden in even the most undeserved trials, and that ordeals were to serve as steppingstones to great achievement. In later years he looked upon his youthful sufferings as a valuable lesson, saying that he had been lucky to pass through such bad times, as they stiffened his happy-go-lucky, indolent nature, and that if he had been born the son of a prosperous gentleman he would probably not have accomplished the miracles that were wrung from his self-education.

But though his natural optimism led him to strike a favorable balance in the long run, he still felt that his success had been rather too dearly bought. He never forgot the drapery period, to which he always referred as "the hell of my life." He describes it in several of his novels. He worked it out of his system with the help of rage and humor. One might have thought the poisonous memories were dead. But they lingered in him, and sometimes rose to the surface at unexpected moments.

One day, for instance, he suddenly announced that he must have a knob-headed walking stick. "Not a stick with a crook handle—what I want is a good, round knob that fits comfortably into the palm of the hand," he told me emphatically. He was often seized by such wishes, childish in their urgency, and which had to be satisfied then and there. They were probably intensified by contrast with the years when so many things had been beyond his reach.

He set out to hunt for the desired walking stick in a big general store. His way led through the drapery department. And there he stopped short, and stood for quite a long time, watching the salesmen lifting bales of cloth from the shelves and unrolling them on the counter. "Have you ever thought how heavy a bale like that can be? Especially if you're young and don't get enough to eat. It strains your wrists and wrenches your arms out of their sockets."

There he stood, a well-dressed, leisurely figure, already getting rather stout, in a comfortable overcoat, his bowler hat tilted slightly to the back of his head—the very pattern of a prosperous middle-class citizen—and gazed at the young salesmen as they bustled to and fro. His hands moved slightly, as though he could still feel the heavy weight bearing down on the frail wrists of his boyhood days. He pointed to the counter, where the lengths of materials were heaping up.

"All that will have to be put tidily away after closing time," he told me. "It isn't as easy as it looks. The stuff is heavy, and the bales are an awkward width to get hold of. And then there are some kinds of material that aren't easy to roll. They cling, they go into wrinkles or twist up like a rope. It makes you sweat blood."

A woman walked away empty handed from the overloaded counter. Another came hurrying up. Wells didn't move. "How one loathes those females who don't know what they want and tire you to death for nothing! 'You might show me that piece, too; I think it's the color I'm looking for,'" he mimicked in shrill, affected tones. He seemed to be talking to himself. "The worst of all are the ones who come along just at closing time. 'I'm *so* glad I got here in time. . . .'" Again the shrill voice, with honeyed accents. "You'd like to kill them, and all you say is, 'Certainly, Madam.' Look. . . . It's getting late. And there's so much to be put away. . . ."

He had begun to walk slowly forward again, his eyes still fixed on the shelves as he passed by. Eyes that were filled with compassion, and with burning anger.

I V

LIFE OPENS OUT

THE LITTLE TOWN of Midhurst was the first bright spot in the gray fog of his existence, and looking back, he saw it as though haloed with gold.

"I suppose it rained there at times," Wells wrote, "but all my memories of Midhurst are in sunshine." He described the place in several of his books, like a painter returning to the portrayal of some dearly loved friend. It served as model for Whortley in *Love and Mr. Lewisham,* with its willow-bordered stream, its great park shaded by ancient trees, and the fragrance of syringa wafted from its gardens. With the wonderful sunsets, too, that made the windows sparkle like diamonds and paved the narrow streets with gold.

Thence comes, also, the strict schema pinned on the wall of Mr. Lewisham's attic—the relentless program that young Wells drew up for himself when he got to Midhurst. For it is Wells's own attic room that he gives to Mr. Lewisham, with its lead-framed skylight, its sloping roof, and the bulging walls from which the accumulated layers of paper were peeling off in patches. As a writing desk he used a packing case, turning it on its side and removing the lid to make room for his knees; another case, painted yellow, held his books. One of the bumpy walls bore a large sheet of paper on which the words "KNOWLEDGE IS POWER" were written in a bold though still childish hand and adorned with many flourishes. To balance this statement, another poster declared that "WHAT MAN HAS DONE, MAN CAN DO."

There was a sense of the greatest urgency about these self-reminders. Pinned to the ceiling where it sloped steeply down toward the washstand was the timetable which fixed the course of Wells's days with unrelenting exactitude. A noisy alarm clock summoned him to work at five o'clock every morning. That gave him three hours' start on the sleepy, the lazy, the unambitious, three hours in which to add to his precious little store of learning. The timetable made no allowance for rest or amusement. Wells mistrusted himself, knowing his tendency toward daydreaming and indolence. So he laced himself up, as it were, into a stiffly-boned moral corset, lest his attention should wander. These precautions were nothing new. Even during his first visit to Byatt's house, at the very beginning of his battle for education, he had decided on a stern self-control, and he had never relaxed it since, even during the nightmare months at Southsea. The employees there had the run of a library that contained chiefly novels, but Wells had sworn to himself never to read a novel or play a game, and he kept this vow for several years. He was hungry for learning, and he had only odd moments in which to assuage that hunger. And he knew only too well how strong the attraction of a good novel or the "disturbance of a game of skill." One day at Southsea, some of his fellow employees had persuaded him to join in a card game to help in passing their tedious hours. He lost money, money that he had not got. With crimson cheeks and strident voice he rushed to his mother, demanding the wherewithal to pay his debt of honor—a little sum that cost her, poor woman, much scraping and self-denial. He was never to forget that dreadful episode. All through his life it came back to his memory as a piece of cruel selfishness, and left him burning with shame.

After his flight from servitude, it was more than ever important for him to make good. Time was short. He was far behind luckier boys of his own age, who had had proper schooling. He must push on with his Latin, one of the keys that had opened the door of escape for him. And then there was that mysterious thing called by the general name of culture. He made the most of every pause in his work at the grammar school. He read during meals. The only exercise he allowed himself was an hour's walk every day, and he strode along at top speed so as to put the short time to full profit. This self-defense against his tendency to absent-mindedness became second nature with him. He was particularly proud of it, as one usually is of an acquired virtue. He was always inclined to spell "Discipline" with a capital D. This idea found expression later on in his concept of the Samurai.

He was driven along his new path by the goad of urgent and unavoidable necessity. He was not setting out to conquer the world, with all that effort of self-control; he was making a desperate bid to escape from the shop and the street.

At Midhurst he did a double share of work. He taught at the grammar school, handling the boys with something of the strictness that he applied to himself. He insisted on discipline; he was perhaps a little resentful toward his lazy, unruly pupils, who did not seem to appreciate the blessings of education. In the evening he became a pupil in his turn. The evening classes were more or less bogus for Byatt looked upon them solely as a means of adding to his salary by examination grants. About most of the subjects that were set, he knew nothing whatever. All he did for Wells was to provide him with textbooks, over which he racked his brains while Byatt sat calmly writing letters at the other end of the classroom. So the seventeen-year-old boy had to work without help or guidance. Some of the textbooks were up-to-date and easy to follow. But for certain subjects he had to be content with outdated books and confused diagrams that he could hardly make head or tail of. His approach to biology and physics was indirect and complicated. There were no experiments that he could watch, to fix a given law firmly in his memory. There were no explanations, even, to start him on the right lines or to clear up a difficult passage. He was heavily handicapped as he started his race for knowledge. But none the less he did start. The burst of energy that had driven him to rebellion was not yet exhausted; it still urged him full speed ahead. Conditions which would have disgusted most students came as a great improvement to him. The attic he shared with the school usher was a room where he could think quietly, not a huge noisy dormitory. His landlady ran a cakeshop, and though he kept his nose so close to his books, Wells thoroughly enjoyed her cooking. He could eat as much as he wanted. His comfortless childhood had left him uninterested in the quality of food; but the landlady's cakes awoke a healthy greediness and gave him his first taste of sensual pleasure. Fifty years later he still remembered her cream buns and whortleberry jam, and kept a warm place in his heart for the kindly creature who had felt so sorry for her young lodger, whom she considered to be overworked and too serious for his age.

Very well fed and, to his own mind, well lodged, his knees fitted comfortably into the packing case piled high with books, Wells was quite satisfied with life. He still wore the black suit he had had in the draper's shop, the cloth was rubbed shiny and there were chalk marks that would not come out, but he was entirely consoled for this shabbiness by the mortarboard with which all the grammar school staff were supplied. Byatt had decided that this headgear would impress the boys' parents. As for the lack of amusements in his life, Wells cared not a jot about that, so long as the certificates testifying to his success in exams continued to add cheerful, greenish-blue patches to the attic wall. There were no loopholes through which trouble could slip in and take him by surprise. No love affair came along to agitate him as his hero, Mr. Lewisham, was agitated at eighteen. Of passion, and the rivalry between love and ambition, he knew nothing as yet. He was entirely absorbed by the struggle to climb up out of poverty. He pored rapturously over the books that had so long been denied him. His imagination, his vitality, his power of enthusiasm and his indignation all found vent as he pushed farther and farther along the paths of learning that he could now explore for the first time. His schema, his timetable, and his loud alarm clock were trusty weapons in a great adventure of the spirit; they helped him to overcome the monsters of ignorance and to win victories more brilliant than those of the conquering heroes of his childish battles. Despite his tousled hair and rather grubby appearance, despite the ink and chalk stains on his hands, he wore, beneath the shabby suit that was getting too tight for him, the invisible armor of a knight of old. There was only one flaw in that armor, only one weakness in his youthfully heroic attitude. Just one cloud loomed in the bright sky of Midhurst, but it was a thick, black cloud.

According to the rules of the grammar school, everyone who taught there had to be a member of the Church of England. Byatt found out that Wells had not yet been confirmed, and insisted that he should put himself right with the church. He must obey, or be cast out of paradise. Bertie Wells had a bitter struggle with his conscience. His nature presented an apparent antinomy—he was cheerful, friendly, tolerant, yet beneath all this lay something implacable, unyielding. His pleasant, amusing qualities grew, untrammeled, out of the hardest rock. Even his sense of humor could not soften that granite foundation. This curious harmony between contradictions lasted throughout his life. He would show the most smiling indulgence, the most genial understanding, and then, when some deep-buried spring in him was unexpectedly touched, there would be a sudden change, a stiffening. You never knew, with him, whether you would come up against soft moss or sharp stones until, in course of time, you found out what subjects he took really seriously and what were of only minor importance to him. He never bargained with his conscience. He was always wholehearted, even when in the wrong. He would make slight concessions, usually for the sake of peace and quiet, but his hatred of compromise was keen and, when roused, ferocious.

In the Midhurst days this combativeness was well to the fore. It was further strengthened by his contempt for social convention and his lack of religion as though having no tradition to buttress him, his convictions hardened like steel to take the strain.

In one of his short stories, "A Slip under the Microscope," he gives it as his opinion that convinced atheists have great difficulty in telling lies; if it were not so, he says, they would not be atheists at all, but broad-minded churchmen. The young hero of this story, who has a great deal in common with its author, is so much tormented by his oversensitive conscience that he destroys his chance of a successful career and even throws away the slender resources that are already his. The theme of the story is, in fact, the absurd and useless triumph of exaggerated scruples, and it forms a sort of reply to the questions that perplexed Wells himself, an attempt to soothe his uneasy conscience. He carries his personal conflict onto another plane. This is what would have happened to me, he seems to be telling himself, if I had kept on refusing to compromise. It is a speech in his own defense, an argument *ad absurdum,* the lancing of a literary abscess to clear the whole body of poison. But in this case the treatment failed.

Kneeling at the altar rails on the day he was confirmed, Wells felt bitterly humiliated. He compared himself to an early Christian who, "for sound domestic and worldly reasons had consented to burn a pinch of incense" to Caesar. He never tried to make light of this act of submission. Neither did he come to terms with his memory and allow himself to forget it. The sting remained. Many years later, speaking at a dinner, he returned to the problem of what he called the first humiliating action of his life. "I swallowed my doubts, I was confirmed—and I lost my private honor." The Church thus became, for him, something huge and stupid that was trying to smother his conscience and intelligence.

He never quite forgave himself for this step, though later events were to prove to him that, at this crossroads, he had taken the right turning. His resentment against the Church endured to his dying day.

The prize candidate, whom Byatt looked upon as a little gold mine, succeeded beyond all expectations. The Education Department was short of science teachers. So students who had passed their exams at the end of a continuation course were offered free training at London University's Normal School of Science, together with a free railway ticket and an allowance of a guinea a week, in exchange for the promise that they would become science masters after taking their degree. This, as Mr. Lewisham puts it, opened the door to all the other great things, success and celebrity.

Byatt had meant to keep his model candidate for some time longer. But no sooner had Wells passed his first year's examinations, which he did in brilliant style, than he received an application form from the Ministry. He filled it out in secret, with a beating heart. Accepted at once, he received the wonderful blue paper that promised unimaginable things—London, and teaching by famous men like Huxley and Lockyer! This was indeed luck!

In a whirl of joy, Wells said good-by to the privately disappointed Byatt and to the quiet haven of Midhurst. He was thrilled at the difference between this departure and his arrival, as a bewildered boy, only a few months earlier. He had come to Midhurst from the draper's on a promise of twenty pounds a year, and a guinea a week seemed like a fortune to him. His natural optimism surged up, leaving no room in his mind for doubts. His future, he thought, was now secure. His great spiritual adventure had taken a miraculous turn. Like the hero of "A Slip under the Microscope," he was at that fine, emotional age when life opens out, at the end of a narrow path, like a wide valley full of the promise of wonderful discoveries and tremendous achievements.

V

THE QUEST FOR CERTAINTIES

AS A YOUTH of eighteen, fresh from the country, he was lost in the sprawling gray immensity of London, realizing for the first time just how small and weak he could still, on occasion, feel. That was Wells's first sight of the great city. Its tragic contrasts were a revelation to one brought up in the shadow of Up Park. He went to live in Westbourne Park, and he puts into the mouth of his hero, Mr. Lewisham, a description of the conflicting sights and sounds that surrounded him in this neighborhood, with its area of brooding gloom, its grim, striking dock laborers, its soup kitchens and ragged, begging children; and then, only two streets away, its rows of glittering, expensive shops, its lines of flitting carriages and cabs.

But these contrasts, noted on his way to the School of Science at South Kensington, did not really sink into his mind as yet. He was entirely given over to happiness and excitement. Years later he still remembered going for the first time into the big red-brick building and signing his name in the hall. It was, he said, one of the greatest days of his life. For the first time he now came into contact with scientific realities. There were well-equipped laboratories with plain wooden tables, sinks with running water, jars and jars of chemicals ranged on long shelves, diagrams pinned up beside objects explaining them clearly, microscopes and retorts, and animals to be dissected. It all seemed to him to be easy, bright, and beautiful. Coming to it after his solitary studies, he felt like some medieval student plunged suddenly into modern times.

It was Huxley, however, who made the most powerful impression of all. Wells once described in an article how he saw the great scientist for the first time. Huxley came into the lecture theater, his hands thrust down in his pockets, scanning the assembled students with the sharp, aloof gaze of a pair of small brown eyes, beneath the deep shelter of his tremendous eyebrows. Seeing him so close was an experience that filled the new student with pride and awe.

Huxley remained for him a tremendous being, whose presence never ceased to inspire pride and respect. They never came into personal relationship. The keen, aloof gaze passed over Wells's head as it passed over the heads of his fellow students. Huxley saw nothing exceptional in the strained attention of this particular young man. He never suspected that the seed he threw out in such generous handfuls was falling on soil that would yield a great harvest. But Wells never tired of proclaiming how much Huxley had done for him— without knowing it. He used to declare that he learned more when studying under Huxley than at any other period of his life, and on this zoology course he spent a year even happier than at Midhurst.

In speaking of this happiness and rating it even higher than the comparative comfort of Midhurst, he had to close his eyes to the painful circumstances of his life in London and forget the wretched discomfort with which he paid for this happiness.

He lodged in a dirty, noisy, overcrowded little house in Westbourne Park, where he was forced into revoltingly close contact with "the coarsest, most bestial and most degrading" samples of humanity that he had ever so far come across. Sarah Wells, filled with motherly solicitude and convinced that London was a den of iniquity, had sent her son to live in the home of an old friend of hers. She never found out that by so doing she had thrust him into the very arms of vice, into disgusting company, to be preyed upon by elderly women of easy virtue. The innocent boy's first sexual experience came to him in distorted form, a thing of cynical lust and hastily satisfied sensuality. It may be that the ugliness, the vile shamelessness of such enticements was more effective than any amount of moral preaching would have been in protecting him against degradation. But these experiences left him with a kind of nausea that made him ashamed even of his own natural, healthy impulses. He remembered the Westbourne Park household as a lot of monkeys, crowded together in a cage that was too small for them.

But thanks to his power of detachment, as soon as he got away from his dirty room, from the lewd women and their continual squabbling, and entered the quiet, well-ordered laboratories, it was as though he had arrived in another planet. By force of contrast, his studies gradually took on a serene and lofty quality that was almost apostolic.

In Wells's poverty-stricken childhood money had been something quite unknown. At Midhurst, a guinea seemed like a fortune to him. In London he soon found out that a guinea a week would not even buy him enough to eat. His midday meal was often no more than a roll of bread, which he ate secretively in a dark corner of the anatomical museum, so as not to be seen by his more prosperous comrades.

By the end of the week, he sometimes did not even have the money left to pay for a roll. A fellow student who was comparatively well off noticed his half-starved appearance, and invited him once or twice to a good square meal, "to make competition fairer" when the exams came along, as he put it, but Wells was sensitive about his poverty and rejected all attempts at charity, however tactfully disguised. There were holes in his shoes, his jacket was out at elbow, his shirt cuffs were frayed. Then there was his collar. A celluloid collar that he washed every night with soap and water. That collar remained in his memory as a feature of his student days, a symbol of the way in which he was obliged to fall into step with his companions, to imitate their starched collars, to wear, as they did, a top hat on all great occasions. A symbol, too, of the humiliating shifts to which his poverty reduced him.

When the collar was shiny and new he considered it a great discovery. But after a time this one and only collar began to show signs of wear and tear; it became covered with a kind of tartar, like the film that discolors teeth. Among all the hardships of his youth, it was upon this long-suffering collar, emblem of pretentiousness and hypocrisy, that Wells concentrated the full force of his resentment.

Resentment began to grow upon him as soon as the first excitement of his arrival at the School of Science had worn off. He had thought that knowledge would solve all problems, but the tragic contrasts of wealth and poverty, to be seen on all sides in the London streets, made their way even into the temple of learning at South Kensington. Wells's alter ego, Hill, in "A Slip under the Microscope," who is also decked out in a celluloid collar, looks enviously at the wealthier students, sons of prosperous families who wear well-cut suits and shirts with flawless cuffs, are always smoothly shaved, and present a picture

H. G. Wells

of calm perfection—men of the world who chat airily with the girl
students in a language that the poor boy from the country cannot even
understand.

Later, when reviewing his early years, Wells had a good deal to say
about the mental stimulus given by poverty. But he soon noticed that
in these sacred precincts of learning, which should have been far removed from material considerations, the wealthier students enjoyed
privileges to which they had no right.

The humiliating experiences that fell to his lot, the swarming
wretchedness of London, the disgusting circle, a symptom of the
diseased society in which he lived, all combined to hasten a reaction
that had been rendered inevitable by past events. His ideas were quick
to take shape, because they rested on a firm basis, like the foundations
dug for a house that is to be built in due time.

During his months at Midhurst, bent on attaining that still mysterious state of grace that went by the name of general culture, he had not
been content just to cram for examinations. Long afterward, he
thought he remembered reading Plato's *Republic* during one of his
visits to Up Park, probably in the school holidays. At the first attempt,
the book was too much for his untrained mind, but, goaded by the
prestige of the author's name, he made a great effort, aided perhaps by
a certain intellectual snobbishness. So soon, however, as he grasped
Plato's theory, he began to realize its revolutionary implications. Until
then there had always been something hesitating and furtive in his
rebellion against the religious, moral, and social systems that were
imposed upon him from outside. From that moment, all his thoughts
rushed out, unconcealed, to uphold the new ideas that he had glimpsed
thanks to Plato.

Every opening mind is marked, once and for all, by the influence
that comes along to crystallize its first confused notions about life.
H. G. Wells was deeply marked by the fact of having drawn his conception of society from the *Republic*. His ideas on the subject would
have taken shape sooner or later, no matter what he read; a young
man of his period and in his position would have been led to the
same path, no matter by what guide. But his future course was determined by this early Platonic vision of a society governed in the common interest.

His premature revolt against social and religious conventions, his
self-education, which made him apt to overprize the acquisition of

knowledge and mistrust any ideas he had not put to the test, had bred in him an aggressive skepticism. But beneath this acquired habit of doubt there lay a hunger for faith which his deliberate rejection of every kind of belief merely served to aggravate. If the philosophy that first broke in upon his mind and formed it had been a materialistic one, his latent, basic idealism would never, perhaps, have asserted itself so forcibly. Plato's *Republic* became the keystone of Wells's spiritual universe. The book which he read for the first time at Up Park, in the meadow where stood a little ruined tower, one of those artificial ruins beloved of the eighteenth century, was to be his companion for the rest of his life. Other impressions, new struggles and interests, may sometimes have overshadowed it; but they never quite effaced it from memory. It could always be dimly discerned, as it were, in the background of the painted over picture; and the background was golden as that of a primitive painting.

Another book, bought by Wells at Midhurst, had an immediate influence on him. This was Henry George's *Progress and Poverty,* which was simple enough to be understood even by a reader still ignorant of political economy.

When he first arrived in London, Wells knew no more about sociology than he had been able to learn from these two works. But personal experience, reinforced by his tendency to generalize, soon ripened his ideas. He used to look back with indulgent amusement at the first phase of his challenge to society. Like Mr. Lewisham, he felt an urgent need to do something that would proclaim his new faith; and like Mr. Lewisham, in a historical moment, he went out and bought himself a red tie—a blood-red tie.

This red tie, which moreover was his first departure from the made-up variety, consoled Wells and his young heroes, Hill and Lewisham, for their threadbare clothes and even for their celluloid collars. Or rather it justified these things, flinging a defiant challenge to the other youths, who were too well bred and too fortunate. A painful necessity was thus transformed into a declaration of faith. But the shy student was soon to prove his superiority on another level.

Nature did not seem to have intended Wells for an orator. His shrill voice had only a small compass and little carrying power. He spoke too fast and occasionally stumbled over a word. Even in ordinary conversation his voice would now and then drop to an almost inaudible murmur. When he was excited, or in the heat of an argument, it was liable to rise almost to a shout, and then suddenly give way. "I don't like hearing myself speak, my voice annoys me," he often declared. He had no use for eloquence. To play upon the listeners' feelings, to work up mass emotion by vibrant speeches, seemed to him an unworthy method of attracting attention, a charlatan's trick. His own gift was for debate. At the Debating Society meetings, which were held in an underground lecture theater, he soon came to the fore. There was no one like him for pouncing on the weak point of an argument, throwing the speaker off his balance by some apt remark, or cutting sharply through the web of a discussion that had wandered from its purpose. His success in this field did much to console him for his humiliating poverty, his growing discontent, and the disappointments that his work held in store for him. "As a speaker in the Debating Society he never had an equal in my time," says a woman student with whom he was then friendly, and who seems to have served, in some ways, as a model for the girls to whom Hill and Lewisham confide their feelings and their hopes. His wit, she says, was lively and sharp, but his sarcasm was never wounding, even to those against whom it was directed, for it was tempered by humor and based on truth. He attacked conventionality, pretentiousness, fraud, with all the youthful courage that never left him throughout his life. He loved knocking over every kind of popular idol and superstition.

Wells was always fond of a fight for its own sake, he reveled in his own aggressiveness. He once confided to this same friend, "Sometimes I fancy that is what gives me my profoundest pleasure—to chuck things at things and break them."

He never grew out of this juvenile love of "kicking up a shindy." In the successful, famous, wealthy writer there still lingered a trace of the hungry, tousle-headed, slovenly student who took such delight in upsetting his more orthodox companions. This was clear to see whenever some battle of words was raging. He would launch himself into it, scarlet with anger, make stinging retorts, increase in fury to the point of losing all self-control, fling out offensive personal remarks; but his eyes would sparkle with a kind of relish that seemed to belie his seriousness. This aggressive spirit resulted from a strange mixture of fanatical idealism and matter-of-fact clear-sightedness, of fierce intensity and smiling tolerance. He was, and always remained, a tilter against windmills. But in his quixotism there was a sreak of Sancho Panza. Rushing forward to attack his sometimes imaginary monsters, he would give them a wink as though to say, "You aren't really fooling me!" He endowed most of his heroes with quixotic features, which create an underlying resemblance even among those who seem quite unlike each other on the surface. From Mr. Polly, breaking a lance for the elderly Dulcinea of the Potwell Inn, to Christina Alberta's absurd father, out to redeem the world, his books are thickly populated with characters who confess to themselves, in their secret hearts, that they are not real knights-errant.

There is another way in which they are akin. They are all, as it were, the ghosts of their own younger days, lingering amid their earlier dreams. Many of them are trying to make up for having shirked the battles of life, to console themselves for having been too sensible.

Wells was immensely sorry for the submissive, for those who never knew the thrill of youthful mutinies, the joy of defiance. Such as these were the favorites of his wrathful moods, together with the poor, the maimed in spirit, the victims of miseducation. To be unable to rebel seemed to him the worst of all privations. Though his own fighting spirit always had ample scope, he seemed to regret every lost chance of a battle, every skirmish that failed to take place. He, too, was still lingering in the boyish world where he used to play at soldiers. He never reached the maturity of caution or the wisdom of moderation. To the end of his life, he was always "spoiling for a fight."

In his autobiography he tells of a typical incident at the Debating Society. Religion and politics were not supposed to be mentioned there. He never tired of protesting against this rule, pointing out that these were fundamental matters and ought to be thrashed out early in life. One day, at a lecture on superstition, he remarked that the superstition about the number thirteen was connected with "a certain itinerant preacher whom I am not permitted to name in this gathering, and who had twelve disciples. . . ." A storm of protest greeted this sally. He shouted in his piercing voice that the words "itinerant preacher" were correct and appropriate. Amid the uproar thus created, he was in his element. He referred for support to the New Testament, describing it as "a most respectable compilation."

He had made a direct attack on British conventionality. It amused him tremendously. Later, he remembered with delight how he had been thrown out of the lecture room by his indignant colleagues. They handled him rather roughly, and pulled his hair with painful energy;

but the scandal remained in his memory as, on the whole, a "radiant and glorious" experience.

Apart from the pleasure he took in annoying his conventional fellow students, there was something deeply and fiercely serious about his obstinate refusal to withdraw the words that offended them. About this time he wrote to congratulate a friend on his declaration of vigorous atheism and added that he himself was striving toward the day when he would have rid himself of the last traces of conventionality— a day he hoped to see before he died.

This hope was destined to be realized more fully than he could ever have dreamed.

Another permanent line of Wells's development was also laid down at this early date. One of the papers he read at the Debating Society bore the significant title, "The Past and Future of the Human Race." Nothing could be more revealing. Because of the narrow bounds within which he had so far lived, his view of the world was incomplete—rather like the barred window of the Atlas House basement, through which he could see nothing except the feet of the passers-by. But although he had so little opportunity of getting a general outlook, he never, even in early life, thought of himself as a lonely individual, launched on a personal venture; he had always a strong sense of taking part in an experiment shared with the whole of mankind. He felt himself to be, like the rest of mankind, issuing from the past and in transit toward the future.

His mind had always a general rather than personal trend. His feeling for the community was to prove stronger than his private leanings; he thought of himself in the first place as part of a multiple whole, and only in the second place as a separate individual. The Darwinian theory of evolution made an indelible impression on him. It came as a revelation, an experience of psychological import, as it had come to all the science students of his generation. But his own particular turn of mind, his own special kind of logic, made the future appear to him as the corollary of the past. A need of balance, which went hand in hand with his fundamental optimism, turned his thoughts to exploring the future, as a counterpoise to the fascinating vista of prehistoric times.

H. G. Wells's path in life, like that of most other people, was often decided by chance; sometimes by good luck and sometimes, more frequently, by bad luck which later turned out to have been simply a blessing in disguise. His lifework, like that of most other people, was built up by fits and starts, by what seemed to be haphazard inspirations, and even by the need to make money. But in his development and his creative writing, these influences, apparently accidental, were nothing more than reagents, precipitating a mixture that already existed, or notes that awoke lingering echoes.

The books that Wells was to write were virtually existent in him when he read his paper on "The Past and the Future of the Human Race" before the Debating Society in the South Kensington basement. Standing under the dim gas lights, amid the shadowy geological models and mysterious diagrams that adorned the walls of the murky hall, young Wells spoke to his audience about the phases through which mankind was destined to pass. A snapshot taken about this time shows him so thin that the bones of his square jaw stand out and his nose looks like the up-tilted beak of some strange bird; his loose-hanging jacket seems hardly to belong to him; his waistcoat and trousers are full of creases; and his tie—it was still a red tie—hangs crookedly from the celluloid collar. He is obviously trying to hide his shyness behind an affectedly offhand bearing and an air of precocious self-confidence.

Later he revised the lecture, but without altering its main lines, and in 1893 it was published, with a very Wellsian title, *The Man of the Year Million*.

Hill, the young hero of "A Slip under the Microscope," was calmly prepared to go through life on an income of less than a hundred pounds a year; Wells mentions this with the touch of indulgent irony that he generally shows toward states of mind belonging to his own past. Hill was determined to become a famous scientist and leave the world a better place than he found it, and to serve in his own person as a proof of this betterment. This program, written down later with a twinkle of kindly amusement, was exactly that of the nineteen-year-old Wells. His eyes being fixed on the future, he was naturally led to seek for some way of improving humanity's lot. His vague feeling of resentment against society gradually took clearer form, and led him, like many of his generation, straight into the socialist ranks. In the following year (1886), he read another paper before the Debating Society; a paper on socialism, and this time he met with resounding success. It was, he tells us, a fairly typical presentation of socialism as understood by the average man of that day. He denounced the waste that came of trade rivalry; he called for what is now known as directed economy, state control of production and distribution.

The young students of South Kensington as yet knew nothing about the facts of political economy. Their minds, trained to absolute exactitude in scientific questions, seemed to approach social problems with a splendid but indefinite glow of ardent generosity and unlimited hopefulness. They looked, says Wells, to a world where the fierce struggle for personal property would be a thing of the past, and where individual creative effort would have nothing to fear from the greed of personal profit. This dazzling vision blinded them to more immediate matters.

The small group that went by the name of the Fabian Society was then the strongest-flowing current of socialism in London. Varied shades of opinion and divergent tendencies were grouped together in it. The South Kensington students walked long distances through the foggy London winter, to meetings at which William Morris and other leaders of the young movement were to speak. Through the Fabians, Wells came to know Bernard Shaw, with his white, fanatical face and straggling, fiery beard. Even in those days, says Wells, G. B. S. was "always explicit and careful to make himself misunderstood." H. G. recoiled instinctively from his elder's flowing rhetoric. Despite his admiration for Shaw's work, and their frequent contacts in later life, the two men never drew really close together. In the days when both had become famous their paths often crossed, but at each meeting, even when the white face had changed to red, and the red beard to white, Wells found Shaw invariably the same. He was aware of Shaw's secret disapproval, and within himself he still felt the concealed irritation that had made him declare, as an inexperienced youth, that he "rather objected" to that "giddy creature," Bernard Shaw.

The meetings of the Fabian Society sharpened Wells's eagerness to delve down further into the socialist theories, looking for their foundations and their exact aims. A light was beginning to break in on him, a light still faint and unsteady, but never again to be absent from his thoughts. Socialism was to be the beacon that guided him for the rest of his life. The search for definite information about it absorbed him so much that he began to neglect his studies. Periods of intense concentration such as this, of single-track exploration, came again and again during his later career. His progress was not a slow, steady climb, it took place in stages, each devoted to one exclusive interest.

For the time being his strenuous if rather short-winded efforts were devoted to building a firm foundation of fact on which to base his own ideas. He read all the socialist propaganda, he read books on history, sociology, and economics. He soon filled up huge gaps in his education. He had been in London for some time, and his socialistic tendencies were already well established, before he even heard of Karl Marx. His first-year biology course, under Huxley, was taking up all his attention just then. His first contact with Marxism had a curious effect, it aroused in him an instinctive hostility. Hostility such as is created, not by a clash of ideas, but by actual meeting between two men of exactly opposite type. Wells's essentially British character bristled up, as it were, in self-defense against these foreign-style arguments; it was a subconscious jerk of protest, rather than a reasoned objection.

He used to say of himself later that as a young man he had passed through the resentful phase of socialism and left it behind. He disapproved, above all, of Marx's attempt to rebuild the world on what he called the merely resentful and destructive basis of the class struggle. Wells himself, in those early days, had a passionate class consciousness; it linked him to all the underdogs. The fighting instinct was in his blood, he felt that he had been sent into the world in order to fight. But in reality his early socialism was not so much resentful as emotional. He needed some support for his glowing faith in human nature and in the future of the human race. Materialism, or rather the Marxist expression of it, was repugnant to his profound, all-pervading idealism. He says in his autobiography that Marx offered to humanity's basest instincts the pretext of a pretentious philosophy, and that the more active-minded among the despairing masses were easily won over by his teaching.

But for his part, he refused to let himself be drawn into the mass of the "desperate." The very word is revealing. Wells was hopefulness personified. He objected strongly to Marx's "axiom of scientific fatality." He himself believed, with all the power of his imagination, in the inventive spirit of the human race—a belief that he had held, unshakably, ever since reading Plato's *Republic*. Seeking the reasons for his dislike of Marx, he discovered that it came from the difference in their aims. He believed in the new republic. As soon as his thoughts began to take conscious form, in his second year at South Kensington, he made up his mind to prepare "the plan of a new social structure." This was destined to be the plan of his life, to which he returned, patiently, at every stage of his development; the task to which he subordinated the work of a lifetime. He always believed that Marxism was the chief obstacle to the success of this plan. He regarded Marxism as a dangerous illness that had smitten humanity while it was trying to emerge from the old social conditions into a new world order.

Despite this latent hostility, he did not underestimate Marx, to whose keen historical sense he paid tribute in his *The Outline of History*. He admitted that there was a prophetic quality about the Marxist theories, many of which had been confirmed as time went by. In the course of his later life, Wells often became involved in disputes with the followers of Marx, and always as a result of the attitude he had adopted from the very first. The new structure of society, planned by him at the age of twenty, took the form of a world state; it was, of course, to be socialist, but its outstanding feature was its universality. Wells was firmly convinced that humanity could reach this goal by the gradual reorganization of existing society. In his opinion a social revolution would lead in the opposite direction. He considered that the influence of Marx was a drag on this steady progress, and declared toward the end of his life that "we should be much nearer to a sanely organized world system if Karl Marx had never been born."

Rarely have a man's life and thought shown such continuity amid so many variations, as did those of Wells. In an essay written at a late date, for the purpose of proving that the integrality of the individual is a biological illusion, he declared that there was no such thing as an original mental unit, and never had been. Though, according to him, the notion of a single self is false, and is dictated only by social conditions, the persona—a word which he borrowed from Jung with great delight—may be firmly established and steadfast. Indeed, his own remained almost unaltered in one chief respect. The variations of his ideas, his spectacular changes of attitude, the twists and turns of his mind could not, perhaps, have been so sweeping unless there had existed in him this solid core, this steady notion of what he himself really was. Throughout his life he took pleasure in dodging any attempt to define his personality and the nature of his work. He was fond of drawing attention to his many different selves, and even tried to make a scientific theory out of this lack of identity. He liked to decline responsibility for his past attitudes, and to shake off all trace of his former states of mind.

Once, when speaking on the radio, he repudiated "a certain sickly and discontented young man" of 1886, declaring that although he still had photographs of that young man and copies of his writings, he could not feel that there was any connection between him and the H. G. Wells of the present day. "I have left him behind me almost as completely as I have left my grandfather."

He no longer sympathized, on the whole, with the reactions of the student of 1886—Wells's reactions were always determined by the conditions of the moment—he no longer approved of the spirit and behavior of that youthful self. But, despite his angry protests, the general trend of his mind was still unaltered. This persistence of a dominant idea was just as typical of Wells as the sloughing of his outworn personalities. He would trample furiously on these outgrown, castoff skins. Yet he remained fanatically true to himself. It is hardly possible to understand him and to arrive at a just view of his work, unless we allow for the fact that the unknown science student still lived on within the man who exerted such an influence among his contemporaries. Wells himself was quite aware that his chief persona still survived in him. Looking back, he could see, running through every stage of his evolution, among all the attractions and counterattractions of his ideological enthusiasms, the scarlet thread, the very strong and clearly visible scarlet thread of one prevailing attachment. He was careful to let the unknown readers of his memoirs into the secret with which only his friends were acquainted, by telling them right away that almost from his childhood he had been drawn toward a particular kind of work and a particular set of interests.

VI

PERPLEXED IN THE EXTREME

WELLS ONCE DECLARED that if brains could be put on show, like cats and dogs, he did not believe his own would win even a third prize.

This was not pretended humility, nothing could be more foreign to him. He was often extremely impatient with himself. Hard work soon tired him. He had the power of tremendous concentration, but he could not keep it up for long. He went forward, so to speak, in jerks, like a motorcar whose engine keeps stopping and suddenly starting up again. He was in a hurry, the road was long and his aim was ambitious, far more ambitious than that of the ordinary man. He made no allowance for this fact. With his innate impatience, he blamed all delays on the engine. He also used to complain of his memory. He had stored up an enormous, encyclopedic hoard of knowledge; but he was inconsolable when for the moment a name escaped him, or when a foreign language became rusty from lack of practice.

His weaknesses he considered to be due to a general lack of vitality. As a matter of fact, his vital instinct was prodigious. Few people have triumphed so brilliantly over so much physical hardship. But his reactions were slow, deferred, as it were. The lightning reflexes of some of his friends he regarded with wondering admiration, and a touch of envy. His attitude toward them was that of a man at table, astonished by the speed with which a fellow diner is getting through the meal. He did not realize that by eating slowly he absorbed at least an equal amount of nourishment. He chewed very thoroughly, reluctant to give up whatever bone he happened to be picking.

He liked to be with those who were more quick-witted and observant than himself. As a youngster at Morley's academy he had admired the son of the Jewish publican, the little cockney who took things in at a glance and then explained, "You see . . ." Wells declared that he owed a great deal to people of this kind. He was quick to strike up friendship with a man—and still more with a woman—who said "You see?" when he was pondering over something that lay before him.

He was as capable as anyone else of absorbing what met his eye. Indeed, he penetrated more deeply into the reality of things than did those who noted all that lay on the surface. But he needed a traveling companion whose exclamations would rouse him and stir his imagination. "There is a slight element of inattention in all I do," he confessed. To tell the truth, there was in him not merely a slight element, but a great faculty for inattention. When he chose he could turn a deaf ear to people and things, closing his mind to them entirely. This was perhaps an instinctive self-defense against his many-sided curiosity, an unconscious safeguarding of his spiritual development. He had the same gift of inattentiveness on the emotional plane. He could withdraw himself completely when he wished. He may have deliberately cultivated this faculty. It was often a great help to him, but now and then it got him into a tight corner. As a young science student, for instance, he wore out his fine frenzy of attention, in his very first year, at Professor Huxley's classes.

The following year (1885-1886) the would-be schoolmaster was told that he must now turn to the study of physics. He was disgruntled at having to give up zoology. To revive his powers of concentration, he would have had to be tremendously interested in his new subject. Instead of another Huxley, fate sent him a professor of physics who was slow and mournful in manner, and seemed never to be quite alive to what was going on around him.

Wells could never forgive anyone for failing to interest him. All through his life he had fits of childish ill temper toward bores. Even when only nineteen he would not make the least effort to get over a disappointment.

Zoology had thrilled him because, with its talk of evolution, it opened up endless vistas of prehistoric life on the earth's surface. Unconsciously, he expected physics to bring him similar revelations about the construction of the world. He was met at once by definitions that seemed to him to have no general bearing. Throughout his later career, he tried to connect up the facts of physics with a vision of the world in which they would play a real part. What was needed, he said, was a bridge across the gulf that separated ordinary people, their ideas and means of expression, from those specialists who set out from the ordinary world to explore the vast regions of physics and mathematics. He never gave up the search for this bridge. He wrestled with physics like Jacob with the angel, but he never reached the state of grace to which he aspired. He felt himself to be surrounded by a mystery, by something inconceivable, "nearer to us than our breath, than our hands and feet." But our life goes on as though this inconceivable did not exist. The mystery may, in the long run, be the only thing that matters, but, within the rules and limits of the game of life, when the purpose is to catch a train, pay bills, or earn one's living, the mystery is of no importance.

His distaste for the study of physics began when he noticed that Professor Guthrie was teaching him only what he could find for himself in textbooks. During lectures he waited in vain for that "You see . . ." which would have caught and held his attention. From one of Guthrie's assistants, well known for skillful handling of his subject, thermodynamics, he now and then gained a vague, disturbing glimpse of a vast universe to which he had no key.

Young Wells had been upheld at first, not only by the energy that had led to his rebellion, but also by his pride in it. With his weak adolescent hands he had broken out of the prison of his apprenticeship; then he had leaped from Midhurst to London. These seemed to him miraculous feats, and for a long time he thrilled at the thought of having achieved them.

But at Professor Guthrie's classes he had a dim feeling of inferiority. He was expected to do practical work there, and he was clumsy. He burned his fingers on the glass tube of a barometer he had been told to make. He got into difficulties while trying to plane a little board. The tools he had to use were full of silent malice, like the bales of material in the draper's shop. He spilled acid over his one and only pair of trousers. He was disgusted with the uselessness of all this labor. The barometer he put together was, according to him, the most awkward looking and the least reliable instrument of its kind that the world had even seen.

The instruments that Professor Guthrie's students had to make were all everyday affairs and could be bought easily and cheaply. Wells was infuriated by the ridiculous notion that a future science master must be able to construct any and every instrument, so that even in the jungle or on a desert island he could deal with the sudden appearance of a night-school class. What with his clumsiness and his bad temper, the instruments he turned out were so ill made that his fellow students decided to put them into a glass case, to remain for years as a general laughingstock. His lack of skill, or some prejudice against manual work, inherited from Sarah Wells, made him feel degraded. Years later he still spoke bitterly of these classes, at which he had felt more like an amateur carpenter and glazier than a science student.

Despite his inner resistance to those who tried to teach him physics, a resistance emphasized in the dramatic manner usual to his bouts of ill-humor, he got through his second-year examination. He was then set to study geology. In knowledge his new professor was superior to Guthrie, the physicist. But he, too, was lacking in militant curiosity. This time Wells was no longer puzzled by the difficulties of the subject. He was bored, with a boredom all his own, an obstinate refusal to let himself be interested. It was an infectious boredom, expressed by yawns, shrugs, impertinent remarks, eyes raised to heaven in protest —in fact, by all the bad-mannered tricks that he used to the end of his days when he wanted to show people that he found them dull. Seldom can any man have possessed such a wide range of expressive gestures.

Geology might have offered Wells a road into the past, a means of deciphering the earth's history, but at South Kensington the students were only taught to recognize and classify fossils. This may have been good training for the memory, but it did little to stir the imagination. From time to time Wells's interest was aroused; he was passionately attracted by crystalography, for example. A section of rock seen through the microscope could suddenly reveal extraordinary beauty. But he waited in vain for an explanation of these wonders created by the earth in agelong travail. So he relapsed into boredom, all the more glum because he had seen a door half open and then close again. He began to cut his classes, going instead to the public libraries to read books on sociology, or visiting friends to convert them to his new social beliefs.

He busied himself, too, in starting a magazine, to be known as the *Science Schools Journal,* but which he and his friends intended to use in the interests of literature and socialism. Wells was now just twenty years old. Semistarvation had made him paler and thinner than ever before, his hair stood on end, his face wore a troubled expression, but he had become a confident speaker, not eloquent, but winning and persuasive. His authority over his comrades was already sufficient for him to get the magazine started, with himself as editor. His faith was infectious enough to make them rally around his ideas. With this college magazine, Wells first ventured onto the path of journalism, a path that he seemed predestined to tread. As a boy of fourteen, dismissed from his first job and staying for a time with his mother, he had whiled away the rainy days that had to be spent indoors by getting up a handwritten newspaper. He had given it a title which already hinted at his particular kind of humor, *The Up Park Alarmist.* The large staff of the mansion cannot have found this particularly amusing (the English lower middle class was never very enthusiastic about Wells's novels, whose characters were drawn from its ranks), and no doubt wondered where their housekeeper's son had picked up his strange notions.

Traveling along the path that led from a childish hobby to the *Science Schools Journal* he had left the conditions of his lonely boyhood far behind. From now on he was never to lack warm supporters. But when in later years he disclaimed any connection with his twenty-year-old self, he also disavowed his first attempts at self-expression, which he said were immature and secondhand. Once he had come into his own, he began to feel very sensitive about these borrowed plumes. He went to the trouble of buying up all issues of the magazine that contained articles by him and destroying them, in order, he said, to save inquisitive searchers from wasting their time on such stuff; and he declared triumphantly that not one copy had survived. He had no patience with what he considered to have been his absurdly slow development, and he was particularly intolerant of the period of confusion from which the magazine had finally emerged.

To its first number, which appeared in December 1886, he contributed an article on Socrates, which he signed with his own name. In later issues he made use of pseudonyms, such as "Walker Glockenhammer" and "Septimus Browne." The style of his essays on Socrates and Mammon, and of a third contribution, "A Conversation with Gryllotalpa," showed strongly—too strongly for his later independent state of mind—the influence of Ruskin and Carlyle. He also tried his hand at poetry, or rather at versification, and it was perhaps for this that, looking back, he found it hardest to forgive himself.

His career as an editor did not last long. The professor of geology was a stern disciplinarian. Wells had forgotten the Midhurst days, when he had been just as strict with his own pupils and even more so with himself. Under the strain of his recent perplexities, the line he had meant to follow was beginning to waver, he was breaking the promises he had made to himself. Like Mr. Lewisham, he had torn up the schedule of his career and thrown his timetable into the waste-basket.

The professor, noticing that he had grown inattentive and was making no progress—two things which could not be tolerated in the holder of a state scholarship—ordered him to hand over the editorship of the magazine to one of his fellow students. This added to Wells's ill-humor. He tried to make up for lost time, but his efforts were halfhearted, and it was too late.

Just now there came a deep disturbance in his private life. A cousin of his father, who worked as saleswoman in a big store, at last found out what an existence the boy was leading amid the unhealthy promiscuity of the little house in Westbourne Park. She protested vigorously, and young Wells, much to his relief, was sent to lodge with an aunt who lived in a tall, narrow building in the dingy Euston Road, and let rooms. Here he found the same conditions he had known so well in Atlas House. A dark kitchen in the basement, a coal cellar, a steep staircase, hard to climb if you were carrying a scuttle of coal or a great jug of water. Every drop of water had to be carried up; there was no running water upstairs.

As a little boy, Wells had helped his mother; now, in his spare time, he lent a hand with the buckets of coal and water that the two old women of the house, his Aunt Mary and her sister, had to carry up at all hours of the day to their lodgers on the second and third stories. These buckets haunted his imagination.

The Euston Road lodgings, like Atlas House, served as a foil for all the Utopias he pictured later on. When her husband died, Aunt Mary had offered a home to her sister. The two women were poor, they had had no special training; all they could do was to let rooms. They worked out on paper a scheme by which they would make a modest profit and be able to hire a servant. But, as with Sarah Wells at Atlas House, this dream failed to come true. To young Wells, their appearance was only too familiar. They were as worn and drab as the walls and furniture. Their Sunday bonnets were just like those that his mother used to wear. They would make extremely polite conversation over a cup of tea. But in their eyes lurked terror of what the future held in store, terror that fought against their patient resignation, it, too, worn down almost to breaking point.

The nephew took a room on the top story. It was not heated, of course. Drafts played over the floor, and the little flame of the candle threw a wavering light on his books and papers. There was no table, he wrote seated in front of the chest of drawers, his feet in the bottom drawer. For warmth he put on all the clothes he possessed and topped them with his overcoat. Like Mr. Lewisham, he thought a great deal about luckier fellows who could work with a will in their comfortable rooms, sitting at their well-lit desks, surrounded by their shelves of books and reveling in the unbelievable luxury of warmth, their hearts and minds at peace.

Visions began to creep between him and his books, visions as absurd as those that haunted Mr. Lewisham. Something very disturbing was beginning to make itself felt. Until now his surplus energy had all gone into the struggle for existence, the battle for education. His imagination had been entirely taken up by this adventure of the spirit, with no attention to spare for anything else. All he knew of love was a kiss snatched from a little kitchenmaid at Up Park and the quivering of her young body as he held her for a brief moment in his arms. From the Westbourne Park house he had brought away horrible memories of leering, shameless lust, of sordid intrigues carried on under the name of love, which had sobered rather than allured him.

Like many very sensual people, he instinctively refused to fritter himself away in furtive pleasures. The hunger that was growing within him could only be appeased by complete surrender to passion. He himself did not realize how exacting he was in love, how difficult to satisfy. He waited with boundless, aimless expectancy for love, the miracle, to be drawn irresistibly into his life. A beacon of passion, ready for the torch. His spokesman, George Ponderevo, describes how he began to be vaguely attracted by girls he passed in the street, women sitting opposite to him in the train, girl students at his classes, shop assistants, barmaids, and even by photographs of girls and women—feeling, more and more strongly, that somewhere in this casual crowd he would find the one particular being who was meant for him.

Wells discovered his miracle—or rather, created it by the sheer force of his expectancy—on his own doorstep. On his very first visit to Aunt

Mary he had been greatly struck by his cousin Isabel. Some idea of her
unusual grace, her grave, strangely appealing beauty, can be gained even
from the bad photographs of that period. A wide brow, shadowed by
a fringe of hair, dark brown, says Wells, whose wavy mass follows
the graceful curve of the head and ends in a heavy knot at the base
of the neck. Below this statuesque forehead, straight eyebrows and
long eyes, the expression is calm and serious. The cheek curves
delicately inward from broad temple to a firm, round chin. The mouth
is very finely drawn; the marked, sensual curve of the upper lip comes
down to meet a full, soft lower lip, like the quarter of a ripe fruit; a
mouth precocious in its womanliness, despite a gentle, childish pout.
Isabel's neck was round and white, her hands long and slender, and
her dresses, of the style then known as artistic, with their simple,
clinging lines, showed her supple form to the best advantage. There
was something extraordinarily suggestive about the long curve of her
body, in contrast to the tightly corseted wasp waist, the "single breast,"
as Wells calls it, and the absurd, rustling flounces with their mixture
of crude colors usual at that time. It seemed to him that under her
dress she was almost naked, and her unrestricted movements fired his
senses. He did not yet understand that these were the throes of physical desire, but from the moment he set eyes on her he knew that she
was meant for him, and he for her. The two cousins were alike in
some ways, they had the same longing to escape from their squalid
surroundings, from the humiliation of poverty, from the drab ugliness
that hemmed them in. Wells was trying to make his escape by way of
the intellect. Isabel had got no further than Pre-Raphaelite dresses, velvet berets that made her look like some medieval page boy, and vague
aspirations, which she believed to be artistic, toward quiet and comfort.
The emptiness of her mind was veiled by her dreamy expression and
the way in which, when everyday matters needed her attention, she
seemed to come slowly down from somewhere in the clouds. Despite
the flowing grace of her movements she was as numb as a statue. She
had been a backward child and her mind was still underdeveloped.
Nothing had happened to shake her out of her mental laziness while
there was yet time.

She was very sweet natured, with an innate gentleness that made
her seem easy to influence, like some precious metal waiting to be
molded into a masterpiece. In reality, however, she was already set
and hardened, a confused jumble of prejudices, odds and ends of ideas,

and blindly worshipped conventions. Anything new alarmed her, as though it threatened her peace of mind. She had not a grain of curiosity. From books she was cut off by the barrier of unfamiliar language, a barrier that utterly defeated her. As Wells pointed out, the average Englishman's vocabulary is sticky with hackneyed phrases and outworn associations, and Isabel never got beyond the commonplaces of her native tongue. Mentally, in fact, she was closer to Sarah Wells than to her son. She talked very little, the movements of her supple neck gave a mysterious quality to her long silences, her vacant eyes were suggestive of strange dreams.

"I think from the outset I appreciated and did not for a moment resent that hers was a commonplace mind," says George Ponderevo of Marion in *Tono-Bungay*.

Thus it was that Wells's first experience of passion was accompanied by great perplexity. There was spiritual perplexity, the desperate struggle of a fresh, keen mind to overcome the passive resistance of a commonplace one. He talked to Isabel in a way that was right above her head, but she listened placidly to the lulling stream of unfamiliar words. His attacks on the social order stirred her to faint disapproval, but she did no more than protest that "people don't all think alike."

Her interests were very limited, and her conversation was made up of maddening platitudes, but when she smiled, her pretty lips seemed to hint at wonderful things; and her young admirer never tired of feasting his eyes on the waves of silky hair that rippled back from her temples. Now and again, when her stupidity became a little too obvious, "I told myself," says his alter ego, George Ponderevo, "that her simple instincts were worth all the education and intelligence in the world." Looking back, he still recognized "something fine about her, something simple and grand," that mingled with her ignorance and outstripped her commonplace limitations.

Further perplexity resulted from the trial of strength that he had undertaken. Believing himself strong enough to shake the very foundations of society, he had thought it would be perfectly easy for him, like a second Pygmalion, to breathe a soul into the beautiful statue he had fallen in love with.

Then there were material perplexities, due to the circumstances in which the young pair lived. Neither of them had much free time. Isabel spent her days touching up photographs, and went to art classes in the evening. The Euston Road house was overcrowded and gave them few opportunities for long private talks. Wells used to walk with his cousin to the photographer's shop where she worked, and rush away from his lectures to call for her there in the evening. Her gentle, serious face turned the diagrams on the blackboard to a blur, her soft voice, whose notes awakened strange vibrations in him, drowned the professor's monotonous drone. Wells was far away from the lecture theater even before he quitted it.

One of the chapters of *Love and Mr. Lewisham* is entitled, "Love in the Streets." They were curious, inconclusive affairs, those nightly walks that he always began in a flurry of vague longings, and that invariably ended with a strange, shadowy feeling of disappointment. There were evenings of misty drizzle and evenings of thick fog, when glorious, gray-white curtains turned each succeeding yard of pavement into a little secret room. They were heaven-sent events, those fogs that allowed a boy and a girl to hurry along arm in arm without attracting any of the usual attention, and undercover of which a host of rash, eloquent gestures became possible—gentle squeezes, and the fondling touch of a little hand in a cheap, much-darned glove. At times like this, that evasive something which would solve all perplexities seemed to be almost within reach. But all too soon the fogs gave place to bitter winter, with its starry skies and bright moonlight; the glow of the street lamps was harsher than before, they sparkled like a necklace of yellow stones, their beams mingled with the sharp, cold glare that fell from the shop windows. Even the stars had a hard radiance that seemed to bite, as it were, instead of twinkle.

Many years later Wells could recall every tiny detail of his long walks across London with Isabel. They had stolen meetings at home, too, when they could dodge the watchful eyes of Aunt Mary and her sister; he whispered fervently in her ear when they met in the hall, or snatched a kiss from her soft lips, which yielded, yet remained cold beneath the warmth of his.

For above all, there was in him a torturing, unfathomable physical perplexity. It was torment to him to watch her lovely mouth, her agitated breathing, the curve of her neck, while his hands were clenched and tense with the wild longing to seize hold of her. He talked to her about love; he talked to her about books that she had not read and never would read; he talked about his future, about the great things he meant to do; he told her that one day he would have the world at his feet. All the time he gazed, fascinated, at her beautiful face with its faraway expression. He was twenty years old, but he did not yet understand what was the matter with him. He wanted this girl who smiled at him with such infinite kindliness. She was the only woman for him, he told himself. With her he could share the ecstasy of complete surrender. She would burn with the same flame as himself. Her reserve was no more than virginal modesty. Her evasiveness and ignorance were signs of perfect purity.

He knew nothing about her and the secret impulses of her womanhood. He knew nothing about himself either. He ignored the physical reality of his desire, with its pressing needs. He wrapped it around in a mist of dreams. He managed to deceive himself. But at the back of his mind there was none the less a painful bewilderment. For a young man of his age he was distinctly backward. He was in the throes of retarded puberty—obstructed and enfeebled by the weakness of his neglected, half-starved body, with its hollow chest, gaunt ribs and flabby muscles, of which he felt deeply ashamed. Everything seemed to conspire to increase his perplexity. He had rebelled against convention, he had thrown off the shackles that weighed him down, only to fall, now, into the bondage of sex. Even the maturity of his mind was a drawback to him. He had no notion that a brain so clear as his could be thoroughly ignorant about the body in which it was housed, or that, in contrast to the boldness of his general ideas, his temperament was still in a state of paralysis.

At twenty he was already, as a thinker, in advance of his epoch; yet his attitude toward love was exactly that of Marie Corelli and her sister novelists. Of all the threads that went to make up the close-woven fabric of his destiny, that of sexual consciousness remained for a long time the thinnest. Right up to his declining years he went on having surprises about himself. Each new sexual experience was a revelation to him. He passed through the childish phase of love during his adolescence, and adolescent love affairs came along after he had reached manhood. Even when he had entered upon full maturity, the lover was the least developed of all the different personalities that went, in his belief, to make him up.

No doubt there were a number of reasons for this backwardness—middle-class timidity, the fact that all discussion of sex was taboo in Victorian England, the tongue-tiedness of the British people as a whole. But the chief cause seems to have been that at his very first entry into love he was met by the slender form of his cousin, so charming, so childishly stupid, and so frigid.

Isabel haunted his life for years after she had vanished from it. He held long imaginary arguments with her. He heaped her with reproaches. He discussed her in his books. Ethel in *Love and Mr. Lewisham* was drawn from her, but Marion in *Tono-Bungay* was a still closer likeness. Sometimes he reconstructed her with an angry pen; sometimes he portrayed her with tender affection. Her expressive face, with its deceptive air of mystery, would rise up before him unexpectedly, even when some other woman was giving him the greatest happiness. The curve of a pair of lips, the line of a cheek seen in profile, hair rippling back from a broad brow—it was no dead memory that these things called up for him, but a feeling of sadness and regret, so sharp as to be almost physically painful.

VII

FACETIOUS DESTINY

AS EARLY AS his second year at the School of Science Wells began to fear that he might not reach his goal. At the examinations held in June, 1886, he had failed lamentably in astronomical physics, and only just scraped through in elementary physics and geology. He knew perfectly well what it would mean to him if he had to leave without taking his degree. He knew that he would have nobody to blame but himself, that he had not been working hard enough, that he had too many outside interests. But he foresaw the catastrophe with a spirit of resignation that was almost expectancy, as though inviting the worst to happen. Something inside him seemed to want him to fail, an obscure impulse, a kind of morbid delight in the idea of throwing up the struggle that he had begun with such rapturous enthusiasm. Clear before him stretched the path along which lay financial security and enjoyable work; but he kept stopping and dawdling by the wayside, as though he no longer cared to reach the goal he had set out for. He seemed to be unconsciously looking for a crossroad. While waiting anxiously for the examination results, he wrote to a friend to say that even if he had the chance of another year at South Kensington, he was not sure whether he would take it—he was so disgusted with his poverty-stricken way of life.

What lay open to a student who failed in his exams? Wells had few illusions on that point. He knew that without qualifications and with no one to recommend or support him, any job he might find would be a wretched one at best. Common sense told him to despair, but his imagination was at work. During that summer of 1886 he illustrated a letter to his friend, A. T. Simmons, with one of the pen-and-ink sketches that often provided an outlet for his unconscious desires. For he always found it easier to express himself through parody, to disguise his secret ambitions by the absurdities of a caricature.

The comic drawing in the letter to Simmons serves as a kind of introduction to Wells's career. It laid down the program of his destiny. His fun turned out to be more prophetic than his seriousness. It was a fantastic anticipation. The little pen drawing gives a humorous outline of his future autobiography. It shows a ridiculous-looking personage, seated in the middle of a field, stroking a restive cat. Cows and sheep, forerunners of Walt Disney's creations, are gazing round-eyed at this meditative stranger. At the top of the page is written in a round, clear, cursive hand, a "copper-plate" hand (which changed very little from that time forward, though all Wells's work was written out by hand, and there was a great deal of it): "Incidents in the Lives of great men!" and below the drawing: "H. G. Wells meditating on his future." Sheets of paper scattered over the grass bear hints of the dreams that were going on behind his closed eyelids: "Secret of the Kosmos"—"Wells design for a new Framework for Society" —"How I can save the nation." On a half-hidden page is written what looks like: "The Whole Duty of Man."

He must have enjoyed himself tremendously over these holiday fancies, which revealed his principal *persona* in the round, without his realizing it. He must have thought the revelation went too far. Up among the clouds he hastily sketched in the ruler of the universe, God the Father, crown on head and thunderbolt in hand, beckoning the figure on the grass to an empty place beside the heavenly throne.

The refractory student, amid his poverty and puzzlement, was all the time subconsciously on the lookout for a crossroad that he could follow as his very own.

But when the blow did fall, it staggered him as though he had never for a moment expected it. The examination he sat for at the end of the 1887 summer term brought disaster upon him. He failed in geology. His professor may well have felt a certain malicious satisfaction in cutting short the career of such an unruly student, and certainly did not suspect that by so doing he was helping the real H. G. Wells to come to life. The birth pangs, however, were to be long and severe, and the issue nearly fatal.

Wells's fantastic daydreams, the little inner voice murmuring incomprehensible things, brought him small comfort now that he was face to face with stern reality. He felt "slaughtered beyond hope of recovery." It was as though he understood for the first time that the college in which he had given vent to his discontent in the most varied ways, had all the same been a paradise of security for him. He described this feeling in writing of Mr. Lewisham's last look back at the School of Science, when he knows that all hope of a scientific career is lost to him, and remembers his first visit there, the hopes and resolutions he brought with him. He tells himself that he might have risen to unimaginable heights if only he had managed to concentrate on one single aim.

From this paradise Wells was now cast out. The house in the Euston Road, which had sheltered his ambitious plans and rung with prophecies of his future triumphs, now witnessed his humiliation. The self-confidence, which had never deserted him since he escaped from the draper's shop at Southsea, now collapsed, he tells us, as suddenly as a pricked balloon.

Only one little guiding light twinkled by the wayside. He had just sold a short story to one of London's most popular weeklies. It had brought him a guinea. This was enough to convince him that he was destined to become a writer. But the twinkling light proved to be a will-o'-the-wisp. He had not yet come face to face with his vocation. Still the friendly welcome received from one editor had pointed the way.

Though he was now twenty-one, his practical experience of life was distressingly small. He was in that downtrodden state of mind where every effort trails off into failure and nothing seems possible except to bow before the storm. But he had a vague notion of what he needed for the time being. He was hungry, he ought to get some fresh air, and he must have leisure to try his hand at writing, which he hoped to be able to combine with teaching. So he decided to apply for a post in the country, remembering that the months at Midhurst had been the only sunny period of his life so far. He agreed to go as assistant master to a school in Wales, in a little country town so cut off from the rest of the world that the absence of a university degree could be overlooked there.

Instead of the romantic countryside he had expected, amid lakes and mountains, he found a shoddy village whose principal feature was a gasworks. The school was a dreary, dirty place. It was called an academy, like Morley's school at Bromley, but the headmaster, ignorant, vulgar, drunken and grasping, was even more like one of Dickens's schoolmasters than Morley had been. The human material into which Wells was expected to instill the rudiments of learning consisted of hobbledehoys, woodenheaded and heavy fisted. The room he shared with two theological students was dirty and dreary too, there was not one chair that could be sat on with safety; the food was badly cooked and not enough for a hungry man. The only intellectual society available was that of the French master, whom he describes in a letter as an atheistic socialist and expert on cuckoldry, and who taught him to *parler cochon* (talk smut).

Wells saw only too clearly that he was in a blind alley. He could not leave his job, in spite of the horrible conditions of life in this isolated village, because he was penniless and had hardly a shirt to his back. He was forced to put up with the filth, the discomfort, and the humiliations inflicted on him by the headmaster. It would have been natural for him to sink into despair, to be tormented by remorse and regret. Yet something braced him up—pride, perhaps, or absurd as it might seem, confidence in his own destiny. His basic optimism made the best of the muddle he was in, just as, if need be, one gets on good terms with a shady traveling companion.

From a glum, troublesome student, swathed in ill-humor, he was suddenly transformed into a teacher who accepted his disgusting surroundings with a kind of merry resignation. All through his life, he was liable to react in this contradictory way; he would be sultry with discontent during periods of calm, and face misfortune with a sort of detached curiosity. This may have arisen from a wish to do just the opposite of what people expected. There was, he used to declare, a perverse strain in him, which made him delight in thwarting predictions about his behavior. But more probably he found deep within himself at the hour of need unsuspected reserves of strength, which had been slumbering undisturbed by the squalls that passed over the surface.

Summer came round in due course, helping him to bear the boredom of his life—decking out the wretched little town, hiding the offensive gasworks behind a screen of leaves, and inviting him to explore the shady banks of the stream. It brought him, too, a holiday companion, daughter of the Vicar of the neighboring parish; she was a schoolteacher, young, pretty and, as he wrote to a friend, possessed of a soul.

The image of Isabel faded; he was deliberately and energetically driving it out, for too many shamefaced memories clustered around it. It brought to mind his ridiculous boasting, up to the very eve of his discomfiture in that geological exam; and his failure, so damaging to manly pride, to bring a tremor to those soft, cold lips. He felt in some way ashamed of having been so deeply moved by an ignorant slip of a girl.

He had frequent secret meetings with the young schoolmistress; they spent hours together beside the stream, under the trees, he talking "grotesquely" to her, and she talking very intelligently to him, as he wrote. His literary ambitions began to stir again, stimulated by the intelligent interest of a pretty girl. He wrote quite a number of short stories and sent them to various magazines, from which they were all to return to him within a short time; he began a lengthy novel, that summer his teaching work left him plenty of freedom; he made other plans which proved too much for his present creative powers. He was as happy as any young man could be while still smarting from a recent setback.

Before long the modest existence that he had built up for himself collapsed like a house of cards. Had he been of a religious turn of mind, he would certainly have believed in teleology, for he said later that his early career had been governed by "the peculiar humor of my Guardian Angel."

The milestones along his road to spiritual freedom already included his father's broken leg and his own, and to these was now to be added a shattered kidney. At the end of the holidays he met with a stupid accident on the football field, caused by one of the hobbledehoy pupils, who were fond of revenging themselves by brute force for the mental superiority of their London-trained teacher. There was a hemorrhage in the crushed kidney. Wells's room was icy cold and he had no proper medical attention. He clung to his job, for he had nowhere else to go, nor even the price of a railroad ticket. The cold affected his general health and brought on an alarming cough that shook his weakened body. Among the events that shaped his destiny he was soon able to include the bursting of a blood vessel in his lungs.

On one occasion when he was talking about his early struggles, somebody pointed out that after all he had never known the worst, most hopeless form of poverty—that which has nowhere to turn for food or shelter, and to which not a single helping hand is outstretched. All through those first miserable years, Wells at least knew that he could fall back on Up Park as a refuge, though its hospitality varied according to whether the old housekeeper happened to be in or out of favor with her mistress. In any case, the word "consumptive" softened all hearts there, as if by magic, and though his brothers were going through a term of banishment from the place, the sick boy was welcomed.

It was a very sick boy indeed who now came back to Sarah Wells. He was very near dying; the long, tiring journey had brought on a violent hemorrhage. His career, scarcely begun, was fated, it seemed, to an abrupt end, and all his boundless ambitions would leave not a trace behind. Before he had tasted life it was over for him, ebbing bitterly, uselessly away.

Judged by the medical standards of that day, he was doomed. The horrible taste of blood was in his mouth. Many, many years afterward he could still remember "as though it were last night" the slight tickling in the lungs, the first, slowly rising drops of blood which preceded the warm, nauseating wave that swept up into his throat. He was very frightened. He was immensely sorry for himself. He was beaten. The world had not played fair. It had beaten him through poverty and hunger. In the luxurious mansion that had opened its doors to him, he looked back over his thwarted, comfortless life. What was the good of having fought so hard to win knowledge that had merely brought him back here to die in a servant's room? The sense of wasted effort was bitterest of all to his very young mind and to his temperament, so positive in its attitude toward life. He was having to pay for all that was best in him, for his most valiant efforts. He was not the only victim of social injustice—he could remember fellow students who had sometimes fainted in the laboratory, really fainted away due to hunger, while rewards fell into the sturdy hands of others who were in splendid health and enjoyed every possible comfort. Summing up the experiences of his long life, Wells once declared that he had paid for his months at South Kensington with the health of all his remaining years.

Rebellion, surging through his fevered veins, began to drive out pathetic resignation and self-pity. The thoughts that tormented him, like the taste of blood on his tongue, he afterward expressed through the revolt of Masterman in *Kipps,* who embodies those moments of his existence when he knew himself to be defeated by the natural consequences of a life which had never, never given him the slightest chance.

Echoes of Up Park's life of ease and pleasure rang in Wells's ears. This safe, confident world seemed to mock his distress even while it gave him charitable shelter. Like Masterman, he felt as though he had been knocked down and trampled by a herd of swine—as though he were far too good for the rough-and-tumble around him. In after days he deliberately drove from his mind the remembrance of this collapse into illness, keeping it at arm's length, as it were, with a kind of instinct of self-preservation. He refused to linger over the sense of defeat that filled him during that period. In his literary work he made great use of the harsh experiences of his early career, but he rarely touched upon these moods of fierce rebellion in sickness, save when creating the episodic figure of Masterman, the dying consumptive.

Yet even in his deepest distress, when his courage was at the lowest ebb, some obscure instinct was protesting against the absurdity, the wastefulness, of allowing his life to end so long before its due time, an instinct which gave the lie to the doctors' gloomy predictions and drew strength from every crumb of physical comfort. The sick, self-centered boy was surrounded by comforts to which he had long been a stranger. In his memoirs, curiously enough, he says nothing about the welcome he received from Sarah Wells—nothing about her distress, which may have been tinged with secret satisfaction at the return of her mutinous son. But he does speak of his pleasant bedroom next to hers, with its gay chintz curtains, its sunshine, and the bright fire that crackled in the grate.

To lighten his despair there was also the relief of being able to give way entirely to his illness, escaping from all responsibilities, and even acquiescing, to some extent, in a defeat more overwhelming than the failure of his studies. Besides, it was considered rather romantic to be dying of consumption, especially if you were young and full of promise. The contradictory streak in Wells's nature, which, as he used to say, always drove him to do the opposite of what people expected, now came to the help of the instinct that was holding out against certain death. Something, he calls it vanity, drove him into persistently playing the part of the gay consumptive. Now that he was to meet his end, he should no doubt, in his mother's view, have turned in penitence toward the God of his childhood. "I have a vague idea," he wrote to a friend, "that God has sent me all this in order to punish me," adding that if so, God had certainly made an error of judgment, for although he had learned some salutary lessons in human charity, he now repudiated the Almighty more firmly than ever.

But whether he ground his teeth in rage, shed tears of helplessness, or forced himself to laugh, he had long, lonely months to spend face to face with death. Those months left their lasting mark on him. His life, and his view of the world, could never again be what they were before this illness. In the shadow of death certain things are thrown into strong relief. Values alter with the shifting light, under eyes that are about to close. There is a feeling of profound indifference toward everything that is still in place, everything that believes itself to be secure and immovable. Those weeks of farewell to life bred in Wells a distrust of stability, so strangely in advance of his epoch that it is generally thought to belong to what is called his prophetic vein. They also left him, as often happens in the case of delicate children who grow up to be healthy adults, with a certain feeling of impunity, as though, having been granted every indulgence while he was sick, he had kept the right to do just as he pleased in the future. The shadow of death, thrown into the balance, upsets the scales of life. Essentials are revealed in stark outline to the dying man who can no longer reach them. Everything takes the place appointed to it by laws from within. Latent tastes are strengthened by regret that they will never be indulged. Fierce hungers grow in a body that can no longer satisfy them.

"I had an angry resurgence of sexual desire," says Wells of this period. Among all that life had denied him, he regretted most bitterly having never known love. His resentment at having been robbed of that crowning touch was to haunt his sexual life long after the danger of death had departed; and because of this, he says, his imagination would often exaggerate the joy of possessing a woman to the point of obsession.

Even worse, perhaps, than the idea of lingering death, was the prospect of living on as a permanent invalid, a burden to himself and his family. He wrote to a woman friend about his dread of dragging on, among "winds, wet days and old women," for another two or three years. He dated his letters to Simmons from "the House of

Captivity, in the Valley of the Shadow of Death." He devoted part
of his enforced leisure to revising his ideas about life and bringing
them into line with his new point of view. "The universe," he wrote,
"is being thought-out thoroughly." This consciousness of a revised
world brought with it a new self-awareness. Another man might,
perhaps, have submitted to live on as an invalid and think out the
entire universe. But there can seldom have been a man so little cut
out for drawing up a system of philosophy in calm detachment from
all worldly matters as Wells. The urge to unite thought and action,
always one of Wells's chief characteristics, was strengthened during
his months of sickness. Thought, for him, was action. As he once
declared, he had no use for life as it was, except as raw material;
it bored him to look at things, unless with the idea of doing something
with them. Action was always the driving power that set his thought
in motion. Now, as strength slowly returned to his body, a longing
for activity began to plague him. He felt very sorry for himself whenever it occurred to him that he might never again be able to take his
place in "the marching column," as he called it in a letter to his
woman friend of South Kensington days.

The longing to do so was in itself a sign of improving health. So
was the irritation he now felt at being an invalid. The gay chintz curtains and the crackling fire no longer delighted him. The letters he
wrote to his friends, and their replies, were no longer enough to save
him from mental loneliness. He had no contact with the higher levels
of Up Park society except through an unusually clever young doctor
who happened to be visiting there and had taken charge of his case.
About the "damned aristocrats" and the life they led, he knew only
the little that filtered down to him by way of the servants, who exaggerated and mimicked their masters' defects. Whenever he went
among them, his mother watched him with the same anxious, disap-
proving eye that had followed him in his childhood. Whenever he
brought out some bitter, critical remark the poor woman would burst
into tears, terrified lest he should endanger the security of the whole
family. During his convalescence he saw nobody except the servants,
who, he complained, were "all dead—purely automatic. Each of them
has fifteen remarks to say over and they get through the lot each
mealtime." A day was to come when their limited stock in trade would
provide Wells with valuable raw material, but that day was still far off.

His youthful nature sometimes got the upper hand, and then his rebellious feelings would vanish, giving way to the enjoyment of life. At Christmas, Mrs. Wells's husband and all her three sons came together at Up Park, much to the envy of the other servants. Frank, the eldest boy, had by this time followed the example of his youngest brother and deserted the drapery business in his turn. He had taken up his quarters in his father's cottage near Up Park; but whereas Joseph modestly but firmly rejected all suggestions that he might do something to earn money, Frank went from village to village, selling and repairing watches and clocks. It was Frank, with his independence, his love of the open air, his stumbling talk and genuine humanity, who served later as a model for the never-to-be-forgotten Mr. Polly.

The young invalid himself, unnatural as it might seem in his sad plight, was in high spirits at this Christmas party. His very personal sense of fun, the irresistible flashes of humor with which he fascinated London society in after years, now made an appearance for the first time, to amuse a group of almost illiterate servants.

He was unwise enough to go for a long country walk, and this led to a relapse. He wrote to his girl correspondent that he was "going down the hill like a toboggan." But amid these melancholy farewells to life, he had begun to hope against hope that he would pull through in the end.

His months of sickness and convalescence at Up Park were not the useless waste of time that they seemed. Until then, his mind had ripened only in patches, as it were. His knowledge of science and his views on social questions were far ahead of his artistic judgment. In "A Slip under the Microscope," he says of Hill, who reflects his own youthful personality, that in obedience to an absurd principle he had never wasted his time on reading poetry. At South Kensington he had been proud of his scientific turn of mind—he never lost this feeling of superiority—whereas for literature he had a kind of contempt, which continued even after he had made it his career and which, indeed, he never entirely shook off. His early writing flowed out with deplorable facility; he was incapable as yet of aiming at anything more worth-while, and even believed that his superficial fluency would appeal to a wide circle of readers. In later years he mercilessly condemned the prolific outpourings of this period, from which, he said, his real self was curiously and entirely absent.

It was the greatest good luck for him that the stories with which

he now began to bombard the magazines and newspapers had no
success. If some absent-minded editor had again encouraged him, he
would have found it much harder to drag himself out of the toils
of banality. The guinea paid to him for the story that had been
accepted before he left London was the only money earned by a whole
year's work, details of which are given in a letter to one of his friends.
This twelve months' output included verses, both serious and comic;
comic prose; humorous essays; a long novel still unfinished; another
novel, completed, 35,000 words in length; and a number of short
and long stories, the manuscripts of which were steadily being returned to him.

By the time these manuscripts came back he had begun to understand why his work was always rejected. During his illness he had
little to do except read. In the shadow of death, he allowed himself the
luxury of reading poetry—Heine, Keats, Shelley, Whitman. He borrowed novels from the Vicar and hailed with joy a batch of books
sent to him by one of his fellow students at South Kensington. For
once he was reading with no particular aim in view, with no preconceived ideas and no wish to add to his knowledge. His mind was
open, as it had seldom been before, to anything that chance might
put within its reach. The seed of literary impressions was falling on
virgin soil. In his receptive mood, Wells very quickly learned to
estimate the relative value of the different things he read. He looked
back upon this enforced halt at Up Park as his real period of professional training. His self-judgment was as harsh as is usual at that time
of life. It led first of all to a tremendous auto-da-fé, which took place
just before he left Up Park. The crackling fire consumed novels, short
stories, such of them as had been returned, poems and humorous
essays—all in one grand blaze.

The chief thing that struck him, in comparing his first attempts
at writing with the good models he had now come to know, was the
inadequacy of his powers of expression. He had been content to
scratch the surface of a subject. He realized that he was not equipped
to delve deeper. His defective education betrayed itself, first and foremost, in the lack of connection between English as he spoke it and
English as he wrote it. Class distinctions are revealed in England by
the quality of the vocabulary, to a more striking degree than in any
other country. Not only by incorrect pronunciations, dropped "h"s
and slurred syllables, but also by the paucity of words, the catch

phrases, the carelessly chosen adjectives, and all-sufficing exclamations that make up the whole store of the millions who come forth from the elementary schools.

It was his limited vocabulary that brought disaster upon Kipps when he tried to climb the social ladder. It afflicted Mr. Polly too, so pathetically "uncertain about the spelling and pronunciation of most of the words" in the beautiful, rich, and disconcerting language that was his by birth. All through his life Mr. Polly went on pursuing the big, beautiful words that would have expressed so well the delicate shades of his emotions and the ideas that haunted his mind. The unaccustomed words kept just out of reach, or else the wrong word would slip mischievously into the place of the one he wanted; he kept on wrestling with them, but he felt they would always get the better of him. Mr. Polly's struggles with his mother tongue make very funny reading, and Wells's account of them is among his most brilliantly successful feats. But there is an angry sadness in it, too.

The English language, the richest in the whole world, is generally used with the most exasperating parsimony. The words that sparkle like jewels in Shakespeare's work seem to be carefully protected from everyday usage; and young Wells had inherited this excessive reverence for the Sunday best of literature. Rather than crawl through the thickets of the vulgar tongue, he hoisted himself, in his writings, onto the stilts of bombast. In his autobiography he quotes a letter he wrote, from Up Park, to his doctor, as an example of "Babu English." But while still at South Kensington he had perfected a style of his own, and used it in his dealings with the other students. A style that was incisive and firm, terse and expressive, through which could be glimpsed a suggestive outline of his future possibilities. All he had to do now was to transpose that style to the literary plane. There was no need for him to borrow from other writers.

After four months' convalescence he was able to leave Up Park and accept an invitation from William Burton, one of his South Kensington friends, now a research chemist with Wedgewoods. By this time, though still very weak and convinced that he would remain an invalid for the rest of a short life, he was to all intents and purposes fully equipped for his career as a writer. The only thing he needed was something to write about, something that would press the right button.

He was hunting for a theme, in the subconscious manner which is always that of the creative process. The industrial setting in which he now found himself had some graphic features which appealed strongly to his imagination. He was breathing the atmosphere of Arnold Bennett's Five Towns, with their pottery kilns and blast furnaces, belching out fire and ashes, and the mighty chimneys of their steelworks towering through the bluish haze of dust and damp that flung a veil of mystery over the long valley. This industrial Gehenna of today and tomorrow, with its clouds and pillars of fire, set him dreaming and let loose upon him, the London suburbanite, a sudden flood of impressions such as he had never received from any country landscape, with its varied tints and the colors that slowly wax and fade in its sky. He was close to what would later form one of his typical backgrounds.

He set to work on what he described as a tremendous melodrama, a kind of *Mysteries of Paris* transposed to the Five Towns district. He already had the idea of the alternation of humor and savagery which he later developed into an unfailing technique. But for the time being he could only make clumsy experiments with a plot that was too loosely knit.

A short story, "The Cone," is the only surviving fragment of the melodrama planned in the Burtons' home at Etruria. It has one feature that was to characterize the whole of Wells's writing in the first period of his career, a strange and unexpected streak of cruelty. Toward the end of his life he made an earnest study of the problem of cruelty, raising the question whether a sadistic instinct is dormant in all men, or whether it develops as the direct result of experiencing cruelty or seeing it inflicted by and upon others. He showed a curious interest in the case of Gilles de Rais, in which he claimed to find conclusive proof that sadism, the delight in inflicting pain, results from a feeling of unlimited power, together with a contempt for the ordinary human being, a loss of solidarity between man and man. He made a clear distinction between sexual perversion and the thrist for power that finds its satisfaction in oppressing the weak. He pointed out, too, that even the disgust we feel at an act of cruelty, the virtuous indignation that comes over us, and whose first impulse is to make the punishment fit the crime, merely arises from the awakening of our latent sadism.

No secret monster lay concealed in Wells. Throughout every ordeal, whether it arose from adversity or from success, he retained his inner balance. In action, thought and feeling he was clearheaded; his being was flooded by the radiance of that consciousness which penetrated far into its depths and lit up every shadowy corner of his mind. But at this early period there seems to have been a poison at work in his system, and it took him some time to drive it out.

"The Cone" describes, with a certain detailed relish, the appalling death of a man who is pushed by a jealous husband onto the cone of a blast furnace. Incidentally, Wells gave to the seducer thus atrociously punished the name of his French colleague at the school in Wales, the "specialist in cuckoldry" who had amused and irritated him with stories of amorous adventure.

Several of Wells's first books are marked by similar streaks of ferocity, a ferocity quite contrary to his placid nature, a kind of harmless revenge for all the suffering imposed upon him by his fellow men and by life itself. Was this the awakening of the cruelty which he believed to be latent in every human being, in reaction to the cruelty he had experienced or seen around him? Or was it the exasperation of a doomed man with an unconscious grudge against the world of the living?

The shadow of death hung over him for a long time before it faded into the sunshine of deliverance and success. The interplay of darkness and light in his books tells of its presence and of its withdrawal. His reaction against death was not caused by a sudden return to health; it came from within, as an act of his will. In the autobiography he describes how, one summer day at Etruria, he lay down in a glade in a wood—a bluebell-covered glade, strangely incongruous in this district of kilns and blast furnaces—and mused about his appointed end and the way it was keeping him waiting. He had had enough of waiting. And he concludes, in the offhand way in which he so often settled the most important problems of his private life: "I stopped dying then and there, and in spite of moments of some provocation, I have never died since."

He then and there determined to launch into what he called his "second attack on London." He did not know as yet that he already held the key to success. Since coming to Etruria, he had begun a novel entitled "The Chronic Argonauts." It was to be serialized in the *Science Schools Journal,* which he himself had founded while at South Kensington; but after the third instalment he stopped it, having decided that his treatment of the subject was wrong. When he constructed his plot he had been strongly under the influence of Hawthorne, from whom he had borrowed, among other things, the idea of the united hostility of a whole village population, directed against one particular man and expressing itself in acts of wanton cruelty.

The description of the village in this story, a Welsh village, is taken directly from reality. The minor characters are to some extent drawn from life, according to the method that Wells followed in later works, where he mingled the everyday world, describing, in minute detail, the humdrum lives of its very commonplace inhabitants, with the most unexpected events, which were rendered more credible by being so gradually superimposed.

The main theme of the book turns on a scientific problem. Wells had often had long arguments with his fellow students at South Kensington about what he called the Fourth Dimension. And he no doubt discussed the subject again with his friend Burton at Etruria. These talks paved the way for *The Time Machine*.

Among the mysteries that had baffled Wells when he was studying physics was that of time, a factor which he felt had been wrongly neglected. His visionary groping out toward the unknown, told him that there was a gap in the system of physics. He was still advancing the usual scientific arguments. But though he did not realize it at that time, the full force of his imagination was bent on the subject.

In the discussion that opens *The Time Machine*—final version of "The Chronic Argonauts"—linger echoes of a debate that must certainly have taken place. The passage from lively argument to scientific hypothesis must have been quite spontaneous. A spark flashed out, and with that spark he kindled the flame of his creative work. Creative imagination evolves not only according to the possibilities of the writer's mind, but also according to its limitations. Achievement depends upon allowing for both. Wells had the extraordinary good fortune to make his choice not only by instinct, but with a clear-sighted awareness of his own qualifications, an exact estimate of his shortcomings.

His literary ambition had awakened long before his powers were ripe for it. Here, he had anticipated upon himself. Creative imagination can work only with the material at hand. Bricks and mortar are needed for building. Wells's store of experience was small, and of no use to him as yet. Because of the particular kind of life he had lived, his horizon was very narrow. He had had no more than a backstairs view of the upper classes of society. As for the underlings at Up Park, the wage slaves, the abortions of the social system, as he called them, he was still too close to them to be able to use them as subjects for fiction; that would come later. A man cannot write with his head leaning against the wall on which he has just painfully bumped it.

Wells brought something fresh into the literature of his day, a scientific education. He made up for his ignorance of human nature by drawing on what he had learned at the School of Science; his ignorance of the laws governing social behavior was compensated by his familiarity with the laws of physics. Physical or biological possibilities gave him the springboard from which his imagination could leap ahead.

He knew quite well why his early work had taken this direction. Speaking of the period when he was planning "The Chronic Argonauts," he mentions, as a sign of growing intelligence in his young mind, the fact that he had known himself to be exceptionally ignorant of the world around him, and had decided, therefore, to look into the possibilities of pure fantasy. This, he says, is a good game for young people to play, especially for those whose lives are too restricted.

But "The Chronic Argonauts" proved to be just another failure, a rough draft. The title was too pompous and the style was uneven. Three instalments came out in the *Science Schools Journal*—April, May, and June, 1888—and then Wells withdrew it. When a friend complained that it had stopped at a most exciting point, he wrote to assure her that there would be a continuation. Indeed, the continuation was already written. But Wells never published it in its original form. When he went up to London he had already a vein of gold, but he had not yet freed the ore from the dross.

VIII

AN AMBITION DISCARDED

ONE OF THE drawings that Wells sent to A. T. Simmons shows him as a scraggy youth, carrying a huge book under one arm, his head crowned with an enormous laurel wreath, his eyes round and puzzled. The caption, written in a flowing hand, but less smoothly than usual, says, "I am in London, seeking work, but at present finding none." In one corner of the drawing is a poster inscribed, "Wanted, 1,000 men to carry advertisement Boards." The scraggy figure is perplexedly sucking a gigantic pen.

Wells went the rounds of the employment agencies, and his humiliating experiences are faithfully set forth in *Love and Mr. Lewisham*. At this time he was more shabby looking than ever, and his wretchedness was made all the greater by the pride born of his new self-knowledge. Loneliness closed over him, the crushing loneliness of shamefaced poverty. He stopped writing to his friends, so as to save the cost of stamps and the necessity of admitting that he had not yet found work. He did not dare to visit his cousin Isabel in his present state and after such a long silence. But now that he was back in the London streets where she had walked with him, the thought of her began to haunt him again. He went over and over the course of their long walks. His eyes ached with longing and summoned up her imaginary figure at every corner.

He was living in utter, penniless desolation, in a slum room with three beds, all occupied, or in an unheated attic, cut into two by a thin partition. His meals grew more and more scanty—a sausage or a herring, fried over the gas jet in a common eating house. He did have, too, the down-and-outer's wonderful stroke of luck—the discovery that the last, blackened coin in his pocket was not copper, but silver.

The first money he earned was in payment for some large wall diagrams for one of his Science School friends who had started a biology class. Months went by during which he just managed to keep alive, thanks to a few pupils sent to him for coaching, now and again, by friends who had taken their degrees at South Kensington. Whenever he was not out hunting for work, he was writing articles and stories that he hoped to sell at once. But the constant worry about the future, and the desperate loneliness of a great city, weighed on him more and more.

He was never to forget the London Sundays when every sign of life vanished behind drawn blinds, and the endless rows of houses looked like the alleys of some vast cemetery; when the step of a living passer-by echoed noisily along the sidewalk; when the shops had blind faces; when everyone but himself had a warm fireside to hurry back to; when only the churches were hospitable to a stranger.

At last, at the end of the year, he found a post, in a private school near London. Sixty pounds a year, with board and lodging. This was as good as he could hope for. His shabby appearance showed that he was at the end of his tether, and his longing to get the job was evident; yet at the risk of losing it, he stipulated that he should not be asked to give any religious instruction. This display of courage seems to have made a good impression on his new headmaster. He also refused to live in. The school was near enough to London for him to go back there every evening, and just at the moment when he got this work London had become irresistibly attractive to him. He had seen Isabel again. His Aunt Mary had taken him back under her wing. They had given up the dingy lodginghouse, but a room next door to their apartment was to let, and they settled Wells into it with a firm hand. Family life began again as though it had never been broken off. All his old tormented desire for Isabel came surging back. As soon as he was with her once more, he says, he forgot how completely he had forgotten her in the meantime.

From now on he had only one purpose—to persuade Isabel to marry him right away. Family life, with its deceptive show of intimacy, was getting on his nerves. But whenever he spoke of getting married, the cautious Isabel retorted, as Marion did in *Tono-Bungay,*

"We can't." For she was scared by the risks and uncertainties of a moneyless marriage, and preferred life at home, with a little pocket money and an outing now and then.

Her hesitations and objections, recorded in the snatches of conversation between George Ponderevo and Marion, drove Wells to such a pitch that he could think only of how to make enough money to get married. "I was keen and eager," he writes in his autobiography, "and she was tepid and rational."

Henley House School was entirely unlike any private school that Wells had come across before. Its headmaster was a reformer, in advance of his time, with a real vocation for teaching. He used to lie awake at night thinking about his pupils. He never punished them or gibed at them. The pupils, too, were different from the boys that Wells had met up to now; they were the sons of professional men—artists, lawyers, writers. The meals were copious, and the headmaster's wife was distressed by Wells's emaciated condition. In fact, the new teacher found himself basking in comfort such as he had never known. There were even white cloths on the tables, and vases of flowers, and "everything is in keeping with this luxurious setting," as he wrote enthusiastically to a friend.

This experience of eating at a flower-decked table with a white cloth made a great impression on him. It meant that he had climbed one rung higher on the social ladder. He never forgot any of the rungs that he mounted, one by one, with such painful effort.

Henley House School remembered him as a master who was very good at teaching the clever boys, impatient with the slow or lazy ones, and apt to hurl pieces of chalk at those whose attention wandered. He never learned to suffer fools gladly. Despite his own mutinous attitude at South Kensington, he was almost as strict a disciplinarian now as he had been in the Midhurst days. But he taught with all the ardor of a reformer, giving joyous rein to his pedagogical gift. He simplified, he tells us, the study of physics, and started a new method of teaching mathematics, which proved most valuable in bringing out the abilities of his pupils and, he adds, laid the foundation for two or three university careers in higher mathematics.

The interest he took in teaching, and his present well-being, were overshadowed by the idea that haunted him unceasingly—the idea of marriage with Isabel. After his experiences with the London employment agencies he realized that his chances would be far better if he had a degree. So he set to work again with redoubled energy, born of his frustrated passion. He deliberately turned his back on his literary ambitions, that long path ended in the clouds.

How could he go on waiting, with all his senses keyed up and starved? He might have to wait for years. Like Mr. Lewisham, he dreamed that at last he was to marry the woman he had so long yearned for. He took her in his arms and bent to kiss her. Suddenly he saw that her lips were faded, her eyes had lost their sparkle, her cheeks were wrinkled.

Whenever Wells wanted anything, he wanted to have it at once, without a moment's delay. He was as uncompromising about practical matters as about ideas.

By the summer of 1889 he was able to get through an intermediate science examination at London University, and at the end of the year he took the diploma awarded by the College of Preceptors, which exempted candidates for the teaching profession from graduation at a university. The ideal candidate, well fed for the first time, had come to life again in Wells. He was going ahead by leaps and bounds.

The Augustan age, the great literary period, was over, he wrote to A. T. Simmons. He was all agog for the next step. After the science examination, he thought of taking his degree at London University. But he heard that the College of Preceptors was offering prizes for the best theses on various subjects. Every pound he could put aside brought him nearer to Isabel. The struggle for money and what it meant, possessed him so entirely that even after many years, almost half a century, had gone by, he could still remember every detail of what he had earned at this time, and how he had done it.

He began a steady bombardment of the College, sending in theses on every subject, covering the whole permitted range at one fell swoop. He won three prizes, one for paper on the theory and practice of teaching, one for mathematics, and one for natural sciences. The only advantage his mind gained from these efforts was that they provided a fresh groundwork of pedagogical knowledge, to reinforce his gift for teaching. He won all the prizes of which he had any hopes, and they brought him in the sum of twenty pounds. Twenty pounds, at one stroke, to an assistant master with a salary of two pounds a week! He felt the thrill of a man who has proved his market value.

"Compliments from the Secretary, enthusiasm at the school, the town Painted Red" he announced.

He got his salary at Henley House School raised at once, and asked at the same time for a reduction of his working hours. He was looking around for an extra source of income, when he received a mysterious communication from a Mr. Briggs, who asked him to come to Cambridge for an interview, and paid his return fare. Briggs was the founder and director of the University Correspondence College; he had set out, writes Wells, to make a few hundred pounds, and had been flung into a position of wealth and influence. He agreed to pay the young man two pounds a week for the time being, promising him a full-time job at a much higher salary as soon as he should have obtained his degree at London University. "Great boom in Wells's!" he announced triumphantly to his friend Simmons.

H. G. and Isabel could launch out into matrimony with the twenty pounds of prize money as their capital. Their future seemed more or less assured. He was so buoyed up by happiness, now that the goal was in sight, that nothing could lower his spirits, not even another attack of hemorrhage brought on by overwork. This earned him a holiday at Up Park, a short rest for a brain that had been soaking up knowledge like a sponge.

He could think of nothing but the absent Isabel; the temptation of her elusive womanhood set his nerves secretly on edge.

The great literary period had only been suffering an eclipse. His suppressed ambition began to stir again. But the respite that he owed to the humiliating charity of Up Park was too brief to enable him to take up any of his more far-reaching plans. He confined himself to dealing with an idea that had been at the back of his mind for some time, as a result of his biological studies; the notion that "everything that exists is unique, no one thing is exactly similar to another." His brain, which seemed to have become simply a machine for passing examinations, went back to its original bent during this short relaxation. The essay is full of statements that bear his typical imprint. He called it "The Rediscovery of the Unique." Written by a man who was engulfed in the banality of his life, his work, and his struggle to make a home, it calls upon human beings to get back their sense of the exceptional.

Man, it declares, allows the watch and the calendar to blind him to the fact that each moment of his life is a miracle and a mystery. This was yeast stirred into the stodgy dough of ready-made ideas. Wells drew conclusions whose scientific bearing was far in advance of his day. He declared, for instance, that the most indisputable corollary of the rediscovery was "the ruin of the atomic theory." Human experience provided no foundation whatever for the hypothesis of similar atoms. This was a forecast, in 1891, of what twentieth-century physicists call "statistical causality." The similarity of atoms and other physical units was a matter of general belief at that time. It seemed unnecessary and unprofitable to suppose that atoms might have their own individuality.

In this essay Wells carries his rediscovery onto the moral plane as well, flinging a challenge to the conventions against which he had been fighting for so long, and the restrictions that hemmed him in. He points out that people are unique, and so are circumstances, which makes it impossible for our conduct to be guided by rough-and-ready principles. For all its air of detachment, this passage hints at the torments of the man. In a striking final metaphor, he compares science to a match that man had struck in the hope of lighting up the walls of the hall or temple in which he stood, and revealing wonderful secrets, only to discover that its flame was too weak to show him anything except his own hand, holding it.

This article was sent out in its turn to make the usual round of the editorial offices. It was given temporary burial by one of the foremost magazines of the day, the *Fortnightly Review*. This journal had been founded by George Eliot and Herbert Spencer, but their sway was now over, and John Morley ruled in their stead. As happens with every famous magazine that attracts aspiring authors, its office had become a graveyard of buried hopes, a huge repository of unpublished manuscripts. These were stored in two enormous boxes; into one went all the definitely rejected manuscripts, and into the other those which, in Morley's opinion, could be used if he ran short of material, but which in reality never were drawn upon. However, into this imposing office, with its solid, unchanging furniture and its ideas to match, there burst one day, like a rocket, Frank Harris.

He took over as editor in chief, appointed by the proprietors in the full flush of his recent success with the *Evening News* and his personal conquest of London society. He came in with the jaunty step of a man who sweeps all before him—his snub nose with its wide nostrils quivered as though he were perpetually savoring a sensational story or a new love affair; his low forehead, beneath the jet-black, wiry hair that a central parting kept in control, was barred by a ferocious frown; his mustache bristled; and from between his full lips emerged a voice that seemed to delight in imitating thunder.

He says in his memoirs that he began his reign at the *Fortnightly* by getting rid of the hoarded manuscripts, and that he kept two of those he found in the rejected box. Harris was a kind of human boiler, always bubbling and seething like an overheated saucepan, and giving forth whistling noises, exclamations, inarticulate growls and melodramatic asides. This high-pressure activity sometimes jostled his memories out of place, or heightened their color in retrospect. But what he says about the manuscripts is very likely true. Anyone who knew Frank Harris can easily believe that his short legs, with their springy calves, danced him right off toward the rejected offerings. He was of the race of pioneers, and though a capricious fate had led him into drawing rooms instead of jungles, he always looked at them with an explorer's searching eye. People have called him immensely vain, but it would be nearer the truth to say that he had a devouring need to be in the right. He was honestly and sincerely convinced that whenever he won a personal triumph he was serving the cause of humanity. In a more heroic age he would have turned with equal readiness to crusading or piracy, or have jousted, with raised vizor, at every tournament. In our degenerate days he displayed his courage by bounding forward, with the roar of an angry lion, to defend some great cause or petty scheme, to herald some neglected genius, or to exhibit what, in his proud opinion, was the appetite of a wild beast.

With his flair for anything out of the ordinary, Harris was bound to be attracted by the very title of Wells's article. And despite his violently contradictory judgments, he had a keen sense of quality.

Wells was in ecstasy when he heard that his article had been accepted by the *Fortnightly*. He wrote to his father about it in the offhand manner of one who takes literary honors in his stride. But in writing to his friend Simmons he overflowed with joy. After so many disappointments he could hardly believe his luck. Frank Harris was loudly trumpeting forth his discovery. Oscar Wilde, whose word was law in literary matters, had been charmed by the originality of the article, despite its immature style, and praised it in no uncertain terms. But Wells, living far away from the literary circles of London, did not realize that he had now made his little mark there. He went on clearing the ground just ahead of him, with the mechanical persistence of a navy. He was preparing for his university examinations. Briggs had made it clear that his salary would depend on the standard he reached in them, for to Briggs, the diplomas he could list on his prospectus were more important than the quality of the teaching in his correspondence course. Wells was the very man for him. There was as yet no routine method of teaching science. The University Correspondence College used textbooks and worked out a more or less foolproof system by which the students learned to answer about a hundred questions that were likely to be set in examination papers.

Wells's first printed book was a manual in this series, based on the model prepared by Briggs, a textbook of biology. It was typical of his freakish destiny that his name, which was later to become a symbol of originality, should appear for the first time on the cover of such a prosaic, utilitarian booklet.

But biology required practical work in addition to the textbook. Wells compressed this into forty hours of laboratory demonstrations, arranged to cover twenty evening classes or, for students who lived at a distance from London, two weeks of the vacation period. He had no illusions whatever as to the quality of his own teaching; it was a series of conjuring tricks, where his skill amused him for a time. There was something in his temperament, he said drily, which responded to the streak of banditry that ran through the whole enterprise. But a secret dissatisfaction was gathering within him; he was on the verge of rebelling against his cut and dried work, and against the dishonesty of a method by which scientific research was deliberately scamped. Like all his rebellions this developed very slowly, in the form of mounting ill-humor, and burst out one fine day quite unexpectedly.

His literary ambitions suffered a knockout blow just at the moment when he seemed to have good enough prospects on which to get married.

Encouraged by the publication of his first article, he had sent in another to the *Fortnightly Review*. This, too, was based on a notion that had come to him at South Kensington, and which he had put before the Debating Society. During that apparently wasted period his mind had stored up reserves that were to last for quite a while. He took the same attitude toward ideas as toward people. He would approach them with an open mind, inspect them slowly from every angle, drop them and then return to them, as though to old friends from whom he had been estranged for a time. He was, in fact, more faithful to ideas than to human beings, more steadfast in his spiritual relationships than in friendship or affection. As he himself put it, his mind never dropped any bone it got hold of without having picked it clean.

His second article, "The Universe Rigid," went back to the idea that he had used as the starting point of "The Chronic Argonauts," the theory of the Fourth Dimension. It gave an imaginary picture of the physical universe as it would appear if the time factor intervened in it; but he himself declared later on that the description was labored and badly written. On the strength of the previous article, Frank Harris had this one set in type at once, and read it for the first time in proof. He could not make head or tail of it. He sent for the author.

In his autobiography Wells describes this interview with Frank Harris. He tells of his rapture and shyness at being summoned by the high and mighty editor, of the careful attention he gave to his clothes, including the top hat which he brushed energetically and which, when his desperate efforts to give it a glossy surface proved unavailing, he damped and smoothed down with a sponge, regardless of his Aunt Mary's cries of protest.

Seldom have circumstances combined so maliciously to bring discomfiture to an ambitious young writer. He was late for his appointment, and when he arrived, out of breath, he was left to cool his heels in the waiting room for half an hour, a thing which is not only hurtful to a man's pride, but fatal to whatever witty remarks he has been carefully rehearsing for the occasion. The big room, with its huge table and the lofty bearing of the clerks, created an atmosphere that was quite new to Wells, and which he felt at once to be hostile. At last the pale, thin youth, painfully aware of his inexperience, his uncertain manners, and the odor of poverty that he seemed to carry around with him, was ushered into the self-confident, aggressive presence of a man who was triumphantly, even insolently successful and prosperous, and had probably been stimulated by an excellent luncheon. The battle of words was fought with unequal weapons. The brilliant young fellow, with his original ideas and daring remarks, had been left behind somewhere or other on the way, or in the anteroom. Wells's piping voice was drowned by the thunderous tones of Harris, rolling over him with innumerable "r"s. A pair of eyes that were perhaps merely inquisitive, glared at him with the ferocious expression that Harris relied upon to subdue his fellow men.

And all at once, Wells caught sight of his top hat, now half dry and beginning to bristle. The pitiful remains of his self-assurance collapsed into horror. It seemed to him that his disgraceful headgear must be filling the thoughts of the great man and his lordly secretaries. He began to stammer an attempt to explain it. Afterward he blamed that bristling topper for the failure of an interview that might have led to vitally important results.

The paths of the two men often crossed in later years, when Wells was climbing, slowly at first, then with dizzy speed, and Harris was going, first slowly and then rapidly, downhill.

But on the day when Wells fled from the office of the *Fortnightly Review,* clutching his unhappy top hat—which he afterward battered into final destruction—and Harris gave orders for the type of "The Universe Rigid" to be dispersed, there was nothing to suggest that the two would ever meet again. As a result of that interview, says Wells, he wrote nothing of any importance for at least a year.

The wound to his pride festered for a good deal longer than that. For the moment it was superficially healed by what he believed to be his greatest victory over the obstacles that life had put in his path. He had reached a position which Isabel thought was secure enough for marriage. He rented a little house in the suburbs, eight rooms, including the bathroom. This was his triumph over Atlas House and the succession of furnished lodgings that had taken its place.

Isabel and he were married in October, 1891.

It is again through George Ponderevo, in *Tono-Bungay,* that we learn of Wells's decision to have a registry office wedding, and his fiancée's insistence that she would only be married in church.

" 'Very well,' I said, standing up, white and tense, and it amazed me, but I was also exultant; 'then we won't marry at all.' "

But like George Ponderevo, Wells gave way in the end, and they were married in church.

Isabel had reached the haven of her dreams—a house with a bathroom, and a church wedding. She was very subdued and very pleased. Frank Wells, the only member of the bridegroom's family who came to the ceremony, unexpectedly burst into tears. For the time being, Wells was in an ecstasy of happiness. But from the church wedding he carried away the secret resentment of a man who could never forgive himself for submitting to compromise.

IX

A TRAGEDY OF IGNORANCE

WHAT GEORGE PONDEREVO tells us about his life with Marian gives, with fair accuracy, the distressing picture of Wells's first marriage. He and Isabel were both very young and, in some ways, unusually ignorant and simple; their natures were in complete contrast and they had not a single notion in common, or ever could have. Isabel was extremely conventional; she seemed to have no ideas of her own, but only those of her class. Wells was skeptical, enterprising, and passionate. They were held together on the one hand by the spell that her beauty cast over him, and on the other hand by her satisfaction at filling the chief place in his thoughts.

In *Tono-Bungay,* Wells presents the story as a single unit composed of several elements, whereas in reality it took place on two planes. He was not aware of this at the time, and even when he put the experience into his novel he had not quite realized it. To the very end of his life he kept on discovering and ridding himself of mistaken notions about sex.

On one of these planes, the external one, the elements that made for conflict were present from the first, and Wells himself most probably knew this. Burning intellectual curiosity was brought face to face with placid ignorance, rebellious impatience with meek acceptance of prevailing ideas. It was the often repeated tragedy of the man who marries, at too early an age, a woman of his own social level, and then rapidly outstrips her and leaves her far behind, like a milestone on his advancing path. Wells was not even comforted, as many young men are when deeply in love, by the deceitful hope of being able to awaken his wife's intelligence and model her on his own lines. He knew her too well. He had lived too long in her company. Their incompatibility of spirit was something that he took for granted even before he married her. He had not been looking for a wife who would share in his thoughts. He had the usual pride of a very young man, believing that he was self-sufficient and had brains enough for two. His physical desire for her was intense. But he longed as well for the sweetness of her presence, the steadying influence of her underlying common sense, her unchanging, uncomprehending kindliness—all that was static in her patient slowness. She was to be the green meadow where the exhausted traveler could fling himself down, the cool spring that would quench his feverish thirst. But when he looked forward to this joy in her mere existence, he had been counting on an entirely satisfactory relationship between them, an intimate and perfect harmony. He knew she was almost illiterate. He knew she was tepid, her senses unawakened. But he thought he would be able to bring her to life. He felt sure that her virginity would be kindled by the flame of his own. He did not know that there was such a thing as a frigid woman.

Still speaking behind the mask of George Ponderevo, he says that what chiefly impresses him, on looking back, is the ignorant, groping way in which they fell into the trap of matrimony. The future of a nation is determined by the manner in which its young people pair off; yet "flushed and blundering youth" is left to stumble on as best it can, "with nothing to guide it but shocked looks and sentimental twaddle and base whisperings and cant-smeared examples."

This indictment of a system that kept young people entirely ignorant in regard to sex, an indictment that Wells drew up as a result of his disastrous marriage, is now the most outmoded of his attacks on society. The problem was further distorted because he had grown up in such unusual ignorance of his own nature. His temperament was exceptionally ardent, though he did not in the least realize that fact; the very violence of his desires no doubt made him clumsy, and fate had thrown in his path a girl who, despite the deceptive appearance of sensuality that nature sometimes confers on cold women, was frightened and repelled by the whole physical side of love. "For all that is cardinal in this essential business of life," says George Ponderevo, "she has one inseparable epithet—'horrid.' " Those few words sum up the disaster that took place on the second plane of Wells's life, the real tragedy of his marriage.

He was bewildered by this first experience of love, vaguely wounded in his manly pride, unsure of himself and therefore angry and unjust. Looking back on the ruins of his marriage, George Ponderevo accuses himself of having behaved like a young brute. But Wells, only twenty-five years old, did not know as yet where the real source of his resentment lay. He thought his relationship with his young wife was going wrong through intellectual incompatibility. They had no interests in common, they did not even talk the same language. Attempts at conversation always faded out. They took refuge in the usual baby talk of lovers, and kept it up even after disillusion had smitten him—him alone, for Isabel was perfectly satisfied with the humdrum life into which she had escaped after the poverty of her childhood. She was proud of her status as a married woman and her skill as a housewife, and equally proud of her husband, who was a little peculiar but really very nice. Her one dread was that children might arrive to throw their existence out of gear. She had not much confidence in the future, or in her husband's brains. She thought it quite wonderful enough that he was able to give her the relative security she was already enjoying.

The University Correspondence College was becoming more and more of a money spinner. Wells's pupils passed their examinations with unfailing success. During the vacations his classes were full to overflowing. Rival enterprises were thrown into the shade, among them, one that was directed by Dr. Aveling, the son-in-law of Karl Marx. Wells's tireless efforts were meeting with their due reward. In January 1893, as a sign of victory over his early tribulations, he opened a bank account. He never forgot the thrill of the moment when his first checkbook was handed to him.

But beneath this veneer of material success he was seething with discontent, not because he regretted the literary ambitions that he had set aside, but because he despised his present work. In his second textbook of biology he could not resist making fun of the type of student, only too often met with, whose one aim was to acquire "as many diplomas and as little knowledge as possible." This second manual was very harshly reviewed in the magazine *Nature*. Isabel could not understand why her husband should be so upset by a few lines of print. She never could understand the fits of rage—the reaction from his disappointing nights—that seized him at the slightest pretext offered by the day's events.

His exasperation knew no bounds. Revolt against his job underlay his irritable impatience. He sought relief in irony, but humor was quite lost on Isabel, and of all mental activities, joking is the one that most needs to be shared. So he began to search for companionship outside the drab solemnity of his home. He found it first of all among his former fellow students. Before long he took on a friend to help him with Briggs's work, and between them they brought out a little publicity magazine, *The University Correspondent*. His new partner, Walter Low, had an experience which was just the opposite of his own, having begun life in easy circumstances and then fallen upon hard times. Thanks to the prosperity of his early years, he had a broader outlook, a more general culture than Wells, and his views on politics and literature were more extensive and coherent. Wells learned a great deal from the long conversations they had together. Their arguments were unending. Walter Low, like so many uneasy Jews, was fond of holding forth on the subject he felt to be the most urgent for him; but Wells would never listen to talk about the Jewish question or allow himself to be affected by it. From his cosmopolitan point of view, he said, it was a question that had no right to exist.

Both young men—Low was the elder—were filled with the sense of failure which can be so acute at that age. They felt that time was rushing by and leaving them behind in a backwater. The ladder of success seemed far beyond their reach.

Wells sank into that kind of defeatism which is the first, lazy stage of the downward path, and invites disaster. He was angry at having allowed himself to be maneuvered into a position from which there seemed to be no escape; he felt as though he were locked up and could only rattle helplessly at the doorknob. In this mood—convinced that he was a failure and always would be a failure, stifled by his own mediocrity—he was ripe for outside help, for the appearance of a miracle.

The miracle slid quietly into his life, in the unassuming disguise that so often masks a great event. It took the form of a girl. She was not really pretty, but she had the delicate grace, the neat, clear-cut features, the radiant complexion and the very fair hair that make up the picture of a typical English girl. She came, with a friend, to Wells's demonstration classes in practical biology. She was not one of those women against whom a man is always on his guard, whose vivid charm is a danger signal in itself. But she had the kind of attractiveness that gains ground, unnoticed, until it is too late to dislodge its owner from the life in which she has become entwined.

The fragile appearance of Amy Catherine Robbins was deceptive. The effect produced by her slight figure, her little face that looked as though it had been carved with the point of a knife in some brittle substance, and her quick, birdlike movements, was contradicted by the expression in the dark eyes that contrasted so sharply with her fair hair and skin. It was an expression of deep, relentless gravity. That aloof, defensive gaze seemed withdrawn into itself, but once it became fixed on someone or something, it clung. The girl seemed as though made of glass, diaphanous, and sharply outlined; but it was a modern-style glass, able to resist the fiercest flame, a glass whose edges cut like steel and which, though it could be cracked, would never break.

Wells had been used to holding intelligent conversation with girls he met at classes and whom he did not look upon quite as ordinary fellow students, or quite as women either. Meeting them in a laboratory, he felt entirely at ease. He would linger beside his new pupil without realizing how much pleasure he gained from her budding mind with its rapt attention and receptive alertness. The outstanding characteristic of Catherine Robbins (to whom he afterward gave the pet name of Jane) was her courage, a courage of the finest quality, persevering and inexhaustible. Left to herself she would not, perhaps, have done anything particularly daring, or broken loose from convention in such a spectacular manner. But she followed boldly along a path that was already traced out; her little feet tripped into the unforeseen as though shod with seven-league boots. Nothing frightened her—neither ideas, nor people, nor the most awkward and complicated situations. Maybe she relied on her gift for putting things in order, methodically, quietly, and with implacable energy. Maybe she knew that she had infinite reserves of understanding and endurance.

She seemed to be utterly transparent and spontaneous, but like the limpid water that makes us feel, when bending over a mountain lake, as though we could touch the bottom with our fingertips, her transparency hid unsuspected depths. It hid, perhaps, the temperament of a gambler, which made her set her whole future at stake without the slightest tremor of fear or regret.

So they had long talks over the dissected frogs and rabbits. She had small, deft hands with tapering fingers, firm and precise in their movements; a childish mouth, its lips tight-pressed with the effort of concentration; a light, distinct voice, crystal-clear in tone. To his eyes, she was hardly a woman at all. He never desired her as he had desired Isabel, and still did. But almost before he realized it, she came to embody "all the understanding and quality" that he wanted to find in life.

For she represented everything that Isabel had failed to give him, on the higher plane—an echo of his thoughts, a definite reaction to his ideas, an unlimited confidence in him. He was so tied down by defeatism that, of all liberating forces, it was this belief in his possibilities that he needed most, a belief that was blind and yet rational, critical and yet absolute. At first, and for a long time, theirs was a purely intellectual relationship. None the less it shed a radiance over his whole life, and lit up all Isabel's shortcomings, her narrow mind, her grasping, middle-class timidity, and the vulgarity of her tastes, which he had not noticed until now.

He might have seen more reason for alarm in his new friendship if he had not, at the same time, been involved in a quite separate and distinctly agreeable affair about which he felt secretly triumphant rather than guilty. A woman more experienced than himself had drawn him into this adventure, and there was nothing remarkable about it, except that it drove away, once and for all, his gloomy fears that love was nothing but an outrage against feminine chastity. It healed his wounded pride, swept out his mistaken notions, and put a happy end to his painful ignorance. But unknown to him, it brought about a whole series of false reactions. For a long time after this incident he believed that the joys of the spirit and those of the flesh, though they existed side by side, could never join and mingle. He split his life in two, as it were, and often found it hard to decide whether his happiness lay in a love affair or in a marriage of true minds. But he was sometimes tormented, like his William Clissold, by a mixture of sexual needs and hunger for a beloved partner in life.

The arrival of Catherine Robbins set him yearning above all for the perfect and stimulating sympathy of a woman. He may have dimly foreseen that it would help him back to his real path, to the true self that lay buried under the cares of the breadwinner. His longing for her was so great that she became the symbol of everything that made life worth while, and he suddenly felt that his present existence was unbearable.

In an atmosphere of comfort and leisure, emotional complications can develop to a greater extent than when hemmed in among petty anxieties. But overwhelming material worries and the crushing weight of responsibility can go far to arouse a longing for escape, a thirst for change, no matter what change. A new burden was laid on Wells's shoulders, before he had been able to attain real security. His mother, who by this time had become very deaf, soured and spiteful, was dismissed from Up Park. She sent him a pathetic message through her son Freddy, to ask whether she could come and live with him and Isabel. He sent his brother a hurried note suggesting that their mother should join their father in his cottage, and saying that he would undertake, with Freddy's help, to pay the old couple's expenses. But now Freddy, the model employee, the only one of the three brothers who had gone patiently along his appointed path, was suddenly thrown out of his rut. Dismissed—to make room for the boss's son— from his confidential post with the firm where he had been employed for a number of years, he found himself at a loose end in London. His savings were very small, and he felt lost among the new methods and the feverish competition that had become the order of the day. Although they rebelled against their paltry surroundings, the Wells brothers had an underlying streak of indolence, a tendency to dreaminess, a casual outlook which, added to the sense of humor that they all possessed, made it impossible for them to achieve the hard and fast efficiency that is needed in the battle of life. They were unable to defend themselves against the cunning and resourceful rivals who jostled them out of the way.

H. G. always bore a special grudge against go-getters of that kind, in all walks of life; he hated them with an undying hatred. He could pick out unscrupulous careerists—"Clever Alecs," as he called them— under any disguise, and in his book, *The Work, Wealth and Happiness of Mankind,* he stigmatizes them as dangerous enemies of society, who sap and destroy its creative efforts.

Thus, at a time when he was feeling discouraged, frustrated, with his emotions all in a tangle, he found himself faced with fresh responsibilities and called upon to make grave decisions. Though he was the youngest member of the family, he had suddenly become its head, both in the material and the moral senses. Not long afterward he sent his mother a scrawl depicting a little man smothered in papers, with the caption, "Little Bertie is writing away for dear life, to get little things for all his little People. . . ." But his sense of humor had not yet come to the rescue at the moment when he saw himself, like Nietzsche's baggage camel, loaded with fresh burdens for the simple reason that he was already carrying more than he could bear.

Then came a knockout blow—or a new trick of his Guardian Angel. Overworked, bitterly resentful, feeling himself trapped in a hopeless situation, he was an easy victim for the sickness that still lingered in his blood. One day in May, 1893, coming home after the first lesson of a geology course that he had just started, and from which he was carrying back a heavy bag of specimens, he was seized by a fit of coughing, and again felt the nauseating taste of blood in his mouth. A violent hemorrhage came on during the night, bringing him, as he said later, very close to death. The shadow was hovering over him once more. But this time it came as a relief. For lack of a better way out of his difficulties, he could take refuge in illness. Fate had intervened and would make his decisions for him. The problems that had seemed insoluble now settled themselves. His marriage would not be disturbed. He had no wish to leave Isabel. He seems to have been still hoping for a miraculous awakening to take place in her. Money matters were not alarming for the time being, his modest saving stood between him and actual want. Freddy had been offered a job in South Africa, and H. G. urged him to take it. His main thought was that slavery had come to an end. "No more teaching for me forever," he wrote to a woman friend as soon as he was able to scribble a line.

He could now let his thoughts, no longer in a turmoil, dwell upon the fragile figure of Catherine Robbins. The perspective of death seemed to alter the proportions of human relationships. Like himself, she was consumptive, and very delicate. They wrote to each other often, and he sent her playful health bulletins, written in the humorous style to which he usually resorted when sick. In one of his first letters he told her that it seemed unlikely he would be able to take up his old work again, so in future, by hook or by crook, he must earn his living as a writer.

She came to see him. Isabel had no suspicions as yet. But she felt the usual mistrust of the illiterate toward anybody who could talk intelligently. Wells knew that a world of worries was growing up around him, to smother him as soon as he put a foot out of bed. But he still had a short respite. He went to the seaside for a brief holiday. He lay on the sun-warmed beach, thinking lazy thoughts, wrapped as it were in cotton-wool by the sense of well-being that comes with convalescence. So far his experiences in trying to live by his pen had not been encouraging. His thoughts drifted on. They were not aimed so high as before. "The Rediscovery of the Unique," "The Universe Rigid," the memory of his visit to Harris still sent a shiver down his spine. Subjects like that were too ambitious, too abstruse. How to live by his pen? He had kept in touch with the University Correspondence College and still corrected the students' papers. But he could not resume his classes in London. He must find some other way of supporting his family.

Sometimes a chance suggestion from outside, which happens to fit in with a man's natural turn of mind, is enough to determine his path in life. That mysterious thing, success, is a mosaic of faint hints and coincidences prepared from within, but which look like miracles to anyone trying to sum up the events of a whole career. This time, a book pressed the button in Wells's brain—J. M. Barrie's *When a Man's Single,* which he happened to buy during his stay at Eastbourne. It was a few "precious words" from this book, he wrote later, that "saved" him.

The lesson he learned is very simple—in the hands of a creator any material may serve, may be molded into form. He can make use of any peg on which to hang his penetrating remarks and vivid imagery. Truth sparkles in a glass of water as well as from the facets of a diamond. The minor incidents of life are common to everyone, easily absorbed. The lesson, applied at once by Wells, opened up the career of journalism to him. "All I have to do is to lower my aim . . . and achieve it," he said to himself as he lay on the beach at Eastbourne, watching the crowd displaying its ridiculous antics around him, as crowds do on every beach in the world, as though stripped by sun and sea breeze of their last vestige of dignity.

But what he had found proved to be far more than a short cut to immediate success. It taught him to look more attentively at people, to take their surroundings into account, and to read the meaning of their gestures and their reactions. He learned to keep a firm grip on reality, to note its changing phases, to find words that would cover the exact impression he had received, and not wander from the point, however slightly. It is very nearly as difficult to describe a chair in such a way as to make the reader see the very chair you have in front of you, as to describe a whole palace. The apprentice must work with common clay before he sets the chips of marble flying.

So Wells set forth on an enterprise that he believed to be very limited—the study of everyday realities—never guessing that he was laying the foundations of his future creative work. He was observant by nature, and his inquisitive mind made him more so. His eyes were far more inclined to twinkle merrily than to screw up in sadness. At their corners, the little wrinkles that marked the passage of his silent smile were quick to form. He registered impressions with the exactness of a movie camera taking close-ups of an actor from unexpected angles. In course of time he stowed away in the great storehouse of his memory enough realistic details to deck out his most fantastic creations, making the impossible seem so convincingly familiar that even the most unimaginative readers were carried along with him.

But at the moment he did not in the least foresee this future use of what he called his great discovery. Lying on the beach, he scribbled an article, at first on the back of an envelope, and sent it to the *Pall Mall Gazette,* which had just taken on a new lease of life thanks to the support of a rich American. This article, "On Staying at the Seaside," was accepted at once. As he jubilantly remarked to Catherine Robbins, it was a real step forward for an unknown writer to get a signed article into a big daily paper.

Even in his days of fame, he remembered the strange joy, the curious little leap of the heart, that comes with the sight of one's work in print. His narrow path soon began to widen. Other articles appeared in the same paper. He had struck a vein that seemed inexhaustible. Barrie, little suspecting that he had helped to guide Wells in the right direction, found his articles very amusing and made inquiries about the author. Wells was no longer frightened at the thought of meeting an editor—and the editor of the *Pall Mall Gazette* was a much less alarming person than Frank Harris. He was asked to write book reviews for the same paper. Books, which he had always been too poor to buy, began at last to come into his home.

The day arrived when he was able to announce to his brother Freddy, now in South Africa, that the *Pall Mall Gazette* had sent him a check for £14.13s, for *one single month's* contributions, though he added, with instant caution, that this had perhaps been a particularly lucky month.

His luck held, and even increased beyond his wildest hopes. Teach-

ing had never brought him so much money. He was able to plan a
home outside London. Isabel began house hunting. For a time they
settled at Putney, where Catherine Robbins and her mother lived. But
before the summer was over, Isabel had already begun to look for
something else. They found a pleasant house at Sutton, the token of
newly won success. A removal is a kind of escape. H. G. wrote to his
brother Freddy that they felt they had already taken root in Sutton.

Though Isabel's nature was not passionate, it was violently jealous.
The emotional crisis in which Wells had been struggling just before
his illness seemed to have passed off so completely that toward the
middle of December he and Isabel went to stay for a few days with
Mrs. Robbins. And there, Isabel realized what could be the strength
of an intellectual bond, woven of so many invisible threads. She realized what a disturbing intimacy could grow up between two people
who spoke the same language. If she had known more about love, she
would have understood that, as a woman, she had nothing to fear
from her rival, that she had a stronger hold over her husband than
this fair-haired girl who was brittle and cold as glass. However, she
may have believed her hold to be so strong that she had only to put
it to the test. To her uneducated mind, the love she had once aroused,
the passion of the past, may have seemed security enough. In the old
days, Wells had always come back to her after every quarrel, she had
always laid down the law to him in her calm, obstinate way. Divided
affections, parallel lines of feeling, the weariness that familiarity can
breed—she knew nothing of all these. She had no inkling of the resentment that smoldered in the man she had disappointed. She still
looked upon him as her rebellious Bertie, whom she could always
bring to reason. Her jealousy, which was not a torment of the flesh,
but an outraged feeling of ownership, did not make her more clear-
sighted or more passionate. Back home after the visit to Putney, she
delivered the usual ultimatum to her husband. Things were said
which youthful pride could never forgive. Wells may have been unconsciously waiting for this state of things to be thrust upon him,
because he was incapable of taking the plunge himself. Anger gained
the upper hand of his lingering regrets, and he walked out of the
pleasant house at Sutton.

He went back to London, and not alone. Catherine Robbins, or
rather Jane, as he always called her, came to live with him. She was a

woman who would never haggle over a sacrifice. It was not a mere reckless impulse, or a surge of physical attraction, that had sent her into his arms. Her surrender was all the more complete and solemn, since it had been made deliberately, one might almost say with cool consideration. In that year of 1894, the girl lost herself, consciously and irrevocably. Perhaps that was just what she wanted, to lose herself through love, as she had flung herself into his love, holding nothing back.

Jane gave Wells all that his cousin had refused to give him—herself, body and soul, without guarantees of any kind, with no thought of money, no need of the past, her own past, her family, and no care for the future, which looked so uncertain for both of them.

History tells many stories of heroines who defied society, religion, and death for the sakes of the men they loved. But it has nothing to say of the less spectacular heroines who defied life, with all its daily difficulties, its insecurity, its small likelihood of lasting passion. Literature, too, has carried to our ears the cries of revolt and of physical desire wrung from great lovers who staked their destiny on a single throw. Those women were swept along by a force stronger than themselves, they were predestined to the fires of passion that devoured them in the end. Often, too, they were magnificently blind, or desperately clear sighted when they weighed their nights of love against the certain doom that awaited them.

Jane had none of their overwhelming frenzy. Her grave eyes looked life straight in the face, and her reason told her that one must often lose everything in order to gain everything. "We were the most desperate of lovers," wrote Wells after her death, "we launched ourselves upon our life together with less than fifty pounds between us and absolute disaster, and we pulled through. . . . And I seem to remember now that we did it with a very great deal of gaiety."

X

EXCELSIOR

WELLS WAS SPEAKING from experience when he declared in an article written about 1894 that an improvement in a man's social position did not bring unmixed joy, although "the young proletarian, playing happily in his native gutter" might not be aware of this. He described the bitterness of leaving real friends behind, friends made at different stages of the climb, and the sting of being looked upon as an intruder by the new class of society to which the young proletarian seeks admission. Quoting Herbert Spencer, he went on to say that "the man from below is not adapted to his environment," and added, "That is not all. He is adapted to no environment."

It was beginning to dawn on Wells that even the enjoyment of life was something that must be learned, and he noted this with a not unnatural feeling of resentment, for he was a young man who had never been really young. Cheated of his youth, he spent years trying to get it back, and in the long run he completely succeeded. The secret of the ageless zest for life that he seemed to possess in his old age, may have been that after mislaying his boyhood he had got it back little by little, like a stubbornly contested inheritance.

But in 1894, when not yet thirty years old, he was flustered, quick to take offense, unsure of himself, and ready, in his discouragement, to jump to sweeping conclusions. He asserted, for example, that the proletarian would find more happiness in a little grocery store, with love and a brood of children, than the Dead Sea fruit of success could ever give him; for though it was "fun to struggle," it was "tragedy to win." When he wrote this lament for success, he had had no more than a peep at it. The victory whose cost he complained of was only a little skirmish with life, that had turned to his advantage. The climb from which he felt so giddy had only taken him up a low hill, not even a moderate-sized mountain. But he had so little experience of life, and his mind was so fresh and receptive, that this gentle gradient seemed quite impressive to him.

His climb began at the same moment as his adventure in love, when his only asset, apart from the fifty pounds already mentioned, was his self-confidence; but that was magnificently stimulated by the very thought of the great adventure. It had as setting the two tiny rooms, divided by a sliding door, which he describes in *Love and Mr. Lewisham*. They were adorned with sentimental color prints in gilt frames, and flower vases of the "given away with a pound of tea" type, and Wells rented them from a German landlady with a great flow of words, most of which could be recognized as English.

Minor factors in his new life with Jane were Mrs. Robbins's tearful protests, the disagreeable curiosity of landladies and servants, the tiresome divorce proceedings, and the isolation of a young couple who had never had any social connections, and were almost without friends.

More important was their courage, the challenging attitude in which they were united, their unspoken agreement to face the world with an appearance of perfect happiness. Most important was their work. Jane, who had passed her biology examination with flying colors, went on with her studies—but not for very long. Soon she gave up all her outside interests, in order to help Wells. She became his copyist, his secretary, his critic, and took all routine worries off his shoulders. She little guessed, when she first began to attend to these literary business matters for him, that the habit would one day grow into a complicated and all-absorbing task.

Unlike many successful men, who soon forget the help and suggestions that benefited them, and come to believe that they owe everything to their own inner resources, Wells was fond of recalling the people and ideas that had guided his early career. According to him it was the editor of the *Pall Mall Budget* who turned him from articles to fiction and helped him to pass from journalism to creative writing, by suggesting that he might do some short stories with a scientific background.

In reality, Wells himself had already thought of using his knowledge of science as a starting point for flights of imagination. He had even given a sample of the bold forecasts that were to come, in the paper, "The Man of the Year Million," which he had read at South Kensington and which he now published, in a different form, in the *Pall Mall Budget* itself. Although, when his editor advised him to try his hand at fiction, he was still a needy journalist, writing articles that were usually unsigned, he already had in him all the elements that were soon to be welded into a brilliant literary triumph. Before his first book came out, he was already in command of the exceptionally wide range of factors that went to make up his success. Before he started on his career, in fact, he had built up his literary capital. It is curious to note that the whole body of his work, varied and often surprising as it proved to be, was pre-existent in him before he began to write. He himself never knew how much he owed to his adolescence —it had been such a groping, uncertain period that, looking back, he did not realize what a multitude of seeds lay hidden in the dark, fertile soil of his mind before it was opened to literature. At the time when his notes and manuscripts were few enough to be kept in a small green box in his lodginghouse room, he already possessed a huge store of invisible records, and could draw upon it as chance or whim suggested.

Wells's boyhood and adolescence are bound to fill a good deal of space in any biography of him, for they provided most, one might even say all, of the material for his literary career. He had a dim awareness of this himself, or he would not have devoted more than two-thirds of his autobiography to the first thirty years of his life.

The story of a writer or a man of action usually shows him increasing in stature as his talents ripen, and often a new, unsuspected figure emerges in due course. The story of Wells is simply that of bringing to light the qualities imprisoned within him, of ransacking the subsoil of his possibilities—a story of salvage rather than of discovery. Some of these pre-existent elements came to light at a very early stage, while others remained buried for a long time. They crystallized or faded, they rose by turns to the surface, and they vanished forever when their usefulness was over.

The principal difference between his numerous works lies in the varying strength of the life that flows through them. Those of his first period are curiously somber. Their atmosphere is sinister, and a note of despairing pessimism is to be heard, ever since the melodrama he drafted at Etruria. Optimism was the cornerstone of his character, but it lay hidden, buried beneath the hard and bitter feeling that came of his early experiences. Most people begin life in a state of happy confidence, which gradually gives way to disillusionment, anger, pity, or disgust of humanity. Wells developed in exactly the opposite manner, by freeing his vein of optimism from the avalanche of disgust and despair that had prematurely swept down upon it.

In his first published story, "The Stolen Bacillus," this is strongly marked. The short dramatic plot, for which he drew upon his knowledge of bacteriology, sparkles, on the surface, with humor. It shows, too, his familiarity with the racy speech of the common people; the cabbies' talk has a brisk, cockney flavor which forecasts the picturesque turns of phrase that came later from Mr. Polly and Kipps's uncle. But more typical of Wells as he was then are the musings of the anarchist, making off with his stolen tube of bacilli, rejoicing grimly at the thought of the power for harm that it will confer upon him, and the terror he will be able to spread among those who until now have slighted him and mocked at him. He will teach them what it means to isolate a man, to deny him any importance.

At about the same time that Wells began his series of short stories for the *Pall Mall Budget,* William Ernest Henley, a leading light among magazine editors, asked him to write for the *National Observer.* The grand old giant with the paralyzed legs was an impressive figure, and Wells determined to respond to this invitation by giving of his very best. He had a sense of quality that was amazing in one so inexperienced. For Henley he brought out his "secret treasure," as he called it—his idea of a journey through time. He knew how much was at stake; this was his strongest card, and he felt that if it failed he would be doomed to mediocrity for the rest of his days.

So an entirely revised version of "The Chronic Argonauts" began to appear as a serial, as yet unsigned by its author. The *National Observer* collapsed, but Henley was soon editing the *New Review,* where he decided to introduce a serial story; and there he brought out *The Time Machine,* after it had been revised yet again. Wells's name now appeared at the head of the installments, and he was paid a hundred pounds for the magazine rights—a fortune to him, for he had never yet received so large a sum all in one lump. The story afterward came out in book form, too, his first published book. This marked the official beginning of his literary career.

The lesson he had learned on the beach at Eastbourne had borne fruit. The "Time Traveller" was set firmly in realistic surroundings, and linked to everyday life by innumerable ties, such as were familiar to all readers. Wells had realized that the more fantastic the story he told, the more commonplace must be its setting. His ability to create such a commonplace setting was quite new, a year ago, or even less, he could not have done it, but now he did it with masterly ease. *The Time Machine* glitters with the same surface irony as "The Stolen Bacillus." But below the surface are depths of gloom and cruel despair. What can have been the matter with the eyes of his contemporaries, that they could overlook the chief problem raised by the book. The notion of a fourth dimension must have dazzled them so completely that they never went on to investigate the nature of the theories that Wells set forth with such relish. His fireworks hid the murky background from their eyes. The book had a curiously sadistic strain, so evident that one wonders whether it can really have escaped even the English, who look upon *Alice in Wonderland,* with its strong undercurrent of cruelty, as an ideal book for children.

The death of little Wena, the greatly loving childwife, in the night, uplifted on the crimson canopy of flame that drifts away into shreds leaving a plume of smoke rising toward the tiny, far-distant stars, while the darkness swarms with white, flabby forms that crawl toward the still, doll-like figure, is an episode so soaked in horror as to be almost physically sickening.

When the book first came out, it reminded some people of Edgar Allan Poe. But Poe's horrific atmosphere, and the shudder which he delighted to provoke in his readers, were for him not only a means but an end, whereas Wells directed his horrors toward a definite aim. The purely imaginative form serves to camouflage what his time called a story with a purpose. The graceful, effeminate little creatures that he portrays, with their silken robes, their curly, flower-wreathed heads—beings whose whole life is given up to pleasure and love, whose idle hands know nothing but play—are surely descended from the idle rich who believed they had inherited the earth. The frightful Morlocks, pallid dwellers in eternal darkness who exist only to serve the children of light, are descendants of the toiling masses of the period. Not only did Wells develop this allegory of social conflict to the furthest possible point, not only did he hint that the reign of injustice might bring terrible penalties in its wake; but he said so outright, speaking in clear, precise words through the mouth of his Time, who sees the key of the situation in the heightened contrast prevailing in his day between capitalists and workers. The chasm was widening and the world was doomed to this so-called golden age—a nightmare of cruelty, wherein the children of light, small and frail as butterflies, unproductive and futile, play among the flowers, until the inevitable day when the ground, beneath which their ancestors ruthlessly imprisoned half of the human race, gives way under their dancing feet and they go down to be devoured by the creatures of darkness. It is a revolutionary book if ever there was one. The tatters of a rainbow-colored veil may help to conceal the theme of retribution that it sets forth with such crude simplicity. The revolutionist wears a velvet mask and a fancy disguise. But his vengeful eyes glare through the slits in the mask.

This first novel by an unknown writer was given a warm welcome by the critics, who were quick to appreciate its value. As the *Saturday Review* put it, this author would have to be taken into account henceforth. W. T. Stead, one of the most eminent critics of that day, roundly declared that "H. G. Wells is a man of genius."

The book was a great financial success, too. For Wells, poverty was now a thing of the past. He may not have realized at first how entirely he had left it behind, but his sudden rise to fame was something that he remembered vividly to the end of his life. Not many men in their sixties would be able to set forth to a penny, in their memoirs, the sums they earned thirty or forty years previously. But Wells, or rather Jane, must have kept even the account books and check stubs of those years. In 1894 he earned £583.17s.7d, in 1895 £792.2s.5d, and by 1896 the sum had risen to £1056.7s.9d.

Nothing succeeds like success, and door after door was now opening to him. The terrible, awe-inspiring Frank Harris, whom Wells by this time found much less alarming, had begun to collect what he called his team of young geniuses on the staff of the *Saturday Review;* and he added Wells and Shaw to the group.

With *The Time Machine,* Wells had broken entirely new ground. The resemblance to Poe which struck some of his readers went no deeper than the veneer of horror that overlaid the tale. Another writer whom it at once called to mind, and whose work really did contain similar elements, was Jules Verne; but as one critic said when making the comparison, Wells's style and ideas were of higher quality than those of the Frenchman.

It was, of course, easy to talk of Jules Verne; it is always easy to point out an external resemblance. But Wells knew that he was aiming at something more than a great adventure of the imagination. He complained that his chief title to fame was to be "An English Jules Verne." Jules Verne, for his part, protested vigorously against being bracketed with the newcomer. After the first few of Wells's tales of fantasy had appeared, Verne declared indignantly to an English journalist, "I can see no comparison between his work and mine. We do not use the same methods. To my mind, his stories have no really scientific basis. No, there is no connection. I make use of physics, whereas he invents."

Jules Verne was right. Science was a secondary consideration for Wells, a means and not an end in itself. He used it like the personal asset that it was, just as other writers, ill at ease in the world of their day and well informed about some particular period of the past, have written historical novels.

But no sooner were his money worries left behind, than his inventive powers, no longer held in check by the need to write for a particular market, burst forth like a mountain torrent from a narrow gorge. He was in the state of creative well-being where an artist feels his powers redoubled. He had struck a chord of such resonance, and struck it with so sure a touch, that its vibrations awoke numberless echoes in his mind. He gives in his memoirs an example to illustrate that curiously inspired condition which permits of divided attention, making it possible to pursue two separate inventions at the same time, without harm to the main theme or to the quality of the work. A state of rare happiness, where the more the artist gives out the richer he becomes—where to divide his energies is to increase them.

Wells recalls one of the summer nights when he was writing *The Time Machine*. He and Jane were worn out by the strain of their emotional adventure; they were both working too hard, they were not getting enough to eat, and this kind of life in their cramped, ground-floor, city lodgings had affected their health so seriously that they were in danger of relapsing into the illness that always lay in wait for both of them. The doctor had been urging them to move to the country. Mrs. Robbins, also unwell, and still tearful, was staying with them. Unexpected money difficulties had arisen. Two papers to which Wells had been a regular contributor had suddenly closed down. Divorce proceedings had begun between him and Isabel, and were bringing the usual annoyances in their train. Their landlady had discovered that they were living in sin. Her indignation increased her disapproval of a lodger who stayed up so late, writing and burning so much midnight oil, a wasteful proceeding that disgusted her almost as much as his immorality.

Despite this crop of unpleasantness, Wells was working on his novel with intense concentration. In describing the Morlocks' grim existence, he could pour out all his own pent-up resentment and bitterness. The night, he remembered afterward, was hot, with a deep blue sky. A faint breeze came through the wide-open window, wafting to his ears the shrill voice of the landlady as she grumbled, for his benefit, about shady lodgers who sat up till all hours. A moth fluttered around the lamp. Into his feverish energy there crept a current of dull rage. The vulgar, nagging voice and the flapping insect became confused together at the back of his exasperated mind. An idea for a short story slipped in between the neatly written lines where he was describing the wrath to come. The story would be called "A Moth, Genus Novo." The idea, inspired almost automatically by the wings that were brushing against the lamp glass, seemed quite unrelated to his personal worries or to his chief work of the moment. Yet it was connected with them by the mysterious chain of associations that leads to artistic creation. It is the story of an obsession. Through it, again, runs a streak of cruelty. It tells of a violent quarrel between two scientists, ending in the death of one of them. The obsession outlasts the quarrel that is thus terminated. It takes the form of an invisible insect which comes to haunt the too ferocious entomologist.

Wells's mind was so well-balanced, so vigorous and healthy, that there is something strange about the pleasure he took in depicting insanity. He liked to trace the wavering line that divided feverish imagination, strained to its utmost, concentrated on one single aim, from the morbid obsessions of a mind that has run off the track and plunged into madness.

For the time being, his own mind was working on two planes. On the practical plane he realized that *The Time Machine* was certain, at the very least, to make a great stir of curiosity, and that he ought to get the most out of this. He told himself that if he could have another book ready before the sensation caused by the first had died down, he would then be able to give up his potboiling journalistic work and earn his living as a novelist.

On the creative plane, he was possessed by a kind of brutal force, a restrained fury that seemed to have no object, but went round and round in his mind like a wild beast in a cage. He felt stifled by the flood of a resentment that could find no outlet. Something was happening inside him, while he and Jane went on with their quiet, almost conventional life, so perfectly united in spirit, upheld by the same courage, brightened by the same humor. He was in the throes of violence. When he escaped from ordinary life and sat down at his writing table, a red mist hovered before his eyes.

A great, unsatisfied hunger lurked in his frustrated body. He himself hardly knew its cause; he could not or would not admit it. Later, in *The World of William Clissold,* he spoke of the wild-beast impulse that haunted him at this period, seeking to carry him away, to send him rushing through the gloom in search of his prey. It was a force deeper rooted than the desire for love, something "more animal, more elemental . . . something a tomcat would understand." Nothing, says William Clissold, is so constantly aggressive as the obsession of sex, so quick to deck itself with unhealthy imaginings, so apt, if constrained or frustrated, to invade and pervert other fields of interest, flinging itself onto substitutes and imitations rather than put up with complete privation.

By the time he came to write his autobiography, Wells had at last attained full knowledge of himself and his sexual needs. This long-delayed knowledge had shed light on many things about himself that he had never been able to understand, as when a lamp is suddenly switched on in a dark room where one has been bumping blindly into the furniture, and shows things again in their familiar, friendly aspect. He could see his life as one complete picture, like a jigsaw puzzle whose scattered pieces he had now fitted neatly into place. He touches tactfully on the disturbing feature of his second venture into love, when he found himself confronted by a being as dainty and fragile as a Dresden china statuette, who was so entirely ignorant of the physical facts of love that it was impossible for him to be rough or urgent with her.

Jane's ignorance, coming after Isabel's frigidity, drove him to the point of wondering whether it was he, with his strong sexual instincts, who was abnormal. He had no one to talk to on the subject, no one with whom to compare experiences; he had to keep it all to himself, pressed down by a leaden weight of shamefaced uneasiness.

There was a monster prowling within him. He made an outlet for it with his second book, *The Island of Dr. Moreau.* He probably got the first idea of this book from an experience familiar to anyone who has ever been suddenly overwhelmed by a feeling of disgust for humanity. He must have looked around him and seen men whose faces were no longer those of men. The secret disillusionment that was poisoning his system had even affected his eyesight. As he stared at people, their features broke up, distorted into brutish masks. Something that the pencil of Leonardo da Vinci could create, merely by thickening the lips, hooking the nose, or giving a jutting or receding line to the jaw. The borderline between man and brute is continually shifting. The hero of Wells's second book describes the visions that haunt him after his return from Dr. Moreau's island. Looking now at his fellow men, he is smitten with terror; for while some faces are wide awake and lively, others surly and dangerous, and others, again, sly and insincere, he cannot find one that has the calm authority of a reasoning mind. He feels the degradation of all these men and women, as if the animal were gaining the upper hand in them.

Like the entomologist who is haunted by the invisible moth, the central figure of this bloodcurdling drama is a man obsessed by his work of scientific research—a genius, whom frustration has transformed into a kind of evil spirit. He has crossed the uncharted frontier that separates the lunatic from the man of sane but overconcentrated mind. He has lost his sense of humanity. In the past he suffered persecution. A journalist's account of his vivisectionist practices roused such a storm of public indignation that he had to choose between giving up his work and leaving the country. Now he lives on an uninhabited island, where he creates monsters—a thing which Wells declares, in an elucidative note to the book, to be among the possibilities of vivisection. Dr. Moreau's monsters are so human in shape that the shipwrecked intruder who tells the story mistakes them at first for men of a debased type. But if their master relaxes his control over them, they soon slip back into their animal state.

When published, *The Island of Dr. Moreau* was looked upon as a chamber of horrors, a deliberate attempt to make the reader's flesh creep. Wells always protested that he had not meant to wallow in atrocities for their own sake, but to depict the bestial side of human life. But his youthful desperation, his overflowing disgust, made him so forceful and convincing that he overstepped the mark. He managed to create an atmosphere so sinister and stifling that his subtle implications were entirely lost. He made horror so credible and brought it so close that no one noticed his outcry against mankind.

In this book he seems to have plumbed the darkest depths of his own soul. People who came to know him later often found it hard to connect him with such a piece of savage cruelty. But those who knew him really well understood that the book had not been just a flight of imagination, but a part of himself—represented a state that he surmounted and left behind him, a wound that was healed.

It is because *The Island of Dr. Moreau* deals with only one subject, presents only one series of images, that it seems at first glance to be the cruelest of Wells's books. But it was not that the depths of the abyss were reached, it was an outside influence that taught Wells to lighten the horrors of his writing and veil his disgust.

The first publisher to whom he submitted *The Island of Dr. Moreau* was shocked, and refused it. But Wells knew the book had value. He set particular store by it because he had entirely rewritten it after the first draft, rearranging the story and tightening it up, which was a thing he seldom did, even at this early period. However, realizing that he had taken a false step with this piece of unrelieved gloom, he set to work at once on another book. Though it was only a short time since the publication of his first novel, he already had a shrewd understanding of public taste. The new book was accepted as soon as the publisher saw its first chapters. *The Island of Dr. Moreau* could wait awhile. It would wait until after the next success.

The rapidity with which Wells changed his subject, and his choice of a new theme in absolute contrast to the one that had been rejected, suggests that he was laughing up his sleeve. So the publisher thought that readers would be too harrowed by the sufferings of animals changed into human beings, would find the animals too hideous and terrifying, the island too sinister in its perilous nights? Very well then, let him have the most radiant and beautiful subject imaginable, the embodiment of his purest dreams, let him have no less than an angel come down from heaven.

The Wonderful Visit really does seem to have been written with a quiet chuckle, as though the author had his tongue in his cheek. It carries a moral that is scarcely more optimistic than that of *The Island of Dr. Moreau*. In fact, it may even be said to be still more negative, more stern in its attitude toward humanity. The plot has a strong resemblance to that of Ivan Karamazov's story of "The Grand Inquisitor." "I shall lead you to the stake," says the Grand Inquisitor to Jesus Christ, "because you came to be a trouble to us. And really, if there ever was anyone, if there still is anyone who deserves to be burned at the stake, it is you, you, you. . . ." And when, moved by Christ's silent kiss, the Grand Inquisitor lets Him out of prison, he mumbles with toothless, trembling jaws: "Go, and never return . . . never, never!"

"I don't want to hurt your feelings," says Dr. Crump to the angel, "but the present situation is really impossible . . ." and he declares that in his opinion, as medical adviser to the community, the angel is having an unhealthy influence and must go away.

"Only now," says the Chief Inquisitor, thinking of the Inquisition, "has it become possible to consider the happiness of mankind. Man was born a rebel? But can there be any happiness for rebels?"

Sir John Gotch, the local squire, hurries indignantly to complain to the Vicar that his strange visitor is putting improper questions to the villagers—asking them why they work, while other people live in idleness, why everyone does not get the same education. He is up-setting the poor things and making them dissatisfied with their lot.

There is no place in the world for the Lord and his religion of liberty, reason, and good faith. There is no place in the world for the angel who brings a message of beauty and happiness.

In *The Island of Dr. Moreau,* even when the lurking beasts had regained the upper hand in a man, the power to rebel was still left to him—the mangled puma breaks loose and kills its tormentor; and so was the sense of loyalty—the dog-man dies defending his chosen mas-ter. But during the angel's brief sojourn upon earth, he meets with nothing but stupidity, cruelty and ugliness; even the village children, pitiless and stubborn, band themselves against him. Just one little tot greets him confidently and slips a bunch of flowers into his hand, the only kindness he had received from a human being except the Vicar and one other person.

The difference between these two novels, one of which seems so somber and the other so shimmering bright, is solely a difference of treatment. Wells had already discovered that the more impossible a story was, the more realistic must be its setting; now he had come to understand that horrors could not be stomached unless they were pre-sented against a familiar background. He had fallen back on the principle that had helped him as a child—laughter is the best protection against an absurd world.

In *The Island of Dr. Moreau* he had spat out his disgust with humanity like a clot of blood. In *The Wonderful Visit* he disguised it with mockery, and his laughter turned away attention from the sadness that lay beneath. Only one touch of radiance lights up this doomed world; it comes from the loving self-sacrifice of a little servant girl. But since faith and love cannot abide here, the angel of beauty and the simplehearted girl have to be released by flames from the narrow prison of human life.

Wells admitted that his aim in this book was to show the pettiness and the narrow outlook of the average life, by bringing typical characters into striking contrast with a being unshackled by the usual human limitations. And most of the characters are types, except the Vicar, who is a real live figure drawn in the round. The representatives of human blindness have certain features that are stressed to the point of caricature. The angel's constant struggles to fit in with social conventions form a thread that runs right through the loosely woven texture of the story. Lady Hammergallow's at home is described at disproportionate length. Wells lingers over the difficulties that lie in wait for the angel during this first experience of a drawing-room function—the awkwardness with which he puts down his hat and manages his teacup, his embarrassment when he scatters cake crumbs on the floor. The disaster that cuts short the angel's social career is a typical Wellsian invention. Having been carefully warned by the Vicar that he must never allow a lady to carry anything, the angel hurries up to the pretty housemaid to relieve her of her tray. The other guests are scandalized, and the Vicar murmurs, overcome with shame, "I forgot to explain to him about servants."

The emphasis that Wells lays on the minor episodes of the angel's visit to earth is a reflection of his own experiences. At about that time the effort to learn correct social behavior was looming large in his daily life. The former shop assistant's fumbling progress into new social circles was attended by some very comic incidents. In later years he used to tell the story of the first big literary reception to which he was invited, when he heaped his plate with a black mound of caviar, a substance he had never tasted before. He then drowned his confusion in drinks that were equally strange to him, and it was in an exultant and muddled frame of mind that he went home to his shabby lodgings. Things of that kind can make a very funny story when looked back upon from a safe and comfortable height, but at the moment they sting sharply. They often continue to rankle long after more serious setbacks have been forgotten.

Catherine Robbins knew little more about etiquette than Wells. They made up their minds to study the subject carefully, dining often in restaurants so that when invited to fashionable houses they would have some notion of how to behave. Many traps lay in wait for their inexperienced feet. He long remembered the day when he asked a certain society man whether evening dress should be worn at an important first night, and how he rushed to a tailor to be measured for his first tuxedo.

He was very proud of moving in a circle which, as the Up Park housekeeper's son, he had only glimpsed through half-open doors. Before the end of 1895 all sorts of people seemed ready to make a great fuss over him, and he wrote with naïve pride to his mother about his social progress for he knew that she would be properly appreciative.

He did not tell her, however, that this new life of pleasure and satisfied ambition had its drawbacks. Social advancement had come to him too late, when he was nearly thirty years old and his plebeian manners fitted him as easily as a pair of old slippers. His new patent-leather shoes pinched him. For a long time he felt like an intruder among all these wealthy people. They did not show him the affection that his sociable, expansive nature always yearned for. The days of brooding resentment were by no means at an end. "It is fun to struggle, but tragedy to win."

XI

THE COUNTRY OF THE BLIND

AT THE BEGINNING of 1896 Wells felt, as he wrote to his brother Freddy on New Year's Eve, that he could look forward confidently to fresh successes and an increased income in the near future, and that one day his work would be known by people from Chicago to the distant banks of the Yangtse Kiang.

The lean years lay behind him. Hunger was a thing of the past. In fact he was beginning to get stout, and had to keep his weight down by exercise like any middle-class citizen. He took to cycling, and bought a tandem on which he and Jane went for long rides around the southern counties.

By this time they had left London. For a very short period Wells had been theater critic of the *Pall Mall Gazette;* he had caught cold on one of his evening assignments, and there had again been signs of slight hemorrhage from his lung. As a result, the couple had made up their minds to go and live in the country. Their first home had been set up with the help of a mortgage on Mrs. Robbins's house, which brought them a hundred pounds. They could not yet afford to be particular, and they made a very modest choice at Woking, which was out of favor because England's first crematorium had been established there. Moreover, their little house was just opposite the railroad, and freight trains rumbled past it all through the night. Still they felt almost independent, living among their own belongings instead of in grimy lodgings where the landlady inflicted on them her shabbiest furniture and most hideous ornaments. Their new home even had a tiny glasshouse, where Wells could dream of exotic plants, of giant, carnivorous orchids, of flowers that he had never seen and that existed only in his imagination. He used this glasshouse, as if it served to call up before his mind's eye unexpectedly subtle visions of faraway things and places.

A solemn event took place in this Woking house, an event which showed to what heights Sarah Wells's son had risen. The great day is commemorated by a drawing where a tiny figure, no bigger than a baby, sits perched on the edge of a chair, watching a procession of fantastic hats, which advances toward her with firm and threatening gait. A caption says, "Jane engaging her first domestic servant."

In this same year of 1896, Wells was able to buy his parents a pretty little house with seven good rooms and a garden. He wrote to tell Freddy, out in Johannesburg, that "the little old lady" was rosy and active, and seemed likely to last for another twenty years; his father, too, was in fine form, so he himself could look forward with a glad heart and high hopes. He helped his brother Frank, too, with his traveling clockmaker's business, and it began to do well.

This was the mood in which he greeted the outer world, as well as his own family. He reveals it in his drawings, which make up a kind of shorthand diary of his life, a humorous commentary on everyday affairs. One of his sketches shows Jane and the rest of the family gazing in breathless pride at their great man, while checks and royalties are heaping up around him. His power of enjoyment, half starved before, was now expanding quickly, and he eagerly absorbed the pleasures, the comforts, and the gratifying compliments that success brought with it.

Now that they were living in the country he was less often reminded of his ignorance of social behavior; he did not meet with so many secret humiliations as in London. He soon began to learn the requirements of his new position, and self-confidence returned to him. Little by little it dawned on him, too, that the fact of being a self-made man had its advantages for there went with it a clearer view of the realities of life, a method of approach that was more direct, fresher and more ruthless, than that of intellectuals. He was positively exuding good humor, naïvely brandishing his triumph like a victorious banner.

The picture he presented to the world coincided with his inner picture. But though to a great extent exact, it was not the whole picture. Deep down within him there still lay traces of resentment, the black dregs of his former bitterness. The feeling of being an intruder, which he never really shook off, had given birth to strange doubts in his mind. He was like a usurper who, having risen to power by means of false credentials, begins to question the legitimacy of all those around him. He now found himself in a world that was built upon rock, the world of unchanging stability that everyone in his generation took for granted. He had no reason to doubt that this stability would endure to the end of time. The social structure of England, in the jubilee year of 1896, seemed to be the most unshakable in Europe. Not the smallest crack showed in its age-old foundations; not the slightest tremor shook the ground beneath them. But a strange feeling began to grow in Wells—a doubt which as yet had no basis, no reasoned explanation, but arose out of his nervous sensibility, the uneasiness that was in his blood.

This uneasiness never left him. The contrast between his intense, acute enjoyment of life, which seemed to bubble up from the very fount of security, and his secret anxieties, lasted until the end of his days. He delighted in everything around him. But when he sat down to write there would come to him a strange presentiment that the ground beneath his feet was undermined.

The obscure forces that ferment in all artistic creation take strangely devious ways in order to express themselves. They channel through the subsoil of the emotions, twisting and turning with the dark river which, like an underground watercourse, now sinks far below the surface, now rises for a moment into daylight. Creative work never corresponds exactly to the impulses of the conscious mind; it draws upon those deeply buried elements of shadow and mystery.

Such an expression of secret reactions is found in his story, "The Country of the Blind." This belongs to the group of fantasies in which he explored time and space. To all appearances it is just a brilliant piece of fiction. But Wells used to claim that all his work was intended to do more than help readers to pass the time. In his view, literature was never a mere amusement. He once wrote from Woking to reproach a fellow author in outspoken terms for having shed no light on any of the "Fundamental Problems of Existence." In his youthful solemnity he resorted to capital letters; but all through his life he was tempted to use capitals for the questions that he looked upon as fundamental. His reproachful words gave a clear hint as to what he himself took to be the writer's mission. He always had an axe to grind; he never left things entirely to chance, or to the inspiration of the moment. Even his most fanciful patterns were always woven around one or another of those Fundamental Problems.

"The Country of the Blind" begins like an adventure story. It is packed with picturesque detail. A man comes by chance upon a path that leads to an almost inaccessible valley in the equatorial Andes, "more than three hundred miles from Chimborazo, a hundred miles from the snows of Cotopaxi." With eyes open to all the beauties of nature, he makes his way toward the fold in the mountains which for fourteen generations has been inhabited by a race of blind people. A proverb rises to his lips, "In the country of the blind, the one-eyed is king." He goes down as a conqueror toward these unfortunates. But he finds that they are stronger than he. For them sight is a form of heresy. They reject all he tells them as the ravings of a disordered mind. Soon he himself is won over to their concept of perpetual darkness, to their belief in a heaven that fits over the earth like a solid lid. He is won over through hunger, loneliness, love. Even to his ears, now, the confident refrain, "In the country of the blind the one-eyed is king," sounds like a mockery. He, who can see, ends by submitting to the ignorance of the sightless, to escape the terrible feeling of being different from those among whom he lives. He is ready to have his sight destroyed by an operation. But at the last moment his mind revolts, and he takes to flight. He climbs up toward the great, free world of the mountain peaks where the snow sparkles in the sunlight. He dies on his way over the crest, but when his body is found it is lying at ease, and there is a smile on his face.

In later years Wells disowned the allegories and the lyricism of his early work. He threw them aside like a worn-out garment that was no longer suited to the harsh climate of the day. But though, in the caution that comes with age, he no longer spoke of it, he never quite lost the sense of being an open-eyed traveler, wandering among a sightless race.

He was strangely haunted by hostile powers. There was nothing morbid about him, yet he was a prey to fears. The life of man is beset by unknown perils. A harmless little man grows orchids in his tiny suburban glasshouse; it is the only hobby of his monotonous existence. But one day, from a shriveled root, there comes up a weird flower, a flower that gives out a heady perfume, and whose uncovered roots, groping like tentacles, like leeches, twine around the man and drag him to the ground. That is "The Flowering of the Strange

Orchid," the death-dealing plant that chance has brought into a sub-urban glasshouse.

From the ocean bed rise huge mollusks, giant devilfish as big as pigs, with tentacles several feet long. They drift in a shoal to the English coast; in some shipwreck they have tasted human flesh and blood; they curl round a swimmer's leg; they cling to the gunwale of a boat, capsize it with their powerful tentacles, and the men, women, and children on board are dragged down below the surface to meet a ghastly death.

The life of man is threatened from every side. All living things are his enemies. At any moment the flimsy fabric of his days may be rent by some new menace risen from the depths of the sea or from the bowels of the earth. Today's familiar things may be tomorrow's merciless foes, as in "The Empire of the Ants," the big ants that lay waste the villages of Brazil, marching under the command of larger-headed ants that seem to plan their attacks systematically. These ants are not divided into tribes, they form one nation; they are inventive ants, and carry with them, fastened to their bodies, crystal phials of poison as slender as needles. They have destroyed towns and villages, occupied whole plantations, entire colonies, killing or driving out the population. They are bent upon conquering the world. One day they will be masters of the whole tropical belt of South America. "But why should they stop at that?" asks Wells cheerfully; and he goes on to calculate that if they can keep up their pace, they should be in Europe by about 1950—or at latest by 1960.

These glimpses of the catastrophes that lie in wait for mankind were only detached exercises, as it were, like the stray notes played by musicians when tuning up before a concert. He was soon to bring out a symphony of horror on which he had lavished all his powers, which were well tested by this time. This was *The War of the Worlds,* the terrible descent of the Martians to our earth.

One mild autumn day, Wells and his brother Frank went for a walk in the sleepy country outside Woking. They talked about whatever happened to pass through their heads, understanding each other perfectly, for they had always been good friends and both had the same roving imagination, the same love of the unexpected. What would happen, murmured Frank, thinking aloud, if a Martian were suddenly to come down to earth? Lazily, as they strolled along, he pursued this waking dream. In doing so he pressed a button in his brother's mind. H. G.'s book on this subject is dedicated, "To my brother, Frank Wells, this rendering of his idea."

It was on a calm day in August that he began to imagine the Martians' arrival. He might have given it the form of a queer meeting between the inhabitants of two planets, with comparisons of their customs and ideas; an enriching experience for both sides. But he saw it as a conflict of unexampled savagery, a welter of atrocities. The Martians set out to conquer the earth so as to drink the blood of that contemptible race, mankind. Their weapons are perfectly fitted to the task of destruction. They bring robots to do the hardest manual work; but they also have terrible armored vehicles, mobile towers, giving out a heat ray that kills and scorches everything within range; and clouds of artificial poisonous smoke. The military skill of mankind is useless in face of this unprecedented attack. The death-dealing robots advance, leaving behind them ruined villages, blazing forests, blackened corpses. The terror-stricken human beings fly before them; the roads are jammed with carts; an old man, half-crushed beneath the wheels, goes on stubbornly hunting in the dust for the gold pieces that he has let fall.

Wells and his wife went riding on their tandem through the lanes among which he had imagined this disaster let loose. With a mischievous twinkle in his eye he picked out the fine houses that were to be ruined, the woods that were to be burned down, the crossroads whose white dust would be spattered with blood.

The Martians' column advances on London, which is as yet unaware of danger. Then comes the sudden panic that smites any great city at the approach of an enemy, the whirlpool of collective madness into which everyone is swept by this unforeseen horror, the fiendish displays of selfishness, the cruelty of the stampeding mob—all described with the most exact attention to topographical detail, and the deepest insight into human reactions. More than forty years later this account of an imaginary panic in London, transferred to the radio by the mastery of Orson Welles, was to spread terror through crowds of Americans who, like the London crowds in the story, rushed panic stricken into the streets.

It is in the description of the Martians themselves that Wells's imagination rises to a climax of horror. With somber relish he portrays the unthinkable, the unimaginable. An enormous head, with tentacles hanging from it: a gigantic brain that has developed at the expense of the body and all its functions, the spirit of evil stripped of its humanity. All his blood-bathed nightmares fade before this vision, so clear to him that he records it in a drawing—a loathsome, spherical creature with evil eyes and a tiny, V-shaped, blood-sucking mouth. Among all the monsters with which human imagination has peopled the earth, none is more frightful than the dying Martian whose mechanical cry comes wailing out from the depths of his armored turret, over the deserted streets of London. Wells seems to revel in describing the havoc wrought by fear in the human soul, from the first instinctive recoil of cowardice to the moment when a man is degraded to the level of the brutes. Once again he points out here the insecurity of life, the helplessness of soft brains and flabby muscles in face of catastrophe. The gunner who tries to rally the survivors to resist the Martians; he gibes at them, telling them to forget their fears and their caution, their humdrum lives and their drawing-room manners, and live dangerously, secretly, to save the human race. His bantering voice rises above the disaster with a note of faith in man's survival.

Wells points the moral of the book in his final comment, where he says that the invasion of the Martians had destroyed "that serene confidence in the future which is the most abundant source of decadence." But this was not the only lesson to be drawn from it. Like every work in which creative imagination is highly stimulated, it left behind it something that had not been developed—material for a new book, arising out of the finished one.

One of these novels, written several years later, seems as though dictated to Wells by an artistic evidence, a sort of half-conscious parallelism, or simply by the mastery of creative potentiality that he had attained. This book is *The First Men in the Moon,* one of his outstanding successes at that time. Having in *The War of the Worlds* described the Martians' descent to earth, he now related the journey to the moon of two Englishmen, an eccentric inventor and an unsuccessful little business speculator. Of all Wells's fantastic romances, this is the one least imbued with sociological implications; it is almost solely a feat of imagination, carried out with supreme skill. So much so that its author, with his disdain of what came overeasily, felt no abiding interest in it.

Thanks to the invention of a substance which can be interposed like a screen between the sun's gravitational pull and that of the earth, the huge ball that has been constructed by the two travelers is able to pass through interplanetary space and reach the moon. The moon turns out to be a sort of vast ant heap, inhabited by complex insects with whiplike tentacles. These insects have soft bodies and can be squashed "like some softish sort of sweet with liquid in it," but they are endowed with engineering genius and have managed to construct a great underground system of pits and shafts, whose walls, like all the objects in use by these Selenites, are of pure gold.

The attraction of the vivid plot is heightened here by an extraordinarily intense power of description. The moment the sun touches the gray, cold stretches of the moon's surface, those vast plains begin to steam like wet linen held before a fire, and reddening tongues of vapor go licking up into the sky, the thawing air boils, like snow into which a white-hot metal bar has been plunged.

Still, *The First Men in the Moon* is no more than a kind of surface continuation to *The War of the Worlds*. As soon as the book was finished, an inner consequence thrust itself upon Wells. Again he was in a state of creative well-being. He said later that at Woking he had enjoyed eighteen months of very happy working life. It was with the spur of this inner stimulus that the logical development of his book arose in his consciousness. The Martian monster had been a monster of the brain, the measureless inflation of selfish intelligence swollen beyond all measure. But the story of egotism's challenge to human feelings had not yet been written. The form that Wells gave to it was one of his happiest inspirations. He was in such close touch with ordinary people that he could share their simplest dreams, their most personal fancies. From this common store of dreams there rose continually into his mind the notion of man confronted with the miraculous—with an angel come down to earth, or with the inhabitants of another planet. From this store there now came to him the thought, or wish, that passes at one time or another through every human mind—"If only I were invisible!"—a thought or wish born of the desire for unrestricted opportunity or secret power. Some of our legends, rising from the dark of time, deal with the adventures of a hero who wears a cap of invisibility. With *The Invisible Man,* Wells took up a subject that was universal in its appeal. Generations of readers have been thrilled by the story, and the motion picture has made good use of its extraordinary possibilities. He gave a scientific basis to the old legend—the theory of the refraction of light, which he took as the starting point of a series of experiments, leading to the final result achieved by the Invisible Man. He knew the experiment was not entirely feasible, but what chiefly interested him was not the scientific theory, nor even its application, its many thrilling incidents of an easy picturesque turn. He never told a story merely for its own sake, and the significance of this book was its picture of one man, a lone wolf, fighting in desperate pride against a close-knit society. His hero has been struggling, as penniless scientists must always do, against attempts to exploit him for mean purposes, against the jealousy of less gifted rivals, against the dictatorship of money. Research is no longer for him an aim in itself; what attracts him is the hope of secret revenge, the lure of power.

His exasperating sense of unacknowledged superiority has given him a thorough contempt for the general run of mankind; his self-centered brain has cast off all scruples; he has no trace of fellow feeling toward anyone. With the exacerbated individuality of Nietzsche's Superman, he is ready to take any step that will help him to reach the lonely summit of occult power. For his experiments he steals a cat which was the only friend of a poor old woman, and kills it as soon as he has managed to make it invisible. To protect his discovery he sets fire to the house where he lodges. He savagely assaults a secondhand dealer whom he has robbed. He steals money from his father, money that did not belong to the old man, and whose loss drives him to suicide. Neither grief nor remorse can soften his stony pride. But the man-hating man is doomed to perish in this solitary battle. Wells fits the strange case of the Invisible Man into the most banal setting, commonplace in its realism. He gives us a village inn, a group of country people who speak in the quaint, inarticulate style he knew so well; he runs through the whole gamut of unsophisticated reactions natural to illiterate men and women when faced with something inexplicable, and reveals their instinctive hostility toward anything that is out of the ordinary. The solitary, secretive man is fated to be betrayed by those to whom, at long last, he gives his confidence— by the tramp who is terrified of him and by the former fellow student whom chance throws in his way and who denounces him to the police. The end comes with a sense of heartrending tragedy; this man, with his brilliant brain, is battered to death by brutal fists in a village street.

Wells's gift for description, his power to make the reader see through his eyes, is used to the full in the passage where the body of the Invisible Man, who lies dying on the pavement, is gradually revealed in the human shape that he had abandoned. This book reaches a level unsurpassed in the author's work. In it he keeps the weird plot subordinate to the inner drama, so that the reader's interest is held, above all, by the psychological conflict. The everyday realism of the setting is made just as vivid, lit up by the shafts of his very individual humor.

Wells was ready to strike out a new line, to adopt a new style, stripped of the fantastic elements that had provided the framework for his early stories. Indeed, he had already started along this unexplored path. His personal life was expanding too, on a firm basis. In a drawing he made to commemorate the publication of *The Invisible Man,* we see him in the garden of his new house, Heatherlea, at Worcester Park, giving instructions to a gardener. Mrs. Robbins, in poor health, had come to live with her daughter and son-in-law. The little house at Woking was too small for the three of them. At Worcester Park they even had a guest room for week-end visitors. This was the home of a successful man, furnished to suit his personal tastes. The wallpaper in the big living room was brown, a neutral, packing-paper shade that made an excellent background for the gay colors of a few Japanese prints. The small, brightly lit dining room had plain walls with here and there the paler patch of a drawing. The pleasures of the table were no longer a mystery to the young couple, and a festive atmosphere was created by colored dishes, bowls of fruit, bottles of wine and long-necked, straw-covered Chianti flasks. The room that Wells used as a study looked onto a pine wood, a dark, silent wood that seemed to be waiting in expectancy.

A constant flow of visitors, neighbors or friends from London, kept the house ringing with eager discussions, egged on by the host who gloried in a brisk argument. Artists, writers, and mere sensation hunters came, and brought their wives, despite the fact that Wells and Jane were not a "respectable" couple. Wells's defiance of religious and social taboos, his dismissal of God as a man-made invention (he still kept up his boyhood habit of referring to the deity as "Mr. G.") were no longer considered shocking, now that he had become a celebrity, almost a "lion" already.

An English woman novelist has recorded, with "astonishing accuracy and acute intensity of expression" (according to Wells himself), a week-end visit to the Worcester Park house. She describes her first impression of her host, who looked more like a grocer's assistant than a writer, with his high-pitched voice, loud and metallic yet indistinct, his cockney accent, his trick of asking questions and then answering them himself, the inarticulate sounds that punctuated his talk—a varied range of sociable noises accompanied by jerky movements of his short arms. She mentions his way of announcing his ideas like Bible truths, as if he were talking not to listeners for whom he had little esteem, but to some invisible presence; that was the secret something within him, which made him, despite his weak voice and his weak mouth, strong and fascinating. She had been a childhood friend of Catherine Robbins, and gives her portrait as well—the birdlike glance of her clear brown eyes, the neat gestures of her small, soft hands, the erect bearing of a woman in perfect command of herself. She describes, with a certain asperity, her absorption in her own life, to which no one else could be admitted, her manner of stressing her own courage, her sparkling conversation and her thin voice, which sounded like a corkscrew "going down into a cork with no bottle behind it."

Worcester Park was an important step forward from the social point of view. Soon after they settled there Wells gained his freedom and married Jane. By this time they were so completely at ease in their new kind of life that they began to make plans for a trip abroad, and discussed them at great length with their friend George Gissing.

Wells was hurriedly putting the finishing touches to a new long novel so as to get it into the publisher's hands before they went. He described it as rather on the lines of *The Time Machine* but on a much smaller scale. The only resemblance between this book—*When the Sleeper Wakes*—and his first novel, is that they both prophesy social changes. But there are no more Elois and Morlocks here. Stripped of its fantastic features, the book is simply the story of a social conflict on the scale of "The Year 2,000" (this was the title with which it first came out as a serial). Later in his preface to a revised edition Wells called it the most ambitious and the least satisfactory of all his books. His ambition had been to paint a picture of the future, showing all the results of mechanization and the altered structure of society. His Sleeper, who had been lying in a trance for two hundred years, wakens to find that, thanks to the wealth which has piled up for him from various inheritances, he is now master of the world. It is a world conceived in a dream of material expansion. London, the immense capital, has eaten up all the surrounding countryside and swallowed its inhabitants. Family life has disappeared, replaced by day nurseries and enormous automatic restaurants, which remind the present-day reader of New York's cafeterias. The windowless rooms of the houses are centrally lighted, heated and air conditioned. Traffic in the monster city is carried along by a system of moving carpets at different levels—Wells was specially fond of this idea, one of those that he was not to see put into practice in his lifetime. Intercapital and intercontinental traffic is served by huge airplanes, making four trips a day between Paris and London (the book was written in 1898). Letters, books, and newspapers have been replaced by the telephone, the phonograph, and the cinematograph. In 1895 Wells had come to know an English inventor, Robert W. Paul, who was then putting the finishing touches on a motion-picture projector. He and Paul, together, perfected an invention regarding which they applied for a patent. Wells gave it the characteristic name of the Time Machine, and claimed later that it had foreshadowed most of the established methods of screen drama. In his world of the future, every room contains a small machine, equipped with a screen and a row of cylinders which, when slipped into the machine, give a sound and color rendering of a novel or an opera. His world of the future even has television, so that people can see what is happening in far-off places—the incidents of a strike, or of a battle in the air. Publicity has been carried to enormous lengths. Even the churches and chapels of the various religious bodies have scenes from New Testament movies shown on their frontages, and exhort the passers-by, in huge, glowing letters, to "Be a Christian—without hinderance to your present occupation," or promise "Brisk blessings for Busy Business Men." Talking machines pour out a flood of news over the city, shrill voices try to drown each other's slogans; one of the rival firms holds the crowd's attention by yelling "Galloop! Galloop!"

The keys of this highly efficient world are in the hands of Mammon. The power of wealth is greater than ever before; it rules supreme over earth, sea, and sky. "The day of democracy is past," says a spokesman of this new society. The propertied classes have a monopoly of all that is desirable in life—beautiful many-colored clothes, culture, the sensual enjoyments provided in the Cities of Pleasure that pander to every human instinct. Humiliating experiences, jealousy, frustrated desires, are wiped out of people's minds by means of a new psychological treatment based on hypnosis, a kind of mental surgery, which is also used in order to impress the memory, in a mechanical way, with useful facts and pieces of information. But the working classes live and labor underground; dressed in the coarse blue linen that is the uniform of servitude, they are uneducated, inarticulate, vitiated—the dregs of humanity, with no hope of escaping from their wretched lot. The Sleeper wakes just as the workers rise in revolt against the Council that has been administering the fortune thanks to which he is Master of the World. Ostrog, a skillful agitator, a cunning politician, aiming at dictatorship, has incited them to rebel, using their resentment as a lever to hoist himself into power. He exploits the Sleeper, who symbolizes the dreams of downtrodden humanity. But the enslaved, victimized masses, once they have broken loose, refuse to be pacified, and Ostrog, whose personal victory has been bought with their blood, sends for black troops to stifle the rebellion.

The Sleeper, who had shared in the democratic ideas of his time, is deeply moved by the distress of these wretched people and by their tenacious hope of survival. He takes off in a monoplane to attack the flying squadron of black troops. In the revised version he dies "as all of his kind must die, with no certainty of either victory or defeat." In tightening up and pruning the plot into its final form, Wells removed a long-drawn-out love story, leaving only the intervention of a girl who is passionately devoted to the people's cause. He admitted later that the whole fabric of the book showed signs of his weariness and haste, of the fact that his attention was being partly given to another novel, and also of the feverish excitement that had descended upon him when he began to get ready for his first trip abroad.

Like any other worthy Briton setting out for the continent, like his own Miss Winchelsea, Wells was so excited when he got to the railway station that he could do nothing but fidget, and to the friends who came to see him off he displayed a naïve delight not unmixed with alarm. "'Abroad' was a slightly terrifying world of adventure for us," he writes in his memoirs.

George Gissing proved to be an enthusiastic and merciless guide to ancient Rome. He was a handsome, fair-haired, leonine man, a mine of classical knowledge, and had an ill-concealed contempt for anyone so ignorant of the subject as Wells, whom he looked upon as illiterate, while Wells, for his part, considered Gissing to be eaten up by too much learning. Gissing took his role of instructor very seriously, describing to his friends the former splendors of the ruins where togaed senators and noble Roman matrons once lived and moved. But on this first foreign visit, Wells had brought all that was most English in him. While Gissing could spare no more than an absent-minded glance for anything that cut into his vision of ancient Rome, and seemed anxious to ignore all the successive layers that helped to make up the city, even those of the Middle Ages and the Renaissance, Wells's eye was caught by the life of modern Rome and the crowds that swarmed in its streets. It was caught still more by the British tourists, zealously consulting their Baedeker; it dwelt with great amusement and secret pity on the horde of dour old maids that England seemed to produce for export only. He imagined to himself the little private drama of renunciation that lay behind each of them, their lives of hidden regret. It was while being led around Tivoli by Gissing that he suddenly saw in his mind's eye the wan features of Miss Winchelsea, and he countered his friend's eloquent descriptions of past glories by outlining for his benefit the tragic effect of snobbery on the heart of an old maid who refuses her only chance of married happiness because the pleasant, cultured man she meets on her travels has a common name.

Fatigued by the month they had spent in Rome under Gissing's wing, Wells and Jane went on by themselves to visit Naples and Paestum. He saw the sun rising across the bay of Capri, the massive forms of the gold-rimmed rocks being gradually revealed as the warm, rose-pink light flowed over them, while a pale moon still lingered in the sky; the sea, scattered with boats that sparkled like tiny flames, and the blue water boiling into white foam through the arch of the Fariglioni rock. But what set him dreaming was neither the thought of Capri's distant past nor the rapture of its present beauty. He had brought to Italy, along with his British realism, his dreams of the future—but of a future entirely taken up by a terrible, world-wide conflict, waged with quite new weapons. In the blue skies of Italy, he seemed to see a great air battle, "A Dream of Armageddon"—the rocks of Capri shattered, a swarm of aircraft flying over Naples. In the deep silence that broods above the ruins of Paestum he seemed to hear the roar of airplane engines and the death-dealing hail of shells.

Soon after his return from Italy, in the summer of 1898, he began to feel curiously unwell. A weariness had come over him, an inability to work; he found it hard to concentrate on the novel that he had planned before leaving England. Since the day when he had seen himself in a scrap of looking glass as a scraggy, untidy youth with ribs that stuck out, he had always felt a sort of contemptuous repudiation of his body, and this had driven him to use it roughly, to demand too much from it. So now, in increasing physical discomfort, he set out with Jane for a long bicycle tour. On the way he fell really ill. His crushed kidney was giving trouble again. He and Jane had been meaning to visit a doctor, a friend of Gissing who lived in a little country town. They were still so little aware of the advantages their new wealth could give them that instead of bringing down a specialist from London, they traveled all the way to this doctor's home in jolting, branch-line trains. Wells was determined not to give in, but the journey was too much even for his obstinacy. He was more seriously ill than he would admit even to himself. An operation seemed unavoidable. But with characteristic humor he made light of his friends' fears. One of his funny sketches shows Jane, horror-stricken, exclaiming "Wow!" while the surgeon brandishes a huge knife. In the hands of his doctor-host he soon began to get better. There need be no operation; he was out of danger. He comments on the fact that his "confounded viscus" had been kind enough to wait until he could afford to pay for medical advice and treatment. But his convalescence was long drawn out, and while it lasted he was strictly forbidden to do any work. He whiled away his enforced leisure by writing and illustrating a story, "The Story of Tommy and the Elephant," to amuse the doctor's little girl. Thirty years later, the sale of this manuscript provided the funds that enabled his little friend to set up in practice as a doctor.

Wells was told that he must leave Worcester Park. He needed a dry climate and a well-sheltered house built on sand or gravel. Jane began to tour the seaside towns. She came back from each trip almost in tears, horrified by the state of the houses she had seen. Wells resigned himself philosophically to the confined, cautious existence that seemed likely to be imposed on him for the future. As he wrote to a friend, his job for the next year or two was to be an invalid, and the world would have to get along as best it could by itself, at any rate until he felt better.

XII

THE DISCOVERY OF THE FUTURE

WHILE EVERYBODY TAKES the past for granted, hardly anyone believes that it is possible to read the future—this was the keynote of a lecture delivered by Wells at the Royal Institution in January, 1902. The memorable occasion is recorded by one of his rapid pen-and-ink sketches. A rather shaky-looking lecturer, whose knees seem in danger of giving way, is gazing with a panic-stricken expression at the semi-circle of seats filled with solemn, bearded individuals, most of whom are slumbering with their heads on each other's shoulders, though a few are glaring malevolently at him; in the outermost seats are a few old ladies, listening with aggressive attention. Like many of Wells's jokes, this one was inspired by an event of the greatest importance to him. It marked a turning point in his life. At the very beginning of his career as a writer, he had fixed his attention, with *The Time Machine,* on the future and not on the past. But the early stories, in which he gave free rein to his imagination and let it gallop toward disaster, had been only a means to an end, a short cut to success. It seems as though he was more or less consciously striving, in those early days, to get onto firm ground, to reach a position of financial security from which he could enter his real artistic domain. He reached that secure position just as the century was drawing to an end.

Having been unable, like his hero Kipps, to find any reasonably comfortable house that came up to his new standards, and being disgusted with the small pretentious villas recommended to him by one agent after another, he decided to build himself a home at Sandgate. (Echoes of his experiences with architects and builders, humorous

and exaggerated accounts of his disappointments, are to be found in
Kipps.) While waiting for their house to be finished, he and Jane lived
in a furnished villa. Wells's gradual progress from cautious invalidism
to fresh confidence in life can be traced through the plans for his
future dwelling. There was a sun-flooded loggia to help him toward
convalescence; his bedroom was on the same level as the reception-
rooms, in case he should have to go around in a wheel chair; but
before the house was finished, the architect had added a day nursery
and a night nursery. Wells's eldest son was born in 1901, and his
second arrived two years later. He was of the opinion that a sterile,
childless existence, however pleasant it might appear, was bound to be
a failure and a perversion. By founding a family, he was giving tangible
proof that he had come to terms with life. The Sandgate house was
also a sign that he was now firmly established in the propertied class.
When he protested against the sentimental device of a heart as decora-
tion for the front door, the architect put an ace of spades there instead. It must have been in some way evident that Wells's fortune was
of very recent growth—he himself must have shown clear traces of his
humble origin, the ace of spades must have fitted in too well with his
sudden rise to prosperity—for a rumor began to spread, to the effect
that the house was being built by a man who had made his money
by breaking the bank at Monte Carlo.

Indeed, just at that time H. G. did rather resemble a gambler on
vacation. He was no longer staking everything on immediate success.
His complete satisfaction with the present expressed itself by a loss of
interest in the passing moment. He began now to divide the human
race, as he said in his lecture at the Royal Institution, into two groups:
the majority, possessed of what he called a judicial mind, turned toward the past, quite unconcerned with the future; and the minority,
who were constructive minded, active in their manner of thinking,
and curious about things to come.

Things to come—the phrase entered Wells's life at this time, never
to leave it again. "Tomorrow is the important and fruitful thing for
us," he declared. He saw the world as a vast enterprise of construction.
A kind of intoxication seized him when he considered the boundless
possibilities of the future. But can the human mind, which is a thing
of memory, pierce through the mist behind which future possibilities
lie hidden? Wells always protested that he was no fortuneteller. The
future of the individual, he said, would always be shrouded in mystery.

But in addition to the general classification of judicial and constructive minds, mankind could be divided into those who had a blind confidence in the future, and those whose concern was to estimate the forces that lay behind individuals. He declared himself to be a rather extreme specimen of the latter species, thus revealing another of his permanent characteristics. By discovering the active causes of things, he said, it became possible "to throw a ray of light forward instead of backward."

Guided by this inner conviction, Wells had found his true path, not that of success or of his artistic self-assertion, but that of his permanent, creative curiosity. The conditions of human life, he pointed out, had undergone a greater change during the past century than during the preceding thousand years. It was henceforth his task, his sacred mission, to foresee, to determine, the trend of future transformations, to give a complete, even a detailed picture of them. He ended his Royal Institution lecture with one of those lyrical outbursts through which, on rare occasions, his mocking spirit revealed an underlying faith in humanity. "All that is and has been," he assured his hearers, "is but the dusk before the dawn."

A great feeling of security had come over Wells. Quite lately, when he first fell ill, J. M. Barrie had called on him to inquire, with the utmost tact, whether he was in any need of financial help, such as the Royal Literary Fund extends to needy intellectuals. But even now, when the Sandgate house was finished, Wells had enough money left to save him from worrying as to whether his new book would have a big sale. He was thoroughly enjoying this respite, he felt that for the time being he could write to please himself, with no need to keep one eye on his public. The new book would be his book, not merely a job done to suit a publisher or to meet the prevailing taste.

This book, his very own, was called *Anticipations*. It is a title that might be used to cover a whole section of his creative work, the most important section. This was only the beginning. A generic title. But Wells was still a timid novice in this enterprise of conjuring up the future. Thinking that the title he had chosen was still too ambitious for him, he added a long and pedantic amplification: "Anticipations of the reaction of mechanical and scientific progress upon human life and thought."

Much later, in one of his last books, Wells declared that the reputation of being a prophet had been thrust upon him, although such a thing lay far beyond his natural capacities. His *Anticipations,* in which he was still groping about on unexplored territory, begin by foretelling mechanical progress of a kind that could easily be anticipated. It was the terrific speeding up of communications that had brought about the most spectacular alteration in human relationships, their complete change of scale. But this speeding up had only just begun. In that year, 1900, it was easy to foresee that railroad travel would expand and increase in comfort and speed, although, as Wells put it, "the ghost of a superseded horse" was still trotting ahead of every locomotive. He prophesied the expansion of road traffic, with motor coaches and special highways built for such traffic, with sloping, asphalted surfaces.

Memories of his own recent disappointments had convinced him that there would also be an entire change in building technique. He writes indignantly about contemporary methods, comparing them for speed with the work of coral insects building a reef, and laughing at the notion that houses must still be built by hand, as in the day of the pyramids. He already imagines prefabricated houses, a kind of machine "running to and fro along a temporary rail, that will squeeze out wall as one squeezes paint from a tube and form its surface with a pat or two as it sets." In those days of kerosene lamps and water buckets, he was already dreaming of homes that would be not only lit but heated from a central power station, instead of individually; that would have a bathroom for every bedroom, electric cookers with thermostatic control, and machines for washing and drying the plates. He even goes so far as to foretell air-conditioned houses. He also draws attention to the servant problem—which at that time had not even arisen—not only because the mechanical household equipment of the future will do away, to a great extent, with manual labor, but also because, in the new society that is to arise, servants will no longer be obtainable.

But it is on the subject of flying that Wells's *Anticipations* are boldest and most accurate. He foresees the transition from the captive balloon to the dirigible and thence to the airplane. Writing in or just before 1900, he says that long before the year 2,000, and very probably before 1950, airplanes will have come into existence—that there will be squadrons of such machines, flying in close formation like a flock of migrant birds in the autumn. With his lively imagination, he already hears the rustle of the expanding parachutes.

From the moment when Wells first wrote of the airplane as he envisaged it, a real plane and not a mere fantastic flying machine, he never tired of predicting its future importance. A few years after this book came out, he described a conversation between an author and his small son, which has a convincingly authentic ring about it.

The little boy begs his father—in the nicest possible way, for he is anxious not to hurt his feelings—to stop writing so much stuff about flying, because his schoolmates are chaffing him about it. The father sticks to his point, and even assures the boy that he himself will fly, often, when he is grown up. But the lad replies despondently that the headmaster himself declared, only yesterday, before the whole class, that no one will ever be able to fly. The very idea was absurd and that no one who had ever hit a partridge or a pheasant on the wing would believe it for a moment. The boy's father was evidently not in the habit of shooting partridges and pheasants.

The most astonishing thing of all on the part of a peaceable civilian like Wells, is the way in which he prophesied a revolution in military strategy. War, he declared, would henceforth be one of the exact sciences. He spoke of machine guns, trenches, subterranean dugouts, artificial clouds, and even of mobile, armored vehicles, a kind of land ironclads.

In a short story written only a few years later, he describes the dramatic arrival, by night, of these future monsters, a few of which succeed in putting an army to flight. A war correspondent who is present at this unexpected attack, and wants a headline for his sensational story, hits on the comprehensive title, "Manhood versus Machinery."

The military officer of tomorrow, said Wells in his *Anticipations,* must be an engineer. But air power would be the deciding factor in future wars. The airplane, which he calls the triumph of man over space, would also be used for the destruction of humanity. Tomorrow's belligerents would fight for mastery of the air. Wells points out the difference between a blind army and one that can see. The savage battle on the ground would be overshadowed by a terrible conflict in the clouds. Everybody, everywhere, would be perpetually and constantly looking up at the sky, with a vague sense of painful anticipations, a terrible fear of approaching catastrophe.

The earth was still cradled in utter peace. A feeling of security passed down from one generation to the next. The grandfathers' world would be that of their grandsons. When Wells looked up from the pages that he was covering with his regular handwriting, he saw only a sky flecked by caroling larks; when he listened, he heard only the wind soughing through the trees and the waves breaking on the beach. But his imagination had leaped across the years that were to come, to the day when man would find no security upon the face of the earth. At night, searchlights would sweep every fold of the country. There would no longer be soldiers on the one hand and civilians on the other, "the tendency to differentiate a noncombatant mass in the fighting State will certainly not be respected."

Britannia ruled the waves. The balance of power in Europe seemed fixed forever. But the harmless little man in his quiet house was already talking about an aggressive Pan-Germanic power, an element destined to become more and more embarrassing. The shade of the Prince Consort was still influencing British minds in favor of his industrious countrymen, but Wells already suspected that the active faculties of the German, as such, might finally prove to be of doubtful benefit to Europe, or even to future generations in Germany itself.

Britannia ruled the waves, proud of her navy, of her officers, of the younger sons who had colonized her far-flung empire. But the strange visionary of Sandgate, though he looked like a tubby, prosperous shopkeeper, was announcing that the days of careless optimism were numbered. In his mind's eye he saw a gray-haired general, with epaulets and medals, spurs and sword, every inch a gentleman—an antiquated warrior, galloping along beside a column of young men doomed to destruction. Wells was not writing for ossified upholders of tradition, but for the thousands, the millions of "boys who will never be men."

It was not only in order to prophesy battle and sudden death that Wells called up visions such as this. Beyond the wasted lives, beyond the nights of horror, he saw the glow of dawn. Whatever disorders, conflicts, centuries of quarrel and bloodshed might lie ahead of mankind, he believed that a synthetic process would lead at last to the establishment of a single, world-wide state where peace would reign.

One word had come to the fore in Wells's vocabulary, a word that he was never to forget. The keystone of his spiritual edifice had been set in place. A world state, "a New Republic, dominating the world . . . a sort of outspoken Secret Society"—this expression, too, now slipped out for the first time at the tip of his pen. A chord had been struck

that would never cease to vibrate in his being. Certain forces, he believed, would prevail, in broad daylight, like an open freemasonry
with no secret code. The world would be brought into unity, despite
all the outdated conventions, all the prejudices that hung on the heels
of reality. There was no such thing as incompatibility between nations
or hostility between races. "There is no Teutonic race and there never
has been, there is no Keltic race and there never has been," he writes;
but "people who believe in this sort of thing are not the sort of people
that one attempts to convert by a set argument."

The most unexpected element in this picture of tomorrow's world
is Wells's criticism of democracy, as a confused form of government
which, in his opinion, was not the first stage of a world-wide movement destined to advance firmly in its present direction, but "the first
impulse of forces that will finally sweep round into a quite different
path."

All this was written at a time when the average man was thoroughly
satisfied with the institutions that he had built up for himself, and
with his rights as a citizen; at a time of faith in evolution, when
people were smugly convinced of their civic powers in their own
sphere of action. But Wells, by this time, had rejected everything that
was of current use, and refused to be lulled by hollow, glittering words.
He suspected that the word democracy was nothing but "a mere
rhetorical garment for essentially different facts." He believed a time
would come when the colorless, hesitant mass of voters, known by
the mythical name of Public Opinion, would make way for a class
of new men, clear-sighted, energetic men with scientific minds. For
years he clung to this faith in the scientist, the specialist, who would
bring order out of chaos; it went hand in hand with his contempt for
political opportunists and for writers who allowed internal problems to
absorb their whole attention.

No one was more astonished than Wells when *Anticipations* became
a best seller, a greater success than even the most popular of his novels.
This was only the first of a number of surprises that awaited him
whenever he left the beaten track and parted with the hope of easy
success. But he was under no illusion as to the quality of the response
the new book had aroused. As he said later, everyone, at the beginning
of the century, shrank from the notion that a great political reorganization was a necessary thing. The mere fact that he had dealt with this

and similar questions put his book outside the sphere of what passed
in those days for practical politics.

All his life long, H. G. Wells strove to bring the evidence of his ideas
into line with the methods of practical realization. A few years after
Anticipations was published, he returned to the same theme with *Mankind in the Making.* He was still upheld by his faith in mankind and
in universal design. He still believed that a great mass of people would
come forward spontaneously to fight for a better world. In riper years
he used to laugh at his former tendency toward overoptimism, harshly
criticizing his hopes and their resounding wording. He was never tired
of correcting himself, throwing back his ideas to be melted down in
the crucible of his dissatisfaction. He wanted to stimulate the imagination of young people. He wanted, first and foremost, to put the final
aim clearly before them, to make it as convincing as possible, so that
it should remain imprinted on their minds. He wanted to show them,
too, that they must prepare themselves, become physically and spiritually braced to hasten the establishment of the world state. He harked
back to the sources of his own inspiration and wrote *A Modern
Utopia,* drawing considerably upon Plato's *Republic* and even adopt-
ing its dialogue form. This book, which appeared in 1905, is a hybrid
affair, a cross between fantastic novel and social prophecy. Its style
seems old-fashioned nowadays, and it has not the dramatic interest
of an adventure story or the bold realism of *Anticipations.* But from
the historical point of view it presents a problem of particular interest.
Wells borrowed Plato's idea of the class of guardians of the Republic,
the greatest possible number of individuals of the social magma,
crystallized as rapidly as possible into groups for the purpose of effective and conscious co-operation. The words "cell" and "nucleus" had
not yet come into daily use. But Wells knew that the question of
leadership was outstanding in its importance. The idea was so new,
however, that he tried, as was his custom, to give it an air of familiarity by linking it up with existing conceptions. At the time when he
was writing this book, the Bushido code, with its principle of utter
devotion to a cause, was exerting a singular attraction upon Western
minds. And he took advantage of this by calling his active elite the
"Order of the Samurai."

"Bushido. It was inevitable," says one of the characters in a later
book, *The Research Magnificent;* but he adds, as though excusing the
failings of a friend, that "it dates." And indeed, a daring conception

was thus coupled with an exotic and outworn title. Wells's own opinion of the idea was subject to fluctuation. At a time when he was strongly influenced by socialist theories, he felt that his Utopia laid too much stress upon organization and uniformity. But when writing it, he believed that there could be no better short cut to universal brotherhood than his Order of the Samurai, which he looked upon as a means of direct approach to the masses. "This dream is a dream," he wrote in *First and Last Things,* published in 1908; but at that moment he was very weary from looking too far ahead, and later he began again to wonder whether, after all, he had really been so completely out of touch with reality. Little groups were forming, inspired by what he had written, and calling themselves Utopians or Samurai; from time to time young men, yearning for action, would come and ask to be allowed to join his army of new republicans. But he did not know how to advise them, or what use to make of their youthful ardor. His theory of a Samurai revolution was "floating in the air," as he put it, and he could not see how to bring it down to earth. For he was not a man of action in that sense. It was perhaps his most precious gift, his power of seeing into the future, that prevented him from being so. His intellectual long-sightedness made him stumble over the first stone that lay in his path. Reality evaded him, became hostile, the moment he tried to make it fit in with his ideas. But toward the end of his life he remarked on the fact that just about the time he made this unsuccessful effort at practical construction, Lenin, "under the pressure of a more urgent reality," was quietly and steadily drawing up an "extraordinarily similar plan"—the Communist party organization. Wells often asked himself whether Lenin's notions had been in any way derived from his own; he wondered, not without a shade of regret, the natural regret of an innovator who cannot succeed in giving shape to his ideas, regret at having disappointed the young people who turned to him with such confidence.

He long remained attached to this still-born idea, and declared in the last years of his life, that if Russia had never done anything else for humanity, the experiment of the Communist party would suffice, of itself alone, to justify the Russian revolution and set it on a higher level than the chaotic stampede of the first French revolution.

His inability to adapt his Order of Samurai to the demands of reality left a bitter taste of failure that lingered for a long time on his lips. He made a further attempt to carry out his project, by means of the

Fabian Society. But before this came his first transatlantic visit. The notes he published about this trip reveal the same shock of contradictory impressions that he was to receive from each of his contacts with the United States. His relationship with America was one that sometimes exists between human beings—an attitude of wrangling friendliness. What chiefly struck him during this first visit was the Americans' lack of national feeling. He calls it "civic blindness." It would rest with Europe, he decided, to give the young peoples of the world the sense of being part of a state, a feeling of civic responsibility. Stimulated, unconsciously maybe, by this journey, he decided, when he got home, to pass to action himself. He had known the Fabians—from a distance and as a looker-on, a fervent believer in socialist theories—during his student days in South Kensington. But one day, just after he went to live at Sandgate, there had arrived at his door, on bicycles, that extraordinary couple who influenced the destinies of British socialism for more than half a century—Sidney and Beatrice Webb.

Beatrice, one of the elder daughters of an extremely rich manufacturer, had developed early in life the self-assurance that comes of wealth, established social position, and the habit of mixing with the pick of the intellectual and artistic world. She was a masterful girl, accustomed to running a large household and shining in society until the day when there took place in her one of those suddden transformations from which saints and revolutionaries are born. That was the day when she realized what depths of distress and poverty lay beneath the gilded surface of Victorian society, and ran away from it to live the life of the working class and watch the girls in the London slums hunting desperately for jobs that were always too few. Wells says there was something "entirely un-English, an unconventional vigor, a brilliance" about her which suggested a gypsy strain; her mind leaped ahead as though, instead of advancing slowly toward her conclusions, she flew to them on a witch's broomstick. With the sure instinct of the self-confident woman, she married an obscure civil servant, or rather a learned sociologist who had somehow wandered into bureaucracy, and his vast learning, retentive memory and objective mind provided exactly what she needed to supplement her brilliant gifts.

Wells's lifelong friendship with the Webbs had a particularly stormy quality about it; it was an affair of strong attraction alternating with moments of passionate revulsion. Their first visit to Sandgate was made with the aim of persuading Wells to join the Fabian Society, to which he would be an asset because of his growing celebrity. Wells, for his part, supposed that through the Fabians he would be able to make contact with the younger generation, the students in the universities and technical colleges, and form them into a stronghold of discipline. He soon lost patience with the Fabians, however, owing to their slowness and their refusal to consider any aim that was not immediate and practical. He lost his temper and made frontal attacks on the very members whose opinions were nearest to his own. As was usual with him, he dragged these disputes onto the public platform. (He says of his own Mr. Britling that "he expressed himself, re-expressed himself, over-expressed himself.") After two years he marched out of the Fabian Society, slamming all the doors that he could find to slam.

His personal disappointment with the Webbs is overexpressed in a book published in 1911, *The New Machiavelli*. Beatrice Webb is depicted there, in all the exuberance that made her so easy to caricature, as the domineering Altiora Bailey. The fury with which Wells assailed his former friends might have been expected to estrange them once and for all. But despite his resentment, he put his finger, in this novel, upon the principal difference between Beatrice Webb and himself. She, he says, was loyal to people and undertakings, sentimental and faithful, whereas his own loyalty was to ideas and instincts, and he was emotional and scheming.

In any case he was one of those rare beings whose friends bear them no grudge for unjust or even insulting behavior. Besides, he never made personal attacks on people except when a cause or an idea was at stake. He would take up an interrupted friendship with all his old fervor, sometimes before the resounding echoes of his departure had faded away. When Beatrice Webb died he wrote, in complete sincerity, "she counted for so much in the scenery of my life that it is almost as if a major planet had vanished from my sky."

At the time of his stormy association with the Fabians, Wells was recommending co-operation with the Labour party, and urging, above all, that the masses must be educated and introduced to the idea of world-wide organization. From 1906 onward he tirelessly repeated that in order to create a socialist society it was necessary "to make Fabians." He tried, with all his fierce energy, to shake the socialists out of their conservative state of mind and out of the tactical rut along which they were plodding. As he declared in *First and Last Things*, socialism, to him, meant nothing more or less than the awakening of mankind to collective consciousness and collective will. His chief objection to Marxism was that it had not begun by proclaiming, as the ultimate and accessible goal of the socialist movement, the creation of a world state.

Most of Wells's books are a kind of heart-to-heart talk with himself. He often wrote in order to convince himself of the truth of his ideas, as well as to win other people's support for them. His writings are not the polished products of long forethought—they are the expression of notions that became clear to him while he was working them out, convictions that grew stronger as they were set down in black and white. He was trying to cut his own path through surrounding perplexities, by making it for other people too. He had his share of that primitive fervor which is common among the followers of a new religion, who find it easier to make public confession than to examine their consciences in private. This tendency to confess himself out loud remained with him to the end of his life. He frankly admitted that a man like himself, irritable, easily wearied and bored, versatile, sensual and gifted with a lively curiosity, was often apt to lose touch with his essential beliefs.

First and Last Things represents the effort of a rather absent-minded believer to call back to memory the articles of his creed. Most of them now show signs of wear and tear. The arguments of his inner voice have been drowned by louder noises. The fact that the book still has a certain interest, is due partly to its descriptions of life at the time it was written, and partly to the biographical details it contains. Wells declared later that it represented an attempt to straighten out his ideas about the world and about himself, at a time when he was still mentally adolescent. He went on to revise his notions in each of his successive books, all of which were records of outdated dialogues with himself.

First and Last Things expresses, above all, a burning faith in the true brotherhood of man, of which humanity was only just becoming aware. It also expresses, for the first time, certain doubts as to the concept of evolution, of an agelong progressive development permeating the various constructive forces of the day. This concept could only be altered, says Wells, by the outbreak of an immense and terrifying war. He is strangely haunted by thoughts of an imminent conflict, which would cause destruction on a scale that no one could foresee, especially now that flying machines would soon make their appearance, to open up "a new world of terrifying possibilities." As was his custom, he worked on two planes, that of reasoned warning and that of imagination. His *First and Last Things,* written in uncanny communion with the future, describes cities flaming into destruction, the sky darkened by mighty airplanes, the explosion of huge shells, roads jammed by a torrent of fugitives, communications cut off, supply trains shattered, ships sunk.

In the same year he brought out *The War in the Air,* as though wondering whether it was as novelist or as author of *Anticipations* that he could make the most effect on public opinion. He had this repeated warning so much at heart that he brought all the resources of his artistry to bear on his readers. *The War in the Air* mingles both the types of writing of which he was now a master, that of scientific invention and that of psychological humorousness. The hero of the story is, like Kipps, the victim of a callous social system; he has still hardly emerged from the sordid conditions among which he grew up, and is tied hand and foot by ignorance. But into his illiterate ken there comes the airplane, the heavier-than-air machine, whose invention is still a secret. The world is on the eve of a great transformation.

The grandfather of Bert Smallways (the name is a portrait in itself) had gone from the cradle to the grave without altering a single one of his ideas; but into his grandson's world there filters a disturbing and dangerous influence—the modernization of patriotism. The dizzy speed with which the rhythm, the scale and the possibilities of human life have altered, has led to the collapse of national frontiers; but instead of giving birth to a new and self-evident fellowship among men, this collapse has brought about a feeling of exaggerated, dangerous proximity. The physical and mental energy of every nation is monopolized by fear of its neighbors. Wells described, in this year, 1908, the position of the great powers. The British Empire, perilously far flung across the earth, threatened by the vigorous and passionately indignant forces of youth that are arising in Egypt and India among the "lesser breeds"; France and her allies, the Latin powers, even more pacifist at heart than the British, nations that are heavily armed but have no will to battle; Russia, "festering toward bankruptcy and decay"; Germany, the most efficient force in the world, with her highly developed administration and a tradition that distorts her political outlook, completely unscrupulous and unsentimental in action. To her misfortune this Germany, just at the time when recent discoveries seem to promise her increased authority, finds, too, a man who embodies her thirst for power, Prince Karl Albert, Nietzsche's Superman in person, "splendidly amoral," a nucleus for the national passion for aggression, whose brutal strength imposes itself on the rest of the world, just as the Napoleonic legend did in a former time. This Prince conceives the colossal plan of using squadrons of dirigibles, constructed in secret, to gain mastery of the air and conquer the whole world by a surprise attack. (Wells perhaps remembered this passage of his book when the blitzkrieg notion arose, some thirty years later.)

By a ludicrous coincidence, the pitiable hero of the tale is caught up in the terrible mechanism of this aerial warfare. Held prisoner by the Prince in a gigantic Zeppelin, one of a squadron that has gone out to conquer America, the terrified Bert looks down at a naval engagement and sees huge battleships ("the weirdest, most destructive, wasteful megathere"), the most costly monsters in the world, sinking after hardly five-minutes' fighting. He sees, too, the attack on the city of New York. Like all North Americans, the New Yorkers had been convinced, even more firmly than the English, that war on their own soil was an impossibility. They feel as safe as spectators at a bullfight; some of them, perhaps, risk their money on a bet, but that is all. The great city capitulates before the terrible threat from the sky. But American pride rebels against this capitulation, imposed by the government; guerrilla warfare breaks out to oppose the German domination and armed bands attack the army of occupation, which replies to this "terrorist" action by an appalling massacre of the New York population.

The little fellow crouching in the enormous Zeppelin looks on at the fearful reprisals. Afterward, in presence of the group of Germans who have perpetrated these unheard-of atrocities, he reflects that "none of them seemed capable of hurting a dog." There is, however, one German officer, English on his mother's side, who cannot rid his mind of that New York nightmare, where his fellow soldiers behaved like brute beasts. He realizes that his Prince, that demigod, is nothing but a lunatic.

Meanwhile, the Americans have been preparing to strike back. Airplanes attack the dirigibles. "The whole atmosphere was a Seat of War." An Asiatic air force suddenly invades the sky. Aerial warfare rages on, horribly destructive, yet indecisive. The economic and financial structure of the whole world crumbles. The hoarding of gold is the sole habit that survives the general collapse. The civilian population, and all the habits and customs of social life, have been swallowed up in the fighting. The entire universe, aggressors and victims alike, is in the clutch of disaster. The cataclysmic spectacle is all the more poignant from being seen through the bewildered little eyes of Bert Smallways, who is driven by terror into actions that he himself cannot account for. He becomes a strange tool of fate by killing the dictator-prince, whose insane ambition brought about this universal catastrophe. Floating like foam on the crest of a tidal wave, he survives the world war, its backwash of epidemics, and the downfall of civilization. His brother, who is also among the survivors, meditating on the reasons for the overmighty and overviolent events that have smitten the human race, says to himself, "Someone, somewhere, ought to have stopped something . . ."

Thirty years later, *The War in the Air* had the sinister accents of an eyewitness's report or a grotesque nightmare; and anyone who failed to notice the date of its first publication might have taken it for the ravings of a distracted contemporary.

In the same year as *First and Last Things*—the year of his break with the Fabian Society—Wells brought out another book, *New Worlds for Old,* in which he attempts, as much for his own sake as for his readers', to define the true meaning of socialism. He declares that socialism is the most inspiring creative plan that has ever been presented to the world. Its chief attraction, according to him, is that it rests on the same firm basis as all genuine scientific research, that it does not consider events to arise from individual will or from the workings of chance. Also that, like scientific research, it calls upon men to step outside the narrow circle of their own ego and their own personal interests. Wells was perfectly aware that certain restrictions had to be imposed for the sake of discipline; he admitted, as one of the temporary imperfections of socialism, that it held out no promise of political and intellectual freedom. But though in most respects so impatient of authority, he was curiously ready to submit to civic discipline and its restrictions. Deep down within him lay a sort of secret inclination toward stringency. His Order of Samurai is disciplined austerity carried to its furthest extreme. His modern Utopia is a police state, where every citizen has his appointed place in society and his description card indexed in the state archives, and has to notify the police of his comings and goings. Under this system, an individualist is simply an eccentric vagabond, liable to die of starvation. The eye of the state follows its citizens even into the shadowy regions of their private lives. But Wells considered that this obedience to control was not too high a price to pay for being rescued from the fatal effects of democracy's free-and-easy methods. What distressed him most in contemporary life was the lack of proper care for children; he decribes slum conditions, their degrading promiscuity, and the sufferings of children whose parents were paupers or drunkards. He considered that individual families were apt to be dangerously irresponsible. Earlier articles and pamphlets in which he had called for state families had roused the conservatives to fierce attacks on him.

The most outmoded part of Wells's sociological writings is, inevitably, that which deals with the suffragette question and the economic independence of women—together with his study of the relationship between the sexes, and his defense (still timidly worded, it is true) of free love, as it was called in those days.

Out of date, too, is his insistence that socialism must never become a political movement, and that to organize it into a strong party under a leader would be to destroy it. His attitude toward socialism, too, was affectionately quarrelsome; there were times when he rounded on it with his usual energy, denouncing its tactical errors much as some people scold their relations in front of strangers. There were times when he looked elsewhere for the faith that must inspire him and set his hopes on an elite instead of on disciplined masses. But after these unpredictable wanderings he always came back to socialism. And in one of his last books, where he summed up all his beliefs, he again expressed the socialist faith of his young days, asserting that an enlightened, world-wide communism was in the very nature of things, like "tomorrow's sunrise or the summer of 1950."

XIII

THE FRAME GETS INTO THE PICTURE

IT HAD STARTED as a timid experiment with something quite new to him. It was hardly more than a joke, begun in the same spirit as his comic drawings. The idea of exploring in a fresh field had occurred to him when he went to live at Woking and had his first experience of comparative comfort.

Wells had a fundamental need of balance. The pendulum that swung him back toward the center of gravity of his healthy, optimistic nature had been thrown out of gear by the humiliations of his childhood and by his frustrated love for Isabel. In the little semi-detached house at Woking, filled with noise from the neighboring railway station, he went on brooding over his old grievances, and shaped with them the terrible, solitary figure of the Invisible Man. Deep-flowing streams of anger broadened out into visions of the blood and flames that would one day swallow up the whole peaceable world, now slumbering in selfish indifference. The horrible, bodiless heads of the Martians would appear one day out of yonder forest, their fearsome, death-dealing machines would come forward along this white lane and kill everything within range.

In search of a realistic setting for the unimaginable, Wells began to explore the neighborhood of Woking, on the rattling bicycle that he had bought with his first savings—the primitive machine of that period, with its incalculable behavior on hills and its unreliable brakes. Before long he had a tandem made for himself and Jane, so that their outings would be less tiring for her. After covering the Woking district—with its wide, empty stretches of heath, its pine woods through which wound a pretty canal whose banks were covered with forget-me-nots and its surface dotted with yellow water lilies—they began to go farther afield. They rode through the soft, golden haze of a southern English summer. The roads, where no cars passed as yet, were silver paths leading to adventure. The unexpected lay just around the next corner.

Wells had now left far behind him the skinny figure of the shop assistant that he had once been, with his hopeless dreams and his absurd ambitions. He seemed to see the shadow of that former self cast on the road along which he sped so easily. It was near enough, yet sufficiently far removed, for him to be able to inspect it with a twinkling eye—young Bertie Wells, dressed in cheap hand-me-downs, with his awkward air and his dreamy, eager eyes that sought pleadingly for some miracle of human sympathy. It was Mr. Hoopdrives, the very essence of vulgarity, who came into Wells's mind on one of those sunny summer days. He no longer wanted to shake off his past. He was beginning to suspect that the very limitations of the world into which he had been born, the obstacles he had met with and the torments his body had suffered might one day be used for literary exploitation. At first he drew only upon the more obviously comic side of his past experience, which supplied him with *The Wheels of Chance,* the story of a shop assistant who goes for a holiday trip on his new bicycle and becomes the knight-errant of a damsel in distress. Most of the minor characters in this novel are dummies. Even the heroine is featureless. Only the hero, Wells's double, is a live figure, clumsy and comical in his efforts to behave like a man of the world, with his excitability and the narrow horizon of his dreams.

Wells was improvising for the first time on a new keyboard, like an amateur pianist who fumbles about with two fingers, trying to capture a tune that is running through his head. In December, 1898, he had announced to his father that he had written a sentimental story of a rather new kind. He was not yet giving up the line he had followed with so much success, the fantastic novel. But he was experimenting more widely with the psychological novel, firmly based on reality. This would not be merely the sketchy story of the cyclist, which he could repudiate at will; now came a meeting with his double from an early period, the period of the famished student, of the job-hunting young professor. His past had come to an understanding with his present, and split away from him; now it stood there in the round, with no tattered edges, no painful bonds like little veins still bleeding.

He and Jane were so perfectly at one in their thoughts that he had been able to get over the painful experience of his first marriage. He even felt strong enough, now, to face the image of Isabel. The texture of his new novel, *Love and Mr. Lewisham,* was interwoven with threads of autobiography. Wells used to declare, indeed, that no author could create characters out of thin air, and that any really vivid figure in a novel must be drawn, either openly or furtively, from real life, stolen from a biography.

It was more particularly during the early part of his career that he was haunted by his own life story, but to the end of his days he never quite stopped relating it. His friends and his opponents, the women he loved, the men he hated, his chance companions, his momentary squabbles—all were transported, naked and unadorned, between the covers of his novels. A tremendous number of people have recognized themselves in his characters, and even in his caricatures, which he could make as lethal as a hangman's rope, because his eyes were always fixed, for creative purposes, on everyday life. His purely literary work really is made up of fragments stolen from the lives to which he had access; and these fragments he scarcely altered, as he often fitted them together under the immediate impulsion of recent interest or unappeased wrath. He regards himself as a sharp-eyed observer rather than an imaginative one. It seems absurd for the man who invented the Martian world and the moon insect to assert that he could not create a fictitious character, lock, stock, and barrel. But however true the statement may be—and it is probably just as true as most artists' self-criticism—the cause lay not in any lack of imagination, but in a lack of interest on Wells's part.

He was an extremely inquisitive man, possessed of what he quaintly referred to as "the beautiful and intrepid curiosity of fear." But that curiosity was aroused by ideas, events, sociological facts, rather than by human beings, who tended more and more, as time went on, to appear in his books as mere spokesmen of ideas, sections of the social strata. When it did turn toward creatures of flesh and blood, it probed into their generic and not into their individual qualities. While still only a lad, Wells had announced his rediscovery of the unique; yet he seldom took the trouble to depict those little differences of character that make a real person stand out—the individual touches, the blur of shadow or the ray of light that brings the picture to life once and for all. He looked at people with the same long-sighted gaze with which he peered into the future. In his haste to create, details were apt to escape him. In the long run, however, this attitude showed itself to be a very personal feature in him, rather than a result of his creative procedure. Despite his curiosity, his interest was limited and sometimes went through periods of eclipse. Despite his passionate feelings, he was liable to intervals of detachment, gulfs of cold indifference and boredom which prevented him from getting close up to his fellow men, or made him weary of them too quickly.

His capacity as a novelist was influenced by this general tendency in him. With *Love and Mr. Lewisham,* his chief purpose was to show the unavoidable struggle between the ambitions of a scientist and the demands of everyday life. He couched his arraignment of society in the most concise and convincing terms that he could find, and what space remained in the book he filled up with minor characters. Even the heroine is only a dim reflection of Isabel, seen in a tarnished mirror. Only the dishonest medium has the clear-cut, picturesque features that Wells always gave to his social misfits. But although his characters are not always consistently drawn, life surges in his books (even those which are outdated)—not so much within the figures, perhaps, as around them, in the London streets with their contrasts of wealth and poverty, their winter fogs, their desperate loneliness. Man's condition was expressed by Wells not as an internal conflict, but as a social one.

In these last years of a century in which the novel was still kept within the limits of a fixed frame, Wells had not yet realized that he was doing pioneer work, helped, perhaps, by his very limitations. He rather felt that he was moving backward, toward an earlier form of the English novel, writing "in the old Dickens style." The novel to which, about the end of 1898, he applied that remark, was not published until 1908. It depicts, in a wider and simpler setting than that of *Mr. Lewisham,* the struggle against spiritual crippling, carried on through the graphic episodes of *Kipps.* The physical appearance and the inarticulate speech of this new hero were drawn from the little, underfed, quick-witted guttersnipe who had taken over Wells's first humble job in the Southsea store when he was promoted from it. But young Bertie himself peeps out from behind the wan features of the little shopboy. Wells called this a humorous novel, and it was welcomed as such by a big public. But only the outlook of that day, the immense self-satisfaction of British society, could have made its readers so utterly blind to the underlying cruelty of the book, the fierce spirit behind the impeachment. Wells made the deeper meaning of his story quite clear with his pictures of the little, stupid tragedies of crippled lives. He shows Kipps as the pitiful sport of fortune, struggling among so much that he cannot understand, ambitions that engulf him, inescapable taboos, all so simple to rich people, and marking him, the ignorant novice, as an intruder.

Wells gave Kipps his own perplexities in an amplified form, making his embarrassment and his blunders into tragicomedies—like that of Kipps' visit to a big hotel, where everything conspires against the young upstart who wears purple embroidered slippers with his tuxedo, where the laughter of the other guests and the contempt of the servants pursue him like a social nemesis. Kipps and Ann are two quite naked and unprotected beings, with no preparation for any life unless it be one of servitude. They go from one mishap to another, under the heavy shadow of a deformed world, where all is proud, lazy or servile, dark and crushing and hostile. "The anti-soul, the ruling power of this land, Stupidity," says Wells. But the page of explanation in which he says it must have had scant attention from most readers. They laughed a great deal at the book, and went on laughing for a long time. Wells had not been mistaken when he hit a vein well known to the general public, which was used to Dickensian humor, shooting golden arrows into the shadowy lives of humble people. But in reality the likeness is only superficial, Dickens's novels, like those of Balzac, gave a picture of things as they were, a satirical portrait of society, with its shadows and highlights, and its immovable barriers which some particular individual strives to break down for his own ends. But Wells questions that society, not merely in the person of Masterman, that brief glimpse of rebellion, but throughout his book. His doubts are never far below the surface, they quiver even in the most laughter-flecked scenes; and the laughter is grievous, like the titters that break out when a hunchback goes by.

Thus it came about that, by deliberately forming his work on an existing pattern, Wells set free his own gift, his really original feature. His continued interest in this particular subject saved him from the rather careless eking out of the story with minor characters who were mere stuffed dummies (Henry James had accused him of doing that). In fact, some of the episodic figures in *Kipps* have their full share of individuality. One of Wells's school friends from Morley's academy, whose gift of the gab still gave him a lot of amusement, served as a model for Chitterlow, that incredibly picturesque teller of tall stories. Besides its careful attention to detail, this book is written with a finer sense of style than H. G. customarily displayed. Like a man in a great hurry, who cannot take the trouble to be brief, he wanted to say everything there was to be said, and usually poured out his treasures, his gleaming jewels, pell-mell, as though they were handfuls of colored pebbles. But on coming to *Kipps,* he disciplined himself and made a careful selection. He even decided to cut out all the first part, the story of the waif's earliest years. Just then he seems to have been very anxious to make a success of his new line. Perhaps he was getting tired of inventing fantastic novels, for like all richly gifted people, he did not care to go on exploiting a profitable vein. Or perhaps he had to take this dive into the past so that he could rise to the surface again, his load of bitterness washed away. His trouble was rewarded by brilliant success. *Kipps* sold more copies, in English, than any other of his novels.

And it did wash away the dregs of his resentment. He moved on with a lighter step. In the year following the publication of *Kipps,* he visited the United States. When he got back home, he flung himself into the political struggle, and took up what he felt to be his most important task, the revision of his own ideas about the world's future course. He was haunted by a feeling that humanity, threatened with disaster, was rushing blindly toward the abyss; and that feeling is expressed in two fantastic stories, *In the Days of the Comet* and *The War in the Air*. These tales may be said to supplement his propaganda work for the New Republic. They are like movies brought in to illustrate a lecture that would otherwise be dull, educational films to teach people who learn better through the eye than through the ear.

As he used to say of himself, Wells was a stubborn and relentless pedagogue. Even in his realistic novels he could never be satisfied merely to describe things as they were; even those that seem most objective all contain criticism and suggest changes.

Kipps was not to be his only arraignment of a pernicious educational system. For the time being he turned away from this successful line. He would not be too easy on himself. But he went back to it a good deal later on, as though he had not said his last word about crippled brains. It was with *Mr. Polly,* published in 1910, that he took up the subject again. Once more he drew largely on personal memories. The central theme of the novel is an event that had made a great impression on him. His eldest brother had been an obedient son, a model employee, always ready to preach to his junior about the need for bowing to one's fate; but one fine day the worm had turned, with the complete, obstinate rebelliousness of a weak nature. Frank Wells had thrown up his job, with its faint hopes of promotion and of security for his old age, and set out to tramp the roads, in the boundless freedom of a man who asks nothing from life. This rebellion had a quality that appealed keenly to the younger brother's imagination. H. G.'s own mutiny had been a conscious one, a striving toward a definite goal, a shifting of his aspirations to a plane which, though different, was still that of practical achievement and security. His brother had shaken off all material considerations, in a way that delighted him because there was something absurd and wanton about it—a sort of courage that he felt to be finer than his own. Wells had always a special weakness for total commitment, for headstrong people who could stake their whole future on a single throw of the dice. He was closer than he suspected to the Russian novelists, who created characters with unlimited possibilities, always absolute in their sacrifice.

Mr. Polly is an apology for escapism. He is another living corpse, filled with that humble grandeur of abnegation that Tolstoy gave to his heroes. But he is a typically British hero, who turns a blind eye to his own nature and to the probable results of his behavior. A dumb hero who underrates himself in the timid, humorous way that is so typical of the British mentality.

Mr. Polly is Kipps's elder brother. He, too, has been cheated of his inborn feeling for beauty, of his dim yearning for something finer than his appointed fate. He is the pathetic victim of a society that enslaved young minds by loading them with premature responsibilities, and left crippled spirits to drag themselves along in its wake. Wells makes him talk in the quaint style of an almost illiterate man eagerly pursuing those big, beautiful words that dart away from his ignorant tongue; a style that Wells had often heard in real use. And he gave him the chivalrous impulses and deep kindliness of an outcast of fortune, always unassuming and ready for self-sacrifice.

The whole story basks, as it were, in the sunlight of H. G.'s half-conscious affection for his model. The tender amusement with which he watched this adventure unfolding gave the book an indulgent atmosphere that is rarely found in his work. He may have written *Mr.*

Polly during one of those restful periods when sheer joy of life made him forget, for the moment, the thrill of fighting and the spur of ambitious responsibilities. He too must have known what it was to dream of escape, of changed personality, of a leap into the unknown; such dreams come to everyone when things seem to be at a deadlock. In his case the dream had been so vivid that it lingered in his mind's eye, with a shimmering happiness that irradiates the whole book. There is a touch of the fairy story in *Mr. Polly,* a streak of improbability such as runs through all the tales of escape that soothe the minds of young and grown-up children.

Mr. Polly shows no trace of the cruelty that is interwoven with comedy in *Kipps,* but only of measureless pity. It is as though the same story had been told twice—first angrily, then indulgently. In this novel Wells rises above his childish humiliations. It is the most optimistic of all his books. Being restricted in scope, telling only of humble people whose horizon stops at the level of their personal interests, it is also the most close-knit and, as regards form, the most successful of his novels. It shows the full range of Wells's talent, his gift for creative writing. In the description of Mr. Polly's father's funeral, which follows the best Dickensian tradition, he reveals all his power of character drawing, his sharp-sightedness, his instinctive knowledge of what should be described. Anyone who wants to know how high Wells could reach when he really did his best, need only turn to the pages telling of this event, which was a great one in the drab lives of those concerned, and of the incongruously festive atmosphere in the little crepe-hung parlor. His ability to draw an unforgettable picture of some minor character is shown by the grotesque figure of Uncle Pentstemon, an ancient, hard-breathing, baleful-eyed man with tufts of hair scattered over all his features except his bald crown. "He seemed a fragment from the ruder agricultural past of our race, like a lump of soil among things of paper."

It is in *Mr. Polly,* too, that we find, at its best, Wells's deep feeling for nature, his memory for everything he had seen, from which he drew his ability to depict imaginary but utterly convincing landscapes. Though he was often driven, by haste and impatience, to set his scene against a mere backcloth, he could work with all the care and skill of a painter when he wished to show day fading into dusk among trails of green and yellow cloud, in deep calm, "as if everything lay securely within a great, warm, friendly globe of crystal sky."

When Wells began to write the story of Mr. Polly, which had been haunting him for a long time, he had just finished a big novel, *Tono-Bungay*. This is the most ambitious of his novels, the largest in scale. Its main theme is the instability of society. Wells had always been suspicious of false security in life. The ground was already slipping from beneath the unshakable social construction of feudal Britain that he describes with Bladesover as his example. George Ponderevo, shooting up like a rocket to his soap-bubble moment of success, shows one aspect of this social disintegration.

Wells seems to have been watching out for some event on which he could base his contrast between changeable human beings and established traditions, his reshuffling of the social order. His story is built around an event of the day, the trial of the financier Whitaker Wright, who committed suicide when sentenced. H. G. had been much impressed by the trial; it interested him in that curious way, sometimes difficult to understand, in which certain events do appeal to the receptive mind of an artist. One feels the scornful satisfaction of a man who had had a hard climb to the top of the ladder, and now saw how readily a suspicious world could be fooled by the lure of easy money. In any case, Wells remembered this trial so clearly that he used it a second time in *The World of William Clissold,* as though he had not yet exhausted all its possibilities. The rumbling of the landslide had far-reaching echoes.

Wells brings into *Tono-Bungay*—which he himself declared to be the story of a "crumbling and confusion, of change and seemingly aimless swelling," of "a fermenting mass of emotions experienced"—in the person of his hero, the only really stable element that he recognizes in life, that of scientific research. He sets the clear, honest mind of the scientist in opposition to outdated prejudice and the taste for shady adventures. Where all is self-defense or collapse, ruin or uncertainty, the only way of rescuing a human being from perplexity is to fling oneself body and soul into the chosen mission, the battle for the future of humanity. "Through the confusion something drives, something that is at once human achievement and the most inhuman of all existing things." George Ponderevo sets out down the Thames on the destroyer that he has invented; the banks of the river rush past him, with their old Gothic buildings, the homes of ancient institutions, that seem to ask, as he leaves them behind, whether man, in his new power, will still respect them. Dizzy with the thrill of speed, George Ponderevo tells himself that this race down the river is like an irresistible drive toward reality—that reality which he sometimes calls Science and sometimes Truth, something plucked with painful effort out of the heart of life itself, something that in other men's hands becomes art, literature, social invention, and that for him is always austerity, beauty.

That is the credo that Wells proclaims in *Tono-Bungay;* there lies the significance of the book. He built it up with the help of autobiographical material—going back to his own boyhood, drawing a lively picture of Up Park, with its large staff of automata, and putting certain real happenings straight into it, for instance, his unhappy return from Southsea. His short stay at the Midhurst chemist's shop provided him with a setting, and the chemist and his wife lent their features and their tricks of speech to Ponderevo's uncle and aunt. By drawing the picture of Bladesover, Wells shook off the weight of Up Park; he rid himself of the burden of his unsuccessful marriage, too, driving out the specter of Isabel by creating Marion. Here are gestures that had remained stamped on his memory, words that had really been spoken, misunderstandings that had poisoned his passionate love. He was draining an abscess.

Among the scenes borrowed from his own experience is the graphic description of the death of his friend Gissing, whose last hours he had watched over in a little village of the French Pyrenees. Molded with rare skill in the clay of memory, this novel gains in breadth through the bold psychological studies it contains, and from its anticipations of things to come. Even the launching of the sham medicine called Tono-Bungay, with its huge publicity campaign, strikes a topical note. The fact that Wells brought in his own sketches for posters—thus linking the subsoil of feelings represented by his little pen-and-ink sketches, with the surface of a literary invention—is enough to show what keen interest he took in that part of his tale. Whenever one of his drawings appeared in one of his books (this did not often happen), it was to act as a warning, like an exclamation mark at the end of a sentence. The same interest in advertising technique is shown in *The World of William Clissold;* one of the Clissold brothers is a modern advertising genius, a worthy successor to the Uncle Ponderevo of twenty years earlier.

Uncle Ponderevo is the prototype of the big businessman, too—the businessman who, though not necessarily dishonest, is swept away, carried off his feet in spite of himself, by the tide of human credulity, the greedy profit seeking of his voluntary dupes. William Clissold regarded high finance as stupid rather than malignant. Ponderevo's adventures are based on incidents of his day, but they show kinship with sensational bankruptcies of more recent times, with the spectacular suicides of Loewenstein, Krueger, and others of that kidney.

The characters are as modern as the social background. George Ponderevo, the first of a line of technicians to be met in Wells's books, is not the only representative of a new generation. There is also the Honorable Beatrice Normandy, an elder sister of Christina Alberta. A spoiled child of society, anemiated by luxury, she can more easily break loose from the moral standards of her rank than from its prejudices. Coming of an aristocratic family, she takes lovers and drugs, because she has not the courage to face independence in poverty, or to live her passion as a social outcast. Haughty even in downfall, Beatrice Normandy brings to Wells's work the enrichment of a new complexity; she is, moreover, one of the few figures that he penned in an outline which suggests more than it reveals.

There are two episodes in the book which hardly belong to the main plot, but seem like short stories loosely interwoven with it. The first tells of George Ponderevo's voyage to an island off the West African coast, in search of a radioactive element whose emanations bring sickness to all the members of the expedition, and end by rotting the timbers of the old hulk in which it is being transported. This is a close-packed, intensely absorbing story, an excursion into a field of scientific reality that had so far been very little explored. The second episode, which fits more closely into the main plot, describes how George Ponderevo's bankrupt uncle makes his escape in an airship constructed by his nephew. *Tono-Bungay* was published in 1909. It was not until four years later that Wells made his first airplane trip, with Graham White. But his description of the Ponderevos' pioneer flight, with all its attendant mishaps and surprises, reads nowadays like the report of an actual experience. The clumsy machine flies over the moonlit English countryside, ventures out above an immensity of gray sea, and is driven by a gale toward the southern coast of Brittany. The primitive cabin, a kind of wicker basket, creaks and groans in the wind that lashes the balloon overhead and sends icy shivers through the passengers. Far off shine the lights of big towns; the rays of blinking lighthouse lanterns are blurred by fog. As the engine stops, there is sudden silence; the machine glides heavily and awkwardly toward the sand dunes that are vaguely outlined against the first dim glow of the dawn sky.

When he gave this novel its vast framework, and brought into it such bold forecasts of the future, Wells was deliberately aiming very high; all he knew about his fellow men and all his confidence in them he packed into these pages. To one of his friends he said that he had risen to a climax with *Tono-Bungay,* so that henceforth he would go downhill, unless he could manage to surpass himself.

The book was not so successful as his high opinion of it seemed to warrant. A big London newspaper refused to serialize it before publication, and when it came out as a volume the sales were disappointing. The public may have found it too new, or been put off by the number of contrasting features that it contained. Yet it is those very features that make it still interesting for today's readers, to whom large-scale plots are more familiar than they were forty years ago. The characters are just as full of independent life as when they were created, and the story still as graphic; only the style has dated a little, especially toward the end, where it becomes rather bombastic.

The semifailure of *Tono-Bungay* may have led Wells to turn away, almost unconsciously perhaps, from that ambitious form of novel that aimed at covering all the perplexity, the longings, the conflicts of ideas and the complex crosscurrents which go to make up the modern man. Though planned in the same spirit, *The World of William Clissold* is really not a novel except by fits and starts—one might almost say by accident—when its characters drift in, as though reluctantly, to interrupt the endless soliloquies, or rather lectures, delivered by the hero. At any rate, when he brought out *Tono-Bungay* and saw how it was received, Wells realized how wide a gap separated him from the artistic standards of his day. He realized what a firm hold the traditional novel had kept on the British public, ever since the days of Walter Scott. It was, he says in his memoirs, a fixed frame, apparently established forever, where individual destinies were played out in an independence that seemed unnatural to the social being of today. So the literary critics began to get annoyed and uneasy when, a period of instability having set in, pieces of the broken frame began to get into the picture. "I suppose," adds Wells, "for a time I was the outstanding instance among writers of fiction in English of the frame getting into the picture."

But those remarks belong to a later-day reconstruction of cause and effect. At the time—during the first ten years of the twentieth century, which were really, in spirit, a continuation of the eighteen-nineties—it had not yet occurred to Wells that he was starting a literary revolution. What urged him forward was his personal scale of values, which turned his interest toward social conditions and traditions in the melting pot, rather than to interior problems. He was trying, as usual, to build up this premature tendency into a system—making it, in his customary pugnacious way, into a must for the artist. He used to have long arguments, face to face and by letter, with Henry James, whose views and ideas were the very opposite of his own; and these arguments upset him more than he liked to admit, even to himself. Henry James complained that Wells's heroes were nothing but revelations of their author's personality, and that "the ground of the drama is some-how most of all in the adventure for *you*—not to say *of* you, the moral, temperamental, personal, of your setting it forth."

Wells was irritated by this relentless and detailed criticism, though it came from a master of words, and was accompanied by assurances of heartfelt admiration; but he had to admit that they were justified. However, he set the argument on a wider plane by pointing out to James that the psychological novel, with its firmly constructed, well-rounded characters and careful choice of words, no more exhausted the possibilities of fiction than the art of Velasquez exhausted those of painting. His presentiment of the future, dimly at work within him, told Wells that something was coming to an end, that certain habits of thought were dying out forever, that something else, which he could not yet see clearly, was being born; that a crisis was approaching, a crisis of which people would not become aware until yesterday's world had collapsed. So far, he could only see his own position as resulting from one of two different aims—to some men, such as Henry James, literature was an end in itself, whereas for him it was, like architecture, a means to an end. Slightly out of his depth in this controversy, Wells could only think of short-term arguments and temporary solutions. He hit out rather blindly at those who held different views.

In his usual emphatic way, he demanded entire freedom of choice for the artist, the sweeping away of all controls. In a lecture he gave in 1912 on the subject of the contemporary novel, he spoke in favor of "an unlimited field of action." He protested against moral restraints and conventional taboos, declaring that there was no point in writing stories about people's lives unless one could deal quite freely with the political and social questions that affected them, with their religious beliefs and inhibitions. But he perhaps already felt, to some vague extent, that however justifiable his demands might be, they were not strictly relevant to the problem that was haunting him. He was not laying down any new conditions for artistic creation. It was easy to point out to him that at earlier periods, social, political and religious questions had already been taken as subjects for literature. He seemed to be championing the story with a moral, which had died a natural death by this time. But when he searched for words by which to define the unconscious creative process, it was not of the raw slices of life presented by realistic novelists that he was thinking.

At the time when Wells seemed quite absorbed by the wish to depict individual reactions in all their complexity, an unsuspected change was taking place in the individual himself; his reactions to the outer world were being radically altered. The expansion of the novel was to be brought about by the thrust of the new forces, and not merely to satisfy an esthetic theory.

The dispute that brought Wells's convictions into such premature conflict with the artistic standards of the day, was really the dispute that a creative writer settles by imposing his work. But to Wells, this battle for the novel was not really of supreme importance. He was not absolutely convinced that everything depended upon its result. He lacked the religious fervor that strengthened him when he was fighting for an idea. He had taken more trouble over *Tono-Bungay* than he did with any other work of fiction, before or afterward. There was a streak of impatience in his character, which rebelled against the slow labor of artistic creation. He was never obsessed by an urge to find the right word, the one and only word that would render the feeling he had in mind, and not just a similar feeling; he never racked his brains to describe one shade of color, and not a shade just slightly different. He summed himself up, with his limitations and his essential quality, when he said: "I write, like I walk, because I want to get somewhere."

He looked upon the novel as a roundabout way to his goal, not a short cut. He was not at all sure that there was any sense in hiding behind fictitious characters, in masking his own identity and giving other people the words that he was eager to speak with his own lips. The ups and downs of a story did not interest him enough to get him caught in the toils of his own imagination. It is unlikely that any

Wellsian hero ever began to live his own life and thus forced his author to make changes in the plot. In fact Wells, despite his huge output of fiction, rather despised the novel as a branch of literature. He went on writing novels, but with a slight suspicion that he was using an out-of-date literary form. Toward the end of his life he tried to compile his own dossier by starting with the query, "Am I a novelist?"

And it was then, while summing up his life's work, that he expressed the conclusion that the novel was unlikely to be very important in the intellectual life of future generations. It was, he thought, quite likely to die out and be replaced by more sincere and revealing biographies and autobiographies.

XIV

THE SIRENS' SONG

IT HAPPENED WHILE Wells was waiting for his new house to be built at Sandgate, and living in another, which he had rented, in a rather lonely position, with only a tamarisk hedge between its garden and the seashore. Until just lately he had been an invalid, resigned to the prospect of a restricted life that would confine him to the house and even, perhaps, to an armchair. But strength was rapidly coming back to him now, and with it, the prick of curiosity, that lust for life whose irresistible urge he did not fully realize as yet. So he listened, with a smile squeezing out from the corners of his eyes, to the conversation of his neighbors, who were prosperous, middle class, intensely British citizens—doughty wives, managing their homes to perfection and issuing dictatorial orders in brassy voices; daughters whose unrelenting purity was worthy of such mothers; quiet, subdued husbands, who took to the boats so as to escape being heaped with wordy or wordless reproaches on account of their inadequacy. Voices carried a long distance, wafting over the hedges from house to house. There were confessions of petty ambition—to make a fortune, to gain a title, to achieve, in one way or another, a position beyond reach of any kind of surprise. These people belonged to the class that delighted in seeing itself flatteringly reflected in the novels of Mrs. Humphrey Ward, whose heroines, unsullied by any touch of earthliness, served as models for its husband-hunting girls.

Wells seems to have written down every snatch of talk that reached his ears, in the inadequate phrases with which the English express their thoughts and feelings.

But the sunny beach was also visited by women whose bodies, freed of all constraint, were becoming aware of themselves; fair-skinned bodies that glided through the water as easily as mermaids. There were eyes the color of sunlit waves, and full of mysterious promises; there were tantalizing smiles that made a man's blood beat faster. It was on this beach that the Sea Lady appeared one day to Wells; she wore a close-clinging swimsuit, and her hair gleamed in the sunshine. Wells said later on about *The Sea Lady* that it contained a certain amount of personal confession, though in disguised form. The plot, like that of *The Wonderful Visit,* is based on a clash between the real and the miraculous, the reaction of selfish human beings to anything that upsets their petty lives. But whereas it was in order to show up the full extent of human savagery and stupidity that Wells had created the radiant figure of the Angel, the similar contrast that he introduced in *The Sea Lady* was nothing more than the stratagem of a man who was still unwilling to look squarely at his real problems. At the very moment when Spade House was being finished, when Wells had decided to start a family, when his life with Jane was building itself up in perfect spiritual harmony, something came filtering into this firmly founded existence and threatened to disrupt it.

Isabel still haunted his life. A year or two earlier—it must have been before his illness—he had gone to see her at a poultry farm that she was trying to run with her usual lack of efficiency. The visit was supposed to be a gesture of sympathy for a woman so childish, an awakening of his sense of responsibility toward her. He found Isabel in her element in this rustic setting; her simple talk was just suited to the work she was doing, and her quiet beauty seemed at one with the gentle landscape. Again he felt the urgent longing to shake her out of her calm, to break through the defenses behind which she retreated from him. He tells of this visit in his autobiography—the sleepless night he spent under her roof; the dread of parting that flooded through him; his fantastic longing to win her back; and his flight at dawn, when his wild despair and the storm of tears that shook him wore themselves out to the accompaniment of Isabel's common-sense remarks, while she, like a careful hostess, lit the fire and put water on to boil so that he should not go away without his breakfast. He departed, through a radiant summer sunrise, with the feeling that he had left his whole life behind him in the little house at the turn of the lane.

His masculine jealousy outlasted their final separation. Though Isabel's senses were still slumbering, her woman's instinct was strong enough to warn her not to tell her first husband when she married again. On learning of it, after quite a time, he was shaken by a tempest of passion whose primitive violence astonished him. He tore up her letters and photographs. Nobody dared speak to him about her. Murderous impulses rose up in him. Later, in *The Days of the Comet,* that dream of a tomorrow's world when jealousy would be miraculously banished, he described the fury that shook him at this time, the desires by which he was obsessed, the visions of the woman he loved, in another man's arms, which haunted him until he became "a thing of bestial fury." The young hero of this book, flouted and humiliated, tracks down the two lovers with a gun that he means to turn against himself when he has disposed of them. The thirst for vengeance, which had driven every other consideration from his mind, was accompanied by an embarrassed self-disgust that made him refuse to face up to what was really wrong with him.

His hero of later years, William Clissold, confessed to having been tormented since adolescence by sexual desire, not concentrated on one particular woman, but taking the form of stark longing, boundless avidity; and accompanied by an inner, spontaneous and acute feeling of shame, and an impulse to conceal any sign of what agitated him.

Wells thought this degree of suffering through sex must be abnormal. He hid it like an infirmity. Not until very late in life did he come to understand himself. At the time when he was still fighting the memory of Isabel, the obsession of his failure to win her completely, he idealized her, transformed his obsession into the longing for something essential that had escaped him, a promise that life had broken.

A siren's song was heard on Sandgate beach. H. G., like Ulysses, tied himself to the mast of his safe home. An upheaval in his private life is related under cover of transparent symbols. He lingered for a very long time in the adolescent stage of development, and *The Sea Lady* is an adolescent's novel, and to some extent a parody. Its characters are not only the neighbors that H. G. had been watching, they are also taken from the pages of Mrs. Humphrey Ward. They talk like the heroes of a cheap novelette. But a man's real suffering lurks, none the less, behind this puppet show. Miss Waters, a beauty with a fish's tail, has bewitched an ambitious young politician. All of a sudden, the promise that he reads in her sea-blue eyes makes everything else seem insipid—his social aspirations, his career, his vague humanitarian ideals, and the girl of good family to whom he is engaged. He yearns for unheard-of delights, for emotions that shall go beyond all understanding. "There are other dreams . . ." says Miss Waters. One velvety summer night, the young lover takes her beautiful form into his strong arms and goes toward the gently lapping water that stretches out beneath the moonlight. Along the empty beach there passes, with the heavy tread of reality, an English policeman, carrying a lantern which lights up a tiny scrap of the dark immensity.

This is an escapist novel too, but on a new plane. For the first time —very late in the day—Wells was debating the realities of passion. He told later what the book had meant for him: it had brought something new to light, a sensual need. The literary debate reflected a private struggle. Chatteris fled from life's petty compromises. He fled, enraptured, into the absolute of death. But in Wells's private life his meeting with the sirens took place under the sign of Catherine Wells's clear-sightedness and indomitable energy. She faced up bravely to this first threat to their happiness. "My compromise with Jane developed after 1900," says Wells in his memoirs. "The *modus vivendi* we contrived was sound enough to hold us together to the end."

Though Wells only partly understood himself, Jane had the insight of deep affection, and it gave her an understanding even of feelings to which she herself was a stranger. They were both ignorant about sexual needs, her ignorance being all the more complete because she was practically free from them. They were both paralyzed by British bashfulness, by that instinctive reserve which shrinks from discussing intimate relationships. They were born of a generation that had dismissed the underlying reactions of sex as something shameful, to be kept for the night hours. More than forty years went by before Wells came to understand how blindly the young people of his day had been groping in the darkness; and then he set Freud side by side with Darwin as a significant figure in the history of human knowledge.

Jane was faced with a problem that, in those early years of the century, was a strange one for a young woman to have to solve. She had only recently embarked on the great adventure of her life, in conditions of utter moral and material insecurity, with nothing to uphold her except her faith in the man she loved. They had just begun to feel themselves on firm ground. And now everything was endangered by a mysterious, hostile power. What was she to do? Should she stiffen her pride and accept the loss of the man to whom she felt so closely linked? Should she give him his freedom, as they said in those days? A painful, silent debate took place within her, and her wounded vanity and possessive instinct had their word to say. Wells remarked later that she revealed not the slightest sign of jealousy. Keen observer though he was, he could be strangely absent-minded in his relations with those nearest to him—short-sighted to an extent that would have seemed deliberate if it had not been so constant. In reality, the eyes with which Catherine Wells scrutinized every new female figure that appeared on her husband's horizon were filled with unsleeping suspicion and an aggressiveness that told of wounded feelings. But she had a self-awareness that assured her she would be strongest in the long run, a pride that was stronger than vanity, and above all, the highest form of courage in suffering—that which denies its own pain. She settled the matter with her pitiless self-knowledge. She considered, says her husband, that he had the right to do as he wished with himself, and that he had been unlucky in chancing on a companion in life who could not give him the response he had expected. She looked at the question, he adds, "with the same courage, honesty and self-subordination with which she faced all the practical issues of life."

But he himself was still wrestling with the perplexities that his own emotions brought him. As usual, he carried the discussion onto the public platform. He imagined a future world from which personal conflicts such as this one would be banished. The Samurai of his *Modern Utopia* practice free love, not with pagan light-heartedness but with the sublimation of intellectuals. This forecast had a most disturbing effect on the rising generation. *A Modern Utopia* was especially widely read in University circles. Students who responded to Wells's ideas found this particular point of his program the easiest to apply. Numerous love affairs were started in the name of the future moral system of the guardians of the New Republic. A leaven had been set at work by a man whose own mind was still fermenting with doubt. A wavering light fell from the lantern of one who was still seeking his own path. But in his last years, Wells had the assurance that his book had done a lot to help the movement that freed women from the rigid chastity that was imposed upon them in Victorian times.

In his own private life, his love affairs gained him the reputation of a Don Juan among the English intelligentsia. This hardly seemed to fit his outward appearance, which suggested the placid, phlegmatic disposition of the average middle-class Englishman. But he had eyes that could sometimes light up with a spark, a fleeting urgency. He paraded his conquests guilelessly, with the ingenuity of a schoolboy receiving such favors for the first time. But in reality, it was long before he fell in love with any of the women that his hungry ardor captured for him. Speaking through the mouth of William Clissold, he admits that his roving sexual impulses prevented him from really loving any woman.

But this revelation of himself to himself did not come until much later, like a torch whose light streamed back to penetrate the shadowy region of his early desires. While actually going through his escapades, he believed himself committed, body and soul—called upon to account, with all his manly sense of responsibility, for the emotional disturbance that he felt or had caused. One of these occasions involved a girl who had the advantage of him, in that she was able to see more clearly into her own nature and put her feelings into words. Wells was always fascinated by audacity, irresistibly attracted by aggressive, fiercely independent people, as though they had something that he lacked. This girl came of good family, and had been brought up amid all the prejudices of her day and class. She had become an out-and-out rebel, had shaken off all restraint. "What do you want?" the disquieted young professor asks Ann Veronica. "You," she replies briefly. Words that he could not have invented—their challenge had actually rung in his ears.

Ann Veronica, whose father had quite recently locked her up so that she should not go dancing, had the boldness that comes of fighting for every scrap of one's personal freedom. She belonged to that intermediate generation which Wells once described as being too free for its innocence and too innocent for its freedom.

The story of *Ann Veronica* is one that Wells himself did not live through to the end, the story of a girl who snatches the man she wants out of his loveless married life. She ruins her career, defies the society that cold-shoulders them, and meets poverty with a brave front. She and her young lover go through to the end of the dream that did not turn into reality for Wells—between the original of Ann Veronica and the consequences of their attraction for each other, there stood the indomitable little figure of Jane. The novel remains from all that might have been. Wells gave it a happy ending. The young couple get married and are thus restored to middle-class respectability; the scientist-husband wins the fame he deserves. Middle-class morality is indulgent toward the successful. At the end of the book, Ann Veronica gives a party in her house for the relatives who had turned their backs on her. All through her struggles and sufferings she has dreamed of one day making good like this. But triumph, complete triumph, turns to ashes in her mouth. Once the thrill of her successful party begins to wear off, she feels sadness creeping over her. The boldest feature of the book is this feeling of defeat in the midst of success. Was it worth going through so much, just in order to make good in the end? The approval of society, material and moral stability—these things are insubstantial as shadows, compared with the reality of love. Will the passion that united her and her lover, welding them together in suffering, endure through their calm days of success?

For today's reader, the real drama is set out on this last page of the happy ending. But when the book was first published, its readers saw nothing beyond the happy ending, which seemed to them to put a premium on immorality. A sinful woman had been pardoned without having repented. A crime against society had been left unpunished.

Ann Veronica is forgotten now, like Ibsen's Nora and her other sisters-in-arms. Forgetfulness is all the more complete because with their rebellion, which today seems childish, and their demands, which were granted so long ago, they paved the way for the generation that was treading on their heels, a generation whose appetite was more violent and its imperative more categorical than theirs had been.

Wells saw clearly how far he had been caught up and outstripped by reality. He believed that of all his writings, the essays, stories and novels that had love as their theme would be the first to vanish from memory. And looking at them with his curious sense of detachment, he declared that as works of art they had no great value and that nobody would ever read them just for pleasure. But despite this severe self-judgment, the stories in question have something more than a historical interest. They are milestones along a road. And they are cairns that commemorate victories.

Ann Veronica was the center of one of the greatest literary battles that took place during that period. It set the whole country in an uproar. The critics seemed to have been lurking in ambush on Wells's path of success. They launched a violent campaign against him. "The muddy world of Mr. Wells' imaginings," wrote one important critic, "is a community of scuffling stoats and ferrets, unenlightened by a ray of duty and abnegation." The book was condemned as a spiritual poison, from which young minds must be protected. The libraries would not have it on their shelves. Prominent clergymen preached against it from the pulpit. Notoriety had arrived before fame. Fuel was added to the fire of scandal by rumors that whispered Ann Veronica's real name and announced her high social position, for the greater discomfiture of her unworthy and indiscreet seducer.

But aside from those who amused themselves by identifying the figures in the story, the reader who was not in the know could see that the heroine was a creature of flesh and blood, sketched from life, with all the surprises that come of genuine reactions, the style that is founded on reality. Ann Veronica is not the mouthpiece of a cause; she is a living, loving woman. She lives on with a life of her own that she has wrested from her author. "From the very outset," he wrote, "Ann Veronica was assailed as though she was an actual living person."

However important the book's impact on the general public, its effect on Wells's private life was still more far reaching. It led to his banishment from society, to which he had hardly been admitted as yet. He underwent a severe boycotting, memories of which were to spoil the eager welcome given to him later on.

He was ill-resigned to this campaign of moral indignation, and met it with injudicious bursts of rage and childish retorts. But he was not alone. The fragile form of Jane was a tower of strength. She stood beside him with all her unflinching courage. Those who came in the hope of seeing a tear-stained martyr, found her to be the impassive ally of the sinner.

This incident gave a sudden fresh twist to Wells's career of rapid progress. Henceforth, *Ann Veronica,* together with his outspoken republicanism, saved him, as he put it, from titles, honorary degrees, and official distinctions of all kinds.

What he called "the peculiar humor of his Guardian Angel" was again at work. Like so many of the setbacks he met with in life, the *Ann Veronica* scandal proved to be a blessing in disguise. It brought unexpected compensations. The young generation, for whom his influence was said to be so undesirable, began to feel a growing interest in him. His opponents, instead of ruining him, had boosted his reputation enormously; he became the symbol of revolt against all that was strict, dull, pompous and generally hateful to young people. Before winning their minds, he had prepared his conquest by rousing their curiosity and gaining their sympathy.

In the defiant spirit so characteristic of him, Wells showed positive eagerness to strengthen the hand of his traducers. Far from repenting or trying to reach a compromise, he laid ever increasing stress upon the postulate of sexual freedom. In *The Days of the Comet,* when poverty and servitude are things of the past, there is a woman who says to the young man she has left for another, "I love both of you." And in this better life, swept clear of our present-day conventions, she will give herself to him too as a matter of course, and to others as well, maybe. She will love unconstrained in a world of lovers.

The book scandalized people just as its author had intended. "Free love, according to Mr. Wells," wrote one conservative paper, "will be the very essence of the new social contract." Nettie, with her divided affections, linked up with the frank desires of Ann Veronica. But Wells's private conflict had hardly started. He still felt the need of public confession. *The New Machiavelli,* which brought the problem down from imaginary regions to the realm of everyday life, came as the true sequel to *Ann Veronica.* In this sequel he extended the field of discussion, and opened wider vistas to the many-sided interests of his fellow men. It is a sequel, too, as a reaction of ill-humor, an outlet for all the bitterness that had piled up in him during the couple of years that separated it from its predecessor. H. G. was always quick tempered, but this book was a real burst of childish fury. He was hitting out all around him.

The New Machiavelli begins with some autobiographical passages. Wells gives it the setting he had known as a boy, and his father hovers in the background (though H. G. would never admit this), with his incredible mixture of incompetence, enterprise, and unshakable optimism. Wells's difficulties with the Fabians also come into this book. In *Ann Veronica* he had still felt able to declare that the Fabians were building a new world. But when the book caused such a scandal, it seemed that his Fabian Society friends deserted him. They joined in behind the yelping pack that was harrying him. The socialists felt that this Fabian Casanova, as he was called, was bringing discredit on them, because people would have it that his ideas were those of the movement. The conservative newspapers made fun of the new social contract, whose chief clause, they declared, was to be free love.

It was in vain that Wells had tried to sexualize socialism, as he put it. At bottom, the Fabians were just as timid and easily shocked as the middle-class moralists. They complained that Wells was bringing their ideas into disfavor. Their personal lack of loyalty was thus added to the disappointments that their ideology had inflicted on him, and which led him to resign from the Fabian Society in 1908. For some time he had been feeling as though he had lost his way, strayed up a blind alley. Now he came out of it, in his own fashion, with a great hullabaloo. He shook the dust of socialism from his feet, denouncing the movement as being nothing but teeth and claws, blind and brainless. The Webbs became his particular bogey. *The New Machiavelli* is strewn from cover to cover with discarded ideas and slaughtered friends. One of the victims was Lord Balfour. Wells had met him during his early socialist days, in the group of enlightened Conservatives who called themselves the Souls. He had been charmed by Balfour's skeptical intelligence, his melodious voice and, in spite of himself, by the easy manner of this aristocrat and his audacious independence. Later, he frankly admitted how much he admired Balfour; but in *The New Machiavelli* he depicted him, as Evesham, in an enlarged and deformed version, as though seen in a distorting mirror, with "a quite wicked unscrupulousness in the use of his subtle mind . . .," his "fundamental lack of convictions," his "diabolical skill."

Wells seems to have let himself be carried away, further than he meant to go, by the resentment that was working in him like a poison. But though bad temper seeps in through every chink, the book is none the less something more than a piece of revenge or a lampoon. It is a bitter argument between a socially constructive passion, the white passion of the man whose eyes are fixed on the future, and the love that holds him like a spell. "I am not in love with her now; I am *raw* with love for her," cries the hero. In Wells himself were two hostile forces—his feeling of responsibility toward mankind, which gripped him with an anguish that seemed strange in that calm, settled period, and the sexual needs by which he was tormented and enslaved. As a responsible member of society he foresaw centuries of confusion, great, stupid wars, despair, catastrophe, fresh beginnings, the tragedy of ill-directed energy. But his eyes, that saw so clearly into the future, could not decipher the chaos of his own life. At times he thought he must be a monster.

He described *The New Machiavelli* as a tragedy of incompatibility

between great collective interests and great individual passions. It was
not until much later that he managed to settle this conflict within his
own being, and realized that the two warring tendencies were, in
reality, a twin force. "The drive," he wrote in *The World of William
Clissold,* "is the drive of what Shaw calls the 'life force' and Schopen-
hauer 'the will to live' . . . It is protean . . . occasionally it becomes
barely and plainly a clamour for woman." But in 1911 he was still far
from this revelation of his own vitality. And far from understanding
that the monster he suspected to be hidden within him, with its un-
faithfulness, its moments of remorse, and its fresh betrayals, could not
be persuaded to fix its choice, to accept one woman, for an allotted
period, as the representative of the life force.

The New Machiavelli gives the reflection of his perplexity—a blurred
reflection. Wells himself said of the book in after years that it was a
queer, confused affair, one of his worst—and most revealing—novels.
The detractors of *Ann Veronica* were on the watch for his new book,
but not with an eye to its literary merits. They supposed that after
having been so severely scolded for his lack of moral sense, he would
be trying to earn forgiveness this time. But sensation-seeking readers
were on the watch too. Both groups were disappointed. The magazine
that serialized the story was in great demand because of a rumor that
Wells's highly respectable publisher had refused to bring it out in
book form. This was so far true, that Macmillans had arranged with
a less prudish publisher to issue *The New Machiavelli* under his imprint. There was a fresh outcry when it appeared, but less violent, since
it was a repetition.

The burst of bad temper to which Wells had given way was hardly
sufficient to relieve his mind. Deep down, he was ill at ease. In moments of appeasement, of emotional void, he had dark moods of discouragement. He lost faith in himself. He lost faith in his work. He
could not get interested in a new subject. He began to find it hard to
concentrate. Everything around him seemed stale. He was laboring
under a sense of overfamiliarity. Above all, he was tormented by fits of
claustrophobia such as occur in every man's life, especially during
the strain of creative work. His house weighed down on him, with the
reality of its brick and stone. The surrounding scene, grown too
familiar, took on the wrinkles of old age as he looked at it. Throughout his life he was liable to be attacked by the sudden fear of being
too firmly settled, the threat of permanence. Possessions were enemies.

He felt caught in a trap. Whenever this feeling came over him, he had to make a bolt from wherever he happened to be. A sort of urgency drove him on. It was as though the walls of his house began to close in upon him. His impatient nature could not tolerate any delay between feeling a need and achieving it. In 1910 he suddenly sold Spade House, because, he says, he felt that otherwise it would become the final setting of his life.

Not until long afterward did he come to understand from what deeply buried source this claustrophobia arose. Then he wrote, in *William Clissold,* of the "imaginations, feverish wishes, rivalries, hostilities, hates, resentments, all arising out of sex," by which mankind is driven, also adding, "and if it were not for that obsession, for its hopes and excitements and collateral developments, I do not know where the great majority of lives would find the driving force to continue."

The need for change, for novelty, was part of his make-up, and in its most usual form—the love of travel. In the summer of 1911 he settled with his family in France, at Pont de l'Arche. The feeling of dread that had caused his flight from Spade House still persisted as a memory of having been caught in a trap—the trap of property, the trap of love, the trap of marriage. That was the theme of *Marriage,* the novel he wrote in France that summer. It is a very distant projection of the emotions that were disturbing him. A more objective transposition of a personal conflict has seldom been made.

Marriage is really a fresh version of *Love and Mr. Lewisham* (Wells often wrote the same novel twice over). It deals with the incompatibility between a scientific career and the claims of love. Or rather, between the demands of daily life and those of disinterested scientific research. It is the tyranny of poverty which, on a higher level, becomes the tyranny of comfort, the preoccupation with money. Love, with its unforeseeable responsibilities, enslaves the mind. The idyllic passion that first united Trafford and Marjorie slips down into the sordid reality of the struggle to earn a living. Wells points the contrast between his scientist-hero's clear mind and the muddle-headedness of politicians and writers. A love-marriage is saved, by sudden flight, from the morass into which it was gradually sinking. But not many people can solve their problems by joining an expedition to Labrador. Wells knew that there was something artificial and unconvincing about his solution, and that some of the minor characters in the story, such as Marjorie's father and her suitor, inclined toward farce.

There are few autobiographical details in this book; the most important of them tells of the birth of Jane's first child, describing Wells's anxiety and his excitement at becoming a father.

In the following year, Wells brought out *The Passionate Friends,* as a sort of amendment to his dissertation on love and society. This time the debate takes place on another plane. Like its predecessor, the book seems to be closely bound up with personal experience. It hinges on the conflict between love and social inequality, a conflict that in this instance is kept within narrower limits than that of *Marriage*. Wells's vehement indictment is leveled against Society with a capital "S," that is to say, against a class which, by its lures and its ostracisms, can enslave even the most independent spirits, the most sturdy characters. In its main plot, *The Passionate Friends* is partly a sequel to *Ann Veronica,* partly a positive and negative reaction, a second telling of the story. This time it is the tale of a woman who did not have the courage to follow up her life and her love, or who imagined that she could keep the special advantages of wealth and social position without giving up her fundamental independence, and who found no solution to the problem except in adultery, with all its sordid and clandestine shifts and its inevitable discovery.

But Lady Mary Justin is not a consistent figure like Ann Veronica. The experiment in the test tube, with its negative reaction, is falsified by a disparity of chemical composition. This is not simply the story of what would have happened to Ann Veronica if she had not had the courage to defy scandal and take the man she wanted. Lady Mary Justin is the finished portrait for which the Honorable Beatrice Normandy had been a preliminary sketch. (Incidentally, Beatrice's name comes up again here, in passing, as though by way of indication.) Wells did not like to discard any story that he had not told in all its ramifications, and *Tono-Bungay* had left him with one whose details had not been entirely worked out. Like Beatrice Normandy, Lady Mary is a bundle of contradictions; she has a fierce longing for independence, yet is cowed by the conventions of her class; she is brave enough to decide on suicide, but cannot face the thought of living in comparative poverty. Like Beatrice, she has a devouring vanity; she clings to luxury at the cost of love, and finally pays for her choice by all-round disaster. She belongs to the series of headstrong women that can be traced through Wells's work from Ann Veronica to Lady Harman, culminating in Christina Alberta. But the story of Lady

Mary Justin, vividly as she is depicted, is really no more than a surface tale, a veneer of polished plywood laid over the thick, hard timbers of an internal debate. So strongly does Wells stress his interest in that debate, that it even takes precedence over the sensational plot, the discovered adultery, the flouted husband, the scandal and suicide that fill the front of the stage. *The Passionate Friends* is a typical example of the frame getting into the picture, almost taking its place.

Lady Mary's lover is a man groping his way through an existing social structure which now and then, due to the twists and turns of his personal love story, caves in on him. One of the chapters is called "This Swarming Business of Mankind," and that might have been the title of the whole book. The young lover, desperate with grief at the marriage of the girl he loves, is traveling around the world. He becomes more and more haunted by the sight of the toiling masses that are still kept down to the level of primitive civilizations by a society bent upon exploiting and enslaving human beings. "This phase of expropriation and enslavement," he says, "has been a necessary phase in human development." But the time for it is long past. The most flagrant abuses, the most shameless injustice, poverty, famine, crime, epidemics, result solely from waste, ignorance, and stupidity. The evils of society are rooted in fanaticism, prejudice, and petty patriotism, and their cure is a universal question, a matter which concerns mankind as a whole. A world state would mean not only peace on earth, the end of "that monstrous European devotion to arms" (Wells wrote this book on the eve of the World War I,) but also the reign of social justice.

The "open conspiracy" against potentates, prejudices, and the disruptive forces of evil is mentioned for the first time in this book, and the expression had come to stay. Wells's hero refuses to give the name of "dream" to his idea of a great State, a World Republic of civilized people, because, he says, it is not a dream, but an obviously reasonable possibility.

Lady Mary Justin loudly proclaims the right of women to share in public life. Wells joined, as a matter of course, in every fight for freedom that took place in his day. Thus, he was associated with the feminist campaign for the right to vote, a campaign which had its heroic and pathetic aspects, and in *The New Machiavelli* he makes due mention of its remarkable effectiveness. He joined it just as he had

joined the Fabian Society—wholeheartedly, demanding absolute material and moral emancipation for women. In course of time he realized
how far out he had been in the margin of his epoch—further to the
left than any of the official leftist movements.

The suffragettes ended, just as the socialists had done, by looking upon him as an embarrassing ally, an *enfant terrible*. His faith
in this movement, and his disappointment with it, are set forth in *The
Wife of Sir Isaac Harman*. On the surface, this is the tale of a very
feminine woman, who begins to look more deeply into herself and,
by logical developments, is led from gentleness to violence. But the
book contains something more than the story of a now forgotten
moment in history. It describes an innocent, penniless girl, faced with
the physical facts of love and the temptations of cheap romanticism.
From the point of view of plot, it has dated more than most of Wells's
work. The lesser figures are caricatures of suffragettes and writers,
who deserve the forgetfulness into which they are crumbling. But
there remains the figure, at first sight merely grotesque, of the poor
rich man, shivering in his unloved solitude, the domestic tyrant in
whom still survives the little boy that his mother used to bully, the
disappointing lover tormented by desires that were too slow in awakening. And above all there is Lady Harman, who faces life with the
silent acceptance of a strong character, drawing sensuous pleasure
from many sources, and protected by her innate courage from being
caught in emotional snares. Her physical presence makes itself felt,
whether she will or no, by the aura of womanliness that surrounds
her. Wells always kept a particular affection for this heroine of an
outdated novel, as though she had been modeled on a woman whom
he had greatly loved.

But Lady Harman was not the emancipated woman around whom
his impatient dreams were still centered, the mistress and comrade that
he sought with boyish obstinacy even after reaching full manhood—
the other half of man, of his mutilated self, of which Aristophanes
speaks in Plato's "Banquet" (this fable was often in Wells's thoughts).
Whether his impatience was appeased or frustrated, it remained just
as strong. He did not yet realize that it was the living spring within
him. It is only with the voluminous confessions of William Clissold
that he sums up a revelation that had come to him only recently, by
saying that "sexual enterprise grows with success," and that those

who had once heard the song of Pan would soon ask for it to be repeated with variations.

Around the time when he was at work on *The World of William
Clissold,* Wells published *Christina Alberta's Father.* After a lapse of
some fifteen years, he had, so to speak, rewritten *Ann Veronica.* The
extraordinary change that had taken place in notions of sexual morality during those years is clearly seen when the two books are compared. Christina Alberta comes along almost too soon to be Ann
Veronica's daughter, yet she makes her look like a grandmother. Ann
Veronica had given herself through love, in a burst of supreme courage. Christina Alberta gives herself through curiosity, and because she
feels her maturity stirring within her. Ann Veronica had aroused
public horror by proclaiming her desire for one particular man; Christina Alberta proclaims an avid longing for everything, she rebels
against the very thought of renunciation, and demands "the world,
from the stars to the bottom of the sea" for her own hungry self. She
is shown as a modern girl whose mind has been swept clear of any
and every positive belief. Neither her thoughts nor her words have
even the smallest fig leaf to veil them. She is completely and out-
spokenly irreligious. She is, at least in theory, antisocial and amoral.
She has no respect for Christian ethics, family life, capitalism, or the
British Empire. And she is always ready to let this be known. It
almost seems as though Wells himself were a little horrified by his
heroine's audacity, as though he were watching her, round eyed, with
the involuntary admiration that he used to feel toward the original
from which she was drawn.

Christina Alberta, like Ann Veronica, is a portrait. The young lover
in the story speaks of "her flare of hungry, rebel individuality." Wells
had been brought face to face with the reality that had so long eluded
him. "She was the boldest enterprise in living that he had ever met,"
says her puzzled lover. She had a vitality that was sister to H. G.'s
own; but her vitality was unflagging, like an engine that never stopped
ticking over, whereas his was liable to slow down at times, to come to
a halt in doubt, because of the devastating frankness with which he
judged his own efforts. She helped him to read himself more clearly,
to solve a contradiction that had been worrying him for years. He
began to perceive the tremendous unity of life. "I suppose all the
energy of life is sublimated from sexual energy; the waters have a
compelling tendency to return to the ocean from which they arose,"

writes William Clissold. This realization ended a long-drawn-out conflict in Wells himself.

The reception given to the book must have been enough to prove to him that that particular conflict was no longer in the forefront of human interests. Ann Veronica had caused a scandal, but it never occurred to anybody to be shocked by the boldness of Christina Alberta. Between the two books there lay a gulf—the gulf of the World War I, which had swallowed up the previous century, from its worm-eaten moral foundations to its watchtowers.

XV

THE WORLD WAS HIS EGG

THE COUNTY OF Essex, said Wells in *Mr. Britling Sees It Through,* was still living in the peace of the eighteenth century. The cottages still had thatched roofs. Rusty inn signs swung and creaked in the wind. The wide acres of Easton Park lay spread out, with the disciplined wildness of a landscape in some old Italian painting, around the long, low, Tudor manor house with its rows of red-brick chimneys. Deer could be glimpsed among the shadows of the great oak trees; a stream wound lazily through the brushwood. Like Up Park, this great estate was maintained in semifeudal style. When Wells bought Easton Park Rectory, about 1912, he stepped into the familiar atmosphere of his childhood. The social changes that had taken place since then were revealed not only in his own person, but also in that of the Lady of the Manor, Lady Warwick, a blond, expensively elegant beauty who had joined the Labour party as "a remarkable intruder into the class struggle," says Wells.

Little Easton Rectory, or rather Easton Glebe, as he renamed it—an old, square, red-brick house, with its great lawn overhung by tall blue cedar-trees, its ancient barn, now turned into a ballroom with parquet floor and Pianola—has passed with photographic exactitude, a loving exactitude, into Wells's work as the Dower House in *Mr. Britling Sees It Through.* For the next eighteen years it was to be the more or less constant background of his life. But it was at the very moment when he had decided to take root again, to make a home for his family and to enjoy stability around him, that Wells began to be haunted by a feeling of general instability, a sense of approaching upheaval. His apprehensions seemed to be at odds with his actions. Later in life, he remarked on the fact that although he had several times foreseen the course of events, he had never taken any measures in his private life to provide against an impending cataclysm.

The sense of social insecurity that had haunted him since childhood, and which he had kept alive in his mind as though it were a gift that ought to be cultivated, now warned him that unrest was rife among the working classes. Another man was also aware of the insecurity, the loosening of the ties that held society together; that man was Lord Northcliffe, then owner of the *Daily Mail*. Before he ever met Northcliffe, who was slightly his senior, Wells had heard a great deal about him and his background. In 1899 or thereabouts, when, after his failure at South Kensington and his farewell to death, H. G. took up schoolmastering again and went to teach at Henley House School, he found that the memory of its most spectacular pupil, Alfred C. Harmsworth, was still fresh in everyone's mind.

Young Harmsworth—the son of a lawyer from Dublin, eldest of a large family, and of a woman who, in her masterful energy, reminded Wells of Laetitia Bonaparte—had not been a brilliant scholar, but he seemed to have been born with a gift for journalism. The headmaster of Henley House, keenly interested in his pupils and in his task of developing their talents, had encouraged the eleven-year-old boy to start a school magazine. On leaving school, Harmsworth had begun work as a journalist, without any particular success at first. He edited a paper made up of articles collected from various other publications, and a cheap magazine for little boys, called *Comic Cuts*. At the age of twenty-four he also brought out a successful book, with the characteristic title of *A Thousand Ways to Earn a Living*. He understood the average little boy well enough to be able to play up to his instincts; and he always understood the man in the street well enough to fit in with his needs, his superficial desire to educate himself, and his wish to be amused.

His fantastic rise to a position of wealth and influence was a constant source of astonishment to himself. His admiration for his own abilities went hand-in-hand with a slightly uneasy conscience, and also with a certain feeling of responsibility. He believed the world could be run with the same efficiency that he had brought to the management of his own life and his great newspaper. And in spite of its apparent stability, the world needed putting to rights—his reporter's instinct told him that. He had a strong presentiment that a new social order was on its way, says Wells, who helped to confirm his ideas on the subject. After reading *Anticipations,* Northcliffe felt that H. G. was a man who could solve the problems he himself felt so disturbing. He had "an almost touching belief" that somewhere, just outside his range, there were numbers of clever people who knew a lot more than he did, and that with the help of publicity, or a competition with a big money prize, any desired aim could be reached.

It was in this conviction that economic puzzles could be solved by a determined approach to them, that he asked Wells to write about the question of labor unrest. Strange stuff, comments Wells, for the readers of the leading halfpenny daily to find upon their breakfast tables. The readers of 1912 did not realize that they were being presented with a plea for something that did not yet exist, and that was later to be known as planned economy. Wells knew that such bold experiments always had met and always would meet with opposition from the privileged classes and from the natural laziness of humanity. But he also knew that the present policy of toleration would not prevent future unrest and disturbance. He called for a national effort on a scale never attempted before, and the preparation of a National Plan. This may have been the first time that the word Plan, so familiar nowadays, was used in a newspaper article. Wells warned his readers that failing such a plan there would probably be a period of social strife, and even of revolutionary outbreaks, that might well leave the nation weakened for a long period, or even ruin it completely.

This was a strange prophecy in 1912, and stranger still was its appearance in a Northcliffe paper. But Wells's attention was distracted from the social problem just around this time, by his feeling that a dangerous international situation was rapidly developing. As early as 1911 he foretold in *The New Machiavelli* that there would be a squaring of accounts between England and Germany before very long. And he added, in that bad-tempered book, his prayer for "a chastening war" that would shake the England he loved out of her state of lethargy.

The Agadir incident had rung an alarm bell in his mind. He wondered to what extent his country was ready to meet the threat. He had doubts about the sense of security behind which Great Britain had taken refuge. The British, as he wrote later, were obsessed by the tradition of the invincible strength of the Royal Navy. He was alarmed

about the vast sums of money that were being swallowed up in building sea monsters, gigantic deathtraps, as he called them. He used the
space that Northcliffe gave him in the *Daily Mail,* to demand the
modernization of military methods. "Put not your trust on dread-
noughts," he wrote in 1913. The readers of the *Daily Mail,* who had
ranked his appeal for planned economy alongside his *Anticipations*
and pigeonholed both as fiction, were shocked that a mere writer
should dare to attack the sacred symbols of British tradition, and to
do so, asserted the Admiralty, without in the least knowing what he
was talking about.

Events took some time to justify Wells's warning. Then, at the
battle of Jutland, one sea monster after another, hit in its ammunition
magazine, sank in a matter of minutes. Great Britain lost the gems
of her sea power, in that one battle she lost over six thousand men.
The Germans lost only two battleships as against seven, and 2,500
men. In 1917, German submarines sank three-and-a-half million tons
of British shipping. But at the end of the war, the British fleet was
still strong enough to face a second conflict with the same mistaken
policy imposed by its chiefs. The catastrophe had not been sweeping
enough to win approval for Wells's views. His prophecy had to wait
almost another twenty years for full justification. It had to wait until
the day when the "Hood," sent in pursuit of the "Bismarck," fought
for three and a half minutes and then blew up, with nothing left to
show for the years of work its designers and builders had put into
it, or the twelve million pounds sterling it had cost.

"As a prophet, the author must confess that he has always been
inclined to be rather a slow prophet," wrote Wells in the introduction
to his book, *The World Set Free.*

In the year 1913, a dread of disaster was growing in many well-
informed minds. Few people, however, foresaw how soon it would
come. But the little man in his studio at Easton Glebe could not take
his eyes off the shadow on the threshold. He wanted to pass his
anxiety on to other people. He had tried to make a direct approach to
the threat, only to find that people were even less ready to believe
him when he dealt openly with reality than when he wrapped it in
a fictional disguise. He wanted to force attention by striking his
readers' imagination with all the vigor at his command.

So he wrote *The World Set Free.* In it he described the Central
European States united in a sudden attack on the Slav Confederation;

France and Great Britain drawn into the conflict; the opening stages of the campaign against the Western Allies, which takes place in the Low Countries; a British expeditionary force sent to the Ardennes, to hold the fortified line of the Meuse. This book was written in 1913 and published at the beginning of 1914. Scarcely six months later, British soldiers were tramping past those golden French fields, those autumn-tinted forests that Wells had described, and Frenchwomen were offering them cool drinks, just as in his book.

Wells's British soldier remarks sadly that no Napoleon or Caesar has appeared among the Allied leaders. The commander in chief of their armies is a French marshal, Dubois, a handsome, taciturn old man with a fixed stare, who always turns his profile toward anyone who talks with him, and overawes everybody by his impassive bearing. Wells gives only a brief sketch of this man—whose "one profound discovery" about the art of war, the key to his career, was that nobody knew anything about the matter, that all action led to mistakes, and that the best chance lay with the man who acted "slowly and steadfastly and above all silently"—but it is a sketch that remains in the memory.

Wells wrote *The World Set Free* with the aim of arousing a horror of warfare by showing it in all its amplitude. But he may have half expected that events would give him the lie, or have wanted to leave his readers time to meditate on the results of homicidal lunacy, for he sets 1956 as the fatal date. Starting from the notion, which then seemed so farfetched, that an entirely new factor was to be brought into military strategy, he knew that many years would go by before science could bring it to the point of practical application. The book was written at a time when he had just been deeply impressed by the work of Rutherford and Soddy. He describes a young research chemist attending a lecture on radium and radioactivity, on the properties of uranium, and the atom, "that reservoir of immense energy." The professor shows the students a bottle containing uranium oxide, about a pint of it, worth about a pound, in which "there slumbers at least as much energy as we could get by burning a hundred and sixty tons of coal," a force powerful enough to blow up the university buildings or to light the whole city for a week.

Stressing the fact that he had been a rather slow prophet, Wells pointed out that, for instance, air warfare had beaten the forecasts of *Anticipations* by about twenty years. The race between reality and imagination, which had made him place the explosion of the atom bomb in World War I, was delayed until the second world conflict. Wells had realized straight away there was a new reality. He knew it partly through scientific deduction, and partly through an instinctive conviction which persisted in his mind, though he would perhaps have been unable to explain his obstinacy. A sixth sense warned him that this invention, still in its earliest phase, would be a dominating factor of the future.

He reacted in the same way to the first experiments in the splitting of the atom as to the first experiments in flight. He knew, too, that the first use of this new force would not be for the good of mankind, but for its destruction, like the use of aircraft in warfare. He suspected that atomic energy would be used to blow up universities rather than to light cities.

Seated at his writing table, amid the soothing calm of the English countryside—the song of a bird or the shouts of a happy child were carried to him now and then by the wind that murmured in the trees —the little man covered sheet after sheet of paper with his small, regular, copper-plate writing. Behind him loomed the gigantic shadow of a new era, the terrible Atomic Age.

He was describing how, in 1933, a chemist discovers a practical method of liberating atomic energy. But after that, twenty years are spent in attempts to make practical use of it. The atomic engine, perfected at last, is used in motorcars and airplanes; the very low cost of this new method of propulsion means that everybody can afford cars and planes. A helicopter is invented at about the same time, enabling fliers to go up or come down vertically, and thus making air travel absolutely safe.

Atomic energy, says Wells in *The World Set Free,* was the most terrible weapon that humanity had ever had at its disposal. The rapidity with which war was becoming impossible should have been quite obvious to the men of the early twentieth century. But they did not realize it, he adds, until the moment when the atom bombs burst in their fumbling hands.

The book shows statesmen and politicians still carrying on with old-time notions, military leaders preparing for war with outdated strategical methods, a war of infantry and trenches. The headquarters staffs on both sides take no account, it seems, of the terrible weapon at their disposal.

The Central European powers are the first to make use of it. An atom bomb is dropped on the Allied headquarters in Paris. "There was nothing else in the world but a crimson-purple glare and sound, deafening, all-embracing, continuing sound . . . A great ball of crimson-purple fire, like a maddening living thing that seemed to be whirling about very rapidly amidst a chaos of falling masonry that seemed to be attacking the earth furiously, that seemed to be burrowing into it like a blazing rabbit. . . ." The boiling waters of the Seine surge over the ruins of the Trocadero that lie scattered over the Chaillot hill. The steam rises in a thick cloud toward the livid, glaring sky. Among the ruins lies the torn body of Dubois, his handsome, cameo-like head undamaged, his face still wearing its expression of sublime incomprehension.

There are allied reprisals on Berlin, counter-reprisals on London; the dikes of Holland are bombed and the sea flows in over the flat land. The world is plunged into the somber glow of destruction, tongues of flame lick earth, water and sky, the world is a drum that echoes with thunder, the ruined towns are hidden behind a fiery curtain, the starving, thirsting survivors wander through the few strips of land that have escaped destruction, like a procession of ghosts in a flame-colored universe.

After World War I, Wells felt that this book was both out of date and absurdly exaggerated. The war had come much sooner than he had prophesied, but despite this terrible blood-letting the world had not been plunged into the nightmare that he had described. He had given birth to a universe that had no connection with reality.

More than twenty years went by.

And then the first atom bomb was dropped on Hiroshima. An unprecedented power of destruction was let loose on the world. Events had caught up with Wells's imagination in the space of twenty years. His book was remembered only by people who had grown up before 1914, in whose minds it lingered like the memory of a childhood terror. The old man, whom the German bombs had not been able to drive out of his house in Hanover Terrace, in the heart of London, must have had a few minutes of strange confrontation with himself when the big newspaper headlines and the first photographs of the cataclysm met his eyes.

But the weird description of world-wide disaster that Wells had put into his book had not been, for him, an end in itself, but a means of stirring men's imagination. What mattered to him was not the scale on which collapse took place, but the lesson that humanity could draw from it. A gulf lay between the outworn institutions, the old-fashioned notions, to which society still clung, and the unification of the world by international science. He declared that independent, sovereign states, divided by frontiers, were among the most outdated of all these lingering relics.

The World Set Free develops along the same lines as earlier fantastic novels by Wells. The shock of disaster is followed by the triumph of common sense, represented in this book by the French Ambassador to Washington, a certain Leblanc. He is a bald-headed, spectacled, insignificant-looking, little man—a typical Frenchman, the son of a provincial grocer, who might quite well have stayed in his little home town, arguing about politics in the local café and going off on Sundays to fish in the local stream. But this little Frenchman is filled with the intellectual idealism which, says Wells, has been one of France's particular gifts to mankind. He also has the faculty of clear thinking, which enables him to simplify the problems that come along, and the political skill of an old parliamentary hand, a shrewd leader of men. Furthermore, he enjoys the advantage of having been in Washington, "and in touch with that gigantic childishness which was the characteristic of the American imagination." It is the Americans who give Leblanc the authority he needs, who enable him to win over the more skeptical European governments to his idea.

Amid the chaos of war, Leblanc is trying to bring together the responsible chiefs of the different states. It is as though a bird were warbling in the midst of a thunderstorm; yet his voice is persuasive and obstinate enough to get across to those who had looked upon him so far as a mere harmless dreamer. And the whole fire-scarred world is calling for peace. In the general bewilderment, the stubborn little Frenchman begins to be looked to as a leader. He succeeds in gathering representatives from all the warring states, he summons them to Switzerland, an oasis of peace among ruins, choosing a spot far removed from the agitated outer world—the little mountain village of Brissago, above Locarno, overlooking Lake Maggiore. Here he brings together nine kings, four presidents, many ministers and ambassadors, and qualified press representatives from every country. From the discussions that he guides so skillfully, a free world is born. A world freed from its nightmares. The terrible atom bomb, and the factories in which it is made, come under the control of the united nations.

Everything turns out to be quite simple, thanks to a great deal of faith and a little audacity—the unconscious audacity that is displayed by the young King of England. Wells's particular brand of humor, never entirely absent from even his most deeply serious moods, gilds his account of this Brissago meeting, which stands out, glowing, amid the horrors that encircle it. Even the minor characters have that liveliness that Wells at his best was so well able to confer. A final attempt to rebel against world union is made by a Balkan king who refuses to hand over his stock of atom bombs. But the candid King of England, a young hero of a very British type, who thinks while he acts, or rather after having acted, manages to get hold of this last threat to peace. A new world begins to rise from the ruins; mankind is launched into the splendid adventure of peace. The moral shock of the atomic bombs had been profound, and "for a time the whole world had been shocked into frankness" by realizing the vital necessity of reconstruction, writes Wells in this book, with his basic optimism.

The author of *The World Set Free* was taken by surprise when the first world war broke out. He saw around him the peaceful English countryside, a trim landscape whose very sky had been tamed, as it were, so that its clouds looked like white sheep being driven across blue pastures by an invisible shepherd. There was his rose garden, in full, rich bloom; there were his romping children with their infectious gaiety; there was the young German tutor, far too serious, with no sense of humor at all, who thought only of improving his mind and was always asking the most absurd questions. Then, suddenly, there was the war. Peace had lasted so long that nobody had the least idea of what war really meant. War was a featureless monster that had come gliding in among all these familiar things. The young German went away, much embarrassed, with the suddenly dignified bearing of a predestined victim. He left his most precious possession, his violin, to be looked after by his employers, those very puzzling people of whom he had been so fond. He never came back to get it, as he had meant to do, for he was captured by the Russians and died in captivity.

The outbreak of hostilities came as a tremendous shock to Wells. This war, which he had foretold, whose early stages he had forecast so accurately, wounded him deeply in his patriotic feelings and roused all his passionate love of his country. Like his Mr. Britling, he was immensely proud of England, although he never tired of criticizing her incompetence and lack of energy. He was truly at one with his homeland during the night when, in the silence of his sleeping house, he sat up writing his first wartime article. He was haunted, too, by a distressful feeling that he had not taken enough notice of the danger, that he had failed to live up to his responsibilities.

In outraging his country's will to peace, the aggressor had committed an outrage against him, personally. Although he was so far in advance of his time, so impatient of prevailing opinions and conventions, he reacted, in hours of heavy trial, exactly like any other man of his time and country. The waves of public emotion passed through him as they passed through any and every man in the street. (He would not, perhaps, have been able to project his thoughts so far ahead of existing conditions if he had been less deeply rooted in his native soil; he might not, perhaps, have been able to explore the future so thoroughly if he had been less firmly established in the present.) During those first months of war he had the exhilarating sense of sharing in the soul of the community—a sense that rarely comes to pioneers of thought in their lonely outposts. He felt that he stood side by side with all those whom war had jerked out of the rut of their personal interests, who were being called upon to give their lives for their country. "I shall insist to the end of my days," says William Clissold, "that the last months of 1914 were a tragically splendid phase in European experience."

The tireless prophet of the New Republic might have been expected to turn a deaf ear to the appeals of overwrought patriotism and to remain outside and above the struggle. But on the contrary he flung himself into it, body and soul. As well as his feeling of union with his homeland, the specifically British feeling of "my country, right or wrong," there was in his nature an undercurrent of liberalism that set him strongly against Germany, against the caste spirit that crushed German democracy, and the criminal militarism that had flung a whole nation into a cutthroat venture. There was his republicanism too, his hatred of the Kaiser's imperialistic aims, which carried the monarchist principle to its farthest extreme. He seems to have imagined that once that cornerstone of European monarchy had been destroyed, the entire royalist structure would collapse. It was to be the people's war. "This is *our* war," repeats Mr. Britling. It filled Wells's mind, driving out all other thoughts; it made him, like his hero, the slave of one single idea. He needed, perhaps, to fill up in this way the great void that the war had created in him. His dreams of world union were dying a silent death. So were his dreams of the brotherhood of the working classes, and of an intellectual elite that would step in to prevent slaughter. His anger was partly turned against his own credulity; his rebelliousness was that of a man who had been fooling himself. He gave way to it entirely, fiercely forswearing the pacifist views he had held in the past. What would become of the world, he asked himself, if those people won the war?

His own particular share of fighting was done by newspaper articles —articles written in the heat of battle, giving a fragmentary view, a forced overemphasis. They reveal a trait which had not been fully tested in his earlier life or writings. He follows his impulses without waiting for events to verify them. He never leaves himself a line of retreat. He never makes reservations to safeguard the future. He does not even pause to wonder whether he may be mistaken. He sets to work, writes, gets angry and prophesies, without a backward glance, like a man with his back to the wall. He cannot forgive those who do not come forward to stand by his side. He thunders against former friends whose attitude is reserved or critical. A note of violent exasperation runs through all the articles, as though their author were settling a private quarrel. He attacks Shaw, comparing him to an idiot child, screaming in a hospital. To those who seek a link with the intellectuals of Germany, he replies that everything worth while in German literature was written by Jews. His admirers in other countries were staggered by the violence of these articles; one American newspaper announced that the writer Wells would like to lynch every German. Hatred, and the sense of sharing in the collective spirit, had heightened his eloquence, redoubled his gift for finding just the right phrase. He had made himself the spokesman of the hour. The hour was speaking through him, finding its most complete expression through his lips. He felt himself to be fused into mass consciousness, as though he were both individual and nation, a bundle of personal reactions and the upsurge of a whole world. He laughed at himself for this tendency to put himself in the place of humanity, to feel himself responsible for its future. "The world was his egg," he says of Mr. Britling, "he had the subconscious illusion of having laid it."

Throughout the allied countries, millions were seeking in perplexity for the fundamental meaning of a war whose causes lay so far outside their own lives—for a reason why they had to sacrifice themselves. Wells set out to provide them with the explanation and the reason. One of his pamphlets was entitled *The War That Will End War.* The phrase gave an only too perfect reply to the crowding, distressful questions. It was one of those phrases that seem to arise from the collective consciousness, rather than from a single brain. The striving multitudes rallied to it as though to a banner—a banner of hope, planted in the midst of a bloodstained battlefield. A day was to come when Wells would be greatly embarrassed by this slogan he had invented. A day was to come when he would feel almost ashamed of having helped to dupe the conscience of his fellow men by that false promise of a war to end wars. The phrase stuck to him with the tenacity born of too much success. His opponents seized hold of it in order to discredit him, to explode his reputation as a prophet. Time and again he regretted having spoken those words! He looked back at them in the way one looks back on a failed examination or a bad social blunder.

His mistake, however, was useful in the circumstances from which it arose. It provided an illusion that served to veil the hideous reality. Blood was shed, in the belief that it was not being shed in vain. Men died, believing that through their death a finer world would be born. Without Wells's contribution, the war would still have relentlessly demanded the supreme sacrifice. The echo he awoke was the echo of a deep need for something to believe in.

A feeling of perplexity, still inarticulate perhaps, remained in his own mind, but he thrust it from him. The writing of articles and pamphlets left him still unsatisfied; his inner unrest called for some form of action that would bring him closer to the terrible reality of the war. He felt sure that his fertile imagination could be put to good use. There was one idea that appealed to him more than any other— that of saving human lives by the use of machines. With his habit of pushing ahead simultaneously on two different planes—of artistic creation and practical adaptation—he had published in 1903 on article on tanks, entitled "The Iron Guard of the Country," after having used this idea in a fantastic short story. He was disappointed at not being consulted when the first tanks were built in Great Britain under the inspiration of Winston Churchill and in spite of Kitchener, who laughed at the mechanical toys. "Leave it to Kitchener" was the watch-word of the day. But Wells could not get rid of his feeling of responsibility.

The war had invaded his everyday life, though in outward appearance it seemed unchanged; the sacrifices and sorrows of the fighting men, the battlefields that he saw in his mind's eye, had become more real to him than the familiar things and people around him. He lay through sleepless nights, gazing wide-eyed at the prowling form of death, at the hardships and sufferings of those who were fighting so far away, fighting for him—men of his own blood, sons and brothers. The lads he saw going away to the front seemed like sons to him, just as much as his own little boys. During one of those sleepless nights, while his eyes tried to pierce the darkness, beyond the dim shapes of the wind-tossed trees, he listened to the rain pouring down upon the slumbering countryside. But it was not the English night that he saw, or the patter of the raindrops in his garden that he heard. He saw soldiers in sodden uniforms, splashing through mud to reach their flooded trenches, and tottering beneath heavy packs that bruised their shoulders. One sleepless night, he jumped out of bed and jotted down on paper the sketch of a mobile teleferic by which supplies could be conveyed right into the firing line.

There was another man who, like him, was obsessed by the war, disgusted by the hidebound inertia of the military leaders. In the studio of Clare Sheridan, Wells met this man—her cousin, Winston Churchill. The housemaid's son and the descendant of the Duke of Marlborough had certain points in common. They both bubbled with the kind of energy that will never keep to the beaten track, but breaks through all routine obstacles. They were both impatient of fools, and full of contempt for anyone too slow to follow their go-ahead minds. They had both come a long distance to meet each other halfway like this, and there were to be many later occasions when each of them fell back to his starting point and they fought savagely, as though wanting to forget their periods of friendliness and the secret affinity between them.

But at the beginning of the war they both had the same sense of waste, the same impatience with the outdated methods that were being used. A new style of warfare was coming along, but the country's leaders were still guided by past ideas. Both these men knew that tanks would play a decisive part in a modern war. On this occasion

Churchill, like Wells, was a slow prophet. The tanks he forced upon the military chiefs, overruling their prejudices, came too late and were too few to have a decisive effect. When some of them got stuck in the Flanders mud, the military experts were secretly delighted at the setback. Another quarter century was to go by before the Churchills would roll over the battlefields of two continents, to face the terrible German mechanized force that had conquered Poland and France with lightning speed.

It was to Winston Churchill that Wells took his plan for a teleferic, and Churchill put him in touch with technicians who gave it practical form. The inspiration of a sleepless night became a reality, but it, too, was used so late and so timidly that no large-scale results could be achieved.

The incident, however, was of psychological value to Wells. It brought him into contact, for the first time, with the responsible chiefs of the army. They were men who believed themselves to be the guardians of an occult science. In outlook they were nearer to their German adversaries than to the civilians of their own country. Their haughty bearing had the effect of thrusting Wells down into his early background; class feeling was reawakened in him. Surrounded by their uniforms, their broad chests, their abrupt voices, he felt awkward, untidy, insignificant; he felt as though his own chest were caving in, and his youthful resentment surged up again. He began to wonder what his war, his own war, had to do with the one that was being waged by these important, gold-braided gentlemen. But it did not occur to him until much later that World War I was "a clash between the old forms and the new." At the moment he was still struggling against his doubts, for, as he said, heroism would be hardly possible if there were no lapses from knowledge into faith.

In defense of his teleferic scheme he came face to face with unexpected difficulties. His system of posts and ropes carried right into the front lines seemed as absurd to the military commanders as all the other mechanical toys that they were being pestered to use. His idea of a life line, he declared, hypnotized the warriors just as a chalk line hypnotizes hens. Meanwhile, on every rainy night, his imagination showed him poor fellows falling into the mud and being smothered. Not only was he disappointed by the treatment given to his own little invention, but he began to suspect that any suggestion for lightening the burden of war would meet with the same fate. He was being worn down by ever growing uneasiness. He hardly slept at all. His hair was falling out in handfuls. He felt that he was caught in the trap of his own powerlessness. Fits of despair drove out his early optimism. Just then he began to learn about the outrages the Germans were committing in Belgium, and to hear the echoes of the hymn of hate against England which was being sung everywhere in Germany, contradicting all his previous notions of a peaceable country and his faith in the identity of human nature throughout the world. Mr. Britling thinks at one moment of writing an "Anatomy of Hatred," in order to demonstrate the function of hate as a corrective of inefficiency.

Another man shared his belief that all the vital forces of mankind should rally to oppose barbarity and reaction behind their German mask. This was Anatole France, whom Wells had met before the war and to whom he was linked by "friendly esteem," as he put it. Anatole France, for his part, considered Wells to be the most intelligent of living Englishmen. At Wells's suggestion, a volume of essays entitled *The Book of France* was published in England in the summer of 1915, to raise funds for the French war victims in the devastated regions. Wells asked Anatole France to contribute an article, and France took up H. G.'s own slogan by calling his appeal *Debout pour la Dernière Guerre* ("Let us Arise and End War"), in place of its first, more academic title, *Horrida Bella*. "The prophetic dreams of H. G. Wells are being realized," he wrote, "they are taking on a monstrous, living form. . . . It is not Martians, but German professors who are doing this. Until today, until they came, atrocious, appalling war did at least retain, among the nations built up from the ruins of the Roman Empire, a human visage, something whose very form recalled the ingenious Greek or the rough Latin, inventors of all the arts of peace and war. War had its laws, its limits; classic natures, like that of Napoleon, could still express their genius therein. The Germans have deprived the art of weapons of every human quality that remained to it. They had killed peace; they are killing war. They are making it into a monster that cannot live: it is too ugly."

A particularly sinister light is shed on these words by World War II. Anatole France himself was not specially well satisfied with this piece of propaganda. To his friend Jacques Lion, who had sent him the request for an article, he wrote: "My lion-cub, you are terrible. I don't know what horrible pleasure you can find in making

me write nonsense to be put into English by H. G. Wells. Here is the
piece. It can be reckoned among the misfortunes of war. Send it to
our friends across the Channel if you have the courage. And may a
submarine torpedo it, always provided no harm is done to the ship
or the crew. . . ."

Unlike Anatole France, Wells issued his appeals with ardent seriousness, all the more ardent because a secret doubt was creeping into
his mind. Later, turning against these articles with the full severity
of his self-criticism, he declared that they had "a curious flavor of
clumsy propitiation or still clumsier menace," and that they were
chiefly remarkable for ignorance, inexperience, and self-importance.
He was, in fact, bound by the attitude he had taken from the beginning, by his entire self-committal. The very effectiveness of his appeals
kept him rooted to the spot he had chosen, in the foreground, the
spiritual front line of the battle. A primitive feeling urged him to
hold on—a man cannot desert his post in the face of the enemy. He
was aware of the response that he called forth, as though he were
talking through a loud-speaker before the German lines. Certain critics
of the war effort, whose articles were jubilantly quoted in the German
newspapers, he accused of sabotage. He made violent attacks on con-
scientious objectors. He accused pacifists of underhanded purposes.
He denied his former friends. They, for their part, looked upon him
as a traitor who wanted to make cannon fodder out of them. He became fanatically uncompromising, like all those who, as he put it
himself, feel that they are in the wrong.

Not until much later did he realize that the Great War had been
a fools' war. But even in those hours of impassioned choice, a struggle
was beginning, deep down inside him. Early in 1915 he was already
at work on the novel called *Mr. Britling Sees it Through*. The name
of his hero is significant. To avoid danger from the libel laws, Wells
always took great care not to give living people's names to his characters, especially to the burlesque minor figures in his books. He
usually picked them out of a railway guide, choosing, as far as possible, the names of small places. But the hero of this novel, with his faith
and his perplexities, is to some extent a self-portrait, and to a still
greater extent a portrait of the man in the street—the Briton. Wells
wrote the book like a diary, drawing scenes from real life. His readers
by the thousand, by the million, came to know that corner of rural
England where trains only stopped when travelers asked them to do

so; friends who came later on were enchanted to recognize familiar views of his house, and of his garden with its scent of roses, thyme and rosemary. He sketched himself, in his everyday setting. Bristling hair, mustache and eyebrows, clothes dragged on anyhow, an interested and yet absent-minded expression—for only when he was to be photographed would Mr. Britling consent to brush his hair, only when he was to be photographed did he wear a martyred air. The sketch is inclined toward caricature. Wells's humor sparkles against the gloomy, confused background that the war had created in everyone's life. He manages to give his slightly absurd, slightly annoying hero that indefinable charm that he himself possessed, and which people never quite knew whether to ascribe to sincerity or inattentiveness, to passionate interest in others or in himself. He also manages, with the utmost skill, to make his hero strongly individual, yet typically English. (Throughout his life, Wells remained conscious of all that linked him with the mass of his countrymen and merged him into his surroundings. One day I happened to catch sight of him in the railway station at Nice. "It's funny you recognized me," he said with his crooked smile, "I'm so exactly like all the middle-class, middle-aged Englishmen who come in swarms to the Riviera.")

He knew that what applied to him would hold good for everybody else. *Mr. Britling Sees It Through* is a running commentary on life in England during the early years of World War I. It is a day-to-day record, and its readers found themselves reflected in a faithful mirror that showed all the successive phases of their reactions—their first boundless astonishment, their unlimited optimism, their bewilderment at the incomprehensible barbarity of German behavior, their slow awakening to the realities of the conflict, their growing doubts about the wisdom of their leaders, their realization of military incompetence, their feeling that lives and hopes were being criminally squandered. Mr. Britling's passionate self-committal was put into words that lingered in the subconscious and rose to the surface at moments of similar emotion: "We'll beat them in the air. We'll beat them on the sea." Did the swing of those phrases haunt Winston Churchill's memory when he came before the microphone in the gravest hour of all England's history?

Every home was turned into a house of mourning. Through the breach torn by death, doubt struck its hardest blow at the suffering survivors. Britling's son is killed in the war. He becomes one of the numberless, sorrow-choked fathers who wonder whether their sacrifice has not been made in vain. Wells described this ordeal with so much power that people supposed he had been through it himself. For years, foreign admirers invaded his house, demanding to be shown the place where he had wept on learning of his eldest son's death. "The world was his egg." What could he give to all these people who had turned toward him, whose only longing was to believe in the certainties that he had held up before their eyes? Certainties that he no longer shared. He was a prey to the most painful form of confusion, that which comes of half-acknowledged responsibility, of failure to keep a promise made in the spirit. He had chosen a road that ended in a precipice. Behind him he felt the pressure of the crowd that had followed his lead. Would he fall to destruction, lead them down after him into the bottomless pit of doubt? The ground was giving way beneath his feet. Like an unskillful tightrope walker, he recovered his balance with a jerk. He had to discover some way out. So Mr. Britling finds God.

Wells himself felt that there was something disconcerting about such a suddenly improvised solution. But it was his own defeat that he strove to avoid by this discovery of God—for it was a discovery, rather than a return to beliefs that had not outlasted his earliest childhood. Mr. Britling's God has nothing in common with the God of Sarah Wells, that Almighty Father, stern, yet just and pitiful, who drew perturbed spirits to Him under the warm cloak of religion as though they were little, frightened children. Wells's God is presented straight away as "the Master, the Captain of mankind." This title is enough to show how closely his appearance is linked with the war and its phraseology. Nevertheless, this "theological excursion," as Wells called it, went on for several years after the war. Wells's wrestlings with God, the Captain of the World Republic, were closely connected with constructive efforts to establish peace. "It is amid the thunder of the guns that the search for a *pax mundi* must begin," he wrote.

The war could end only with the exhaustion of Germany, the crumbling of the Hohenzollern regime and its replacement by a republic. Wells also foresaw the changes that would come about in economic conditions; he predicted rising prices and a revaluation of gold. And as early as 1916, before the United States had entered the war, he began to glimpse the imperative necessity of a great council or conference, some kind of permanent institution, superposed upon the various states.

This institution would deal with problems in a broader spirit than could be expected of any form of nationalism or political imperialism. This was the first time that the idea of a League of Nations had been expressed by his pen. The idea was already in the air. Early in 1915 a League to Enforce Peace had been founded in New York. Many people claimed to have originated the title. According to Wells, its true author was the English writer Lowes Dickinson, who, with a group of friends, formed a League of Nations Society in London at about this time. Wells joined it, but he did not agree on all points with his associates. After having been carried away by emotion, he was now gradually getting back his natural lucidity. "The return to complete sanity took the greater part of two years. My mind did not get an effective consistent grip upon the war until 1916," he writes in his autobiography. He grasped the realities of peace too. His friends were dreaming of a democratic league in which all nations, great or small, would have an equal voice. Wells already knew that only five or six countries had sufficient resources to wage a modern war. A short visit to the front in the late summer of 1916 confirmed his belief that the increasing mechanization of warfare made it an impossibility for any country that did not possess considerable sources of raw material and a highly developed industry. An agreement between the great powers could put an end to war forever. Wells pointed out these facts in a series of articles which were republished, in 1917, in a volume entitled *War and the Future*. From that day forth, he never ceased to drive home this idea, with his usual tireless persistence.

While the war was losing its first aspect—that of an easy victory to be gained over a nation led astray by evil counselors—losing its soul, as Mr. Britling said, Wells was trying to ensure that peace would have some meaning. As early as June, 1917, he asked for a declaration of imperial policy, and he returned again and again to the need for a clear statement of war aims. He outlined them himself in an essay, *A Reasonable Man's Peace*. This title responded to a deep-seated craving, to a kind of lassitude by which many people were being overcome. When the essay was reprinted as a pamphlet, a quarter of a million copies were sold. Though his prophecies had not always come true, Wells was still the spokesman of his time. The average man was revolted by unnecessary bloodshed; but he felt a paralyzing fear of what victory might bring in its wake, a fear of incomplete victory for the allies, a fear of an imposed peace. (It was not long before the legend of the Diktat of Versailles arose in Germany, and therein lay the seeds of the second world war.) "Few men have the courage to reach their own convictions. They must be led to them or helped to them. They fear the greed of their antagonists, fresh wars, fresh outrages, and an unending series of evil consequences, if they seem to accept anything short of triumph," wrote Wells in November 1917, to an American who had asked him for a letter that could be given to President Wilson.

A great hope was beginning to dawn over the benighted world. Anxious eyes were strained toward the vision of a man who seemed to symbolize the approach of happier days. The war had discredited the statesmen of Europe, worn them threadbare. Only America could raise the question of peace without surrendering any claim or condoning any outrage. Only America could call the Allies together for a peace conference, suggest the establishment of a League of Nations, decide the future of the Austro-Hungarian Empire, group the liberated countries under a covenant of mutual defense, draw up another, similar covenant for the German states, found international organizations for the control of transport, trade and armaments, revise colonial legislation, provide higher education for colored peoples—in fact, make something real out of the League of Nations. Wells realized that beneath its war-torn surface, Europe was seething with the unrest that would force an outlet when fighting stopped—Great Britain and France were rent by the quarrel between reactionary and progressive elements, between aggressive nationalism and modern liberalism. He suspected the existence of secret agreements binding the allies. But his deep-rooted optimism arose once more from the ashes of his disappointed hopes. He believed in mankind, in the victory of common sense, with a faith as tough and hardy as a desert cactus.

He seems to have looked upon Wilson as the incarnation of Leblanc, that world-saving figure of whom he had dreamed on the eve of this war. He was perhaps the first to feel an enthusiasm that spread, later on, throughout Europe; the first to dream a dream that was taken up by millions of other anguished mortals. Seldom in the course of history has such unlimited confidence been bestowed on one single man. Disgust with the past, horror of the present, fear for the future—all these bore Wilson up as though the wings of the wind, carrying him higher than any other of the mighty ones of this world. The hopes of mankind shed a glow around him, like the aureole set by early painters behind the head of the Saviour. As an English historian has said, he seemed for a time to be a new Moses, who would "lead the nations towards the Promised Land where wars are forbidden and blockades unknown." When he came to Europe he was welcomed like Jesus Christ preaching the gospel of peace. (A tin-can Jesus Christ, said Clemenceau savagely.)

Some of Wells's friends claimed later that his letter provided a good deal of the material for Wilson's Fourteen Points. Wells himself did not remember if this had been so. He had thrust back his letter into the shadows of oblivion that covered all his dead dreams. But he kept on with his efforts to prevent a patched-up peace, a peace as badly planned as the war had been. "Peace is an empty cup that we can fill as we please," says a pamphlet issued by the preparatory committee of the League of Nations, to which Wells belonged. He pressed for the name to be altered to League of Free Nations. The adjective was tremendously important to him. It expressed the difference between Wells's outlook and the general tendency of that day, whose superficial optimism gave birth to the League of Nations. Wells did not believe that there could be any world-wide peace until revolutionary movements had taken place in all countries. These movements meant peace, in his view. When the Russian revolution first broke out, he persuaded Northcliffe to print an article by him in *The Times,* appealing to republican feeling throughout the world. The article caused a scandal. Society, and the army, which until then had looked upon Northcliffe as an ally, avoided him like the plague from that time forth. "There goes my earldom!" he whispered in Wells's ear.

The two men had drawn increasingly close together during the war. In its last year, Northcliffe was made Propaganda Minister, a newly created post. He summoned Wells to his magnificent headquarters, Crewe House—which, with its beautiful period furniture and the stately proportions of its rooms, seemed to have survived unaltered from the eighteenth century—and asked him to write some anti-German propaganda. Wells, moved by his instinct to improve the shining hour, began again to speak about his theory of social revolution; but Northcliffe interrupted him, saying in his low, confidential voice, "Isn't our sitting here social revolution enough for you?"

Just when Wells was thus entrusted with an official task, he brought out a booklet, *In the Fourth Year,* which made a vigorous attack on the whole principle of national sovereignty. The League of Free Nations must, he said, not only put an end to the new German imperialism, which was fighting so hard to gain possession of the earth, but also liquidate British imperialism and French imperialism, which possessed so great a part of the earth. The new international organization would have to be given authority over the army, navy, air force and armaments industry of every nation, and power to check all militarist propaganda and to suppress all incitement to war, as a threat of rebellion against the League of Nations. Until patriotism ceased to uphold the man in the street in his dislike for international control of armed forces, he could never be anything but a slave, helpless in face of threats from abroad; and peace could never be anything but an empty word, a name given to the pause that divided one war from the next.

It was with these distinctly unorthodox ideas in his mind that Wells became an official propagandist. The routine of propaganda consisted in having tracts distributed by secret agents, dropping leaflets by plane, and bringing out fake German newspapers. Wells insisted that the war aims should be set down on paper, as a beginning. A memorandum was drawn up, and submitted to a consultative committee. Wells's personal contribution to it was his energetic protest against the pseudo-parliamentary form to be given to the League of Nations, with votes conferred upon small nations which, in the event of any difference of opinion, would probably be drawn into the orbit of the great powers. The League of Nations was not born as yet. But Wells could already lay his finger on its essential weaknesses: the illusion of a so-called democratic vote, despite the overruling influence of the great powers; the maintenance of national sovereignty; and the lack of the military strength to enforce its decisions.

The war was creating a vast backwash. It had shattered old standards, uprooted past habits, jolted people's thoughts out of their rut. The prewar world had vanished forever. A will to peace had been born, fully conscious, for the first time, of how much there was to safeguard or to build up. Boundless hopes were rising now, as the war drew to an end. It was time to think in a new way, a big way. The superstate, the world state of which Wells had long dreamed, might become the reality of tomorrow. The expression "citizen of the world" came from his pen, a new name for the Samurai, guardian of the New Republic. Wells flung himself body and soul into the great illusion.

But in the day of victory his eyes were opened. He tells in his memoirs about that Armistice Day, when he mingled with the wildly excited crowds in London's flag-hung streets. Victory is a strong wine that clouds the brain. All doubts as to the wisdom of the nation's leaders were scattered to the four winds. The horror of useless bloodshed faded from the survivors' minds. Tears flowed easily. Resentment was concentrated on beaten Germany. Hang the Kaiser and make the Huns pay. The future was to be nothing but comfort and ease. Triumph had paralyzed the people's will power. The average man trusted to the fate that had brought him out of that nightmare war. Credulity hampered all constructive efforts. On that Armistice Day, Wells already saw how fragile the new international construction would be. He saw that people had "not even begun to suspect the real meaning of the project for a League of Free Nations." They had not begun to realize that peace has its price.

XVI

THE RACE BETWEEN EDUCATION
AND CATASTROPHE

BY 1921, WELLS had decided that the moral shock of the war might
not have been great enough to touch off the trigger of world revolution. But he felt none the less certain that to preserve the old system
of independent states would be to bring "disaster after disaster" upon
mankind, and perhaps to wipe out the human race completely. This
was to be the central theme of his work in years to come.

He came out of the war with a deeply troubled spirit. He knew, as
he said in a letter to a friend, that for many years to come, life would
consist chiefly of making a world, "or patching it up." Though he saw
the aim, he did not yet see how it could be achieved. He was like a
man shut in a dark room, seeing the ray of light that creeps in under
the door, and groping his way toward it. Mr. Britling had kindled a
flame of religious faith to guide him through darkness and despair.
Wells carefully tended that trembling light, which gleamed amid the
nightmares of wartime. *God: the Invisible King,* is the sequel to Mr.
Britling's discovery of the Presence. Wells said later that he could no
longer make out how much, in this theocratic phase of his life, had
been simple and genuine, and how much had been a matter of policy.
The Invisible King, as a matter of fact, is a very unorthodox God. In
turning to religion, Wells once declared that a Communist might have
accepted his God, as a metaphor. But that was just an interpretation
made up after the event, to lessen the importance of a stage that he
had left behind and now found embarrassing. During the time when
he was passionately seeking for certainties that evaded him, his re-

ligious fervor had a deep, somber seriousness. A bitter struggle was going on in him between traditional forms of belief and this new faith of his. This struggle was reflected in a novel, *The Soul of a Bishop,* which he published in 1917. This is one of the most completely forgotten of his books. He brought it out with the following comment: "A novel (with just a little love in it) about conscience and religion, and the real troubles of life." A man who has grown up in simple faith, undisturbed by the faintest doubt, becomes Bishop of an industrial diocese. A conflict arises in his mind between his personal faith and the hidebound tenets of the religion he professes. A strike shows how greedy and stiff-necked the employers are, and how little the Church can do to appease social unrest. He suddenly realizes that God does not dwell in the forms of religion, or in the magnificent cathedral; but he is more than ever sure that God exists. God appears to him over and over again in visions. Now of all human states of mind, the one most shut off from Wells, most foreign to him, was that of mystic rapture. The Bishop of Princhester's visions must surely be among the least convincing that ever found their way into creative literature. In order to explain these visionary states, Wells has recourse to a drug, administered to the Bishop by a mad doctor. He could describe lunar landscapes, bring Martians to life, but his imagination is strangely inadequate to the portrayal of religious ecstasy. The Bishop, after having renounced the Church and its rites in a sensational manner, declares that "faith is a tour de force" (Wells uses the French expression). And he brings off this tour de force. His God is the God of things to come. He is a new arrival. All the sorrows of humanity converge upon this God, who is to sweep away all kings and all national quarrels from the earth, and weld mankind into one great brotherhood. Wells discusses the theological arguments of the established churches in his usual direct, aggressive way, as though trying to beat down a political adversary. The world-wide brotherhood of the faithful, for which his hero pleads in the pulpit, is simply the Order of the Samurai in a rather different form. Its God remains Captain and King; the world republic under its aegis has become, in this theological phase of Wells's development, more vague and indistinct than Plato's Republic. Even when he makes an about-face, Wells carries with him part at least of his old loyalties and his old grudges. Even Wells the believer cannot forgive the Church for having once forced young Wells the atheist into a humiliating position. The Bish-

op's experiences tend to loosen rather than to strengthen religious ties.
"Are we still Christians?" his daughter asks him toward the end of
the book.

Wells saw all around him a marked slackening of traditional and
moral bonds, caused by wartime confusion. Mr. Huss, in *The Undying
Fire*, declares that God calls upon man to struggle against this confusion of mind. *The Undying Fire*, which came out two years after *The
Soul of a Bishop*, forms a kind of resumption, on another plane, of the
earlier work, whose poor literary quality its author himself admitted.
He had a special liking for this second version of his debate with God,
and ranked it among his best books. It is written with great care, deep
seriousness, and an occasional glint of mischief. He had already been
criticized for the monologues or dialogues into which he was apt to
launch his heroes, who expressed his views at great length for the
reader's benefit. *The Undying Fire* consists almost entirely of dialogue.
Wells thought this was a new departure. But the public wearied of
these endless discussions, and the book was severely handled by the
critics. Nevertheless, Wells kept his taste for the dialogue form of
novel, and returned to it, undaunted by several failures.

The Undying Fire is a modern adaptation of the Book of Job, of
which Wells was particularly fond; it harmonized with his underlying
optimism, his faith in man's final triumph over all ordeals. He even
used the names of the biblical figures in his novel, merely giving them
an anglicized form; and he followed the order of the original discussion. The modern man of Uz goes through all the afflictions of his
biblical namesake. The world is a place of suffering and injustice.
Nature is an old witch whose claws are stained with the blood of the
weak. Man's hand is turned against his fellows. But in the soul of
Job Huss there burns the undying fire that he calls God. He is the
headmaster of a boys' school, entrusted with "the greatest of human
tasks," that of educating the young. Like the Bishop, Huss comes face
to face with the vision of God—a thread of rainbow-colored light
above a crystal floor. A voice replies to his doubts, his sense of failure,
telling him that if he will take courage, victory shall be his at last—
however dark the night, however fierce the battle, however strange
and sad its end. "Only the courage to live upholds heaven and earth."

With this vaguely comforting observation, the personal God disap-
pears from Wells's work. He said later that *"The Undying Fire* was the
sunset of my divinity." Having arrived suddenly, at a moment of deep

distress, his heavenly Captain withdrew quietly, like a visitor smitten with shyness. Wells returned little by little, on tiptoe as it were, to the atheism of his youth. Not for some time did he openly repudiate his "period of hypocritical phraseology," as he called it. It had arisen out of the torment of war, and it filled him, afterward, with the same embarrassment as did the memory of his chauvinistic outbursts in the press. He felt that many readers had been led astray by this mood of his, and that it had turned him aside from his search for mankind's future path.

Between *The Soul of a Bishop* and *The Undying Fire* comes a long novel, planned on a very large scale, *Joan and Peter,* published in 1918. He subtitled it *The Story of an Education.* This is one of the novels in which he tried to hammer out everything that was occupying his thoughts for the time being—his spiritual and emotional perplexities, scattered memories of past years, events and episodes from other people's lives that had struck his imagination—and to bind all the varied elements into one compact whole. "But it is pathetically unfinished, like a Gothic cathedral," to quote his own words.

Joan and Peter takes a place beside *Tono-Bungay* in Wells's work. From the literary standpoint, it is one of his most careful pieces of writing. Its characters, carved in the round, live their own lives, severed from the author and his personal background. Through this independence of his Oswald Sydenham takes a special place among Wells's heroes. As a twenty-year-old naval lieutenant, during the bombardment of Alexandria, he threw a live shell overboard, to save his men's lives. The shell exploded in the air, and half Sydenham's face was blown away. He groped his way back to life with the Victoria Cross and a glass eye. Love was out of the question for him, and he went off to look for adventure in the still-bubbling caldron of darkest Africa. The girl he had been in love with married and had a son, Peter, and he became Peter's godfather. Peter's father is a sketch, or rather a caricature, of a type that Wells particularly hated: the writer, the aesthete, the agreeable egotist, tyrannical in his weakness, who can always make stronger characters give way to him. (A study of minor literary movements in Britain could be written by picking out these caricatures of men of letters from Wells's works—beginning with Mr. Magnet, in *Marriage,* and going on, by way of Aubrey Vair in the short story called "In the Modern Vein," or George Brumley, Lady Harman's admirer, to Rowland Palace in *Brynhild*.) Peter's father manages, at the last moment, to persuade his wife, whom he has deceived, not to leave him for Oswald Sydenham. He takes the disillusioned and regretful young woman off to Italy for a second honeymoon. During a sailing trip, when he stupidly and obstinately refuses to take shelter from a storm, they are both drowned in the bay of Capri.

Peter and a little orphaned girl who had been brought up with him —the illegitimate daughter of his mother's brother—come under the guardianship of Oswald Sydenham who is now home from Africa. Sydenham is wealthy, with plenty of time on his hands, and decides to give the children the best education that can be obtained.

Wells describes Peter's experiences in a private school—a setting that he had known of old—the scanty and mechanical teaching, the absurd punishments, and the tyranny that turned the older boys, by contagious example, into bullies. Sydenham tries in vain to discover a school where boys' minds can be trained for real life; he finds nothing but worn-out machinery through which flows a torrent of wasted youth. This part of the book, dealing with the defects of the educational system, grew to such inordinate length that Wells had to cut out whole chapters, describing Peter's experiences at school and university, before the manuscript took final shape. Peter is typical of a new generation, no longer restrained by moth-eaten beliefs and out-of-date conventions, and so exasperated by the social stalemate he sees around him, that the prospect of a general upheaval, on a scale sufficient to shake fixed ideas out of sclerotic brains, has no terrors for him. But though Peter stands as the representative of a change that is taking place, Wells gives him a strong individuality and a life of his own. The lad's emotional education comes to him through the short-lived experiments of an easily awakened sensuality. Soon, with his problems still unsolved, he is whirled into the war and into the Air Force. The book has striking pages about this young pilot who cannot quite overcome the fear that haunts him, the dread of the unknown, the ever present thought of death.

Peter crashes and is taken to a hospital, badly wounded and delirious. Like the dissident Bishop and the modern Job, he comes face to face with God. Wells's characteristic humor gets the upper hand of his religious seriousness, that earlier tour de force. Peter finds the Lord God, with some difficulty, in a small office at the far end of a huge building. It is the drabbest, grubbiest office imaginable, the unwashed windows darkened by cobwebs, the table scattered with dirty test tubes. The Lord God is an elderly gentleman whose thin, tired face has "an air of futile friendliness masking a fundamental indifference." To this indifferent God, Peter hotly proclaims his disgust at the ridiculous cruelty, the waste of life, the murderous lunacy that is driving a splendid world, a world good to live in, toward its final ruin. "You don't like it? Then change it," replies God wearily. "I leave you to work out your own salvation . . . why don't you exert yourself?"

Wells's faith in a better world had outlived other beliefs that were now crumbling—belief in the spontaneous generation of common sense, in the victory of scientific certainties, in the almost automatic effect of progress. "Belief in inevitable progress is the end of progress," he said more than twenty years later. The vision of a heavenly captain who could rally the hosts of his followers to save mankind, had faded too, making way for the figure of this Old Experimenter, glimpsed through the mists of fever, who demanded that men should themselves make the effort that would bring order out of chaos.

While writing *Joan and Peter,* Wells was readjusting his ideas, revising his notions as to how mankind could be saved. "This immense disaster that has come upon the world is nothing more or less than the failure of education," says Oswald Sydenham, bringing the book to a close. These words pointed out Wells's future path. His great novel, which had only moderate success, represents one of those discussions with himself, one of those adjustments, that it was his custom to carry out in public.

The end of the war had left him with a sense of failure, as poisonous as an abscess. The gap that yawned between the certainties of which he had been the spokesman, and the results actually achieved when peace came, was so wide that he could not but be cruelly disappointed. He soon saw through "the pseudo-settlement of 1919," as he calls it in his memoirs. He became indignant, angrily outspoken, insisting that wartime demands should be pressed and wartime promises kept. But as an exasperated critic, he stood alone in an atmosphere of general enthusiasm, where the self-seeking were well pleased and the idealistic were momentarily blinded. He protested with an energy inspired, perhaps unawares, by the uneasy conscience of a man who had helped, in all good faith, to put across what he now saw to have been a mere travesty of peace. He was a man who could not live in a state of turmoil without trying to find a way out, or at any rate to discover what caused it. He gave at the end of *Joan and Peter* what he took to be one of the most important causes: the disaster of the war and the breakdown of the peace resulted, he declared, from the failure of the educational system.

Unlike Oswald Sydenham, who tried in vain to find a suitable school for his ward Peter, Wells, just before World War I, discovered a modern teacher and a model school for his own sons. From the day he first met the "great schoolmaster," Sanderson, Wells followed his experiments, his successes, and his difficulties, with the most enthusiastic interest. He was not in the habit of overestimating the significance of individual efforts or isolated ventures. It is typical of him that only one experiment, that of Oundle School, should have received his special attention. He never closely followed the career of any individual, but he did write one biography—that of Sanderson. In it he gives an arresting portrait of a passionate man, violent in temperament, stuttering and yet vehement in speech, a born educator, fundamentally idealistic, but endowed with great common sense and a felicitous power of giving practical shape to his ideas. Above all, he shows the progress of certain notions, developing through this man's temperament. He shows Sanderson up in arms against the leaders of the young who "led them backwards." He shows him at work, introducing scientific, experimental methods, developing a collective instead of a competitive system. Sanderson used to declare that Nemesis lay in wait for those who tried to live for themselves alone. Wells also showed him preparing future administrators of the British Empire to take a fresh view of the duties that awaited them, a view based on the spirit of co-operation and on unselfish devotion to their task.

During the last years of his life, Sanderson became more and more convinced (doubtless influenced in this by Wells) that unless educational methods were revised, it would be very difficult to alter human ideals. In his last lecture, he made an appeal—rendered all the more moving by the fact that almost as soon as he had finished speaking he died from a heart attack—to all brainworkers, and first and foremost to all scientists, to come out of their seclusion and devote themselves to setting up a new economic and social system for the world. As Wells said, he and Sanderson were united in the belief that the average human life, based on sterile motives, "stupidly cruel and cruelly stupid," was not worth living, except as a necessary step in the progress toward a more noble form of existence.

This problem of spiritual evolution seemed to Wells to be particularly urgent. The World War had proved the interdependence of men, for good and for evil. A further conflict could only bring universal disaster, universal, blind destruction that would not spare even the babies in their cradles. Peace, like war, could be nothing if not worldwide; prosperity must be universal prosperity. But it was impossible for men to have peace and prosperity in common without having "historical ideas in common."

Amid his postwar bewilderment—while he was carrying on endless arguments at committee meetings about the need to establish peace on a broad basis, to drive it home as a reality, into the conscience of mankind; while innumerable conferences were being held for the purpose of founding League of Nations Unions in the different countries—he realized that most disagreements arose from the fact that each person concerned "seemed to have read a different piece of history, or no history at all." Urged on by his need to take a hand, by the sense of responsibility that was so typical of him, Wells concentrated his attention on one immediate aim. History, he decided, must no longer be considered as a list of wars and kings, a series of events taking place in separate countries, but as an adventure in which all mankind had shared. He summed up his ideas in a pamphlet entitled *History is One,* published in 1919. He expected that these ideas would be put into practice. Meanwhile, he went on making notes. He suggested to various postwar pacifist organizations, and in particular to the Research Committee of the League of Nations Union, that they should draw up and publish a history of the human race. His private notes grew more and more bulky, for demonstration purposes. His idea was greeted with general approval—the Platonic approval that is so readily meted out to big ideas. He began to lose patience. With his usual eagerness to follow up an idea, he found the delay maddening. He could see the absurdity of his insistence about a work that was right outside his own line, but he was bent upon explaining to someone else, some ideal historian or group of historians, what he meant by this great historical synthesis. His plan was already drawn up, but he still felt that it was not for him to prepare such a book by himself. He was a novelist. He had his public, which might easily desert him if he wandered off into a path that was not his own. The work would be long and tiresome; there was not much money in it. He was barely able, at present, to keep up his standard of comfort. His savings had melted away during the war. But he was haunted by his new idea. Finding nobody to take it up, he decided to tackle it all alone, even if he had to make sacrifices to carry it through.

A woman had come into his life, one so full of vitality that it seemed as if the world had been created for her. She had a memory that registered everything in bright, distinct images, a concrete imagination that never shrank from facts. "Don't you see?" she would ask the man she loved. And he saw things as if for the first time, in quite a new light. Wells had found what he had been looking for all his life, a woman who would complete him. But the meeting with her came too late. His life was no longer quite his own. Jane had taken root in it so deeply that to tear her out would mutilate his own existence. "Our alliance was indissoluble; we had intergrown and become parts of each other," he says in his autobiography.

The indissoluble quality in their marriage was due to Jane's limitless understanding and to her capability, which was most impressive to a man like Wells, who was apt to be overwhelmed by everyday trifles. She was the delightful friend, as well as the mother, of his sons. She was the perfect housewife, relieving him of all household cares, and setting things to rights with almost maternal patience when, as often happened, he came to cross purposes with the people or the objects around him. From the very first, she had taken his business affairs into her firm hands. Her death left him childishly, pathetically at a loss concerning the management of his own fortune. She handled his translation rights in foreign countries; she was thoroughly discouraging to any male or female admirers to whom he gave vague promises of this or that; she threshed out his contracts with the exactitude and vigor of a shrewd business executive. No literary agent could have done it better, as he said. She began by typing his manuscripts for him. For the first twenty years of their married life she continued to act as his secretary. She always read his proofs, bending over the sheets with the set, serious expression that sometimes hardened her face into sharp outlines. Her taste was surer than his, her literary judgment better, her artistic sense more delicate. In close touch with the best literary circles of her day, the little biology student had been quick to respond to its aims, its striving after perfection of style. She was the sternest critic of anything hurried, slapdash or commonplace in her husband's work. He was so much interested by what he had to say, that he often rushed ahead, announcing a discovery or shouting a warning, without regard for style. He himself declared that he had to "overwork, with all the penalties of overwork in loss of grace and finish," in order to get his work done at all.

She liked subtle psychology, delicate shades of feeling, hesitant words choked by emotion, echoing silence. She admired minute descriptions of people and things, literary jeweler's work where detail was lovingly displayed. Her favorite authors were among those that Wells held in the greatest contempt and who, for their part, looked upon him as a barbarian. She greatly admired Proust, whose works her husband compared, to their disadvantage, with a twenty-year-old store catalogue or a provincial newspaper. Most of all she liked Katherine Mansfield, whose form of expression, with its vague, broken contours, she felt to be nearest to her own feelings and most easily approachable.

At the back of Jane Wells's mind lay the desire, not fully conscious perhaps, but keen, to build up a life of her own. This desire reflected all that life had denied her in the way of wholehearted affection, constancy and faithfulness. The sacrifices to which she had forced herself, the bitter feelings she had concealed, the humiliations she had bravely thrust behind her—all these demanded to be compensated by spiritual independence. She thought she would be able to find compensation as a writer. The atmosphere of creative tension in which she lived had given her that sensitiveness that amateurs often mistake for the gift of literary expression. Although she was so clear-sighted, she must have had illusions about her own talents. She achieved a style that her husband described as "delicately characteristic"; but as he also says, she was not driven to self-expression by any uncontrollable urge from within. In an age when letter writing flourished, she would probably have been content to write letters, which, because she was so observant, would have been precious documents. Her wish to assert herself was so strong that she persisted in writing short stories, and sending them to magazines through agencies, or under false names, in order not to gain advantage by using her own. Catherine Wells, the unfulfilled writer, was perhaps the only illusion that H. G.'s wife ever allowed herself in the whole of her life. A novel, never finished but never relinquished, was her permanent, secret retreat. Yet in her everyday life at her husband's side she had, perhaps without quite realizing it, succeeded in creating a place of her own, asserting her own personality.

She had done this not only by her unfailing competence—which, taken singly, would have wearied even those to whom it was the greatest blessing—but also by the atmosphere of gaiety that she maintained just as skillfully as she coped with day-to-day problems. Very few people noticed that her gaiety was somehow forced, that her apparently flighty humor had something deliberate about it. "If only she would stop being funny!" exclaimed Dorothy Richardson, writing about the time when the Wells couple was just beginning to rise in the world. Indeed, it was neither an irrepressibly merry nature nor a special way of looking at things, that gave rise to her drollery.

By mutual agreement, Wells and his wife had put their relationship on a humorous footing from the very first, as soon as they discovered that they were sexually ill-attuned to each other. They thought that a gay atmosphere would do more than anything else to reduce emotional complications to a minimum. For Jane it became, too, a constructive element in her life—like her well-run home, with its ready and apparently casual hospitality. Besides, her inventive turn of mind helped her to social success. Wells mentions the party games she used to get up, from charades to improvised comedies and dramas. In *Mr. Britling* he describes the big barn converted into a ballroom, where Jane could indulge her love of dancing to her heart's content, and the cupboards full of the brightly colored materials and strangely assorted garments that she collected to use at fancy-dress balls or comic performances. Her greatest triumphs were the charades, which she often prepared in secret, under her husband's eye, or sometimes with the help of her sons. The playful streak that runs through every grown-up mind, especially if the grownup is British, lent Wells's guests a childish gusto, a disconcerting eagerness to vie with each other at these entertainments. Almost every famous figure of the period visited their home sooner or later; and all of these celebrities took their turn in the charades in which Jane's inventive skill rose to its greatest heights. Philip Snowden, solemn as ever in the purple robes of Rome, Arnold Bennett, Noel Coward, or Charlie Chaplin himself, as Noah. Amid the laughter that greeted their appearance, none was so loud or cheerily youthful as Wells's own.

Even he perhaps did not understand quite how much lay beneath Jane's humor, her trick of twisting reality just enough to turn it into caricature, her love of dressing up, and the valiant gaiety that was her armor against malicious gossip and, above all, against pity. Perhaps he only suspected, without, in his masculine egotism, frankly admitting the fact, that there was something hidden behind what he himself called the "smiling mask" that she turned toward the outside world. It was this essential part of herself that Catherine Wells tried in vain to express in her short stories and in her unfinished novel. She was too self-controlled, too deeply entrenched in her reserve, to indulge in even partial literary confession. Imprisoned in her own armor, she did not even allow herself to drop hints or to set out her confidences in a disguised form. But every one of her stories or poems is written around a central idea which is either bitterness or melancholy resignation. She dwells on the loneliness of human beings, with their heavy-hearted loves; the loneliness of gardens on summer nights, when a woman waits for the sound of a footstep that she knows she will never hear; or lovers drowning themselves in a moonlit lake because they are too poor. She tells about unfulfilled dreams of a too perfect house or too beautiful clothes, or about a jewel that a child drops and loses. Through all her writing runs a sense of waste—wasted gifts that no one accepts, or wasted love, set upon a goal it can never hope to attain.

These longings and this bitterness she kept to herself, closely guarded secrets. To the outside world she seemed invulnerable. She had the calm that comes from a sense of permanence, the security of an assured position. From the very first she had taken up an attitude of indulgence, tinged with a great deal of humor and a little contempt. "She managed to sustain her belief that I was worth living for, and that was a harder task, while I made my way through a tangle of moods and impulses that were quite outside her instinctive sympathy." It is in this rather embarrassed sentence that Wells sums up his wife's personal tragedy.

The invasion of H. G.'s life by his new love was probably the hardest of all Catherine Wells's trials. She had always found patience to wait for her husband to come back to her after absences caused by deeply or not-so-deeply passionate attractions, brief or comparatively lengthy explorations of the unexpected or the picturesque. The curiosity of literary circles, and his own selfish taste for comfort, brought considerable publicity to his escapades. His new love affair was particularly unfitted for secrecy. The young girl had all the fierce independence that marked the emancipated young women of her generation. She felt strong enough to defy the drawbacks and inconveniences of a liaison such as theirs. Wells's life was split into two parts. To all those who were in the know, the liaison was recognized and widely discussed. The fact that Wells was able to establish it on this basis, coming to terms with scandal, as it were, gives the measure of his fame. It also gives the proof of Jane's skill, her flawlessly tactful behavior in a situation that required exceptional self-control in everyday life.

Charades still went on at Easton Glebe. Jane's comic inventions still called forth bursts of laughter. The roses still came to rich bloom in the garden. Now and again the master of the house went away, but the calm gaiety that reigned in the country retreat, the determined, smiling little face of the hostess, seemed to deny the existence of any painful secret.

The ties between Wells and his wife were still further strengthened by a work that they shared together.

He had discussed his plan with Jane. She had agreed that he could afford to give up a year or two to this hard and unprofitable task. So he flung himself into it as though it were a great adventure. This enterprise, which he began in a spirit of self-sacrifice and carried on through sheer, unremitting hard work, had a happy end, as comforting as a story of rewarded virtue. Contrary to his own expectation and to his publisher's cautious skepticism, this *Outline of History* proved to be one of his biggest successes, a world-wide best seller.

He had asked certain friends, specialists in various branches of history, to go over the manuscript with him. Despite these precautions, other historians raised objections to certain passages of the book, criticizing its construction and disparaging the achievement of its author. The welcome it received throughout the world was a sufficient retort to all this quibbling. Once again Wells had been in such close sympathy with the general public that his need to shed light upon the vestiges of the past had proved to represent a need for knowledge that was felt in every country in the world.

The Outline of History was, to some extent, another conversation between Wells and himself, an answer to the questions raised by his own curiosity, a way of solving his own perplexities—his curiosity, his perplexities, were those of the average man in every country.

Only one of the fears with which Wells had started this work proved to be justified—he did indeed lose his following as a novelist and his contact with the literary critics. This loss was not soon made good. Since then, he declared when writing his autobiography, he had vanished forever from the horizon of the regular novel reader. This result probably arose partly from a weariness that had descended upon him and was preparing him unawares to give up writing the usual kind of novel. When he made up his mind to devote himself to *The Outline of History,* he may well have been driven by an unconscious need to escape from the beaten track. The mere fact that after so much success he could give up his literary work without a pang, seems to show that he was already drifting away from it even before this chance of trying his hand at a new task. In later years he felt that he had left it altogether behind him. The autobiography speaks of his novel-writing past as of a chapter that was closed forever. In fact, he submitted to this deluge of general ideas, which had always threatened to submerge him, as though he had actually been longing for it. He welcomed the new possibilities that lay before him, like a man giving up a well-paid but not entirely satisfying job in order to turn, at last, to some branch of work that he really enjoys.

That Wells could drop out of the literary field in this way seems to show a fundamental lack of interest in imaginative writing; it is a negation of all his past career. Nothing could be more characteristic than the pleasure he drew from the success of *The Outline of History.* It was his smiling boast that the book had sold more copies in America than any other except the Bible. It put him on firm ground from the financial point of view. He used to speak of it as though it were, at one and the same time, an adventure that had happened to someone else, and an inheritance that had come to him as a surprise, setting him free from money worries and permitting him to write for his own pleasure.

The guiding idea that inspired his *Outline of History* is summed up in the last paragraph: "Human history becomes more and more a race between education and catastrophe." His optimism triumphs, here, over his forebodings of possible disaster. From mankind's past, with its ruins, the squandering of riches, the useless bloodshed, the wounds inflicted by man upon man, is to emerge the man of tomorrow, the student-teacher of the universe. He will take over the management of a world that will be "unified, armed with the secret powers of the atom and with a knowledge as yet beyond dreaming."

Wells saw the mighty and manifold powers of evil, incorrigible as ever, stirring again to provoke fresh disasters; but he believed that they would be held in check by a still greater power—the free and growing intelligence of mankind. It was this faith in the triumph of man's common sense that sustained him throughout his life, deserting him only at the very end. It rose again, victorious, after each successive collapse of his hopes. It hovered over a mangled universe. Seldom can faith have been so stubborn and triumphed over such disastrous rebuffs. Although Wells's compliant fellow countrymen looked upon him as an unbelieving rebel, there was really something deeply religious about his belief in mankind—in man's intelligence, perfectibility, and thirst for knowledge. The nobler existence of which he dreamed was to be an uninterrupted process of education, continuing right through life.

While he was working on the *Outline,* his former passion for natural science began to stir again within him. A good deal of the book (about one-sixth) is devoted to the evolution of the prehistoric world. His enthusiasm for the tremendous adventure of science, which had revealed the immemorial past of the human race, extended also to its patient, unselfish representatives. He believed that men whose brains were trained to carry out strenuous research work, who were in the habit of arriving at practical results, would show greater skill than others in unraveling the tangled skein of social problems. He looked upon scientists as the embodiment of human intelligence, and contrasted their clear minds and their courage with the muddleheadedness and love of compromise displayed by party politicians. It was a long time before he lost this juvenile vision of a righteous man quelling confusion, driving out all that was base and greedy—a St. George armed with laboratory apparatus. As the years went by, he must have noticed that contact with science did not, in itself, suffice to change a man or to purge him of his defects. He must have seen abundant proof that scientists were just as liable as writers to be swept into the current of mass emotion, to give way to political passion, to help in the betrayal of mankind. But curiously enough, he never admitted this disillusionment. His belief in scientists died a silent death.

The Outline of History proved so successful that after it had sold two million copies in English, not to mention translations in every imaginable language, Wells brought out an abridged edition. The immense popularity of these two books had a tonic effect on him. It revived his self-confidence, which, as he remarked with the condescending irony that he often turned against himself, had "a great power of resurrection." A new path opened ahead of him, broad and straight. He conceived the ambitious plan of preparing a work to which he gave a high-sounding (and borrowed) name: "The Bible of Civilization." He developed the idea in a series of lectures written for use in America but never delivered and which he published in a little book entitled *The Salvaging of Civilization*. History, he declared, was only one of the subjects with which it was essential for man to be acquainted. To secure the communion of ideas, the heritage of identical concepts, from which alone, in his view, any constructive future could arise, the study of history must be supplemented by that of every other branch of learning. *The Outline of History* was to be completed by an outline of biology and an outline of political and social science. After announcing this principle, Wells, encouraged by success, set to work to follow it up without waiting for other people to take the lead. In preparing his outline of biology, which he called *The Science of Life,* he was helped by his eldest son, who had become a professor of biology, and by Julian Huxley, grandson of the great Professor Huxley of South Kensington days.

The Science of Life came out in 1930. It was closely followed by the outline of sociology, to which Wells gave the title of *The Work, Wealth and Happiness of Mankind*. This third part of the new education was, he said, in an even less advanced state than the history of biology—less developed, yet even more urgent and necessary.

The third of his outlines, like the first, was written not only for the reader's benefit, but for that of the author as well. It was, again, an answer to certain questions that he put to himself. But they were questions arising from a complex state of puzzlement, and the facts were capable of varied interpretation. His *Outline of History* had been pervaded by his general views on historical evolution, on the progress of events that tended to unify the world. The facts of biology had given a firm framework to his *Science of Life,* which was based on indisputable scientific certainties. The outline of sociology is an attempt to explore a region where confusion still reigns, where the too familiar lies alongside a vast no man's land, where mysterious upheavals are apt to take place, and where the relationship of cause and effect is still a matter for violent debate. Ill-fated attempts at collaboration were made and abandoned before the material was finally assembled. The book came to definite shape only after fierce arguments, broken contracts, and a partly finished version that had been rejected or completely revised. Its different sections are sewn together, as it were, with stitches that are not quite invisible. Its lack of unity is also due to the fact that in it Wells is no longer describing the past, but writing about a transformation that is going on before our very eyes, a continual progression whose end is uncertain, like a river that flows swiftly on, eating away its banks and silting up its estuary.

Neither *The Science of Life* nor *The Wealth, Work and Happiness of Mankind* was to meet with as much success as *The Outline of History*. The lively curiosity that had marked the first postwar years had by now given way to weary apathy. The spread of general ideas immediately after the war had been followed by a return to private worries, to the selfish outlook forced upon people by the increasing difficulties of everyday life. The technical nature of the outline of biology was bound to narrow down the circle of its readers; the third outline led up "almost in spite of itself," as Wells said, to views so advanced that they displeased some of the people who had enjoyed the *Outline of History*. What Wells liked about the book was the originality of its plan, which represented a more vigorous effort of co-ordination than he had made before. He quite realized how ambitious was this effort, this first attempt to give a complete picture of mankind at work, at play, or idle.

The book reflects the doubts and misgivings of a whole epoch. Only a generation earlier, life had been easy to understand. Wells and his contemporaries had been born into a world whose inhabitants went from the cradle to the grave in an atmosphere of complete security. The economic and sociological upheavals of the following years took these people, whose minds had been set in the mold of that security, completely by surprise. The men of the late nineteenth century found themselves in much the same situation as the population of Pompeii and Herculaneum when the river of fire and the flood of ashes overwhelmed them at their peaceful labors. But these later men survived their political earthquakes and financial eruptions. Wells's book may be said to mirror their survival. It contains biographical sketches of certain great financiers—from the amazing figure of Hetty Green, the very symbol of monopoly, to John D. Rockefeller—which shed a revealing light on the shaky moral code prevailing in big business, the unsound situation created by heaping up unproductive wealth, or, in a minority of cases, the stimulus given to progress by the vast possibilities of the modern world.

The dominant idea in his *Outline of History* had been that the world had, as it were, shrunk in size, owing to the abolition of the distance factor and the formation of ever larger groups of human beings—beginning with the family and leading, through the tribe, to the federation of states. This evolution must logically culminate in the unity of the whole world. The guiding principle of his third outline was that of an ever growing interdependence of nations in the economic field. During the age of security, it points out, there had been men, communities, and countries that were self-sufficient. But in the present epoch of great international exchanges, the everyday needs of the individual were supplied from the four corners of the world. Technical progress knew no frontiers. The simultaneous arrival, and practical development, of certain inventions in different parts of the globe was enough to show that all the human race had something to contribute. Social progress, the improvement of working conditions, could not be regarded as an isolated problem, either. Man did not take kindly to work, and social history was, in great measure, the record of successive attempts to make him submit to it, or rather, the record of some men's attempts to force other men to work. From the days of captured and enslaved enemies, or serfs, up to modern times, men had never ceased to pursue this aim. Gradually, over a period of about twenty-five centuries, the old system, servitude and tyranny, had yielded, step by step, to the substitution of money for other methods of constraint.

Neither this unification of method, nor the ever strengthening organization of the working-class forces, was to lead the world into unity; and unity remained, in Wells's view, the highest aim of human society. All through *The Work, Wealth and Happiness of Mankind,* written in 1930-31, there runs a subdued note of apprehension which is rarely found in his writings. His mind was visited by flashes of perception that inspired him to make forecasts which nothing seemed, at the moment, to justify. He stressed the alarming and unprecedented instability of economic interactions. He analyzed the threat of disaster that was overshadowing the world, saying that if Soviet Russia met with success and began to prosper, or even if it only managed to "survive and give a semblance of success," the "insurrectional tension of the Atlantic peoples" would increase and the resistance of capitalist circles might harden into the beginnings of a panic. He feared that there might be a conflict between the brutal elements among the wealthy section of society and the brutal elements among the poor section. The wealthy brutes, with something of the gangster in their nature, might resort to illegal violence. They would try to find a strong man who could seize power and keep order among the embittered, threatening masses of workers. Reasonable men, with constructive minds, would be caught in "a cross-fire of misunderstanding, suspicion, panic and class hatred." In this book, which came out in 1932, Wells adds, "The age of dictators and popular 'saviours' is on its way."

Despite these fears, he clung, with his unconquerable faith, to the possibility that a collective consciousness might stir in enlightened minds, and that man, seeing his knowledge, his powers and his possibilities increasing, would pass to the next stage, "co-ordinating his knowledge and systematizing his future power" in order to adapt them to a definite purpose. In Wells's view, the light of human thought sheds its beams unfalteringly over the chaos of the modern world. The mind, like a lighthouse, sends messages through the darkness and watches for the answers that come from other lighthouses, star scattered across the seething ocean below.

XVII

RUSSIA IN THE SHADOWS AND AMERICA IN THE LIMELIGHT

WELLS HIMSELF SAID that Russia had always exerted an almost magical sway over his imagination. Yet his character offered no clue as to why he felt attracted by that immense mass of contradictions, the soul of Russia. He was not a man to linger in the twilight of emotions; he hastened toward the broad day of self-awareness; introspection soon wearied him. Neither did he care to pause for long on the threshold of his ideological conflicts; he would bring his arguments out onto the public platform while they were still brand new. The world as he saw it was a solid construction, with no holes and corners for northern mists to wreathe around in. His habits, even his idiosyncrasies, were in strong contrast to the indecision and exurberance of the Slav nature. His sidewise smile discounted excessive emotion, total surrender to a personality or an idea. Even at times of the most vehement self-committal, he stood as it were a little apart from himself, a detached and mocking observer. His impersonal sense of humor, with its tinge of cruelty, was a safeguard against the temptation to take himself too seriously. He declared that he did not like Dostoevski or Tolstoy and hated "the epileptic temperament"; he was, in fact, "the antithesis of a Slav." He even had his share of that obscure feeling of superiority that leads the British to look upon Slavs as charming, backward children rather than adults.

But the attraction did exist. It may have been an attraction of opposites, but it seems rather to have been the urge toward something irritating, yet familiar, the yearning after a lost communion, the search for an impossible fulfillment, like a dream forgotten on waking. A cord vibrated in him, as though independently, against his will.

In the period before World War I, British travelers seldom ventured into Russia, whose frontiers were guarded by a figure never seen elsewhere in those days—the passport official. Russia was not only off the beaten track, it was practically outside the European community.

Wells went there for the first time in 1914, arriving when winter was still at its height. He was vividly impressed by the barbaric grandeur of what he saw—the wild landscape; the vast plains covered with sparkling snow; the roads, full of potholes beneath their white surface; the villages, whose wooden shacks huddled on the ground below the greenish domes of their churches; the streets of St. Petersburg, fringed with brilliantly lit black-and-gold frontages; Moscow, with the mighty, red walls of the Kremlin and its cluster of gilded domes. In his novel, *Joan and Peter,* the hero, visiting St. Petersburg, feels the whole pressure of the north, with its hunger, its frozen savagery; and Wells tells himself that here are the boundaries of humanity. He is surprised by the number of oriental costumes in the Moscow streets, and especially by the crowd of Chinese. From here to Vladivostok stretches all Russia and all Asia. To north and south, east and west, lies an endless stretch of territory. Coming of an island people, he feels the pressure of this mass of firm ground, this solid earth.

Sunset over Moscow—the houses gleam purple between patches of snow; the river twists like a silver eel through the crimson city; the gilt crosses on the painted, onion-shaped domes point up into the glowing sky and glimmer like pale flames on the horizon. Oswald Sydenham, watching this, feels himself nearer to an understanding of Dostoevski; he sees Holy Russia as "a sort of epileptic genius among nations." He realizes, too, that Christianity, for Russians, means the brotherhood of man. Peter, who stands beside him as the typical representative of a prematurely embittered generation, materialistic and disillusioned, sees only the familiar realities that lie beneath this picturesque surface, the dull tragedy of Russia, akin to the dull comedy of his own country.

Wells was greatly struck by the sitting of the Duma that he attended in the old Potemkin Palace. The council chamber, a big glasshouse transformed for this purpose, was dominated by a huge portrait of the Czar, which attracted his attention first of all. A vacant face, four times life-size, topped a uniformed figure standing four square in cavalry boots, just above the head of the president of the Duma. This portrait seemed to Wells to be an insult, a challenge to the self-respect of the Russian people; it seemed to be saying: "You, and all the empire, exist for *me*."

Though he stayed only a short time, Wells realized what a corrupt, oppressive system was weighing on Russia, supported by the outdated authority of indolence and dishonesty. Oswald Sydenham meditates on the comparison between Russia and Great Britain that his ward suggests to him, seeing a closer parallel between those two countries than between either of them and France, Italy, America, Germany, or any other great political system in the world. Russia was like a landlocked Great Britain. Great Britain was like Russia on an island and on all the oceans of the globe. Both were striving to express themselves, to pursue their aims, by means of forms and symbols which were steadily losing their value. "And each appeared to be moving inevitably towards failure and confusion."

While in Moscow, Wells saw performances of Chekhov's *Three Sisters* and of *Hamlet,* at the Art Theatre. They were given by a perfectly trained company with the help of excellent stage equipment, and attained a dramatic vigor that far outstripped the possibilities of any London theater. "In untidy, slushy, sprawling Moscow shone this diamond of co-operative effort and efficient organization. It set Oswald revising certain hasty generalizations about the Russian character." * Wells's attention was caught, too, by the audience, which consisted chiefly of young people, critical, alert, and passionately interested. He felt that their attitude toward art was more personal than that of their British contemporaries. His brief voyage of discovery made such an impression on him that he asked Sanderson to engage a Russian teacher at Oundle. This was the first time Russian had been taught in an English public school. Wells's sons thus learned the language in their early years, and the elder of them acted as interpreter for his father.

When the Russian revolution broke out, Wells first of all looked

* It is curious to recall that at one of these performances, Wells was watching the work of a fellow countryman. The *Hamlet* was "Gordon Craig's fantastic setting— which Moscow in her artistic profusion could produce when London was too poor to do so," as Wells comments, and which had by that time been in the repertory of the theater for two years.

upon it as heralding the collapse of the monarchist system—the sytem
for which he nourished a purely personal hatred—in every country,
particularly in his own. He managed to persuade Northcliffe to print
in *The Times,* in March 1917, an appeal to republican feeling
throughout the world. The letter scandalized official circles. Northcliffe himself was appalled at the effect it produced. In 1920, Wells
went out to Russia again. This was an act of deliberate courage. A
nightmare of bloodstained terrorism was oppressing the world of
stability. Military intervention had turned out to be a costly failure.
But economic forces were banding together to oppose a system that
threatened their domination. Moral forces were rallying to oppose the
man with the knife between his teeth. It was felt that a burst of general indignation might drive out the evil spirit. At that very moment
Wells accepted Kamenev's invitation to visit Russia. He accepted it like
a challenge.

His first impression was one of utter and probably irremediable
collapse. Ruin, he wrote, was the primordial fact in Russia, a terrible
reality that could not be hidden. But he was quick to understand that
the revolution was something that had happened "among the ruins
and because of the ruins."

Like everyone who set out to visit Russia, he had been warned
before leaving home that he would be, to some extent, the prisoner of
a police system. He found that he was able to go around freely and
to talk quite frankly with people. He collected stories bearing on the
details of the Russian breakdown. With memories of his first visit
still fresh in his mind, he could understand how, under the fearful
strain of war, the worm-eaten fabric of the State had crumbled and
fallen like a house of cards. But the outdated governmental system
could not be saddled with the entire blame for the immense devasta-
tion. The British Admiralty, "perhaps from mere cowardice," had
failed to come to Russia's help when she was exhausted. After the collapse of the Russian power, a torrent of violence had been let loose
over the country. In this reign of lawlessness and bloodshed, the Bolsheviks alone had been able to set up a semblance of authority. The
resistance they met all over the world had prevented any attempt at
consolidating their position. "The vindictive French creditor and the
imbecile British journalist" were just as much to blame for this distress,
these death pangs, as any Bolshevik, declared Wells.

However, what he saw in Russia did little to awaken his sympathy for the new regime. He had always considered Marx to be "the worst type of bore." During this trip his passive objections were transformed into active hostility. He noted the ignorance of the Russian leaders, their lack of training for their task. He disliked their clumsy propaganda, of which he had at least one personal example. He was taken to visit a school at Petrograd. The children who were studying English literature began to extol the merits of one writer, and one alone—himself. He became as furious as he always did when anyone took him for a fool. He swore that never again would he go any place where his visit had been announced beforehand. He was disgusted, too, by the defects of Russian bureaucracy. He stormed because he had to waste eighty hours in order to obtain an hour and a half of conversation with Lenin. Most of all, he was repelled by the younger Bolsheviks. "I dislike the type actively," he wrote later on. In an angry mood he once declared that he had no use for the "Revolutionary of the Communist placard type, that pithacoid Proletarian, dishevelled and semi-nude." But despite his private misgivings, he gave the Soviet leaders the benefit of his fundamental honesty. He was still feeling a secret annoyance when, after the maddening delay, he came face to face with Lenin.

It was a strange meeting that took place between the instigator of a gigantic revolutionary experiment, with his crushing weight of responsibility, and Wells with his aggressive curiosity—between the man who was already very sick, and soon to die, and the British traveler, with his insatiable energy and his machine-gun fire of questions. It was Wells's pugnacious doubt, its force doubled by his fear of being fooled by Bolshevik propaganda, which dominated the interview. To the chapter of his book in which he tells about it, Wells gives the title, "The Dreamer of the Kremlin," which minimizes the importance of the encounter. He was resolutely on his guard, but Lenin's personal appearance shook his inner defenses. Wells was astonished at the man's small stature, the simplicity of his words and gestures, and his free and easy manner. With a quick movement, Lenin pushed aside the books that were heaped on his table, and propped his elbow on the space thus cleared. He sheltered his stricken eye with his hand. But in the shadow of his fingers there shone a gleam of lively curiosity. At the moment of the interview Wells felt, as usual, more interest in general problems than in the man sitting opposite to him. He was bubbling with a sense of immediacy, overflowing with the impressions that he had collected during his trip.

The talk was nearly all about the replacement of peasants and factory hands by intensive agricultural methods and modern machinery.
Lenin, like his visitor, was a man who could concentrate enthusiastically on one subject. What interested him most just then was the idea
of transforming Russia, step by step, into a great industrial storehouse.
He had flung himself—with the energy of a young man, said Wells—
into the study of a subject that was quite new to him, the possibilities
of electrification in Russia. Wells thought it ridiculous for a man to
be making plans for the distant future when heaped-up ruins were
lying all around him. They seemed to be talking at cross purposes.
Wells was thinking only about the difficulties inherited from the past.
Lenin, who knew himself to be a very sick man, was thinking only
of things that would endure. "Our minds were tuned to different
keys," Wells said later. Seeing the skeptical smile on his visitor's face,
Lenin smiled too, with serene confidence. "Come back in ten years
from now, and you will see," were his farewell words to Wells.

Not until long afterward did Wells grasp the full significance
of this interview. When he looked back and considered Lenin's lifework across a vista of years, his personal memories took clearer shape
and impressions that he had registered unawares stood out boldly
from their shadowy background. He began, he said, to realize for
the first time what a remarkable part Lenin had played in history;
although he had a horror of so-called Great Men and their influence, he felt bound to admit that if the word "great" could be applied
to any of the human race, Lenin was one who deserved it.

At the time, when contradictory impressions were flowing in upon
him, and he was judging events from the special angle of day-to-day
experience, he arrived at one general conclusion—communism was
the only stable form of government that was possible in Russia. He
made up his mind then and there, amid the confusion that still
reigned; and to those who supposed that the Bolshevik regime was a
temporary evil, he gave warning that it was "as firmly established as
any other government in Europe" and pointed out that Trotsky had
put fresh life into the Russian army. The articles he wrote during this
trip were collected in a book called *Russia in the Shadows,* and there
he emphatically repeated his warning that there was no alternative to
the present form of government in Russia. If generous help were given
to the Bolsheviks, they might be able to set up a new order of things.

The only alternative was total collapse, and that would leave a gaping wound in Eastern Europe.

Western hostility carried with it a threat of a different kind. Wells was warned of this by a man who, like himself, was so typical of his own country that all its anxieties and all its future tendencies were mirrored in his mind. Wells had met Maxim Gorky before, during his first visit to America in 1906. That was when the exiled writer was at his lowest ebb, living penniless and hopeless on Staten Island. After meeting in these distressful circumstances, the two men were linked by a firm bond of sympathy. Gorky was a close friend of Lenin, and fired by enthusiasm for the great Russian experiment, but he clearly saw the dangers that lay ahead. He talked to Wells freely, as a tried and trusted friend. A big conference of Soviet republics had just been held at Baku—one of those impressive performances that the Russians know how to arrange in masterly fashion. It had been a great parade of representatives from the Asiatic tribes that were suddenly awakening from their centuries-old sleep. It had also been a sign that Bolshevik policy was taking a new turn. Finding the Western gates barred, Soviet Russia had flung itself in the opposite direction. Gorky, said Wells, was "obsessed by the nightmare" of an Eastward-inclined Russia. So far this was only a figment in the mind of a visionary, but it impressed Wells deeply enough to make him tug with all his strength at the bolts of those Western gates.

Russia in the Shadows had a stormy reception in England. One Conservative journalist wrote some violent attacks on Wells and published them in a volume where he included H. G. among the thinkers who "think against their own country," the would-be destroyers of England. He accused him of criminal tolerance toward a land that was passing through a reign of terror, a land where "a pitiless militarism, more brutal than that of the Germans," had rallied its famished, tattered hordes to destroy Western civilization; a land from which the semblance and even the memory of freedom were banished. Russian exiles, such as the great writer Merezhkovski, attacked Wells too, reminding him that not only Russia, but the whole world, was henceforth divided into two camps—those who were for the Bolsheviks and those who were against them.

Winston Churchill joined in the hue and cry. With his usual fiery eloquence, he made a comparison between cancer, destroying a healthy human body, and communism, devouring the political and social economy of a country. He and Wells engaged in a battle of words, made all the more violent by the antithesis that existed between them. Wells lashed out against the anti-Bolshevik mentality which "pays no attention to reality and learns nothing from experience."

But he did not rest content with having set forth his impressions in a book, or with fighting back at his infuriated adversaries. The conclusions he had reached during his stay in Russia seemed to him to be so important that he tried to draw practical results from them. Much as he disliked making any approach to officialdom, he went to see the Foreign Secretary, hoping to persuade him that it was urgently necessary to arrive at an understanding with the Soviet. As ill luck would have it, the man he was dealing with had an even greater aversion than most of his countrymen for the ideas that Wells set before him. The contrast between different types of Englishmen can seldom have been shown so clearly as at this meeting of two who were as unlike each other as could well be imagined. Lord Curzon was a triumph of British insularity. He had survived from a past age, and did not even know how completely it had vanished. Even in his younger days there had been a rhyme about him in England, beginning:

> I am Sir Nathaniel Curzon,
> And a most superior person.

His years in India had had a considerable effect on him. England probably never had a more regal viceroy than Lord Curzon. Beside the portrait where he was depicted in full official splendor, the reigning sovereign looked puny and awkward, like a commoner in fancy dress. An invisible coronet seemed always to be hovering above his head of smooth, glossy black hair. He used to address Parliament in the tone of an absolute monarch—he had a fine English style, whose very perfection made it seem old-fashioned; the slow, pompous periods rolled forth, while his eyes gazed solemnly over the listeners' heads, as though he felt it would be too painful to look at their insignificant faces. In his own home, he moved as if robed in invisible scarlet and ermine. He asked for a cup of tea in the manner of one giving orders to an army. Even his hands seemed to forbid the hands he shook, and the things he touched, to advance beyond the tips of their disdainful fingers. He was all of a piece, impressive in his determination to overpower everyone around him, and his lofty sense of superiority was so flawless that it kept ridicule at a respectful distance. His mind, which really was exceptionally brilliant, brought its entire resources to bear against anything that threatened to shake the foundations of British society or the unchanging structure of the British Empire. He protected that Empire and that society with his own person, feeling that he was strong enough to be their sword and buckler. He braced himself to meet the onslaught of a new world, not because he underestimated its strength, but because he foresaw what would be the result of any departure from traditional policy.

It was to this man that Wells turned. Even before they met he was probably bristling with annoyance at Curzon's lofty manner and irritated by his calm. He explained that there was no alternative to the new regime in Russia, that it was bound to last, and that as the Bolsheviks were in urgent need of manufactured goods, scientific instruments, and money, the smallest gesture of goodwill would win concessions from them.

Lord Curzon listened as Wells poured out his statements—they came faster and faster, in an unavailing effort to bring a gleam of life into the stony face opposite to him. Lord Curzon listened, said Wells, "as a man listens to a language he does not understand, but is unwilling to admit is strange to him." Or perhaps it was like a judge listening while a rather shady lawyer pleads the cause of a hardened criminal. Then he answered, slowly, bringing out his words one by one, in his usual manner—emphatically, like the judge passing sentence: "But so long as *Russia* continues to sustain a *propaganda* against us in *Persia,* I do not see how we can possibly do anything of the sort you suggest."

Wells realized, there and then, that a great turning point in history had been missed. As he said bitterly after the interview, he had wanted England to come to terms with Russia two years before, in 1918; and he believed that if that had been done, Russia would by then have returned to civilization and the Bolsheviks would have been already thrust aside. But now, after his interview with Curzon, he knew that a unique opportunity had been lost forever. Through all the experiences that came later, all his disappointments, and his own changing viewpoints, he kept to that unshaken conviction. Many years afterward he still maintained that Soviet Russia had been "the best moral and political investment that had ever been offered to Britain. And our Foreign Office turned it down, like a virtuous spinster of a certain age, refusing a proposal to elope and bear ten children."

While Russia always had and always continued to have an irre-sistible attraction for Wells, America both irritated and fascinated him. His dealings with the country and its people went through ups and downs, in the way that dealings with distant relatives are apt to do. It might have been expected that, with his complete absence of mysticism, his mixture of impish realism and idealistic faith, his awareness of being a new man, self-made by his own works, he would have felt very much at one with the citizens of the United States. But curiously enough, whenever he came into contact with Americans, he felt particularly and thoroughly British. A half-hidden note of con-descension ran through his relationship with them, a certain hesitation before their unpredictable reactions; a little embarrassment too, per-haps, such as a man feels when catching sight of himself in a distort-ing mirror.

On his first trip to the States, in 1906, he was annoyed by the exaggerated national pride he found there, which could not tolerate the slightest criticism or admit the least imperfection. During later visits he found that the American mind seemed to be ripening, that the nation was becoming conscious of its strength and wishing to get rid of its possible weaknesses. He noted that a new school of literature was coming to birth too. But he still considered that "half an Ameri-can is in a loud glare and the other half is darkness." In a study of the American people, published in 1914 with the title, *Social Forces in England and America,* he drew attention to one of the most positive features of the American character, the one which first strikes every visitor from the Old World—a new consciousness of humanity. No-body there, he explained, would submit to being downtrodden, no man or woman would take on a job that carried with it a sense of inferiority. Servile traditions had not managed to take root in the country. The population was continually being increased by a flood of peasants and serfs from Europe; but as soon as these people set foot on American soil, their backs straightened with a confidence they had never felt before. This awareness of their human status had the drawback of making them interested only in immediate personal success, in material achievements.

Wells was stimulated, almost in spite of himself, by the rapid tempo of American life, which satisfied his insatiable hunger for living. But when he confessed his own appetites, it was always by way of defying British taboos; he failed to recognize the moralist hidden deep down in his nature, interested only in things outside his own circle, in things more important than his own hunger for experience. He accused the Americans of "burning to live and living to burn." What discouraged him most in the United States, however, was the corrupt and undignified political system, slogan fed, darkened by violence and illiteracy. The essence of Americanism, he declared, was cheaply satisfied morality and insincere sentimentality. He reproached the Americans, above all, for their civic blindness, as he called it, though he considered that this was the natural, almost inevitable product of a middle-class society that had never been called upon either to rule or to be ruled, but had concentrated, solely and successfully, upon private profit.

This accusation of civic blindness continued to be the keynote of his relationship with the American people (a relationship which had its ups and downs, but was always lively). From the very first he was attracted by their spontaneity; the frankness of their attitude toward him; their utter lack of standoffishness and solemnity, which seemed to wipe out the distance separating a man from his fellows, to scorn the precautions of European society, and to accept people at their genuine face value, without official references.

On his very first trip to America, he was invited to luncheon by the President of the United States. (He once remarked, later in life, that he had been four times to the White House, but had never set foot in Buckingham Palace and was never likely to do so.) Theodore Roosevelt was then President—having, as Wells pointed out, achieved that position quite accidentally—and he had more influence at home and greater prestige abroad than any of his predecessors since Abraham Lincoln.

At this time, in 1906, Wells was still looked upon in his own country as nothing more than a rather successful novelist. His influence on public opinion was negligible, as if, he said himself, he talked unheeded, amid general indifference. But as the London *Tribune* had commissioned a series of articles from him, he was received by the President of the United States. In America, a journalist was already looked upon as a man of might, not to be fobbed off with well-worn clichés, and Theodore Roosevelt was too strong a personality to suffer from that dread of saying something indiscreet, which haunts the ordinary, colorless politician. A true American, he felt quite capable of forming his own judgment about his visitor; and besides, Wells, as author of *The Time Machine,* interested him particularly.

As for Wells, strolling with his host, after luncheon, in the grounds of the White House, he was impressed by the man's determination to see things for himself, not to let his mind get into a rut, not to deal in ready-made phrases. Theodore Roosevelt was the first prominent man Wells had ever met. His faith in man and his possibilities was unshadowed by the faintest doubt. He belonged to that race of fervent individualists which, in America, has so far survived the most world-shaking catastrophes, and whose inveterate optimism still expects miracles from the creative will power of mankind. Out of sheer contrariness, or rather out of the secret annoyance provoked by a sense of spiritual kinship that he was unwilling to acknowledge, Wells launched an attack on this buoyant cheerfulness. He afterward confessed that during the whole of the day he spent at the White House, he was haunted by a secret skepticism. Theodore Roosevelt had perceived, perhaps more clearly than British readers, how much cruelty and despairing pessimism lay below the surface of *The Time Machine.* With all the strength of his belief in the future, he braced himself against Wells's nightmare vision. When his guest was taking leave, Roosevelt, kneeling on the seat of a garden chair and clutching the back of it with one hand, held up the other hand with clenched fist and said slowly and emphatically, in his grinding, metallic voice: "And suppose, after all, that should prove to be right, and it all ends in your butterflies and morlocks. *That doesn't matter now.* The effort's real. It's worth going on with . . . even so."

This last moment of the interview, set in the shadow of the White House, with all America for a background, made a strong impression on Wells. Theodore Roosevelt remained in his memory as the embodiment of good will toward men, the true representative of his nation and of the human race—with his hastiness, his lack of discipline, his prejudices, his occasional unfairness and his frequent mistakes on the one hand, and his strength, his steady courage, his honesty and open-minded intelligence on the other. But even this impression, favorable as it was, could not drive out Wells's misgivings. He went on wondering whether America was "a giant childhood or a gigantic futility."

His faith in America had periods of eclipse, but it blazed out once again, with still greater force, during those few months when, as he said in his *Outline of History,* the world was lit up by faith in Wilson. Wilson's failure, when it came, seemed to him to be a typically American tragedy; he saw the man's limitations as those of the whole nation. He found a certain short-sightedness, a touch of egotism, in Wilson, which he considered to arise from something superficial, inherent in a generation of Americans born to security and brought up amid plenty, ignorant of history and remote from the problems that confronted the European peoples, and then suddenly brought face to face with tragedy on a scale that they could not grasp. This was the permanent misunderstanding between two different worlds, the clash between the new age, with its crude, juvenile idealism, and the old epoch with its ripe experience; a clash that found its echo in thousands of individual cases, and would do so again at every turning point of history.

Wells's mind was still dominated by the distressful query: "Where is the world going?" He was surprised to find how few of the people around him felt any share of this obsession. With a feeling of helplessness, he sought for a reply to his question in Russia, and then in America. He realized, though perhaps only dimly at first, that the future of the world would depend on the solution arrived at by one or the other of those two countries. From this time forward he always felt the need to follow up a visit to Russia by a trip to America, or to compare impressions gathered in Washington with those that he formed in Moscow.

In 1921 he attended the Disarmament Conference in Washington, as special correspondent of the *New York World.* Here, what exasperated him most of all was the survival of old-fashioned notions and selfishly nationalistic views, which blocked the way to any lasting settlement. France was the country that irritated him beyond all others. The tragic inability of the French to give a constructive form to their sense of insecurity revealed itself the moment the war was over. Their feeling of being permanently threatened expressed itself in outdated precautions and demands that did not square with general developments. French thought was out of step with the rest of the world. In his reports on the Disarmament Conference, Wells attacked France so sharply that the *Daily Mail,* which held the English rights in his articles, felt obliged to cut out the most violent passages.

The Washington conference marked only the beginning of the

efforts made to found peace upon the ruins left by war. High hopes had not yet been crushed by the series of failures that was to follow. But Wells saw, by now, that the world was moving toward a disaster that it could avoid only by learning to think as a world and to take a constructive view of its future. He was already haunted by the sense of failure that was to descend, years later, upon the young people of Europe. He was painfully aware of his own helplessness, but he felt that he must struggle onward, through "this present world of disorder and darkness, like an exile, doing such feeble things as I can toward the world of my desire, now hopefully, now bitterly, as the mood may happen, until I die."

XVIII

MEANWHILE

WELLS LOOKED AT his daily life and saw that it had become intolerably threadbare. He had reached a point where the all-pervading familiarity of things was a torture to him. People and things that are over-familiar tend to become hazy, as though seen through a fog. They make their presence felt, none the less, like ghosts flitting around a haunted house. Even inanimate objects seemed to claim authority over him and demand too great a share of his attention. He had been born with a need for change, a need to throw everything overboard now and then, no matter what the cost, and make a fresh start. In later years he realized that it was this urge to flight that had led him to break out of bondage in his childhood; that had afterward driven him to divorce, although he was so deeply attached to Isabel and missed her so painfully. He also realized that this sudden, overwhelming weariness, which can make use of the most trifling incident as a pretext to fling a man out of his rut, was something that came to everyone at times, and especially to people with sensitive, creative minds. But it is doubtful whether he was ever aware to what extent his own yielding to the escapist urge, his own obedience to impatient impulses, had helped him, despite the false situations and blind alleys into which it sometimes led him, to renew himself and kept him spiritually and emotionally young and resilient. He was, however, not the kind of man who is always ready to follow the secret call that echoes within him, to commit himself entirely and pay the price un-grudgingly. Poverty, or perhaps a lingering trace of middle-class tradi-tion, had left him with a need for security that held him back from

235

rash decisions and sudden departures. He always had to touch the very depths of forlorn perplexity, be overcome by profound uneasiness or half choked with the tedium of everyday things, before he would yield to his aching desire for flight.

In the background of his personal uneasiness, there was the general uneasiness of the whole world. Every morning the papers had some piece of bad news to announce—there was a lockout in the mines, disturbances in Ireland, the League of Nations was sinking into a mood of complacent futility, discord and injustice were rife. Seven-eighths of the world, as Mr. Barnstaple, one of Wells's heroes, remarks, were a prey to chronic unrest and social disintegration.

As usual, the urge to escape found its first expression in a fairy story that Wells told himself on paper—*Men Like Gods*. Mr. Barnstaple, in that story, finds life too monotonous and the world too gloomy, and feels discouraged, like Wells himself. He has lost all hope, and he is a man who cannot stomach life unless it is spiced with hope. Threatened with a nervous breakdown, he slips away from his home and family—feeling as wicked as a criminal and as excited as a boy playing truant from school—to sample the thrills of a holiday on his own. Suddenly he finds himself in the midst of Utopia—a world of wise, beautiful people, who live in perfect harmony with nature and their fellow men. (They are, in fact, so beautiful and so virtuous that they go around among the flowers and animals like Adam and Eve in the Garden of Eden, clothed only in the mantle of innocence, thus giving a great deal of trouble to the illustrator appointed by the Hearst press, which had bought the serial rights of the story with a rash disregard of its characters' nakedness.)

These Utopians have had their own century of confusion, with violent struggles around the question of private ownership, over-burdened economy, waste, stupidity, and greed. The intrusion of earth dwellers causes a great disturbance in the Utopian paradise. At times the book becomes wildly comic, yet it always has an underlying note of secret melancholy. As representatives of the human race, Wells chose his favorite *bêtes noires*. There is the Catholic priest, bursting with indignation against a world where churches are no longer built and marriages no longer celebrated; the Utopians consider that his indignation springs from an unhealthy and disordered sexual imagination. There is the conservative politician, an enlightened philosopher: even a miracle is hardly enough to lead his thoughts out of their beaten track; he is surprised at nothing, he believes in nothing; he just harangues the Utopians in the phrases that have already served him for hundreds of speeches. There is the statesman, vehement and volatile, reactionary and reckless, who looks upon the Utopians, with their peace and harmony, as degenerate weaklings. There is the monocled aesthete, lionized in London drawing rooms, who is quite at a loss when faced with genuine beauty. There are the high financier, who has sold his conscience and bought a title; the American movie magnate, who has stolen other people's inventions; the cocky, chauvinistic Frenchman, who still demands, on this Utopian soil, appreciation of the tremendous sacrifices made by France in the cause of civilization.

This handful of mortals is soon put into quarantine in a lonely spot, for the Utopians, like the Martians before them, have no acquired resistance to the illnesses which earth-bred microbes are liable to cause. Thereupon, the reckless statesman, dreaming of a universal empire, declares war on the Utopians. Warned by Barnstaple, the only mortal who has appreciated the nobility of their world, the Utopians crush this revolt and, by repeating the atomic experiment, which has put them into contact with another universe, send the mortals back to earth. Barnstaple is the only one who grieves at losing their perfect world—a world where such things as constraints, supreme authority, and police methods are unknown. "Our education is our government," explains one of the Utopians. Since their long-past age of confusion, their mentality has gradually altered. The supporters of the educative state had to fight stubbornly to defend their ideas against persecution, slander, intrigue, firing squads, and bombs. More than a million martyrs lost their lives. But the progressive party had conquered one position after another, until the day when the notion of self-advancement had given way to the notion of creative social service.

Wells was still dreaming that the human race would come to its senses in this direction. He dreamed of it aloud. To a book he brought out in the following year, he gave the title, *The Dream*. It was another vision of the future, but much less ambitious in design; another drama of jealousy, but handled rather as a diversion from serious concerns. A citizen of tomorrow's world, the world of fully evolved, entirely uninhibited human beings, lives through again, in a dream, the life he had led before he was killed by a jealous husband with a revolver.

It had been a wasted life, lived in an epoch when people had nothing but fears, "blank prohibitions," and ignorance instead of ideas, a time of contempt, an age of confusion, which seems incomprehensible to men and women who have learned "the art of being human," who live out their own lives to the utmost and are full of loving-kindness toward their fellow creatures.

The Dream is to some extent a repetition, a return to the autobiographical elements of his childhood, looked at from a distance—the distance at which he himself now stood, and that of the happy beings of tomorrow, whose astonishment and horror at our present-day conditions form an amusing embroidery to the plot.

The figure of a woman with the weaknesses of a sensual nature, yet poignant in the misery of her expiation, stands out as a memorable creation among the other, already familiar characters, with all the emphasis of disturbed and disturbing actuality.

But underneath these shimmering dreams with which Wells was diverting himself, an idea was coming to birth in his mind. He felt increasing impatience at merely daydreaming about a better world, which could not be constructed unless a man's life were put entirely at its service. He was exasperated with politicians who floundered in the morass of day-to-day expediency, and with leaders who ignored their real responsibilities. After his long period of dreaming, he felt eager to test himself in action. He suddenly decided to take a hand in the struggle of contemporary affairs.

He thought the Labour party would give the best response to his constructive suggestions, so despite his past unfortunate experiences with the Fabians, and his dislike of public speaking, he entered the political battle under that banner. He stood as socialist candidate for London University in 1922 and 1923. In support of his campaign he brought out various pamphlets, such as *The Educational Aims of the Socialist Party*. He spoke at public meetings, and hated the sound of his own voice, which rose to shrill heights in order to drown the objections made by hecklers. He argued at committee meetings, trying in vain to make himself understood by the old hands, who had risen to party leadership despite the handicap of a sketchy education, and who thought that all this fuss about teaching was just highbrow nonsense. On the one hand, again, was the day-to-day wisdom of the party men, tempered by experience; on the other, the clumsy impatience of a man concerned only with promoting general ideas. Wells's secret irritation led him into continual friction with the Labour leaders. His contempt for the second-rate and his disgust for party politicians made him blind to the patience and persistence with which they were plowing onward.

Eight years previously, when reviewing the social situation in Great Britain, Wells had stated that he did not expect to see the Labour party come to power during his lifetime. He was still dreaming in terms of centuries. But when he himself took action, he expected that the results would be immediate. After the event, he said that he had never had the slightest chance of being elected. But his defeat rankled, like the disappointment of a secret hope. He was angry with himself. He declared that on reading reports of his speeches, he could hardly believe he had talked to so little purpose, and that when he gave an interview and saw it in print, it always struck him as completely futile. His restlessness increased. A wave of uneasiness and dissatisfaction swept over him. The urge to escape was becoming irresistible. He made furious onslaughts against everyday events, like a prisoner shaking the bars of his cell.

These bursts of frustration-born anger, spectacular and childish rage, signs of a bewilderment that could not quite be accounted for, are described in *The Secret Places of the Heart*. This book is a conversation that Wells carries on with himself, aloud, without the slightest indulgence and even, it seems, with a shade of cruelty toward his own weaknesses. The hero, Sir Richmond Hardy, is a wealthy business magnate, faced with important tasks, possessing everything that life can offer, yet now undergoing a sort of psychoanalytical treatment which he hopes will restore the energy and clear-mindedness that he is beginning to lose, and curb his growing irritability. He can hardly be described as suffering from frustrations, however. His libido, as the specialist assures him, is extremely uninhibited. He is a sensualist who, unhampered by scruples or regard for other people, has always sought his satisfactions—as he says himself—like a thirsty beast making straight for water. Is he abnormal? No. But excessive—this, too, he admits. He is married, and also has an attachment to a remarkable, brilliantly intelligent woman by whom he has a child. Wells gives a striking portrait of his hero's mistress, though she herself does not appear until the last pages of the book. In words of rare psychological insight, he explains the capacity for self-surrender that is sometimes shown by self-restrained women. The more creative is a woman's imagination, he says, the more she will be tempted to give herself up completely to the man around whom her imagination begins to crystallize.

It is in vain that Sir Richmond Hardy shakes off all the restrictions that oppress him. By chance, while traveling, he meets a woman with whom he falls deeply in love, and who loves him; but no solution is possible, and he goes back to the confusion of his former life and dies of pneumonia as another man might commit suicide—dismissing the women who love him, determinedly alone at this liberating end.

According to Wells himself, the central theme of this novel is love as a source or as a waste of energy; but the story born of his bewilderment is rather, with its somber conclusion, the tale of an impossible escape, of the inevitable contrast between the urge to live life to the full and the blind alleys into which it leads.

Himself confronted by complications in his personal life, by conflicting loyalties, and relieved, perhaps, of part of the poison by the half confession in this novel, Wells went away, rather at random, as his hero had done. He believed he was thirsting for distant scenes, that what he wanted was to travel, but in reality he was driven by a need for complete change, no matter what kind. His wife knew the symptoms of this exasperated impatience. She stood aside, with the wisdom of a woman who knows that in order to retain the man she loves, she must be ready to part with him for awhile.

After wandering about for some time, he settled near Grasse, in a region where nature seemed beautiful, fertile, and soothingly gentle. He made his home in a lonely farmhouse, backed by olive terraces; he was determined to live like the local people, undisturbed by tourists. He had come on a trip, but he stayed for years, like so many unconventional Britons who settle in some corner of France, untiring in their enthusiasm for the landscape and for the unchanging life of the peasants.

In the silence of Lou Bastidou he began an interminable monologue —or rather, a contradictory dialogue with himself. He was to continue it for three years. So great was the confusion in his mind, so numerous the problems that had been collecting there and the uncertainties that were clamoring for attention, leaving him no peace, that he took much longer than usual to thresh out his difficulties on a public platform. He was rebuilding a world whose framework had collapsed and whose ruins lay scattered across his path. His dialogue with himself took the form of a novel, but he deliberately kept its plot very slight. In his introduction to the book, *The World of William Clissold*, he claims that this minutely detailed discussion of his personal opinions had the right to be considered as a creative work. "Is it not quite as much 'life' to meet and deal with a new idea as to meet and deal with a new lover?"

The transposition of his ruminations onto the literary plane was rather haphazard and hesitant, for he first of all thought of writing the book like an autobiography, in the first person singular. He admitted later that he had cast himself in the character of William Clissold, the retired businessman, with an exactitude worthy of the Prophet Hosea. But once the transposition had been made, his disjointed and somewhat rambling self-confession gradually turned, as he worked at it, into the form of a novel, and its fictitious passages belong among his most carefully polished pieces of writing. Its leisurely development was favorable to this; Wells, who was often careless about style, shows here how well he could write when he chose. But the story of William Clissold, his childhood, his marriage, and the extraordinarily vivid figure of his mistress, are like so many islets, scattered in the wide stream of a debate on general subjects.

Into this book Wells poured all his momentary confusion, his passing perplexities, even his recent mortifications. In one angry outburst he liquidated his quarrel with the laborites. *The World of William Clissold*, like *The New Machiavelli* before it, was a squabble between friends, fought out in the literary ring with a ferocity that came of white-hot indignation. He later admitted having written the book while still too full of the disappointment he had received from the Labour party. His usual pugnacity expressed itself so vehemently that he even seemed to have changed sides. He, who had always stood shoulder to shoulder with the downtrodden in their thrust toward freedom, now declared, There was nothing in the masses, as masses, but an unreliable explosive force. Society would come to its new form through the work of an intelligent minority; it will be effected without the support of the crowd and possibly in spite of its dissent. "Rather the dukes than the doctrinaires!" exclaims William Clissold.

After his quarrel with the party politicians, Wells considered that socialism had ceased to be a creative movement, and become a mere pretext for the disinherited to give passionate vent to their inferiority complex. He looked upon communism as nothing better than the

narrow souled, defective and malignant child of this distorted socialism—a parricidal child at that. Wells's temporary alter ego now asserted that the first steps in a true revolution were more likely to be
taken by America than by Russia. Yet as though against his own will,
his perpetual striving toward the union of mankind managed to
assert itself even here. William Clissold carries on the impossible
dream of a reconciliation between the opposing forces. He suggests
that many apparently hopeless contrasts, such as that between communism and international finance, may develop in the next half
century in such a way as to become good neighbors, advancing along
parallel lines. William Clissold's meditations, though they seem to be
based on a realistic outlook, often have this Utopian flavor about
them. Wells was afterward very glad that instead of writing this
book in the first person he had followed his second thoughts and taken
a mask; for once his mood of irritation had passed off, he began to
reflect upon his hero's world from a standpoint closer to that of his
permanent convictions.

In addition to Wells's political perplexities, the book records his
experiences as a man struggling amid the conflicting impulses of his
emotional and sexual life. In this report, he is completely identified
with his hero. He makes his confession in this impersonal form, with
all due frankness. At a distance, in France and alone, he can see things
in their proper perspective, and rid himself of the innate reserve that
prevents the inhabitants of Great Britain from discussing the facts of
sexual behavior. *The World of William Clissold* marks the end of
his retarded adolescence. While writing it, he faced up to the two
contradictory forces within him, his sexual hunger and his need of
freedom. He saw, now, how large a part the obsession with sex had
played in his life. He recognized, too, that he was incapable of complete self-surrender. "I have never given myself to anyone," he wrote,
"I have never wanted to give myself to anyone." He was nearly sixty
years old when the tangled skein of his past was unraveled before
his eyes and he began to see clearly into his own inner history. His
youthfulness seemed to be imperishable. So far, as he said, he had had
scarcely any physical evidence of the passing years. He welcomed any
adventure that came along, with as much warmth as ever; a woman's
presence could stir him just as deeply as in his youth—and bore him
just as quickly. He was still eager to learn a lot about himself from
every woman who crossed his path.

Most useful of all in him was his lingering, persistent dream, the dream of perfect love meeting with a perfect response. He confesses in this book that he had been haunted for years by an undefinable conviction that somewhere, among all the women in the world, there must exist one who would complete his own nature—the other half of his androgynous self, which he had lost and must now find again. He found it surprising—this surprise was another very juvenile trait in him—that active, creative men did not usually fall in love with women who were active and creative, or at any rate capable of being a real help to them. This attitude testifies not only to the youthfulness of his mind, but also to his strength of character, the confidence that lay, like firm ground, below the cluttered surface of his doubts and perplexities. He was so sure of himself that he did not need admiration or helplessness at his side to give him a feeling of superiority; and he was not vain enough to be annoyed by a woman's independence, or by any success that she might achieve without his help or against his wish.

The women he loved and the women who lived with him were always free to show what they were made of; and he was all the fonder of them if their personality kept its highlights, and even its sharp angles. He admired their way of standing aside from him and living their own lives, doing their own independent work. His deep affection for the woman whom he now loved and lived with was partly made up of respect for her creative self-sufficiency, the individual nature of her inspiration.

The ties that bound him to Jane had been strengthened, not by the similarity of their views, but by their points of difference. She stood firmly by his side in every one of the skirmishes that he provoked, though she felt by no means certain that such battles were necessary, or their outcome important. "I do not think she believed very strongly in my beliefs," he wrote after her death. "She accepted them, but she could have done without them." This made him all the more grateful for her support, as though it put him under a debt that he could never pay in a lifetime. There was one thing about her which he never ceased to find deeply touching, and that was the strength underlying her apparent fragility, the frank, challenging spirit that counterbalanced her tendency to dreaminess and her love of beauty. A novel called *Meanwhile,* a sequel to the self-confession of

William Clissold, stands as a milestone marking his return to Jane, the Jane of his early years.

Through his examination into his own character and his past preoccupation with sex, which is recorded in the long, meandering chapters of *William Clissold,* Wells had freed himself from that sense of urgency that had so often spurred him to flight. It was as though he had laid his ghosts by letting daylight in among them. His obsessions were no longer to receive more than their fair share of his attention. His outspoken dismissal of the sexual problem must have struck him as particularly daring. But it came as no shock to the postwar generation which, in the space of a few years, had swept away every vestige of Victorian convention. He may even have been surprised to find that he had been hammering on an open door.

The World of William Clissold displeased the great novel-reading public because of its form, and the literary critics because of the ideas it expressed. The sharpest disappointment of all, however, was felt by the large group who had expected that this book—preceded by a resounding publicity campaign and announced as the masterpiece of its author's ripened mind—would show Wells once again as the prophet of coming events. It did nothing to smooth matters between him and his adversaries, either. His supporters, like his detractors, considered that the path he had so laboriously traced among the ruins of a shattered world was leading nowhere. In fact, as he himself put it, his first attempt at a general announcement of policy came back to him with numerous corrections, mostly in red ink; and he made up his mind to profit by them.

He was the kind of man to whom failure is more stimulating than success. His youthful disposition included the faculty of drawing benefit from well-founded criticism. He was always ready to admit to himself that he had made a mistake, whether of form or content. He now set about rewriting his long novel, in the most compact form that he could achieve, and as a piece of pure fiction in so far as he was ever able to escape from the clutches of immediate reality. Yet although *Meanwhile* is a work projecting outside himself, as remote as possible from his personal problems, it none the less gives, by transposition, even more revealing evidence of his development than William Clissold's confessions had done.

The book is one of the juiciest fruits of Wells's rich humor, yet it has a core of bitterness. Its chief character, Sempack, the "Utopographer," is both pathetic and absurd; he is a rounded-out, independent personality, not a mere dramatization of the author. But in making Sempack a member of his own calling, or rather a representative of his own chief convictions, Wells also gave him certain of his own features, in an exaggerated, caricatural form. He turned this fictitious character, living with a life unrelated to his own, into the battleground of his personal perplexities. When Sempack declares that the struggle for progress is to him the most important thing in life, and that he would lose all desire to live if he lost confidence in the improvement of existing conditions, he is expressing Wells's own feeling. Wells himself believed that life was worth living only as a transition to something better, and reality only if it opened out into Utopia. Even Utopia is valueless if it remains a vague, impossible dream. Wells was painfully aware of the gulf between the world of the future which he had so often pictured in his books, and the practical possibilities of attaining it. Sempack points out apologetically that constructive Utopianism is of very recent birth. He and his author are rather like medieval geographers, drawing up the map of a still-unexplored continent without knowing how it can be reached. "We have at last made it seem extremely credible and possible," says Sempack, struggling against his own doubts. He knows that this intellectual exploration of the future is about to enter on a new phase; he is tormented by the longing to put his ideas to the test, but realizes at the same time that he will never be a man of action. In laying bare the contradictions in Sempack's nature, Wells is very hard on himself. He shows a man who seems quite unconcerned with material questions and professes a glib contempt for social pleasures, yet leads a snug, pampered life; a man who holds aloof, priding himself on his solitude, a monk of his religion, yet in his own home accepts all that attentive devotion can do for his comfort; a man whose masculine self-confidence can be disturbed with ridiculous ease, who is thrown off his balance, at sixty years old, by a glamorous woman, and becomes her mere plaything. But, as the young hero of the novel explains, the man had reached a deadlock in his work. He was worried about the world situation, and an active mind in distress turns to a love affair in the way that timid people with low vitality turn to drink.

The subtitle of *Meanwhile* is *The Picture of a Lady*. The book seems like a memorial to a very small, very brave, and clear-sighted woman. She is of delicate fiber and lowered vitality, with none of the superfluous energy that torments her husband. This portrait of a lady is painted as though against the golden background of memory; it has a strange radiance that seems to come from regret or from a presentiment of loss. It is a memorial of something that has not yet happened.

The young hero of the book is the spiritual heir of William Clissold, created as a gesture of defiance to Clissold's detractors. The son of wealthy and highborn parents, he had the incapacity to express himself and the dread of showing emotion that are common to well-bred Englishmen; he belongs to a social set where fools lay down the law and stupidity is a recommendation. But in an hour of crisis he awakens to a sense of responsibility and begins to grope his way toward a truer vision of the world. *Meanwhile* is in great part a diary. It is the story of the great coal strike that took place in England in 1926 and was followed by a general strike. The coal owners—young Philip Rylands explains to his wife—seeing that world markets are shrinking and that Britain's influence is dwindling, would like to make the working classes bear the whole burden of the country's economic crisis. They imagine that the decline of the Empire is the result of a conspiracy— or of a spell cast by "the wicked men in Moscow." If the Bolsheviks did not exist, the miners, instead of being mere tools of Moscow, would be only too glad to work longer hours and get less pay. Bolshevism should be taken by the throat and strangled, and then everybody would be happy. Philip Rylands describes Wells's spiritual counterpart, Winston Churchill, bustling about with his usual vigor, in the belief that he is fighting against an attempted revolution, and proud of having stifled it. Wells found this story of the general strike so exciting that he adorned Philip's letters to his wife with some of those little comical sketches that he himself used to illustrate what he thought important, to underline certain passages as though with an angry stroke of the pen. One of these little drawings shows Churchill, a ball of explosive energy, rushing along between a double row of stolid lookers-on, and the caption says "Winston doing Everything."

Rylands describes the communists, too, the stubborn clumsiness of their demands, their ardent faith and self-sacrificing spirit, and contrasts them with the helpless labor leaders and timid trade-unionists, who seem more alarmed by possible victory than by certain defeat. He describes the government's shifty attitude, its ruses and provocative behavior. Angry thunder rumbles through the book. *The World of*

William Clissold had been left somewhere by the wayside; its dream
of an agreement between high finance and communism had faded
before the reality of social strife. Wells's chronicle is marked by partisan indignation. Galsworthy used the same theme in the story of the
Forsytes. He described the mobilization of all who supported law and
order, the public spirit of the English, their magnificent sense of solidarity, which came to the fore in opposition to the working classes.
Those stirring days, when volunteers saved the country from economic
paralysis, remained as a vivid memory in the minds of the younger
generation, and had a dire effect on British policy in general. The
comparison with Galsworthy's books makes Wells's keen insight into
social problems and his shrewd political instinct particularly evident.
Behind the defensive reaction of British conservatism, he glimpsed
lurking forces which were ready to use it for their own ends. The
British fascists were mere puppets as yet. The ridiculous figure of
Oswald Mosley struts through the book, and another, less sketchy
character is a retired officer who reveals his ignorance in aggressive,
barking tones. In Wells's eyes, Mussolini's British imitators were just
so much raw material for caricature; their direct action was not nearly
so dangerous as their influence in shaping the country's future policy.

In the beautiful garden of the Rylands' villa in Italy, an Italian
liberal politician takes refuge, pursued by a savage pack of young
fascists—another topical incident in this record of an epoch. The
onrush of actual events was damaging to the success of the book. The
reading public felt too close, still, to the events described, which went
past like a film serving as background to flesh-and-blood characters.
Sometimes the living characters blocked out the moving shadows,
sometimes they drew aside and the film ran on without them. But in
the last twenty years the perspective has altered. The once topical
incidents now stand out with strange clarity; they no longer form a
chain of fleeting, familiar pictures, but a page of history whose importance was underestimated both by those who acted in it and those
who looked on. The things that happen in the book and the people to
whom they happen are now undivided, all of one texture. *Meanwhile*
is one of several books by Wells which the passing years have shown
in various aspects, which have gone through periods of oblivion and
bursts of curious popularity. These books now gain added interest
through the very defects that spoiled them as novels—their excessive
topicality, their lengthy presentation of general ideas, a current of life

that runs through them, hidden from contemporary eyes. They will be of great value to future historians, to whom they offer one of the most reliable records of our period. In Wells's personal history, *Meanwhile* represents a revision, a kind of precipitate of his ideas. The time for dreaming had gone by, so had the time for mapping out the world of the future; what must be done now was to discover how *to* get there. *Meanwhile* is a crystallization of its author's perplexity, his weariness of makeshifts. Sempack compares happiness, as it now exists, to a wild flower, growing on stony ground, which some day men will cultivate in gardens all the year round. "Meanwhile . . ."

Someone else, listening, remarks, "I perceive I have been mean-whiling all my life. . . . Have I been living? No, I have been mean-whiling away my time."

XIX

THE OPEN CONSPIRACY

"THIS CONCEPTION OF an open conspiracy to realize the World Republic is the outline into which I fit most of my social activities. It is as much a part of me as my eyesight or my weight," writes Wells in *The World of William Clissold*. The term "Open Conspiracy," the idea it expresses, came into his mind quite suddenly, and completely filled it for a long time. It not only defined the goal toward which all his thoughts were directed, but also revealed his growing tendency to operate what might be described as a decentralization of his personality. General ideas had always seemed to him to be more important than private interests, and this conviction had strengthened as he grew older, especially since financial security had set him free to follow whatever notion was uppermost in his mind at a given moment, and to write the books he wanted to write, without having to ask himself whether they would sell. The direction in which he was moving is revealed now and then through the soul searching of which *William Clissold* is the written record. He was not only running away from himself; he was also running toward something bigger than his own personal existence.

It was not an individuality but a community that he wanted to find. His own disquiet made him realize that the man of today can no longer find satisfaction in completely selfish gratification, and that to provide for all his own needs is no longer enough to bring him happiness. Humanity was outgrowing the intense individualism of its romantic adolescence, just as it had outgrown the fears and superstitions which haunted its infancy. Wells began to feel a need to unite with those who shared his aspirations, for he saw how necessary it was that all their efforts should take the same direction.

The path—the final, definite path—now opening before him turned out to be the same along which he had traveled in early youth. But he had left the region of Utopia and passed on to that of urgent reality. The "Republic of Humanity" was no longer to be the inevitable goal reached by gradual progress; the pressure of immediate danger had made of it something that must be achieved in the nearest future. "Why are there no Fascisti of the Light to balance the black Fascists?" asks Philip Rylands. The "Fascisti of the Light" are a revival of another old notion, the men of good will, united in the discipline of shared labor, the Samurai of an earlier book. Wells foresaw that the Western democracies would lose face to an ever greater extent, owing to the muddleheadedness of their politicians, the concessions they were always ready to make for vote-catching purposes, and their way of bowing before public opinion instead of guiding it. This was still only 1927. The parliamentary system seemed more firmly established than ever. Even in Germany the Social Democrats had won a victory at the polls. The political fabric, with all the bits and pieces that went to make up coalition cabinets, seemed likely to outlast the present generation, despite the strain put upon it by the continual changes of government in France. But Wells was in such close spiritual contact with the rank and file of humanity, that he could foresee with uncanny precision the weary and rebellious mood that would make itself felt before long. He really seemed to be at one with what he called the mass mind, to share in collective thought and yet stand in its forefront, giving it definite expression before it had consciously formed.

When, in the spring of 1927, he was invited to lecture at the Sorbonne, he decided to take as his theme the apprehensions that were haunting him, and set them down under the heading of "Democracy under Revision." This seemed to him to be an important occasion, and he took great care in preparing his lecture. Jane went with him to Paris. She too had been preparing for the occasion, taking French lessons without her husband's knowledge. She astonished him by the ease she showed in talking with French scientists such as Madame Curie and Jean Perrin. "They made much of her," he notes with naïve pride.

The lecture was listened to with considerable interest. The audience recognized that Wells's criticism of democracy was justified, but his

constructive proposals seemed far removed from present possibilities—
just another Utopian scheme, drawn up with his usual skill. People
did not understand how serious he was; the need to alter existing conditions was not sufficiently obvious to make them realize what dire
anxiety prompted him to speak as he did. He had indeed anticipated
the coming confusion—but only by a few years.

At the time when he was thus pointing out the necessity of revising
the democratic system, people were still in the habit of expecting the
younger generation, almost automatically, to give the world some kind
of miraculous fresh start. This younger generation, which had not
taken part in World War I, had grown up with a grudge against
its elders because they had not given it a better start. The young people
were fond of describing themselves as a realistic generation, in contrast
to the muddlers who had made a mess of the past. They were proud of
their lack of education, their lack of background, of the fact that hardship and bereavement had made them callous. The previous generation
having been decimated during 1914-18, old men were still controlling
public life, and the need of new blood was becoming more and more
evident. So evident, that to be young seemed in itself to be a virtue.
The atmosphere was charged with a sense of guilt, a confession of
helplessness, without which the myth of miraculous youth could not
have gained such a firm hold.

Wells had been one of the first to question the generally admitted
superiority of youth. He pointed out that lack of maturity is a form
of deficiency, and that the adolescent young man or woman is a natural
barbarian, whose dearest wish is usually to revive all the cheap romanticism that adults are trying to do away with. "Young people are
not conservative perhaps, but they are instinctively reactionary"—their
outlook is medieval, a throwback to the epoch of religious persecution
and terror.

Turning his back on the most convenient source of hope in the
contemporary world, Wells was all the more puzzled as to where to
find recruits for his open conspiracy. In planning this revised version
of his Samurai, he had embarked on the greatest enterprise of his career. He devoted himself to it entirely, until the moment when his
private life was shaken by unforeseen disaster.

The Paris visit seemed to have tired Jane more than it should have
done. For some time before that she had not been feeling well, but
with her usual courage she had hidden the fact from her family, and

continued to show an unfalteringly brave face to the outside world. She could not bring herself to abandon the decided, pugnacious, cheerful personality that had become second nature to her, the personality of a woman who was master of her own fate. She must have felt that to admit illness would be to admit defeat, to fling the door open to a host of suppressed regrets, unacknowledged humiliations, and dead dreams. She insisted that she would soon be well again. And before Wells went back to France she promised him that she would see a doctor. She arranged to have an operation while H. G. and his eldest son were away; but it was too late—the cancer from which she was suffering had become generalized.

In *The Book of Catherine Wells,* writing with the pent-up emotion in face of death, which has an accent of its own, Wells describes the last months of her life, and the perfect self-possession that she maintained until the very end. Impressed by her unflinching courage, the doctors had not tried to hoodwink her, and she made her plans for dying as others make plans for living, methodically, anxious not to overlook anything that still remained to be done. She wanted "to have a beautiful death," as people used to say when she was young, with calm features from which all trace of suffering should so far as possible be wiped out, listening to her favorite music, Bach or Mozart, while the roses were in full bloom in her garden. True to herself, she tried to console the doctors in their distress at the bad news they had to give, and to comfort her husband with assurances that he had always made her very happy. This may have been almost true, for life had brought her every possible outward satisfaction, and even, toward the end, the belated triumph of an act of renunciation. She knew the choice that had faced her husband, and the decision he had made when he parted from the woman he loved and who had borne him a son. Thanks to her wisdom, she had not been left to meet death in loneliness.

Absolute harmony shed a golden radiance over those last months. Her husband was with her all the time, hiding his deep sorrow, attentive to her every need; and in the silent dusk hours of closest understanding between them, she could tell herself that all this was as much the result of her own patient effort as were their lovely home and their social successes. If she felt a secret bitterness at dying thus prematurely, she showed no sign of it. Catherine Wells died as she had lived, with an inscrutable expression on her heroic little face.

Carrying beyond the gates of death that dream of beauty that had gone with her all through her life, she asked her relations and friends not to wear mourning for her. Wells himself wrote the words that a clergyman spoke at her cremation service: "The best and sweetest of her is known only to one or two of us; subtle and secret, it can never be told." It was this, the secret of her valiant wisdom, that weighed most heavily on him. Her death left him in a state of bewilderment—he was confused by the everyday matters that she had dealt with so efficiently, and by the sense of a terrible gap in his life, now that two women he loved had left it at almost the same moment. He, who had always insisted on freedom, was terrified at suddenly finding himself without ties of any kind. He felt a fear of growing old, together with a very youthful panic at the thought of the unfamiliar life that lay ahead of him, and that might bring either thrilling adventure or dreadful, overwhelming loneliness. He began to travel around, as though driven by every chance breeze; and he flung himself, with an energy born of deep distress, into the search for a way by which the world could avoid the disaster that threatened it.

The life and ideas of H. G. Wells make up, as it were, a film that ought to be run off backward. The sequence of events, and the warnings that he gave out, draw their greatest interest from subsequent happenings and future trends.

In December, 1928, the general mood was one of optimism. The failure of various disarmament conferences was offset, to all appearances, by the strong revival of the will to peace that found expression in the Kellogg Pact. War had been outlawed, and though it was only morally condemned, everyone believed that the condemnation would be reinforced by the people's ardent and universal demand for peace. The Franco-German conflict, that everlasting source of discord in the heart of Europe, had subsided. Stresemann, though gravely ill, had himself come to Paris to put his signature beside Briand's on the Kellogg Pact. The final report sent in by Parker Gilbert, America's financial representative in Germany, laid great stress on this high peak of the peace effort. American loans had stimulated German economy to a fantastic pitch—modern highways were being constructed throughout the length and breadth of the country; even the smallest towns had taken advantage of the generous shower of dollars and built themselves splendid city halls, huge stadiums, and luxury hotels for nonexistent tourists. Basking in well-being, people dismissed all thought of war.

Wells was invited to give a lecture in Berlin; the invitation came from a society whose ranks included representatives of all the political parties, of finance and industry, of science, literature, and art. The mood of the hour was favorable to international meetings. Paul Loebe, Socialist President of the Reichstag, allowed them to use its assembly hall, where the members of the Society took their places on the government bench: General von Seckt, gazing icily through his monocle, sat next to Professor Einstein, and Loebe, the Socialist, had a von Siemens for neighbor. Wells spoke from the tribune whence Bismarck had addressed the house in days gone by. It was perhaps rather ironical that a man who had so violently preached hatred of Germany, and war to the death, should now have the cream of the country as his audience. The hall was packed; the demand for tickets had been far greater than the supply. Wells seemed surprised and slightly alarmed, as he looked across and down at the sea of faces that filled the great amphitheater. He felt he ought to apologize for his bellicose attitude in the past, by saying that in the agitation and heat of the moment he, like many others, had spoken a great many hasty and unjust words. He admitted that he was responsible for the slogan, "the war to end wars." But there was no need for him to excuse himself. Repudiation of war was in the air just then. *All Quiet on the Western Front* had stirred the dregs of bitter memory by depicting useless slaughter in all its horror. Besides, there is always indulgence for a celebrity.

The audience listened to Wells with an attention that arose chiefly from curiosity. Silent concentration and bursts of applause gave evidence of the Germans' zeal for improving their minds. But only a part of what he said was within their grasp. As he spoke, the audience followed the German translation that had been handed out. They expressed approval of certain passages, but the main warning passed over their heads. It seemed to have no connection with the present day, to be just another *Time Machine* whose aimless flight had landed it in the middle of a nightmare.

Wells pointed out the hollowness of the Kellogg Pact, that "beautiful nothing" which merely skirted round the real difficulties of the situation. He declared that it was just as impossible to ensure peace by merely wishing for peace, as to feed oneself by merely concentrating one's mind on the fact of being hungry. Real, world-wide peace could only be attained through a complete transformation in the very nature of all existing governments and in the basic principles on which each government was founded. The chief difficulty confronting all constructive efforts for peace was the sovereign independence of the various states. That fully independent sovereignty implied an aggressive attitude, a muster of latent hatreds, which was bound to lead to war. The only possible way to save peace was to set up a world-wide federation of states. If it was mere utopianism to imagine that the world could unite in the interest of mankind as a whole, then any effort to ensure peace was mere utopianism. It was the nationalist spirit, a product of the last few centuries, a thing that man had bred and that man could destroy, which was resisting the formation of this world state. Wells confessed, with a wry smile, that he himself was tainted with this nationalist spirit, and sometimes had difficulty in keeping it down.

The future Nazis in the audience smiled too, full of indulgence for this piece of self-criticism, as though it could not possibly be applied to them. Wells went on to point out the great error committed by the League of Nations in treating the national question, from the very first, as though it were an essential factor in human society. The real struggle for peace had not yet begun. But in the confusion of our social and intellectual life, where could we turn to find the leaders of that struggle, its saints and martyrs, its troops, its discipline, its spirit of unity? He himself, he said, had been awaiting some such movement for the past twenty-five years. But he was neither a leader nor an organizer; his task was to announce coming events, by trying to read the next, still unturned page of the book of history. And what he read was gloomy indeed: despite all pacts and all promises, the world was undoubtedly moving toward fresh wars.

His words did not even send a ripple over the audience, a movement of fear or indignation. Germany's conscience was at rest, untroubled by the faint stirring of unhealthy agitation on the outer fringe of her political life. But the little visionary was still speaking from the rostrum: soon, he was saying, the guns would begin to go off of their own accord, and the corporal would be driving men again into the barrack square. This prophecy contrasted strangely with Wells's restrained manner of speaking, his cheerful rotundity, his gesticulating hands, and the twinkle that never quite disappeared from his bright eyes. His matter-of-fact appearance in no way suggested that of a seer, in fact, it combined with the current mood of "all's right with the world" to defeat the purpose of his speech. His warning that "the new cycle of war," when it came, might wipe out civilization for a thousand years, and his fervent appeal to those reasonable men, who still had one last chance to save the world, were applauded only as an effective piece of oratory.

He may have already known, only too well, the sensation of speaking to deaf ears; or he may have been suddenly wearied and disheartened by the mingling of attentive interest and profound indifference that he sensed in his present audience. In any case he ended on a note whose solemnity found no echo even in the most sagacious of those around him: "But I must admit that the chances are against us . . . that they all seem to tend toward a conflagration that will destroy the future of our race." A tragic light was to be thrown on these words by the flames that gutted the very Reichstag building in which they were spoken. But the full meaning of this unturned page of history was perhaps not understood until many years after Wells had expounded it.

Everything he himself did and wrote from that time forth was influenced by the premonition of approaching disaster. For years, all his thoughts and all his efforts were engaged in a desperate struggle to save the last chance. It was, too, a struggle to preserve his own faith in mankind.

In 1928 he brought out a little book, a crystallization of all that had been taking shape within him during the previous years, to which he gave the title, *The Open Conspiracy,* and the subtitle, *Blue Prints for a World Revolution.* He presented his subject with befitting emphasis: "This book sets forth, as simply and clearly as possible, the essential ideas of my life, the perspective of my world. Everything else that I have done until now seems to me to do no more than contribute to these ideas and suggestions, or illustrate them. . . ." On the very first page he warns the reader that "This is my religion." This religion was the undying faith in a New Republic that had persisted in him from the very first, the belief in a world-wide commonweal that would have control of all the moral, biological, and economic factors that lead to war. Wells clung to this belief, which alone could save him from the depression which was consuming most of his contemporaries. A community that was no longer held together by the bond of faith was, in his view, like a building in which the mortar had turned to sand. The old beliefs had lost much of their power of persuasion, their substance, their sincerity. The structure of society was disintegrating. A new faith was arising amid all this confusion, but it had not yet achieved the clear expression and firm organization that would enable it to influence human affairs. "The essence of a religion is the subordination of self." The actual creed professed was less important than this voluntary submission to something that transcended selfish aims and personal triumphs. The first article of this modern faith must be, not "I believe," but "I give myself," and it must find expression in a complete change of attitude toward life. Unlimited possibilities and tremendous dangers had paved the way for this new morality. World unity had become the necessary condition for man's survival and the outcome of his religious instinct. But this unity must take one definite form, the liberation of human thought and creative effort. From the point of view of progress, a world Caesar would be little better than world chaos.

The Open Conspiracy is directed first and foremost against the policy of letting things slide, it flings a challenge to fatalistic resignation. It would begin, said Wells, with little groups of friends or fellow workers. These would then be organized like the Fascisti or the *Sokols*. Members would be drawn from all sections of society, but communism and Christianity, being already full-fledged associations, would be left outside for the time being. Communism, as a world-wide propaganda organization, was "manifestly the inspirer and precursor of the Open Conspiracy," but the movement could not be founded on mere resentment. In Wells's opinion, the antithesis between capital and labor was not and never had been the essential problem facing mankind. Private property, he declared, could not be an evil, if only for the reason that it was able to overstep political boundaries.

The real enemies of the Open Conspiracy were muddleheadedness, lack of courage and imagination, laziness and wasteful selfishness. "Professional patriots," nationalists, and imperialists, would be automatically excluded from the first group of "conspirators," but the majority of people in Europe, and an even higher majority in the United States, could become citizens of the world without their present occupations being in any way disturbed. The aim of the Open Conspiracy was to awaken mankind from the nightmare of struggle for existence and inevitable war. Wells's concluding words are: "The final decision as to the fate of life on our planet depends today upon man's own will."

The little book has the restrained emphasis of deep conviction. It is Wells's most sober and succinct piece of writing, with no digressions and no rhetorical flourishes. In fact it is, as he himself said, a summary of ideas that had gradually thrust themselves upon him. He knew that these ideas were incomplete and far from final. He had ceased to hope for the sudden birth of a new mentality, the sudden appearance of those who would guide the new world into being and give it a social and economic framework. He knew now that failing a great, dynamic movement to achieve peace, led, like communism and fascism, by an active minority, the human race was doomed to suicide. But he could not do more than throw the seed of these ideas into the teeth of the wind. The *Blue Prints* are adapted to the moment, ready to be taken up again, completed, and adapted to any changes in the international situation.

Once such revision came in a little book called *What Are We To Do With Our Lives?* For Wells, this question by itself alone formed the boundary mark between the old world and the new. What used to make up the whole of life had now sunk into the background. The change that has taken place is illustrated by the fact that, as he says in his autobiography, it is quite possible to ask a man, nowadays, a question that would once have been meaningless: "Yes, you earn a living, you support a family, you love and you hate—*what do you do?*"

When Wells began to write his memoirs, five years had gone by since the publication of *The Open Conspiracy*. The idea itself still survived, in spite of all the disappointments that those years had brought. He still looked upon his religion—or particular moral system, as he was henceforth to call it—as representing his special mission in life. He still felt that life would not be worth living if he could not carry on what he felt to be his appointed task. During the past five years, attempts had been made in various directions to put his plan into practice. Several journals had been founded in support of it. Little scattered groups of people had formed here and there and taken up his arguments. The words "Open Conspiracy" had hovered in the air for quite a time. But deep down in his heart, Wells knew that the effort on which he had concentrated all his strength had been made in vain. No army of conspirators had sprung forward to answer his call; not even a small advance guard had responded. He was not one of those whose thoughts work like yeast to leaven the lump of humanity. His general ideas had perhaps reached a wider audience than he would have supposed from the visible results; but the chief one of them all had vanished like footprints on shifting sands. With his peculiar tenacity, however, he still clung to his belief, even in the teeth of the evidence. In his autobiography he asserts that the Open Conspiracy, whether under that name or some other, will sooner or later have its way in schools and colleges, winning the support of the best type of young men and women, of the specialists, of those who are simple and straightforward, confident and resolute, and that in the long run it will spread to all mankind.

This is the language of a man who is trying to convince himself. For—and therein lay the secret tragedy of his eminently successful life—H. G. Wells was the single, solitary member of the Open Conspiracy.

XX

APROPOS OF DOLORES

TRAVELING AROUND AT random after his wife's death, Wells arrived one day in Geneva. For some time past he had been receiving letters from an ardent admirer, who expressed herself with unusual liveliness and whose amusing turns of phrase appealed to his strong sense of humor. The letters were written in faultless English, but with oriental fervor. The unknown correspondent pressed for a meeting. With his native prudence, Wells had so far avoided this encounter; but after a further interchange of letters, it took place in Geneva.

Having thus abruptly entered his life, Dolores turned it upside down and made such a cleavage in it that his later, aging existence—he was now in his sixties—never quite re-established contact with the middle period which had immediately preceded her tempestuous arrival.

Seldom has a connection between two human beings received such wide and resounding publicity as that of Wells and Dolores. However, a relationship may be just as thoroughly falsified by glaring limelight as by enshrouding darkness. Verbal explanations and literary transpositions have thrown the "Dolores case" out of perspective. Some years later he wrote that resentful novel, *Apropos of Dolores*.

The Dolores of Wells's novel is a creature so farfetched that we can easily understand how the hero is driven to murder her, but not how he could ever have been in love with her. Yet the portrait, or rather the caricature, is convincing in its savage power. Where there is direct portrayal, as in certain shades of character, it is a grim depiction, with not the faintest rim of light to alleviate it. The few concessions added by way of afterthought, as though grudgingly, on the last page of the book—"she was a great stimulus to him," for instance—seem to be the results of a hasty touching up.

In real life, Dolores amused him vastly, and this amusement was the strongest bond by which she held him. But the humor with which he depicted her after their separation was a sinister humor too.

Dolores, the figure in his book, is placed obliquely between fiction and fact. Her physical appearance is dwelt upon with the careful realism of a Flemish painter rendering a repulsive wart. The tall, angular figure; the thin, eager, heavily made-up face framed in locks of black hair; the air of rather wild animation; the bony arms, overloaded with heavy bracelets; the expensive, showy clothes, always in the vanguard of fashion; the wave of heady perfume that preceded and announced her entry were all precisely described. From the tense planes of the face glowed a pair of jet-black, piercing eyes whose expression was both provocative and troubled. The long, sinuous mouth, never still, seemed to be constantly disturbing the arrangement of the features, whisking them from tragedy to farce, and from farce to melodrama. The author of *Dolores* maintains that this personal appearance was a complete fabrication, designed to attract attention at all costs. But whereas the synthesis might have been merely grotesque, its flagrant artificiality was rendered impressive by the strangely primitive forcefulness of crude will power.

Probably no one knew exactly what races mingled their warring blood in Dolores's veins. In the book, Wells gives her a Scottish father and an Armenian mother. The terrible public prosecutor who wrote *Apropos of Dolores* declares that the very essence of her life was affectation and boastfulness. But even her delight in shocking people, which she tried to pass off as aristocratic indifference or absent-mindedness, may have been simply the expression of an unacknowledged and thoroughly middle-class yearning for respectability.

To Wells, the discovery of Dolores opened a whole new world. The Eastern hemisphere forced itself upon his insular existence. Despite his cosmopolitan outlook, he was repelled, in his heart of hearts, by this unfamiliar way of life, by the habits, fads, and fancies that Dolores had accumulated during her years of roving. Repelled, yet at the same time he was attracted and intrigued, like a traveler in an unknown land. Everything that was foreign or inexplicable jarred his thoroughly English character to its foundations, but this shock value was none the less a part of Dolores's attraction for him. It was not only the East that he explored through her personality; she also opened his eyes to France, her adopted country. Though he had lived for years on the Riviera, Wells had never really taken root in France; he was greatly hampered by his insufficient familiarity with the language, and his British shyness made him shrink from taking part in conversation whose finer points eluded him. "You don't really know a language," he used to declare, "until the little words begin making faces at you."

Through Dolores he discovered Brittany, and Finistère with its inflexible limpidity, where "everything is definite, finished" and where "one reaches a sort of conclusion." He settled down on the Côte d'Azur. Lou Bastidou was too primitive to satisfy him any longer. "A craving for an efficient bathroom, electric light and a small car, it may be, was my undoing," he writes in his autobiography. He bought a piece of rock-strewn ground where there was a vineyard with a stream close by. The building and fitting up of a house afforded him that pleasure, keen and yet exasperating, which is so closely allied to the joy of creation. But as usually happens in successful instances of this kind, his new house, Lou Pidou, proceeded to live a life of its own, making exaggerated demands on him and entangling him in a network of habits and obligations.

Before long he sold Easton Glebe. "My life ended there when my wife died. I should soon be an old man there. And I don't want to be old. It's not going to be a pleasant world for the venerable pose," he wrote at that time.

He also took an apartment in Paris and for the first time he came to know Paris otherwise than from a hotel window and through the mediations of a hall porter.

His relationship with Dolores was an unending duel, a constant flashing of crossed swords. He asserts in his indictment of her that she considered a negative attitude to be the sign of a distinguished mind. "To contradict is to be original. But to approve, for her, is to abdicate." He admits, however, that she had a brilliant, eager brain. In the preface to one of his most important works he pays public tribute to the help she had given him, to her keen, critical intellect, to the persistence with which she urged him to define his ideas and explain them with the greatest possible lucidity.

One of the most spectacular events in their relation was Dolores's clash with English society. At the bottom of her heart, in the corner where lurked her yearning for respectability, she also concealed an

admiration for the unshakable calm, the natural courtesy, the relia-
bility, and the sense of humor of the English people, all these being
the permanent qualities that went with a feeling of impregnable
security. But her own uncertainties put her instinctively on the defensive in face of such inaccessible superiority, so that in self-defense she
aggressively stressed the fundamental differences between these people
and herself.

Wells describes Dolores's contact with his native land as a series of
catastrophes: her showy elegance, so out of place in the depths of the
English country; her unconcealed curiosity, a trumpet blast of deliberate challenge. He found it hard to forget the horror she aroused
when, in conversation with a Conservative cabinet minister, she took
up the cudgels for birth control, which was her favorite theme. But it
was Wells's favorite theme too. This urge to defy British conventionality was his own, but reflected, as it were, in a distorting mirror.

His life was henceforth split into two parts. In fact, his duel with
Dolores was a kind of exteriorization of the duel that went on within
himself. Like every open conflict, it served to appease his inner restlessness, his secret embitterment. In fact, amid the growing irritation, the
exasperation of their approaching rupture, Dolores was for him a zone
of tumult in which he could recover his underlying calm. The exploration of that emotional jungle led him back with all the more
security to his native surroundings, like a man returning from an
adventurous journey to the enjoyment of peace at home. In the long
run, the association with Dolores served to consolidate his most essentially English qualities.

The first literary evidence of Dolores's impact upon his life is provided by Wells's unfairly neglected novel, *Mr. Blettsworthy on
Rampole Island*. The book is marked by a new seriousness, a more
vigorous approach to reality; even its style is more biting than hereto-
fore, the incisive phrases drive with tooth and claw into the very heart
of the human problem. Wells himself described this novel as an attempt to escape from established literary forms, an attempt which he
considered successful, in spite of the cool reception given to it by
critics and public. The book is not only new in form, it also has a
more carefully constructed plot than the works of fiction written by
Wells during the preceding years. The action is rapid and varied, with
a close-packed succession of episodes, and the interest is maintained by
unexpected developments of the central theme. *Mr. Blettsworthy on*

Rampole Island offers the same hearty fare that was provided by *Tono-Bungay*.

This time the book is not a thinly veiled dissertation by the author on contemporary problems, an experiment conducted in an intellectual laboratory; its personages are not merely pasted on a background of current events; they are fashioned in the round, we can look at them from every angle, and we have to go back as far as *Kipps* in order to find minor characters drenched in so much color. It is a cartoon like the one which portrayed the group of visitors from the earth launched suddenly into Utopia amid the "Men like Gods." But a comparison between these two books clearly shows the new element, the depths that now open behind that caricature of humanity. Wells is no longer content to sketch his puppets in bold outline, black on white; he feels a need to justify this transposition of reality into nightmare, to raise it to a higher, more convincing plane. "I laughed while I was writing that book," he tells us later. Indeed, his story is full of humor. The hero is the scion of an ancient, typically English family, but inherits from his mother a mixture of Syrian and Portuguese blood. "I am divided against myself," he says. He feels that he is not one piece, but a collection of fragments; not at ease with himself, he is all the more anxious to acquire the balance that is natural to an Englishman. "I am consciously a Blettsworthy because I am not completely and surely a Blettsworthy."

Youth is depicted as though against the gilded background of a legend, against the stability of life in the prewar period. Among the tightly packed assemblage of typical Britons with whom Wells peoples his book, Blettsworthy's uncle, the Bishop, stands out, a luminous figure drawn, it would seem, by a nostalgic hand. "He seemed to diffuse kindliness as a hayfield in good weather diffuses scent." His benevolent gaze did not range beyond his own world, which was bounded by an indulgent God, a simple, good, and wise queen, and a social hierarchy of the best intentioned men. This gentle gaze sought out the vein of pure gold even in the soul of a criminal, and surrendered itself with that confidence which disarms the most wicked. This kind of lamblike innocence which lingers in the English soul with all its ludicrous and touching simplicity, has seldom been so well represented as in the few pages devoted to the worthy clergyman. Young Blettsworthy, brought up in this sheltered atmosphere, meets at an early age with the faithlessness of a woman and the treachery of a friend. The tendency to excessive emotion, derived through his foreign mother, threatens his reason. When he recovers, an indifferent guardian ships him off for a voyage round the world. This leads to contact with everything that life had so far concealed from him—the aggressive jealousy of uneducated minds, the power complex at work in a brutal nature, the servility of the coward, and the ferocity of the ignorant. The captain who locks his young passenger into the cabin of the sinking ship represents, in his murderous hatred of an intellect superior to his own, a specimen of humanity diametrically opposed to the Bishop uncle, a narrow-minded incarnation of evil contrasted with the narrow-minded incarnation of good.

The shipwrecked Blettsworthy is washed up on Rampole Island, among cannibals. The note of cruelty, previously struck in *The Island of Dr. Moreau* and *The Invisible Man,* is heard again. Wells gives an absolutely convincing description of these savages, with their filth, their rancid stench, their bloodthirstiness, and their unpredictable taboos; they stamp themselves on the imagination as ineradicably as the beasts that Dr. Moreau transforms into men.

But Rampole Island is also, as Wells has told us elsewhere, "a caricature of the entire world of humanity." Some of the characters in the book are described with a sort of impish humor. The savages avoid calling things by their real names, so everything they said meant something slightly different, and everything they set about they did with an air of really doing something else. Their life of daily terror is dominated by gigantic Megatheria, age-old brutes which had forgotten both how to die and how to bring forth, but which continued to devour the substance of the human inhabitants—like those states, organizations, and institutions which become entirely unproductive yet cannot resign themselves to a natural death.

Blettsworthy lives among the savages as a sacred lunatic, like the man of genius in our modern world, "with his remarkable privileges of unorthodox suggestion and his conspicuous immunity from responsibility." Indeed, Rampole Island is the mere figment of a disordered brain, or rather, the flight into sickness of a man prostrated by the blows that life had dealt him. Reeling beneath the weight of his own disappointments, Wells always found particular interest in such transpositions of reality, occurring in a brain too weak to confront it squarely. Blettsworthy's consoling dream is related to the dream of greatness that haunted Christina Alberta's father.

The young hero is brought back to sanity by a woman with a troubled past—in the world's eyes a wretched adventuress, selfish, greedy and vain, but capable of tumultuous and disinterested affection. Blettsworthy awakens from the nightmare of his life among the cannibals, only to be plunged into the nightmare of war. Amid the horrors of the trenches, under the red glare of bursting shells, swept by enemy fire, trampling on the dead and wounded who lie sprawling in the mud, he cries out, before he too falls wounded, "Rampole Island was sanity to this. . . ."

Wells was fond of establishing a parallel between man's insanity and that of a world gone mad. Another of his stories, published in 1930, has this same basis, the ravings of a mind unhinged, a monstrous dream. It links up with the two previous novels, which mirror the tragic absurdity of contemporary society. But whereas *Mr. Blettsworthy on Rampole Island* is a transposition of the past, *The Autocracy of Mr. Parham* is a strange and disconcerting projection of the present into the future. This is one among several novels by Wells which are not only thrown into strong relief by the light of subsequent events, but which seem to draw from those events a fresh purport and even a fresh substance. It is particularly characteristic of what has often been referred to as Wells's prophetic faculty. This faculty was based on the penetrating diagnosis of a given situation, a particularly clear-sighted analysis of the prevailing psychological tendencies by which public opinion was being guided. Wells recognized what forces were at work, and foresaw what direction they would follow and what the repercussions would be, almost before the first faint signs of those repercussions were perceptible. This "discovery of the future," whose feasibility he proclaimed at the very outset of his career, was to manifest itself by some surprisingly accurate forecasts, not only in science, but also in the political field.

The workings of Wells's mental apparatus are particularly easy to follow in *The Autocracy of Mr. Parham*. He notes the existence of a mentality loathsome to him, perceives its connection with the stirring of mightier forces all over the world, depicts an exaggerated form of it, and carries it to the point of absurdity. But this monstrous absurdity is tomorrow's reality. Is he himself aware of that? Probably not. Despite his intermittent gift of prophecy, he was slow to credit his own predictions. He used to seem rather astonished when they were realized. In 1933, writing about *The Autocracy of Mr. Parham,* he says,

"It still amuses me, but not many people share my liking for it." A time was to come when certain characters in the book would no longer amuse him.

From the literary standpoint, this novel is inferior to *Mr. Blettsworthy on Rampole Island*. The people in it seem to have only two dimensions. The story fades out into interminable political arguments. Considerable sections of the book are mere glorified journalism, written in the ironical style of a pamphleteer. The whole thing smacks of farce. But at the heart of the folly lies a great bitterness. The hero is one of Wells's favorite laughing stocks, the modern British imperialist of the university type. Around him move figures, or rather cartoons, taken straight from the daily newspapers and hardly disguised: for instance, the socialist prime minister, "like a lonely, wind-stripped tree upon some blasted heath," the League of Nations official, and a number of others. An aimless skepticism is in fashion. The country is weary of parliamentary government. The League of Nations official realizes that nothing can be achieved on the basis of current mentality. A scientist who, as usual in Wells's books, is the spokesman of a new international conscience, declares that the existing governments are automata, preparing for war and preparing war. Economic and financial forces are tending toward the unification of the world. But in America, as the banker says, one cannot fight popular clamor or the mischievous politicians who stir it up; and least of all can one fight the press.

For men like Parham, the ultimate peril, the most redoubtable enemy, is Russia, which must be encircled in order to eliminate the danger that she represents, whereas Mussolini is his idol, because luggage is no longer stolen from Italian trains. "Why are there no such men in Great Britain?" he asks himself despairingly.

In a dream, during a spiritualist séance, Parham sees himself as dictator of the country. He summons his followers to a mass meeting at the Albert Hall. He harangues an excited crowd in a style of "colossal simplicity." Four years after the publication of this novel, Mosley held a meeting of his black shirts in the Albert Hall, and Parham's dream might have been the straightforward report of an eyewitness. Parham takes over the government. The time has come to unite Western Europe. Germany, in his view, constitutes the barrier of the West against Asia, and only by agreement with her will it be possible to strangle Russia. Germany has now appointed her own

dictator, hailed as a reincarnation of Bismarck, "and in a day Germany
became again the Germany of blood and iron that had dominated
Europe from 1871 to 1914. Liberalism and Socialism were swamped by
patriotism and vanished as if they had never been." (This book came
out in 1930.) The British fascist visits the German dictator; but in
spite of England's desire for an understanding, the awakening of
German nationalism and the accumulated resentment of ten years of
humiliation and frustration lead inevitably to war. It breaks out after
a plane has been shot down. Bombs of unprecedented explosive force
are dropped on London, Paris, Hamburg, and Berlin. Bombs rain
down on Trafalgar Square. "People torn to bits, mixed indifferently
with masonry and thrown about like rags and footballs and splashes
of red mud." Did Wells reread his own description of the bombardment of London when, ten years later, the house next door to his was
destroyed in a German air raid?

Parham awakens from his bloodthirsty dream, to find himself just
an ordinary little man who had hoped in vain to play a leader's part
and defend the immutable traditions and institutions of his country.
"If we don't see to it," his former protector says to him reprovingly,
"these Old Traditions of yours and all that will upset the whole
human apple cart, like some crazy old granny murdering a child.
Foreign offices, War offices, sovereignty and clutter like that. Bloody
clutter. Bloodstained clutter. . . ."

It seems as though, in this year of 1930, a sense of urgency had
crept into the book, almost against its author's will. Taken all in all, it
was simply the ravings of repressed ambition, of emotions run to seed.
Loud laughter echoes from its pages. Wells was telling himself a story
to make grown-up children's flesh creep. And once it was finished,
he apparently forgot all about it.

There was as yet no sign foretelling the arrival of a German
dictator in the sumptuous nakedness of a new chancellery. The cum-
brous mechanism of the League of Nations was still working by
accumulated impetus. Constructive ideas were making their way in
the world, tending to unify it. Wells's own life was passing through
a constructive period. Lou Pidou was a brand-new vision of beauty.
The Open Conspiracy might yet be the reality of tomorrow. In
America, his idea had aroused a certain interest. Wells always believed
that the Americans saw things big, although he referred to "that
strange mixture of forward-reaching imagination, hardy enterprise,

exalted aims, and apparently inseparable cynicism which makes the American character a wonder and perplexity for the rest of mankind." In 1932, at the request of some influential Americans, he prepared a memorandum on the world situation. Confronted with the increasing stubbornness of reactionary ideas, he also published, around this time, a series of articles under the general heading, "There should be a Common Creed for Left Parties throughout the World." But his principal activity was the laborious preparation of the third part of that mighty work, intended as a bible for the civilized world, that vast sociological compilation, *The Work, Wealth and Happiness of Mankind.*

The exhaustion that comes when a lengthy task is finished, the blank feeling that follows a long-sustained effort, made him especially sensitive to the unsatisfactory aspects of his private life. Lou Pidou was no longer a wonder and delight, but an ever increasing burden. Wells found his life invaded by people he had no wish to see, by telephone calls that made havoc of his working hours, by all the parasitic elements whose importunate tendrils were stifling his creative impulse. Like Henry James, he dreamed of a "Great Good Place" where he might retreat and work unharassed by material problems, inaccessible to all the people and things that laid persistent claim to his attention.

The spiritual backsliding of society which he had depicted, by way of a joke, in *The Autocracy of Mr. Parham,* was now a reality. In that summer of 1933, a dictator had come to power in Germany, a man both more ridiculous and more formidable than the dictator in his novel. The first visions of terror were rising from the unfathomable abyss of human cruelty and corruption.

Wells shared his countrymen's inability to believe in utter wickedness, in evil for evil's sake. But though he underestimated the horror, its duration and the peril it represented for the outside world, he was profoundly disturbed. His own task, his self-appointed mission of warning, now seemed more hopeless and yet more urgent than ever. He felt the need to reassess all his accumulated store of experience, his failures and successes, in an attempt to discover their hidden meaning. The meaning of his own life must surely be that of all lives which reach out beyond the narrow circle of private interests. He became more and more detached from himself, a normal happening, for as he said, the young are completely and passionately self-identified, but

individuality is a sort of innate obsession from which we free ourselves as our spiritual development proceeds. In his mind was arising
the conception of what he called the immortal soul of humanity, in
which the individual existence is swallowed up like a passing thought.
But this absorption of the individuality in some vaster evolution
seemed to him to render the sense of human will both more evanescent
and more important. "Interests far transcending mere individual survival take over the will and consciousness and direct them to ends
that go far beyond the limits of the individual life."

It was with this guiding principle constantly in mind that he turned
to the scrutiny of his own life.

He was sixty-six years old. He was familiar with the recurrent
heartsickness of seeing a period of his life drag to its end in discontent, like a played out record. But would there be another new beginning for him, at sixty-six? This, he said to himself, was the last stage
of his journey. And as people do who are uncertain of the future, he
turned back toward the long stretch of years that lay behind him, to
unravel the tangled skeins and trace the crimson thread of permanent
feelings and ideas, the order, as yet unperceived even by him, which
would lead every scattered piece in the game to its appointed place.

In a restless moment, during a night of irritation and sleeplessness,
he began to write the first chapter of what he later called *Experiment
in Autobiography*. But it was a premature attempt. In order to free
his mind and recover its full vigor, he would have to make his escape
once again, in the physical sense, as so often before in the course of
his life. At the same time, the general disquiet was increasing to a
degree that thrust it into the forefront of his concerns. The sinister
light of the menace hanging over the world served to clarify his own
muddled situation. He realized where his immediate task lay. And
with this discovery came the courage to make a clean sweep. He
parted from Dolores.

He gave up Lou Pidou. It was not without a pang that he uprooted himself from a place he had loved so deeply. He took a last
stroll in the light shade of the olive trees on the hill, lingered beside
the rose bushes, sad for a moment to think that he would never see
them blossom again; he looked at the row of irises that he had
planted along the stream, under the weeping willows; he gazed with
intensity at the view from the terrace, absorbing it into his memory.

The stately black cat, which had so long been the silent companion of his meditations, seemed to understand all about this final separation, and it was to him that Wells made a little gesture of farewell, as he set out toward the station, walking with the rapid step of a man who has shaken off a heavy burden.

XXI

THE SHAPE OF THINGS TO COME

THE YEAR 1933 was drawing to an end in a mood of puzzled apprehension, a kind of icy silence, the dead calm that sometimes falls before a storm breaks, as Wells described it in his novel, *The Shape of Things to Come*. For the sake of this new novel, which he felt to be an important task, he had freed himself from all ties, rallied his scattered forces and called upon all his skill. Now he felt sure of his ground and could give free rein to his imagination. Later he declared that the hardest work and the deepest thinking of all his career as a writer had been put into this book.

It came out in the fall of 1933. Rereading it nowadays, one is impelled to check this fact by the date on the title page, so closely entwined is imagination with the reality of future happenings. Wells's description of that year's approaching end was in itself a prophecy. "War was manifestly drawing nearer in the Far East; in Eastern Europe it loitered, it advanced, it halted, and no one displayed the vigor or capacity needed to avert its intermittent, unhurrying approach." This reads like a record of events, yet it was only a forecast.

The novel begins with a kind of supplement to the *Outline of History*. Certain events need to be stressed, while others have sunk into the background. Certain lessons need to be drawn from the confusion of the past; the chief currents of history have to be traced in their main lines. The essential thing is to bring the *Outline* up to date, carrying it right forward to the present and supremely grave moment of time. But nowadays no one is any longer interested in history, no one wants to read outlines, and Wells is particularly anxious to capture the attention of a large public. He emphasizes that he has gone to considerable trouble to make this new book as readable and absorbing as possible without sacrificing what, for him, were the essentials. To keep the reader's interest from flagging, he uses a rather obvious trick. He imagines a League of Nations official, a man concerned with international questions, who dies in 1930, leaving the unfinished manuscript of an "Outline of the History of the Future"—a "Book of Dreams." Wells was anxious and impatient to put his message across. This setting was merely intended as a stimulus to lazy imaginations.

The first part of the historical outline is entitled "The Age of Frustration Dawns." Wells describes how the notion of the modern state dawned in the minds of a half-enlightened generation, unconnected with any real forces that could have imposed it. He goes on to speak of the spendthrift economic system and the progressive militarization of the world. According to him, the Boy Scout movement had been the first to set up a semicivilian, semimilitary organization of uniformed adherents. The Black Shirts and Brown Shirts were flagrant examples of that collapse of the boundaries separating civilian from military life, which had been going on ever since World War I. This collapse would sooner or later be completed by the introduction of bombers, gas-diffusing airplanes, and long-range air torpedoes.

What he was describing was neither the past nor the present, but the future. "The militarization of the European multitude reached a maximum during the Polish wars. About 1942, gas masks, either actually worn or hanging from the neck, were common for a time." Towns are plunged into pitch darkness, as a precaution against air attacks. "Before the Polish struggle," writes Wells, "general architecture was very little affected by military needs." But the panic caused by bombs and poison gas brings about as complete a change in architecture as the deepening impoverishment of the market permits. People begin to construct huge subterranean shelters, human life takes refuge under massive armor plating that follows the curves of the ground.

After the 1930 depression, the world had seemed bewitched and all progress had come to an end. Everywhere and in everything there had been a lowering of vitality. The disorganization of the monetary system had led to a breakdown in public morality. People had ceased to respect society, because they felt it had betrayed and fooled them. In the old days, observes Wells, it was famine, pestilence or invasion that caused social collapse, but recent signs of dry rot seemed to be due to an increase rather than to a decrease of material and energy. This expansion of the social framework was hampered and checked by incapable governments and outdated laws. A crime wave was spreading throughout the world, the age of insecurity had set in. Criminal gangs were being formed, and terrorist gangs with political pretexts, both resulting from the same dissatisfaction, the growing restlessness of pent-up energy seeking an outlet. In a troubled world, military strategy and scientific armaments were being developed with a terrible and shameless logic of their own. The changes in methods of warfare that had occurred between 1900 and 1930 were the most important, except for the invention of firearms, that had taken place since man first turned his hand against man.

Wells mentions certain of these new weapons: the amphibious tank, the fighter plane, used with particular success by the English and Germans, the long-range aerial torpedo, guided by remote control, chemical warfare, gas warfare, and bacteriological warfare. Most of the men who worked to prepare chemical warfare, he says, were serious, respectable individuals; but considered as a group, they were dangerous lunatics, destined to bring atrocious death, suffering, and mutilation to millions of human beings.

This war, for which every kind of horror has been enlisted, breaks out in 1940. (Wells said later that it was quite by accident that he had hit on this date, early January, 1940.) The whole of Europe had been undermined for a long time. "That ignominious invention of President Wilson, the Polish Corridor, was the first mine to explode," says this book of 1933.

Wells outlines the psychological factors which had been at work inside Germany, for, he writes, the whole of European history from 1900 to 1950 could be written from a study of the German mentality and the reactions it called forth among neighboring countries. "Adolf Hitler, as the decisive product of Germany in labor, is one of the most incredible figures in the whole of history." This judgment is remarkably accurate for 1933, especially in Great Britain, where politicians were so slow in taking Hitler's measure. Wells supplements it with a shrewd psychological portrait of the man, with his vague, rudimentary ideas and his swastika symbol, "the idiot's own trademark." He adds a note on the influence of hatred upon the relationship between the various sections of mankind; this was a form of social insanity to which he had given special thought and which he looked upon as a disease, capable, like many other mental diseases, of being cured. He foretells the harm wrought by such hatred, "There were many thousands of suicides between 1930 and 1940—suicides of sensitive men and women who could endure the dreadful baseness and cruelty of life no longer."

This outline of future history is a strange mixture of prophetic insight and inaccurate forecasts. It shows war breaking out after an incident at Danzig. From the very beginning, this war of 1940 arouses less enthusiasm than that of 1914. Wells imagines a localized conflict between Poland and Germany, Italy—which this time takes the German side—and the Balkan States. The Russian army seizes eastern Poland and Bessarabia, which are transformed into Soviet republics, and halts at the frontier. France is soon drawn into the war. It is a war of raids and reprisals, a war of scorched earth—total war. Every adult who is not fighting in one branch or another is recruited for forced labor, constructing underground shelters or clearing up ruins. Wells gives a vivid word picture of a group of gaunt, ragged Frenchmen, working under the lash, while those who are overcome by exhaustion drag themselves aside and die unheeded.

It is a war fought out mainly in the air. The airmen seek for crowds and bomb them. The great air raids begin amid the hideous wailing of sirens, while panic-stricken crowds jostle their way to the nearest shelter. One often almost forgets that it is not an eyewitness who is writing, but a man whose dreams are haunted by tomorrow's nightmare reality.

Wells's future war is a war of poison gas. He might have made it culminate in atomic warfare, for as early as 1913 he had been obsessed by visions of the atom bomb; but he either underestimated his own prophetic gift, or else overestimated the time that would elapse before the atom could be split.

One wonders whether the man who in 1913 had been haunted by premonitions of the atom bomb, was not obsessed twenty years later by some nightmare conflict of the future, horror that dominates the world. Wells describes the various gases with which experiments had already been made during World War I—the chlorine compound used at Ypres, the arsenical gas invented in America in 1918—and thus leads up to the latest invention, the permanent death gas which destroys all living things. The stricken towns, where corpses rot among ruined houses and the spectral survivors are tortured by famine, are fit breeding ground for the epidemics that come later and range from influenza and cholera to bubonic plague and yellow fever. The future war comes to an end through the sheer exhaustion of mankind. Twenty years after its start, the population of the world has fallen by fifty per cent. In the ruins, life is at a standstill. Transport no longer functions. Governments have collapsed. The whirlwind has swept away a bankrupt civilization, with its economic and monetary systems. Private capital no longer exists. Here and there, groups of people are still living, in primitive conditions. Berlin has dwindled to a few villages, scattered among ruins. London has been partly destroyed in a landslide. A citizen of the future cycles along the deserted roads of the French Riviera, where the big hotels and country houses stand empty, the towns are a mass of rubble, the lovely gardens have grown into tangled thickets, and water gushes out from broken conduits. America has slipped back into the rough life of the pioneering days. Wells certainly enjoyed himself a lot in these descriptions of the little islets that remain amid the wreckage of civilization.

One idea has survived the universal cataclysm—Wells's guiding idea, the Modern State, as forecast in his persistent dream of an Open Conspiracy. One man sets about to assemble the scattered men of good will and clear mind into groups. This is the reappearance of Wells's former heroes, the incorruptible scientists, the "revolutionary technicians." Aircraft provide the one fragile link between the separate parts of the shattered world. So the young airmen, the favorite children of Wells's imagination, take the management of public affairs into their capable hands.

Wells gave his book the subtitle of *The Ultimate Revolution*. It is a creative revolution, the contrary of a mere insurrection. It overcomes all resistance to the Modern State. Isolated rebellions are stifled in bloodshed. In its early days, the Modern State is a militant state; it passes through a phase of dictatorship, exercised from the air, before arriving at the removal of all governmental controls and the sovereignty of public opinion, which functions through a world-wide agreement between active thought and imagination.

Wells attributes the success of this ultimate revolution to the fact that from the very beginning it is essentially an educative movement, in which politics play only a secondary role, and is thus able to make a particularly deep impression on the public mind. In this part of the book he is dreaming aloud about his ideal future world. Man's inventive faculties, freed of all constraint, can turn aside from destructive work and concentrate on improving the condition of mankind. Scientific discoveries lead to a hitherto undreamed abundance. Men discover unsuspected wealth beneath the earth's surface. Thanks to the tremendous progress of meteorology, they can control the winds, redistribute rainfall, and greatly extend the habitable regions of the globe. Average expectation of life is increased by physical security and by new measures of hygiene. Now that hunger and fear are driven out, the human mind can turn to loftier interests. Life has become a pleasant thing, and man discovers his true self in his increased working capacity, his thirst for knowledge, his creative enthusiasm, and the infinite possibilities that lie ahead of him.

Such is Wells's vision of human happiness. *The Shape of Things to Come* is his most elaborate and definite declaration of faith in mankind. Amid apocalyptic conditions, man gropes toward his destiny. A note of profound fervor runs through the book, as though its author were deliberately crowding all his knowledge, the results of a lifetime of reflection, into this fresco of future existence, that it might become a goal for all men's scattered dreams. This is the same spirit in which faithful believers raised their eyes toward the heavenly Jerusalem, the city of the future. *The Shape of Things to Come* is written with testamentary earnestness, like the dying message of a man in full possession of his faculties.

But Wells emerged from these dreams to find himself faced with a reality that confirmed his worst fears. Galsworthy had recently died, and Wells now succeeded him as International President of the P.E.N. Club. On leaving Lou Pidou and bidding farewell to a slice of his past, he went to Ragusa, where the annual P.E.N. congress was being held. There he found overwhelming evidence of the way in which individual thought and creative effort were being shackled. He heard first-hand accounts of the persecution of Jewish and liberal writers in Germany. The most celebrated among them had gone into exile, to escape being tortured in prison or thrust into the degrading conditions of a concentration camp. They had sent representatives to Ragusa. But a Nazi delegation had come as well, to speak in favor of this brutal campaign against liberty.

Wells the private individual was never on an equal footing with Wells the prophet, and he did not fully realize, either at this Ragusa congress or at the Edinburgh congress of the following year, that he was witnessing the first skirmishes of the world war he had just been describing. He thought all this was just one more professional struggle for the maintenance of literary freedom and dignity, whereas it was really a first urgent and unavailing appeal to the conscience of mankind. He always loved a fight, and these impassioned arguments had a tonic effect on him. Even in his autobiography he writes of the Ragusa congress as "stormy but very amusing." It marked, too, a turning point in his private life.

At the end of the novel *Apropos of Dolores,* just at the moment when the hero feels most keenly that he has made a mess of things, Wells brings in a fair-haired, broad-browed, golden-skinned young woman with frank blue eyes. She appears for a brief moment, then vanishes. She embodies for Wells's double the dream of an immortal and unattainable goddess, whom he was expecting to find just round the corner.

As usual, this dream was a forecast of reality. Soon, at the Ragusa congress, Wells was to meet the woman who would be the last love of his life. Later, he depicted her as the heroine of his novel, *Brynhild.* Brynhild revised her lover's scale of values and gave him, too, a final, abiding sense of security. She appears again in his novel *The Brothers,* as Catherine. Wells describes the feelings she aroused in the hero of this book, feelings that were his own: "He had an intense affection for her, an admiration, a belief in a sort of textual wisdom of body and impulse in her."

Brynhild (the name went well with her tall, strong, statuesque body; and she carried herself like an armed Valkyrie) or Catherine (that name avoids the suggestion of a Germanic streak, of which she had none whatever) summed up in her nature all the women Wells had ever loved, and yet was at the same time a unique experience in his life. When he met her, he was nearing his sixty-ninth birthday. He might have been content to live on memories. But the Dolores incident had left a painful void in him. He could not bear to return to a life that was already all too familiar, a world he had explored to its farthest horizon. And as good luck would have it, the woman he now met had another new world to throw open to him, the Slav world, with its limitless possibilities which had always held such attraction for him. His last love had in it something of the astonished admiration of an explorer penetrating ever farther into the unknown;

and also there was a touch of exasperation, expressed at times with childish impatience, at the presence of something he could not understand. Now and then he felt lost, as though amid the boundless Russian landscape, and retreated, grumbling, to the safe, familiar ground of his ineradicable Britishness. These fits of bad temper and perplexity made Catherine laugh, a deep-throated laugh that baffled him because it seemed to come from very far away and to tell of things that were beyond him. There was a kind of detachment about her laughter too, as though it came from outside herself, rather like the rustling sound when a big tree shakes its leafy branches in the wind. She seemed to be still closely linked to the earth, the rich, light, fertile soil from which she sprang. Her broad, lively face, with its lofty brow, was like a landscape, composed of expressions rather than features. Grave or gay moods drifted across it like the play of sunlight and shadow over a plain. From her deep roots, her inner harmony with all that grows and progresses—earth, sky, the primitive strength of natural feelings—she drew an independence which was revealed, without the least aggressiveness, in her amused aloofness and utter lack of self-interest. She was immune from the considerations that govern most human lives; she preserved her independence, but not out of bravado nor thrift; she did it as naturally as though marking the boundaries of an estate.

Wells was considerably disconcerted by her alternation of surrender and withdrawal, her air of living her own life with carefree bohemianism or aristocratic indifference. He himself had never entirely surrendered to anyone, but now he was irritated by someone else's self-possession; he had made his escape so often, and now he was impatient to grasp something that eluded him.

In the light of this final experience, the nature of the relationship that might exist between a man and a woman became clear to him for the first time. Partly out of conviction and partly as a matter of personal convenience, he had worked out long ago a theory of free love, and only now did he perceive that it was misleading, superficial, making no allowance for the possessive urge or the gnawing pain of jealousy. He was a little like a scientist, taken aback by the discovery that real life contradicts the results of his laboratory experiments. For a long time he had looked upon human beings as mere biological specimens. He had even given the title "Dissection" to the chapter of his memoirs that dealt with the emotional side of his nature. Now he suddenly felt that he had overlooked, there, an element of pain, as though mistaking living tissue for the prepared specimen with its dried-up veins. His interest in people, as individuals, was now aroused. He seemed to become more human.

The meeting with Catherine gave him new zest for finishing his autobiography. In giving this book the subtitle, *Discoveries and Conclusions of a Very Ordinary Brain,* he was not displaying false modesty, he was simply bringing into focus the events he had to relate. He has been described as "a glorified edition of the ordinary man." His personal experiences drew their chief interest from the fact that they were understandable and convincing to all of the vast numbers of people who resembled him. He identified himself quite consciously with the great mass of the public. But his personality and that of the ordinary man did not entirely square with each other. He stood head and shoulders above the man in the street; the difference lay in his penetrating awareness of himself, of other beings and things, of present events and their future repercussions, and also in the frank courage with which he tried to explain what he saw, disregarding the risks that he ran in being so outspoken.

It was in Catherine's country house, on the shores of a lake in Estonia, that he settled down to write these memoirs. Everything around, from language to landscape, was strange to him. He was beginning a new slice of his life. He needed to shake off the weight of a past that was now too long and too burdensome to permit him to make an entirely fresh start. "I began this autobiography to reassure myself during a period of fatigue, uneasiness and annoyance. It has done its work of comfort," he wrote.

In this book, he speaks as freely of personal matters as consideration for other people allowed him to do. He conceals nothing of his past, his humble background, or the repeated failures and disappointments of his early career. But while his book contains a very large measure of truth, it also has its share, not of poetic license, but of deliberate omission. There are more snatches of self-confession in his novels than in this story of his life. His cool, rather inhuman lucidity never quite left him, even in moments of passion; but he often remained silent out of respect for human feelings. In this book of memoirs, his mother's figure stands out a little softened by affectionate pity, but his father's, like those of his sons, is left in the shadow. He goes as far as possible in the exploration of his sexual experiences, but dwells chiefly on recollections. Most detailed are those concerning his two wives—because he had been married to them and because they were both dead by that time—though he refers in passing, very tactfully, to the scandal created in England by his private life as well as by the articles he wrote. This experiment in autobiography is a sort of web where his life story has still to be filled in, along the guiding lines that he himself has fixed.

Begun amid agitation, the book ends serenely on a conciliatory note. He had made a clean sweep of his past. So much so, that he now shrank from all that he used to cling to and seemed afraid to settle anywhere or to have any possessions. His present adventure was so full and satisfying that it needed no stage setting or properties. On getting back to England, he went to live in one of those absurd beehives where wanderers make their brief halts between journeys: a block of service flats, standing on the noisiest crossroads in all London, at the corner of Baker Street and Marylebone Road.

The place was a maze of corridors laid with pinkish rubber matting on which one's feet made no sound and leading past innumerable green-painted doors, all exactly alike. Despite the unsuccessful attempt to induce cheerfulness by this color scheme, the atmosphere was that of a clinic; one had the impression that people must be dying, silent and forgotten, behind all those closed doors. The building echoed like a hollow shell with the clamor of the double stream of traffic outside. The rattling windows were kept tightly closed, but conversation was punctuated by the hooting of motor horns, the crash of metal, and the screeching of brakes. No kind of confidential talk could ever be held in a place thus delivered over to street noises. There was a semblance of privacy in his cramped study, where shelves of books lined the walls from floor to ceiling. But books and pieces of old furniture seemed out of place in this clearing-house atmosphere. The gray London sky hung like a curtain before the windows. Everything was impersonal, the negation of a home. A restaurant on the premises supplied food for the dwellers in this hive, and horrible food it was. A dish of shellfish would contain more shell than fish, in broken pieces that the assembled guests spat out as unobstrusively as possible; the meat and vegetables tasted of the water in which they had been overboiled. But Wells, though something of a gourmet, did not seem to notice all this. He merely raised his falsetto voice to be heard above the noise of traffic. He even seemed to enjoy the lack of comfort, to be delighted by the impermanence of his surroundings.

Just at that time he was feeling like a child who had discovered a new toy. His book, *The Shape of Things to Come,* had been taken up by a cinema firm, and he was going every day to the Elstree studios to watch the work. He stormed and raged at the ignorance of the directors, their short-sightedness and wastefulness, but he had tremendous fun. The cinema was another of his anticipations that had been completely realized. The talking machine and the picture box of *When the Sleeper Wakes* were now within reach of everybody. Most people of his generation, born in the days of horse-drawn traffic and kerosene lamps, had become gradually accustomed to modern inventions and comforts, by advancing, as it were, step by step along an unknown road. But for Wells everything new was something already seen. Today's achievements were old friends. They took him back to his own earlier dreams, dreams outstripped by reality. He was like a sower, watching the growth of an amazing harvest. Seldom has a man's imagination been so richly fulfilled within the space of his own lifetime. But Wells lived so much in the present that he gave little heed to this gradual materialization of his past visions. Besides, his own writings seldom lived long in his memory. Still, from time to time some present-day picture would surprise him by its striking resemblance to some long-past figment of his brain.

One such moment came during his plane journey from London to Moscow by way of Berlin, in the summer of 1934. He remembered that in 1900, when he wrote *Anticipations,* such a journey was still as improbable as a flight on a magic carpet. Now, arriving over Moscow, he saw huge airdromes on the ground below and hundreds of airplanes lined up outside the hangars. There was for him something curiously familiar about this sight that he was seeing for the first time. Twenty-six years before, in a book called *The War in the Air,* he had described just such a wide open space, with aircraft scattered about it "like a herd of cows in a pasture," and the hangars and storehouses between which tiny human forms could be seen bustling to and fro. He remembered how, when writing that book, he had given free rein to his imagination, which had conjured up that clear-cut vision of present-day reality. But even in his boldest moments, he declares, he had not expected to live long enough to see such things with his own eyes.

He was never given to boasting about this prophetic vein of his; he considered that his "guesses," as he called them, had in most cases hit the mark by sheer good luck. But he was naturally driven to the conclusion that since reality had caught him up and even outstripped him in the field of practical invention, his great idea of world union was also destined for fulfillment in the not too distant future. He remembered the skepticism that had greeted his forecasts of the future role of aviation in war and peace. Why should not his more important phophecy be fulfilled in its turn, despite the short-sighted politicians and cynical profiteers who were interested in maintaining the present state of chaos? His belief that common sense would triumph in this hour of unprecedented gravity, was strengthened by finding that his pronouncements had called forth an enthusiastic response from a man with tremendous power of action.

Wells had for some time been watching the policy of Franklin D. Roosevelt with attentive interest. In an article written in this same year of 1934, shortly before a visit to Washington, he had expressed the opinion that any attempt that President Roosevelt might make to reorganize the political and social system of America in such a way as to halt the present headlong rush toward disaster, would be met with such powerful opposition that it could not possibly succeed. But this pessimistic conclusion was somewhat altered by the impression Wells gained from a personal interview with the President. He went to the White House armed with "his own credentials," and was welcomed not only with the curiosity that greeted him everywhere, but with an evident interest in his ideas for their own sake. Most of the politicians he had known so far had been men who, when they rose to power, had tried pompously to appear equal to their lofty situation. So when he met Mr. and Mrs. Roosevelt, he was all the more struck by their curious independence of mind, and by a simplicity that seemed to be based on inner security. They did not, he said, seem to be concerned with the impression they were making; they were simply interested, in a manner that was keen and yet detached, in the general world situation.

Wells found them exceptionally forthright and unprejudiced, ready, as he put it, to do as they thought fit without excitement or apology, and apparently not even aware how exceptional was this attitude of theirs. Franklin D. Roosevelt was not a man whom he would have called an "open conspirator" but, according to him, a shrewd and even crafty politician, skilled in the handling of crowds and individuals, never straying too far away from the majority opinion and never losing sight of current possibilities. He was, however, always ready to strike out along a new path, to speak to the great American public, over the heads of the political parties, in his own direct, spontaneous manner, as man to man. He was eminently reasonable and fundamentally indomitable and, concludes Wells, the best possible means of transmission for a new world order.

The shadow of war was looming on the horizon. But while Wells saw it more clearly than most people, he knew, too, that it could easily be driven away by an agreement between all the peace-loving peoples of the world. He declared that only the purely mechanical factors of international politics—the out-of-date traditions, the childish mentality prevailing at the Foreign Office, and so on—stood in the way of an understanding between the English-speaking peoples, Russia, and France; and that if those three groups declared firmly and unanimously that they were determined to maintain peace, peace would be maintained.

Such was the waking dream that he related as he sat in the White House watching his host, the man who could smile so confidently, his heavy body suspended on crutches. This dream of an understanding between East and West, which seemed so fantastic in peacetime, was to be achieved amid horror and bloodshed. Wells seemed obsessed by the approaching nightmare, as though all the great host of those about to die was on his heels. He did not pause to wonder why he should have been singled out to sound the alarm. He looked upon himself as just an adventurer, thrusting his opinion, unasked, upon influential men. But he went ahead with his peace crusade, always dogged by the specter of fatality. When he left Washington, he felt himself to be the bearer of an important message.

He went to Russia. He went there for a definite purpose, in his capacity as International President of the P.E.N. Club. Russia still stood outside this international organization, refusing to allow her writers to rub shoulders with the enemies of communism or to accept the principle of freedom of thought for the individual which is one of the articles of the P.E.N. Club charter. Wells had flung himself and all his authority into the turmoil of the last two P.E.N. Club congresses, in an effort to obtain the right of free speech for the exiled German writers, including Communists such as Toller; and he expected to find in

Russia an atmosphere more friendly to the P.E.N. He relied above all on the personal support of the most powerful man in the Russian literary world, Maxim Gorky, the writer who had passed into legend while still alive. He went to see Gorky one lovely summer day, and found him on the white, sunny porch of the fine house that the state had put at his disposal. Wells could not help being reminded of the exile with drawn, hopeless features whom he had met and helped on Staten Island so many years ago. The eyes that then had been filled with tears were turned upon him today with a piercing, suspicious gaze, as though trying to penetrate the capitalist plot that must lie concealed behind his proposal. Wells, always very sensitive to suspicion, was deeply wounded by this mistrust, coming from one whom he had regarded as an old friend and a comrade-at-arms in the fight for liberty. He had the bitter feeling that the other man had betrayed their common ideal. As usual when his feelings were hurt, he became aggressive and tactless. He was left with the impression that Gorky now, at the height of his glory, was justifying those who had driven him out of America in 1906.

A few days later he received a warmer welcome, from Count Alexis Tolstoy and the Writers' Club of Leningrad. He supposed this difference in atmosphere to be due to a difference of spirit between Leningrad and Moscow. He did not realize that Gorky, like all other members of the Russian official circle to which he belonged, was in the grip of war psychosis. Rearmament was going on at a tremendous pace all over Russia, both material and moral rearmament. Wells, who had just hurled at an apathetic world, sunk in fatalistic resignation, that great cry of warning, *The Shape of Things to Come,* might have been expected to understand better than anyone the Russians, with their mentality of a besieged people. Had he not himself foretold that a period of dictatorship and dogmatic intolerance would precede the victory of the Modern State? But owing to his curious habit of thinking in the future and living in the present, he failed to understand the Russian psychology, although Gorky stated definitely in his hearing that, unlike the English-speaking countries with their assured stability, "Russia was like a country at war. It could not tolerate opposition."

It was like a country plunged in war that Russia continued to marshal her resources and to carry on the series of large-scale, bloodthirsty purges that revolted the Western world. Only much later did other countries, ruined by fifth-column activities, understand to some extent what had happened in Russia. Wells looked upon this Russian psychosis as nothing but a flagrant infringement of individual liberty, and he was bristling with resentment when he bade farewell to Gorky.

His disappointment was increased by a meeting with Stalin. This was an important interview which began with a revision of preconceived notions. Wells had expected to find in Stalin an unbending fanatic, an incorruptible and lonely despot, a dark, tortuous mind. He found instead a man whose undistinguished, rather heavy features wore an expression of commonplace amiability and whose gestures suggested real shyness, or at least the dread of seeming self-important. Stalin's peasant costume, with its embroidered shirt and heavy boots, accentuated his countrified appearance. The interview was supposed to last for forty minutes but Stalin insisted on prolonging it for three hours. When it was over Wells decided that he had "never met a more candid, more honest or more just man," and that it was to these qualities, and "not to anything occult or sinister" that Stalin owed his tremendous and undoubted ascendency over the Russian people. With a rare understanding of the psychology of the Russians, he saw them as a race both subtle and childish, quick to mistrust subtlety in others, and trusting Stalin because of his exceptional lack of subtlety.

This was a meeting between two typical representatives of their respective nations—two men of the people. All that was genuine in them, deeply rooted in their native soil, simple and human, made itself felt in a kind of involuntary flow of sympathy. If they had been able to speak as man to man, they would perhaps have come to an even better understanding. But between them there was a skillful interpreter, well accustomed to international conversations, whose eyes gleamed from behind well-polished glasses, and Wells felt an instinctive distrust of him, as of all professional diplomats. The flow of sympathy was a silent one, and interrupted at intervals by Umansky, reading out the translation of the copious notes that he was taking. But the two men would have had no common language, even could they have spoken the same tongue. For Stalin was an out-and-out Marxist, while Wells was imbued, more thoroughly than he himself realized, with the American spirit that refuses to pin down an individual to one unchanging place in society, and therefore was impervious to the notion of class warfare. Stalin must have looked upon Wells as an infidel, attacking the most sacred tenets of his religion, for Wells declared that outdated propaganda about class conflicts was one of the most disastrous of all the oversimplifications introduced by the Russian revolution. And his injunction not to estrange valuable intellectual and technical circles must have seemed to Stalin like a bourgeois trap, a retrograde notion, an insult to the dogma of the proletariat.

But the shrewd politician in Stalin felt his interest quickened by the picture of the world situation that Wells drew for him. Japan, said Wells, possibly but very improbably allied to Germany, was the only dangerous reactionary threat to civilization. Yet Germany's political delirium, Japan's imperialism, Italy's aggressive nationalism, could be easily disposed of by an understanding between the great Eastern and Western powers. This was a message from President Roosevelt, his first message to the Kremlin, brought to Stalin by Wells.

On the plane of international politics, Stalin seemed ready to admit the truth of these ideas. But Wells wanted more, he wanted to go further. He could not rest content with proclaiming the possible coexistence of two divergent social systems, two ideologies which, though hostile, would be ready to unite for mutual defense. His ruling idea was that East and West should move toward a common goal, a world-wide socialist state. He pointed to the continual extension of economic planning. But Stalin refused to admit the slightest resemblance between the procedure, methods, and aims of Washington and those of Moscow. In vain did Wells emphasize the special position of Roosevelt and that of Stalin, which would make it possible for them to address the whole world with one united voice. In vain, striving to remain patient in face of this exasperatingly slow means of conversation, did he plead for a revolutionary process on a universal scale. Stalin just shook his head and went on explaining patiently, as though to a backward child, the fundamental and irreducible cleavage between a socialism that was merely disguised capitalism, always ready to make a comeback, and the true proletarian revolution. Very much at home in his arguments and quite sure of himself, he sat there, pulling at his pipe and answering all his visitor's exhortations with a calm and positive *nyet*. The interview ended on this note of fundamental disagreement.

This put a stop to Wells's dream of a reconciliation between East and West, between Western socialism and Russian communism. It was the end of his self-appointed mission as mediator, the mission that had been intended to hasten the arrival of the world state and to fend off the horrors that loomed ahead. He admitted, with deep discouragement, that he had failed in an undertaking that was far too vast for him.

XXII

FRUSTRATION

"I HATE BEING seventy," declared Wells when the P.E.N. Club gave a birthday party for him on October 19, 1936. He did not feel he was growing old. Life, it seemed, could never be long enough for his boundless vitality. He went on to compare himself, in this speech, to a little boy who, at a grand party, has been given a lot of lovely toys and is just beginning to spread them out on the floor when his nurse appears and says, "Now Master Bertie, it's getting late. Time you began to put away your toys." "I don't in the least want to put away my toys," he protested, "I hate the thought of leaving."

He spoke with a smile twinkling along the little lines that spread out fanwise from the corners of his eyes. But the joking tone covered a deep feeling, a kind of astonishment at having already reached this advanced milestone in life. His whole appearance belied his age. His cheeks were round and smooth, his glance keen, his movements alert. His only wrinkles were those that laughter had engraved on his face. He still felt the sharp prick of curiosity, and a very juvenile, impatient eagerness to be active and creative. His life had been one long struggle for knowledge, a fight for education. Now he had come to realize that, as he said, three quarters of present-day troubles were due to the intellectual confusion prevailing among bewildered young people; seven eighths of the butchery at present going on in all parts of the world was committed by young men, lads whose minds had been fed on old, outdated theories, or not fed at all. Education had not kept pace with recent needs. In his opinion, a new intellectual and moral impetus, both powerful and free, a kind of encyclopedic education, was essential in order to restore the shaken morale of the human race and set all these confused minds to work in one definite direction. He was still pursuing his great encyclopedic dream. He felt that his own attempts to make a summary of human knowledge had been mere straws in the wind, and that a mighty and urgent task remained to be carried out.

But, as a "frustrated encyclopedist"—an expression he applied to the hero of his next book—did he really believe that the battle for education, the race against catastrophe, could still be won? The book he was writing in that year, 1936, bore the title *The Anatomy of Frustration,* a title which deliberately recalled Robert Burton's *Anatomy of Melancholy.* As in *The World of William Clissold,* Wells hides behind an alter ego, Steele, author of a voluminous work whose title is also *The Anatomy of Frustration.* Steele protests against the implications of the comparison with Burton, declaring that it is no longer possible to speak of life in the same despairing tones used by the seventeenth century writer. Exasperation may be permitted, but not melancholy. The universe is irrational, he goes on, but it is not devoid of hope. Wells almost seems to be trying to reassure himself through the mouth of his hero. It is difficult to alter the attitude of a lifetime. He had always predicted catastrophes, but he had always foretold ultimate salvation. The optimist had invariably got the upper hand of the prophet of disaster. And his new hero still assures himself that although for centuries failure has resulted from every effort to unify the human race and bring it to co-operate, this story of frustration is nothing but a story of birth pangs. He knows too, however, that man is a timid, suspicious creature, and man's history is that of an excessively quarrelsome monkey that is gradually being tamed. At the bottom of his heart, Wells's alter ego no longer believes that ignorance and faulty education are the cause of the evil. He recognizes that in man's subconscious mind there is a firmly rooted and powerful hostility to the idea of a peaceful world. This admission appears here for the first time in Wells's writings. The cornerstone of his Utopian construction seems to have been shaken.

In this book he digs down deeply, more deeply than ever before, into the psychology of the human species, with its secret contradictions. The common denominator of all living beings is their desire for freedom. Peace means, for mankind, freedom from the anxieties of war. Abundance means escape from want and toil. The day came when

Wells's words, "freedom from war and freedom from want," found their place in the document that for a time expressed humanity's great dream—the Atlantic Charter. But man also feels the desire to free himself from initiative, to escape from isolation. And then the desire for freedom becomes a snare, since it leads men to turn their backs on freedom itself, in order to feel more free, more pettily free, in one single respect. Steele also discovers that one of man's principal motive forces is agoraphobia, a form of flight from responsibility toward collective discipline.

The Anatomy of Frustration marks the eclipse of the superman of Wells's various Utopias, with his clear, constructive mind. Writing the biography of his alter ego, he describes Steele as being almost ready to admit that man is incurably a short-sighted, cheating, self-frustrating fool. He can escape final frustration only by setting his will and his hope upon some transcendental aim. As long as he can sincerely believe in an eternal divinity, a nation, a private interest such as scientific research or intellectual progress, he reduces death to a matter of secondary importance. He survives himself only in that which goes beyond himself. But anyone who is unable to rise toward an invincible, immortal life, must submit to frustration. Wells emphasizes the current of defeatism that runs through Steele's concepts, despite his insistence on the limitless possibilities of mankind. Man can find salvation only by renouncing his private aims, by merging into immortality as into a torrent or a river that flows into the sea. The antithesis of finding salvation is suicide. The conclusion of the book is governed by the implications of that last statement: Steele dies by his own wish. We are left uncertain as to whether his death results from momentary weakness, or is the logical culmination of his despair. This is the first of Wells's books to end on such a gloomy note, and it marks a break in his faith in the future.

He himself struggled against his all-invading presentiment of defeat. To commit suicide is to accept frustration, to desert in the heat of battle. And the battle to be waged was a stern one, demanding every ounce of a man's effort. Wells declares, through the mouth of his hero, that the only effective reply to violence is force, that the noncombatant is of no use to civilization at the present time, and that a tolerant, kindly man is as harmful as a policeman who turns his back on a riot and goes away.

The author took up the cudgels that his hero let fall. He continued to plead for a permanent world encyclopedia. He started from the conviction that "the history of human thought is essentially a history of human error," and tried to present a synopsis of everything that the citizen of a democratic world ought to know. He repeated himself deliberately, hammering in his principal ideas, as he put it, however much he might irritate the delicate-minded.

He delivered an address to the Educational Science Section of the British Association. During the year 1937 he did his utmost to spread his idea of a new encyclopedism, but, as he admitted later, with very little success. He still firmly believed that a world encyclopedia would take shape sooner or later, but he was beginning to suspect that progress would not be rapid enough to meet the present urgent need.

As often when at a loss, he now turned toward America. He believed the United States would be the best place in which to set up his encyclopedic world organization. In the autumn of 1937 he crossed the Atlantic and delivered a series of lectures, which were published in 1938 in a little volume entitled *World Brain*. But he said later that Americans are people with profound and generous feelings, who listen to lectures with more eagerness than discernment. They will listen, he added, to any kind of lecture, and as long as the lecturer speaks clearly it matters little what he says.

He met with a still sharper disappointment when, still bent on spreading his ideas, he accepted an invitation from the Australian and New Zealand Association for the Advancement of Science. Even now, in 1938, he still clung to the belief that there would yet be time to change the mental attitude of the world. The date for which he had predicted war was close at hand, but he continued to speak and write as though mankind could still pull itself together and avoid disaster. During that summer of 1938 he was seized by impatience—impatience at the thought that his idea might not be realized, that he was unable to put it over convincingly. At Canberra he spoke on "The Role of England in the Development of the World Mind" and on "The Poison Called History." Urged on by impatience, he spoke more pugnaciously than ever. His success was tremendous and the large gathering gave him a wild ovation. Prominent scientists congratulated him on the vigor of his statements. He had stimulated his hearers, jolted their thoughts out of the usual rut. In the debate that followed, distinguished members of the audience made some highly intelligent observations and gave vent to philosophical utterances adorned, says Wells, with abundant biographical details, none of which had the remotest connection with the vital subject on hand.

At the end of his principal lecture the eminent Australian statesman who was in the chair invited those present to strike up "God Save the King." So after listening attentively to the gloomy prophecy that the human race, having passed its zenith, was now sinking through successive disasters toward final extinction, the earnest audience "lifted up their voices in simple loyalty to things as they are." This reminded Wells of the legendary passenger who went to the bar of the "Titanic" and ordered a drink, with the remark "The damn boat hasn't gone down yet." However, he made no boast later of being superior to his audience, for he remembered arguing at great length about the fee he was to receive for repeating his lecture in Sydney.

Disaster seemed to be marking time. Violence, persecution, and systematic defiance, though they had disturbed people's minds, had not sufficed to call the conscience of the world to arms. Realistic policy was all in favor of coming to terms with the forces of evil. Terrorism presented its letters of credit, and the swastika's ambassador saluted the King of England with "Heil Hitler!" It was a dreary period of compromise, when humanity closed its eyes to approaching catastrophe, and prepared its thoughts to admit capitulation. "History," says Wells, "became an attempt to humor and appease a lunatic who after all— and that was the worst of it—was not always quite so mad as he seemed."

At the time, perhaps, even Wells himself was not fully aware that paralysis was creeping over the world. Perhaps he did not admit to himself that he and those who fought by his side had suffered defeat. He only felt that the present was an abject thing and that daily life held no more zest for him. As though trying to find his way out of the general stagnation, he turned to a fresh activity.

On his seventieth birthday he had remarked that there was a time to write novels and a time not to write novels, that the novel was not one thing, but many, and that every age had its own type of novel. And he had added in conclusion, "I do not see why, after seventy, one shouldn't attempt to write a novel of experience and reflection."

So now, after a long absence, he returned to purely imaginative writing, to the psychological novel. He claimed, however, his personal share in his characters' discussions, the proof of his own presence. The controversial themes of his youth, long forgotten by the public, still lingered in his memory. In the introduction to his last work of fiction, he referred to the protests that had met him, during his early years as a naïve and spontaneous writer, from the vigorous champions of *the* novel, as they called it—the kind of story that eschewed all explanation of the ideas by which its characters were impelled, and never so much as hinted at the presence of the author, who was expected to remain mute and invisible, like God. Wells, on the contrary, had always claimed the right to reveal himself in his writings. He had told the whole world about his joys and disappointments, about the human beings and the ideas that came his way. He felt wonderfully enriched by his latest experience, and was as impatient as a young lover to draw the portrait of the woman he had met. In 1937, for the first time in many years, he brought out a novel that was not linked to the umbilical cord of a current political or social event. This book, *Brynhild,* depicts a woman, the ultimate haven of man's eternal disquiet, the appeasement of that restless craving that flings him, unsatisfied, into all the snares of adventure. Someone in the book observes that the greediness for life, or at any rate, the frank release of greediness, is something quite new and modern, "though perhaps it is rather that quite different thing, a greediness for reality."

The explanation of Brynhild's influence, the secret of her unwavering stability, lay in the fact that she could always withdraw into something that belonged to her and her alone, something whose essence was deeply mysterious and deeply real. It is this reality that Wells brings into contrast with the puppets that make up the rest of his book. He sets a living, three-dimensional being in a group of shadow figures. He had meant to write a book of experience; he wrote a book about one of his very recent experiences, the settlement of a personal feud. Brynhild's lover had fled from a woman who considered herself as the embodiment of the *grande amoureuse,* and who pursued him with her incessant and excessive volubility. Brynhild's husband, the chief figure in the book, is a man of letters, an entirely self-centered intellectual, an old-style aesthete who adopts a fashionably cynical pose, agrees with everything and believes in nothing. An unscrupulous agent raises him, by devious ways, to the heights of fame. In passing, Wells makes a ferocious attack on publicity. Describing the ballyhoo that is needed to build up an author, the agent declares that "Wells at his best was a discursive, unteachable writer, with no real sense of dignity," and that "a man is not called 'H. G.' by all his friends for nothing."

Frustration 295

Brynhild is a story compressed around a quickly moving plot, and the psychology of the central characters, the wife and her lover, is explored in careful detail. Even the superficial puppets sparkle with wit. But as he had foreseen, Wells had lost the attention of novel readers and he was never to regain it. To be labeled by the public is the greatest possible danger for a writer, it confines him behind invisible bars. Wells's earliest readers had been estranged by his obstinate attempts to mingle the most incompatible literary styles, and the new readers he had won by his anticipations and outlines were not interested in the ups and downs of a literary career, or in love affairs.

Was Wells trying to recapture his early, lost public, when he persisted in writing novels that he was afterward to describe as arguments carried on through living people? Or did he feel that he had not yet exhausted the lessons of his experience? In any case, he continued his public confession.

The minor character of Frieda in *Brynhild* was never more than a rough sketch of that whirlwind of a woman who had swept across his path. He followed it up by the savage full-length portrait, *Apropos of Dolores,* which he called a novel about the happiness and solitude of souls. Despite touches of caricature, it presents a flesh-and-blood woman, painted in harsh light and sharp, sudden shadows. A corner of Brittany stands out against the vast, empty horizon. Some minor French figures are drawn in careful outline. There is the French peasant woman in all her stability, a woman whom nobody and nothing can impress and who possesses the instinctive, silent understanding of simple people. The novel is steeped in his special humor, and in the vestiges of resentful bitterness. It cauterized a wound. From that time on, Dolores belonged definitely to the past.

It is a long path that leads from the English girl, Ann Veronica, to this oriental exhibitionist, a lifelong path. Wells now held a position of his own. Anything, it was felt, might be expected from him, so nothing could be surprising. His widespread bad reputation sheltered him as securely as a veneer of respectability would have done.

The psychological novel was only an episode in Wells's career, his neglect of topical events did not last long. After a brief pause the major problem confronting humanity laid firm hold of him again. The world was divided between two ideologies, split by the antithesis of America and Russia. Wells already felt the weight with which this

problem was to bear down on the future. But perhaps he was not quite
clear as to his own position. He carried this still unsettled ideological
conflict before the public in the form of a novel, or rather in a hybrid
form, as sketchy as a radio play. He evidently sensed the risk of the
transposition, the amplified simplification, for he gave this novel, *The
Brothers,* the subtitle, *A Fairy-tale.* The basis of the story is deliberately symbolic. The brothers are enemy brothers. The scene is laid
in a vague, Balkan country, like the setting of a musical comedy. A
dictator is about to seize power, supplanting the king, who has been
defeated in an attack on the Reds. The dictator is a man of liberal
opinions, a "Master-Citizen" who wishes to establish a corporative
regime. His men capture the redoubtable Red leader—his twin brother,
American like himself, whom he believed to have been drowned as a
child, in the Missouri floods. The construction is so clumsy that its
obviousness seems intentional. The communist leader expresses his
personal views on his native land, declaring that "We Americans are
the most lawless and revolutionary people on earth, but we don't like
to give it a name. In our bones we know that we are really a new
people, and it frightens us." Americans, he adds, would sail straight
into socialism if they were not stopped by the Red flag being waved
at them.

The dictator advocates order, evolution imposed from above, a new
world which will be easier to construct on the existing foundations
than on tomorrow's ruins. But it will not be a world modeled on capitalist lines. The dictator tells his ally, the banker, "Like so many of
your American friends, when you say democracy you mean unfettered
finance, private police, controlled newspapers and so on." The dictator's mistress, Catherine—Brynhild in a new guise—sums up the dispute between the two brothers by remarking that they seem to be
putting forward the two separate halves of one scheme. The representatives of reaction—the aristocrat, the priest, the banker, the general
—range themselves beside the dictator. They turn against him when
he decides to come to terms with his enemy brother and to get rid of
foreign help. The dictator arranges for the captured communist chief
to escape. But in the meantime the Reds have launched an attack. The
dictator's friend and right-hand man fires at the escaping leader; the
dictator flings himself between them and is killed in his brother's stead.
Wells himself must have felt the weakness of his fairy tale, the inconsistency of its characters and the childishness of the plot. But the

problem was not rendered less acute by his failure to create flesh-and-blood beings to convey his general ideas.

The storm was gathering on the horizon. Wells regarded the Nazi movement, with its destructive possibilities, as the most serious challenge to human thought that ever had arisen or would arise in the future. Yet it was inevitable. The postwar generation in Germany had been fed on explosive material and was bound to explode. Hitler's madness, Wells pointed out, would have been of small consequence to the world if it had not fitted in so well with certain essential requirements of the German situation. But for that, he would by then have been yelling and ranting, foaming at the mouth, in a lunatic asylum.

After World War II, UNESCO was asked to inquire into Nazi and Fascist methods and to investigate the technique that had enabled them to gain such a hold over the masses and to come into power. But Wells in 1938 was already seeking to discern what economic and sociological conditions were most likely to lead to dictatorship. He was trying to take the mechanism to pieces, to analyze its essential parts. All social unrest seemed to him to be due to the surplus energy of a young generation that could find no outlet. He listed all the other elements of discontent that came to strengthen the initial movement. The Nazi poison was filtering into every country. In Britain Oswald Mosley gazed into his mirror, blandly comparing himself to Julius Caesar, and sent out his ruffians to wreck Jewish shops. But the danger would not come from him or from his actions. What were the reasons and what the circumstances, wondered Wells, that gave birth to a dictator? What were the factors that influenced a necessarily primitive spirit, a necessarily limited mind? What forms of stupidity and what kinds of resentment could conspire to engender violence? What were the forces that believed they could make use of a dictator, only to find that he was making use of them? What part does humanity play in the creation of a monster? The inquiry might have resulted in a sociological study, a far-reaching investigation into mass psychology. But as though to make up for the inadequacies of *The Brothers,* with its cut-and-dried formulas, Wells embodied this interplay of forces in a realistic being, familiar and credible. His new novel, *The Holy Terror,* appeared in 1939, on the eve of World War II. He might have drawn upon the life story of the fantastic lunatic with a reputation for genius thrust upon him who was darkening the horizon. He might have made use of him rather as Charlie Chaplin did. But he seemed to be hinting that the danger was lurking everywhere, that the evil might declare itself even amid British common sense. Unlike Sinclair Lewis, who called one of his books *It Can't Happen Here,* Wells maintained that "it can happen here."

The story tells of a tiresome, bad-tempered boy, a holy terror, a victim of spiritual undernourishment, of miseducation. This is a far cry from the comical, illiterate Kipps, innocent of heart despite all the unfair tricks of fate. Wells no longer believes that society's victims can survive, except to wreak vengeance on a doomed social and economic order. Whether accidentally or deliberately, he gives this young brute for mentor a social failure, one of those picturesque beings whom society throws on the scrap heap. This is just as he had done with Kipps. But the day of happy endings, of rehabilitation through success, has long gone by. The mentor, too, is destroyed by the brute in a fit of panic. Wells shows unaccustomed vigor and great psychological insight in depicting this narrow-minded creature, concentrated on a few simple ideas, drawing bad-tempered strength from his obsession with one single aim—unbridled brutality, that cowardly form of courage.

In a normal period, Wells's hero would probably have developed from an unruly child into a low-grade employee, dreaming limitless dreams, harmless except in his own circle. At worst he would have been a petty criminal, at best a middle-class citizen with repressions, tyrannizing over his family. But this is an age of accumulated resentment, of social instability, of economic privation and moral uncertainty, providing excuse for every kind of rebellion. The framework of life has collapsed, the foundations are shaky, traditional beliefs are dead wood, private property is a worm-eaten institution—so much fuel for a coming fire. If any readers of *The Brothers* were tempted to believe that with advancing age Wells had lost his grasp of reality, this new book showed them that he was still in full possession of all his powers. He had drawn upon memories of his poverty-stricken childhood, his "blasphemous and unsaintly" rebellion, to provide the elements that feed the bloodthirsty instincts of shiftless and unsuccessful beings. Kipps had represented a danger that H. G. had narrowly escaped, a state into which he might have fallen; the young criminal of this book is a nightmare that might have been reality for thousands of children who whiled away their mutilated lives on plots of waste ground, dreaming of battles and conquests.

Young Rudolf, who later becomes Rud, the dictator, is another familiar monster. The dissertation on cruelty which can be read between the lines of *The Time Machine* and goes on through *The Island of Dr. Moreau* and *The Invisible Man* to *The Shape of Things to Come*, finds its ultimate embodiment in the Holy Terror. But not content with such a remarkable psychological study, Wells chose to supplement it by an evaluation of the forces that pave the way for a dictator, only to be destroyed by him in their turn. Here is the American who exploits the mental confusion of his country, the soldier who enjoys the game of forming semimilitary battalions, the born organizer with his passion for planning, the nondescript individuals who settle their private quarrels under cover of party strife—all steps that the dictator uses in his climb to power. Wells also analyzes, piece by piece, the technique of a movement that begins by appealing to the man in the street, flattering the instincts of the underdog, feigning to represent the claims of the people, only in order the better to enslave its dupes. He describes the English fascist movement, drawing a ferocious portrait of its leader with his exploitation of social snobbery and his vanity carried to the point of sadism, imitating the Nazi methods of persecution. With the help of a traitor, the budding dictator seizes the forces and headquarters of the English fascists, whose leader, Lord Horatio Bohun, has to seek safety in an ignominious flight.

Against a background of fiction Wells sets the contemporary tragedies of conscience. The plot is lively and rapid, with unexpected climaxes. Wells's dramatic sense, so much in evidence when he described the descent of the Martians or the explosion of an atomic bomb, comes to the fore again in this fresco of a great social adventure. Terror is weighing on the world, the dictator has swept everyone from his path. He has no sexual needs, no power to love, and solitude has been his strength. But now he falls into the loneliness of a beast at bay. After the blood-stained horror of dictatorship, as after a violent war, the world recovers its sanity. The dictator dies from an injection, given in charity by the only man he could ever bring himself to trust.

A straight line of evolution leads from Wells's first rebels, Dr. Moreau, for instance, or the Invisible Man, to Rud the dictator; a line determined by the varied events of an epoch. Yet there is a fundamental difference between the early figures and the late one. Wells's scientists were exceptional men, who drew their fierce egotism from a proud consciousness of their own value. Rudolf's strength lies in his failings, which are those of the ordinary man—his ignorance, his laziness, his vulgarity, his knowledge of all that is basest and most vile in human nature. But the men of overweening intelligence and the man who is still a hooligan boy are alike in that they are rebels, out to avenge a personal affront, a cherished grudge. When Wells wrote his first books vengeance could still be an individual matter—man enjoyed the luxury, the tragic luxury, of being a lone wolf. But nowadays the individual destiny is no longer a closed circuit. The avenger raises armies. A whole wolf pack howls in chorus with its leader. A day will come when future sociologists will find in this novel a deal of valuable information about a troubled epoch when men's minds were glad to capitulate—an age of contempt when men renounced their human dignity.

Wells knew that war was close at hand, just as he had known it in 1914. It had not yet been declared when he wrote, "At any moment of the day or night, sirens may wail and high-explosive or incendiary bombs may burst around us." All clear thinking had become offensive and intolerable. There was no more hope of a return to mental health. There would be no unification of the world. He anticipated that this war would be shorter but far more destructive, both in the moral and in the material sense, than World War I. Vast resources would be squandered; the earth and the sea bed would be scattered with broken fragments of airplanes, tanks, twisted rails, burned airdromes, and an enormous number of ships sunk with all their cargo. The flight from home of the civilian population in the different countries would be no less terrible than the pitched battles. There would be many wanton bombardments of great cities. Human dwellings would be burned and destroyed to such an extent that no one would have the heart to re-build them, and there would be such wholesale destruction of beautiful buildings, works of art and things of matchless beauty that the exploits of the Huns and Vandals would seem like boyish pranks by comparison. Wells even expected bacterial warfare, in which epidemics would result from the disorganization of the medical services.

Such was the prophetic vision announced on the eve of war. But the prophet was not listened to with the confidence that he deserved. It may be that even he himself did not grasp the full teaching implicit in this prophecy—under a sky that threatens to fall, man is condemned to live like a hunted fugitive, surrounded by perils on every side. The choice no longer lies, as in Goethe's day, between building a house and setting up a tent. Just as Wells had announced before the first war

that the epoch of social and economic stability was gone forever, so
he now knew that no nation, not even among the neutrals, would be
able to preserve its old level of civilization. But his certitude seemed as
though divorced from reality.

His life continued along its old lines. Habit was stronger than conviction. Stubborn middle-class instincts dwelt in him unawares. On the
very brink of war, he settled down to pass a peaceful old age in a
large house in Hanover Terrace. The Baker Street apartment had been
a temporary lodging, a tent that could easily be folded. The Hanover
Terrace house was a challenge to his own misgivings. He seemed to
have a superstitious feeling about stability, as though by fixing himself
down in this way he were braving a tidal wave. Perhaps it was a sort
of childish reflex, as though he had only to close his eyes in order to
dismiss the nightmare.

A P.E.N. Club congress had been planned for Stockholm, for the
fall of 1939. It was obvious that it would have to be canceled. But he
went to Sweden and stayed there up to the last moment, despite
warnings from friends, stubbornly awaiting the arrival of the other
delegates. The outbreak of war found him still there. It was from the
standpoint of a neutral country that he saw the conflict become a
reality. The reactions that took place around him were those natural
to selfish interests that had suffered a rude shock. The hero of his
book, *Babes in the Darkling Wood,* describes, in a letter from Stockholm dated August 25, 1939, feelings that were Wells's own. These
people, he says, "have been accustomed to look on on wars, sell munitions and supplies at tremendous prices, and disapprove highly. But this
Russo-German treaty has knocked them out of that. Never have I
seen a land so fair and so frightened."

It was in this neutral country that he awoke once more, as he had
done twenty-five years previously, to the consciousness that he was
an Englishman. The Swedes would hardly venture to speak to him,
for fear of compromising their neutrality. Opportunism always aroused
his fighting spirit. But he went back to England in a state of deep
disquiet. He was far from the early certitudes of his Mr. Britling. His
young hero declares during that last autumn of peace, that the war in
which everyone was about to be swallowed up will be "a war about
nothing, because the sense has gone out of everything." One thing
was as rotten as another, there was nothing left to hold onto.

Wells began this war in the mood of disillusionment in which he had ended the previous one. He tried to discover a real meaning in it, something to justify the lives that had been lived and the deaths that would be met by all these young men and girls who were, as his hero put it, the heirs to a bankrupt world. *Babes in the Darkling Wood,* where his bewilderment found vent, was, according to his foreword, a novel of ideas. Human thought and vision had been overwhelmed by a change greater than any that had taken place so far. To express this changed mentality, this new contribution to philosophy, Wells chose as his chief characters a group of intellectuals, who discuss their feelings and actions out of habit, by profession, or from necessity.

The hero and heroine of the book are a young couple on their last peacetime vacation. The girl is not yet twenty, the young man is scarcely four years her senior. They both belong to the upper middle class and have been educated in the same way and read the same books; and they communicate with each other in a kind of mental shorthand. They are two very young people of unusual intelligence. But they admit to each other that no one ever taught them anything worth while, anything real. They are as though suspended in a void. They feel that the religion and the moral code on which they were brought up are nothing but exploded myths. But living forces are stirring within them. They feel an urgent need of action, an irresistible longing to see their way through the surrounding chaos. A world is coming to birth; skeptical, rebellious youth believes in Soviet Russia, in something more primitive and more fundamental, and yet wiser and more scientific than the outworn egotism of the West.

Communism, according to Gemini, Wells's young mouthpiece, has been to a great extent paralyzed, especially in the West, by the ossification of its doctrines. The new revolution (1939 version) would keep its beliefs living and flexible. It was to be a new kind of revolution, "Post-Communism." Even now, on the verge of war, Gemini still believes in the existence of a Common Human Imagination which is only waiting to be aroused. During one of their holiday outings, the young couple, looking through a hedge, catch sight of a sculptor who is standing, motionless and in a dream, before a block of marble; suddenly he makes a wide gesture, as though caressing the invisible. One day, muses the girl, he will take up his tools and bring a statue out of that shapeless block. This idea becomes, for this boy and girl, the symbol of their own task—to bring a yet unrevealed world out of the

monstrous block of their epoch. But they are soon caught up, both of
them, by the everyday world that threatens their love: Gemini's parents, Stella's mother. They are caught up in the nightmare of war.
Toward the end of August, Gemini sets out for Russia, regardless of
the clouds in the Polish sky. He goes with an American journalist. In
Warsaw they find that everyone is very excited and pugnacious, and
quite confident of winning the war, a war of personal prowess and
cavalry charges. Who could have foreseen that the Poles would be
swept aside the way they were? They were sold beforehand by other
Poles, comments the American. The two foreigners are in Warsaw
during the bombardments, which Gemini takes as a personal insult.
He wanders fearlessly about the streets and comes across some shattered
bodies. A civilized man has his first, terrible experience of barbarity.
The son of an English judge, full of the ideas about human decency
that have been handed down to him from generations back, suddenly
comes into contact with a shambles of savagery; he finds himself
looking into the abyss that is swallowing up the whole of humanity.
He joins a team of stretcher bearers and helps to dig victims out of
the ruins, shoulder to shoulder with a foreign people, linked by chance
to their fate.

The American manages to get him out of the besieged city. Their
train is bombed and machine-gunned by planes. The Nazis "went
after some poor devils who were running. . . . Then they went away,
waving their hands like schoolboys." And realizing how monstrous is
his story, the American insists, "Like schoolboys . . . it was fun for
them."

Twenty-five years earlier, Mr. Britling had listened to the stories told
by Belgian refugees. Twenty-five years earlier, Wells had brought out
anti-German propaganda pamphlets. But he had never seen any Belgian children with severed wrists, or met anyone who had seen any.
His activity as a propagandist had left him with a slightly guilty conscience. But this time he talked with people who had escaped from
bombarded trains in Poland. He looked into the eyes of survivors and
saw, still lingering there, the incredulous horror that had smitten
them when the German airmen made their playful gesture. So this
was the culmination of centuries of human effort? Gemini admits that
he had never realized how artificial and accidental a thing our ancient
civilization was, how fragile a prey for the forces of destruction, how

easily it could be thrown back to the age of dry earth and bestial, naked humanity.

Wells himself felt this terrible, suffocating astonishment, as keenly as though he had never described the heavens pouring down destruction and man the enemy of man. He never quite recovered from the shock, never quite reassembled the scattered fragments of his faith. From now on he lived with all his sensitive perceptions alert to the experiences that every occupied country was going through. Something withered within him, as in all survivors of those dark years, his faith in an enduring light, in justice or truth, or perhaps just his confidence in life. The weight of some dead thing remained in him, like a tombstone.

"Civilization!" sneers Gemini. Routed soldiers are pillaging the bombed train like rats gnawing at a corpse. But Gemini still believes that in Russia he will find a new order, he still persists in his intention of getting there. At Riga the American journalist leaves him, making off with his money—a rat on the run.

Gemini vanishes completely. But his mother and his mistress still believe he is alive. He is found in Sweden, in a clinic. He had been in Finland when the war with Russia broke out, and had seen Russian airplanes, planes from the promised land, come to free the Finnish proletariat by making mincemeat of it. He had seen a house split open by bombs, a house where the little clock was still striking, where an old lady was still seated at her sewing machine, where a man's head, torn off and dashed against the wall, still had a cigar sticking to the blood-stained flesh, and where broken furniture was all mixed up with children's scattered limbs. He had managed to escape to Sweden. But at Flens station a wagon load of munitions had blown up a few yards away from him. He was taken to a clinic, suffering from severe shock. The result had been a complete nervous breakdown, with paralysis of the motor muscles. He is now sunk in comatose apathy. He refuses to see his relations. In his ravings he shows chiefly a hatred of Stella. But his mother comes to Sweden to bring him home. Stella's uncle, a well-known scientist, a professor at Cambridge, agrees to take Gemini into his house and try to cure him. Dr. Robert Kentlake, the reasoning chorus in this drama, is a born lecturer, whose conversation takes the form of a discourse on philosophy. In his mouth Wells put long biological and social essays.

The novel is forever slipping aside into dissertation and even into magazine or newspaper articles. But Wells was determined to pack into it everything that lay within his field of vision, even reviews of books that had particularly struck him. The living substance of the novel is not stifled by this patchwork of ideas. Its flesh-and-blood characters emerge unharmed from the long tunnels of monologue. Uncle Robert strives patiently to save Gemini's reason. He tries to counteract the shock that the young man suffered when his illusions collapsed. When Gemini declares that he and those like him had placed all their hopes on Russia and those hopes have come to nothing, Dr. Kentlake replies that the Russian revolution was about the only good thing that emerged from the 1914–18 war. The League of Nations had been rotten from the start, but the Soviet regime had stood firm and achieved a great deal. He even takes up the cudgels for "the ineffable Joseph." "I am convinced," he concludes, "that he is still as devoted to the revolution as a good mastiff to his home." This was a strange full-length portrait to paint during the "phony war," when the Allied governments were toying with the notion of bombing Baku, a strange defense to publish in the month of September, 1940.

Gemini sticks to his point: "He bombed civilians and refugee trains in Finland." Dr. Kentlake replies, "He probably knew nothing about it," and maintains that all Stalin saw in his mind's eye was the imperialism of Germany and Western Europe, ready at any moment to stop their present conflict and turn on him. And Finland, with its guns pointing toward the Neva, would be the spearhead of the attack. But Kentlake says, too, that Gemini and the rest of the young Communists are the worst enemies of the revolution, for to refuse to co-operate with anyone at all is "not exactly in the party line." This dialogue between the sick man and the doctor was Wells's own inner monologue. He brought it out, still disjointed and full of contradictions, and put it before the public with the noncomformity which was so characteristic of him. The courage he had shown throughout his life was still with him now, at seventy-four years old. He was still the man who refused to take sides, to look at only one aspect of a question, to see everything as either pitch black or snow white. This binocular vision was expressed even in the very last of his messages to a world where there would have been no place for him any more.

But this political discussion forms only part of the texture of his book. His chief concern is with the bewildered younger generation represented by his hero and heroine, whom he depicts so convincingly that the reader's spontaneous interest in them never wavers, as sometimes happens with characters that Wells left like unfinished sketches in full evolution. Gemini's hatred of Stella is due to an instinct of self-defense, because he believes himself to be impotent. The doctor gradually brings him back to reality, soothes his fear-born complexes, assures him that at the bottom of their hearts all intelligent young people are afraid of life. But one night, in blacked-out London, Dr. Kentlake is run over by a truck. Stella inherits his fortune. She suggests to her lover that they go through a form of marriage. She takes him back to the little house where they spent their brief days of love. His paralyzing terror melts away in these familiar surroundings. He returns at last to the conviction that sexuality "is really the essence of life," the source of all vital impetus. But what are they both to do with their lives and the love that has been reborn between them? The war is still going on. "We are fighting because there is nothing else to be done," says Gemini. He has a presentiment that this war will be the end of the old England, leader of the nations—she is not crumbling into dignified ruin like a mighty pillar, she is melting away like an old tallow candle in a draft.

When Wells was writing this book, Britain still had what he called its "stupefying pro-Nazi government." German strength had not yet proved itself in the collapse of France. But Wells knew that the Nazis could not stop now, any more than a homicidal maniac escaped from a lunatic asylum. He declared that they were bound to continue their venture, and that it "can only end in failure, when the destruction has reached its culminating point." Although the war is the most immediate fact in life, the thoughts of young Gemini reach out beyond the conflict. If a better world does not emerge from all this dross within a reasonable time, if Homo sapiens fails to keep his promise, "it will mean the death sentence of everything that gave life a meaning for us."

On this note of doubt the book really ends, though Wells added a short chapter to it after the invasion of France. It is a dissertation on the future destiny of Homo sapiens. But it is a novel all the same, a living, vibrant piece of imagination. Even the minor characters stand out clearly. Through the book there flits the extraordinary figure of Gemini's mother, a fragile, silky, unreal creature who had been married very young to a man of domineering temperament, had been badly treated by him, and had rebelled against the ugly side of life, from which she was always in flight. There is the stern man of law himself; there is Stella's mother, who was deserted by her husband and has since clung desperately to what she believes to be her love for Stella; among the transitory figures there is the journalist who reduces every ideological concept into propaganda slogans; and many others.

This is one of Wells's most ambitious books, written by a man who felt himself to be in full possession of his powers, and was using them with keen awareness of his task. Amid the universal conflict, he was still gazing into the world of tomorrow. He still believed that modern educational possibilities were untouched as yet. But if no practical world federation were to come after the fighting, if humanity were to remain at its present level of education, it might either sink into a rut of perpetual warfare, or scramble out, as luck would have it. Perhaps there might even be a few more decades of peace, he hoped so; but mankind would be unable to hold back on the slippery path that was leading it, totteringly, to final extinction. Wells still asked himself whether the human race could succeed in making the extraordinary effort of adaptation which was required of it.

This question, which he had taken as the theme of several essays, he now repeated in the form of a novel. It was to be his last novel. He brought it out in November, 1941, with the subtitle, *A Sample of Life, 1901–1951*. The title itself, *You Can't Be Too Careful,* expresses an attitude toward life which he found particularly hateful. He had always loved risk. He knew that everything worth while had to be won by daring and self-sacrifice, by total committal. His last message as artist is a repudiation of selfish conservatism, of paltry prudence, of middle-class timidity. All around him he could see that timidity crawling, that instinct of conservation walling up human beings in a precarious present, like rats in a cellar that is in danger of collapse.

The hero of this book is the final variant of the social misfits that Wells had depicted in the old days. Like Kipps, he is what our civilization has made of him. Like another reflection of Wells himself, he is the son of parents who have lived in a feudal world. But Wells no longer feels the old, overflowing pity for the spiritually starved, the intellectually maimed, such as Mr. Polly. He is beginning to suspect that they are legion, that they make up a force whose cohesion is a danger to mankind.

His Edward Albert Tewler is irresistibly comic, but he is sinister as well. In a world of security, Kipps or Mr. Polly made some people laugh, while others wept or clenched their teeth. In our threatened universe, Tewler seems the embodiment of evil, the antagonist. Wells drew him in black strokes. Tewler, like his forerunners, is the victim of dishonest education, of sexual ignorance, of social maladjustment. But unlike those dissatisfied beings whose rebellion against society is only partly conscious, he deliberately chooses to withdraw into mediocrity: you can't be too careful. He is utterly hateful, rather in the manner of the Holy Terror, in fact, one of the thousands who have helped in the creation of a monster. His instinct, says Wells, had always driven him to detest new ideas, but in the past he had been a little afraid of them. Now he despised them as powerless. "In all this he was essentially English."

Homo Tewler Anglicanus. Wells tells his sorry tale with biting humor, the grim humor of his later years. He takes his minor characters from a circle he knew well, those lower middle classes who are protected from want by a narrow margin of security and who do their utmost to conceal their social servitude. But though he had so often drawn upon this class, Wells here shows little sign of repeating himself, of copying any of his past successes. Among his new happy inventions is the ancient servant of a dissolute Duke, who throughout her long life has never understood what was going on before her very eyes. Then there is the young clerk who has been deeply impressed by a brief trip to Paris, and murders the French language in an excruciatingly funny manner; there is the verbose, inescapable bore who tyrannizes over quiet boardinghouses; the professional backbiter; and a number of others.

This last of Wells's novels is not a portrait of society, however; it is a cry of warning, on a note between laughter and fury. He warns his reader: this is meant for you; you are Tewler and I am Tewler—Homo Tewler versus Homo sapiens; an inert mass which has weighed heavily on the past. Wells describes a state of mind that existed on the eve of World War II; the Bolshevik, the Jew, the "inspired" Führer, all essentially fictitious creations, are, he says, becoming the three cardinal personages in a new mythology of flight from thought, firmness, courage. A solid mass of Homo Tewler was still blocking up all paths toward the future, an impenetrable mass, which perhaps would never awaken to that idea of the cosmopolis that alone could save mankind.

Wells's last humorous novel thus ends on a note of bitter disillusionment, hardly lightened by the persistence of his old dream. He saw that the great wheel of man's destiny was turning faster and faster, striving to fling off its human burden into the void; and he doubted, now, whether the burden could develop sufficient tenacity to cling on and be carried toward the new phase of "infinitely more vigorous life" that could be its reward.

XXIII

MIND AT THE END OF ITS TETHER

THE WAR HAD become a permanent obsession with Wells. His days, as he said, were filled with war efforts. What could he do? What ought he to do? And what, he wondered, were the dangers that lay in wait? He asks these questions in *The Happy Turning,* a little book in which he seems to slip away from reality, but which is just a roundabout approach to the problems that were haunting him. He was living the war with an intensity born of his usual complete surrender to the immediate; but he was already thinking of the afterwar period, and thinking of it with ever increasing dread; his dreams were nightmares in which he battled fiercely against the scourges that were ready to smite the human race. According to him, it was practically impossible to hope that the present series of world wars would end in anything better than a confused alliance against the military power of the lawless states, whatever might be the resultant nominal victories or defeats. He foretold that the constant strain of these struggles would lead to a progressive lowering of moral standards; this, in his view, being the blackest feature of the second world-shaking tempest of war.

He was a very angry old man, standing his ground, defiant and sometimes alone, against the world's folly. He understood how greatly people's minds had been disturbed by the Russian attack on Finland. But he knew, from the very beginning, that Russia would soon be in the allied camp. He knew, too, that the British government had refused to guarantee the independence of the Balkan States. Stalin had been forced to realize that Russia was isolated. He had done everything he could to gain time. It was the British Foreign Office, maintained Wells, that had forced Russia to conclude a nonaggression pact with Germany. But the English conservatives could not forgive Stalin for the pact. Wells tried to prepare people's minds for tomorrow's change of attitude; this seemed to him to be the most urgent task of the moment.

Despite the protests of his family and friends, he obstinately refused to leave London during the blitz. Through all the infernal nights of the Battle of Britain he stayed at home in Hanover Terrace. The house was near the junction of five main railway lines. Incendiary bombs came spattering down all around it. One night, one beautiful, moonlight night, the gasoline tank at a nearby station was hit, and a shower of fiery sparks was carried far and wide. Wells and his servants became expert at discovering and quenching outbreaks of fire. He got used to the sleepless nights, the wailing sirens, the rumble of falling masonry, the clang of twisting metal, the crash of broken glass. He seemed to feel no fear, only a very violent indignation. When the din of the explosions became too unbearable, he would begin to swear, all the long-forgotten oaths of his boyhood days came back. Hanover Terrace was emptying around him, as its other inhabitants yielded to the persuasion of the evacuation authorities. But Wells remained, and each day brought fresh food for his anger. One night a huge bomb hurtled past the Terrace; the house next door collapsed, and the blast of the explosion might easily have destroyed Wells's own home, but the bomb went down so deep that it merely sent up a spout of mud into the sky. Thanks to these chances of war, he acquired, he declared later, a sense of precarious security. But he also acquired a conviction that the war had become intolerable and must be ended at the earliest possible moment. He set his hopes on the possibility of Russia joining in.

At the end of September he left for the United States. For three months he tried to explain to his numerous American audiences the reasons that had led Russia to sign a treaty with Germany and to invade Finland. He often came up against sharp opposition. He found that economic and financial circles everywhere, but particularly in America, were "almost insanely anti-Bolshevik." He persisted, none the less, in pointing out the necessity of co-operation with Russia, whole-hearted co-operation, sufficient to smooth away suspicion not only for the duration of hostilities, but after the war as well. Once again he had gone ahead of public opinion, and consequently shocked it. He said in 1942 that it made him giddy to see how rapidly the British and Americans had adapted their minds to a new point of view.

His anger found vent in vigorous onslaughts against half-witted politicians and inefficient military leaders. Except for Bernard Shaw, he was the only man who could venture to use such virulent language. And Shaw was content to take a negative attitude behind a screen of verbal fireworks, whereas Wells had a positive and immediate purpose. No paper would have dared to print the things he wrote while the war was at its height, had it not been that they bore his signature, and that implied a very special kind of liberty, a licensed audacity. One of his articles, published in 1941, bore the title: "Why Generals Deteriorate." In it he bluntly stated that so far in the war on the Western front, Britain had thoroughly disgraced herself. He wondered how "this remarkable level of military incapacity" had been achieved. He attributed it to the survival of those old-fashioned ideas of which he considered Pétain to be the living embodiment—Pétain, who had capitulated "as one soldier to another," and expected to be granted full military honors. But the day of professional wars had gone forever. This was either a war for world revolution, or yet another senseless carnage. It was a war where no quarter could be given, a war to avenge millions of slaughtered victims. There would be no Elba for Hitler and his gang. They were criminals who would be executed, like Quisling and all the other Quislings who were still carrying on their treason and setting up barriers against the rising flood of human indignation. "V for Vengeance" was the slogan of the day.

These articles aroused strong resentment in military circles. Wells's humble origin was recalled; what, it was asked, could a onetime shop assistant know about strategy? He answered his detractors with bitter sarcasm. Above all, he accused the governing classes of having drained the war of every vestige of meaning. It had become a stupid squabble about questions of secondary importance, which was delaying or even preventing the world-wide settlement that should have been arrived at long before. The fact that it might kill millions of men made no difference. A lunatic with a revolver could kill a whole family, but he remained a lunatic.

In those dark days, in that discouraging atmosphere, Wells still kept on with his mission of shedding light on the future. He clung to the remnants of his faith. He fought against the surrounding gloom by planning a series of pamphlets whose purpose would be to give an account of everything that the human race had already achieved during its passage through the ages. As though in challenge, he chose resounding titles for these little books—*The Conquest of Time, The Conquest of Distance, The Conquest of Power, The Conquest of Hunger.* Only the first small volume was actually written. Published in 1942, it replaced his old, outdated book *First and Last Things,* which had appeared in 1908. Much that he had foretold in that book had come true in the meantime. He himself commented that the passage on modern warfare, its methods and consequences, was so true to present experience that it might have been written only yesterday. But the general ideas that he had then expressed were no longer in harmony with this winter of discontent. Present-day intellectual life, he declared, with its racial illusions and preponderances, "its American Way of Life, its Dictatorship of the Proletariat, etc.," was as fantastically unreal as some grotesque film by Walt Disney. The conquests that he had thought of describing had been the rapid and astonishing conquests of our planet. But man had trusted entirely to luck and had shirked the facing of reality. Yet this avoidance of all facts that implied danger for oneself and for others, was sheer madness. According to this definition, mankind had indeed slipped down toward lunacy and was now, as a species, mentally unbalanced. The book that still remained to be written by Wells should have been called *The Conquest of Sanity,* without which all the other conquests would be mere hollow deceits.

The Conquest of Time touches on the various factors that had upset the mental stability of the human race. (Later he returned to the same theme with increased energy.) It also analyses the chances of humanity's survival. Its final note is one of forced optimism, one of those lyrical outbursts with which he used to veil his own uncertainties: "The stars in their courses are fighting for the new humanity." *The Conquest of Time* is a mere outline of the themes that he was to take up again, one after another, in the coming years. The relationship between the individual and the species was still in the forefront of his philosophical preoccupations. He looked upon this relationship as the necessary starting point of any journey of exploration into the future of mankind. He felt that the thing to do first of all was to define the notion of the individual as precisely as possible. Despite the fact that before and during the war he was absorbed by completely topical considerations, he found time to prepare a thesis on individual life, which he submitted to London University. He was moved, not only by a sense that the problem urgently required to be solved in the light of strictly scientific data, but also by the desire to revenge those youthful humiliations that he had not even yet forgotten. He could have had all the degrees that the shabby young Wells had striven for in vain, and had them for the asking, *honoris causa*. But it was by a rigorously scientific work that he wanted to gain that D.Sc. that had eluded him in the old days, as though he would thus be bringing together the two ends of his life, or closing a wound.

This work, which he published in 1944 as an appendix to a further volume of reminiscences, bears the title: "A Thesis on the Quality of Illusion in the Continuity of the Individual Life in the Higher Metazoa, with Particular Reference to the Species Homo Sapiens."

He develops his theory on the following lines: The integrality of the highly evolved individual is an illusion. There has never been such a thing as mental unity, it can never be attained. Among the various reactions of the human mechanism there are many behavior systems, loosely connected with each other, which take over the control of the body and share in the illusion of the single self. It is the body that holds the mind together, not the mind that maintains the unity of the body. The body obeys the dominant system of the neuro-sensitive apparatus, but a tremendous variety of other reactions are constantly altering that dominant system. There is not just one John Smith, but five thousand John Smiths, perhaps, all grouped around a central nucleus, the concept of self, the persona of Jung. They are really "a collection of mutually replaceable individual systems held together in a common habitation." A silent struggle is going on within each one of us, a struggle to establish the most coherent system of conduct that may be possible between our dissimilar and often mutually antagonistic selves. Like governesses or policemen, these conduct systems, these dominant neuro-mental reactions, exert an impossibly uniform discipline in their sphere of influence, thrusting all our contradictory impulses down into the subconscious. "An extraordinary amount of unhappiness has been and still is caused in the world by the failure to recognize the fluctuating quality of personality." A great deal of hatred, jealousy and ostracism would vanish from the world if people would only realize the fact of this personal inconsistency.

To grasp the fact that the notion of individual integrality was an illusion, would do more than any amount of "inflamed egotism" to achieve true continuity in life. There is something greater than the individual, something that is older than he and will outlive him. From the ideological viewpoint, an individual is a unique experience. It is by his individual differences that he helps to alter the life of the species. Wells investigates the survival of groups and species, the factors which have determined migrations, the herd instinct, the outdated concept of a collective soul. His thesis ends by predicting the arrival of an elite whose members, like religious mystics, will experience the ecstasy of complete surrender of their jarring selves, a fusion with something mightier than the individual purpose, something that belongs to the whole human race.

In *The Conquest of Time* he had dealt with the interdependence of the individual and the group or species, the contribution made by each to the life of all. Here he stated that every individual life, without a single exception, did something to change the race, and the contribution of the individual endured as long as the race itself. This was an assertion made to defy those dark days when one is tempted to believe that life is really nothing more than "a tale told by an idiot, full of sound and fury." The upheavals, the savagery, the overruling demands of the present hour must not be allowed to conceal the fundamental insignificance of these events, which were only "the birth-pangs of the human release," said Wells emphatically, as though trying to override his own misgivings. But the salvation of that race that we prematurely call Homo sapiens depends on its realization of the dangers that threaten to destroy it. Henceforth this was to be the leitmotiv of Wells's work. Did the present bewildering return to destructive violence mark the beginning of the end of the human race? That was the question he asked himself all the way through a bulky work entitled *The Outlook for Homo Sapiens,* published in 1942, in which he summarized and revised two of his previous books, *The Fate of Homo Sapiens* and *The New World Order.*

The human race was no longer in harmony with the new conditions of life. Within a relatively short space of time it had experienced an unprecedented increase of power. For instance, the total energy expended in the battle of Agincourt was less than that of one single high-explosive bomb. Each new discovery had increased man's power—his power of destruction. The cornucopia, pouring out a flood of inventions, had revealed itself as more dangerous than beneficent. On the eve of the discovery of the atom bomb, Wells admitted his fear that scientists might even now allow themselves to be caught in the net.

The abolition of distance, Wells repeated yet again, had been even more fantastic in its degree than the increase of power. Man had not succeeded in adapting himself to the scale of the new world that he had created. If he did not do so very soon, for this was no time for slow methods, he might easily be exterminated, as other, earlier species had been. Wells considered that the survival of mankind depended essentially on three conditions: the idea and tradition of warfare must be eliminated; the squandering of natural resources must be stopped and their distribution assured by collective economy; and the surplus energy of youth, which had so often upset the peaceful progress of history, must be directed toward loftier aims, worked off in constructive tasks.

These three points were fundamental and inseparable. Wells analyzed the chances of achieving them. He wished to pass on to his readers the sense of urgency that seethed within him. He admitted that he was impatient, and that he could not find the way to hasten matters. But, he added, this was not simply a case of the distress of an old man in a hurry; in the present-day world haste was fully justified, for the human race might, "after all, prove a walkover for disaster."

It exasperated him that other people's minds should be so entirely absorbed by current events as to forget the permanent aspects of the problem. As early as 1942 he wrote that to win the war would not be enough. The disease of the world could no more be cured by getting rid of Hitler and his Nazis, than measles could be cured by scratching. It was, he said, one of the most amazing things known to history that there should be the possibility of death and destruction on an incalculable scale, controlled by a governing class that seemed to have no notion of what was to be done when Hitler had been overthrown. For even if Hitler disappeared tomorrow, Germany would still be "the problem sister among the European States, an embittered and crazy sister clutching the high-explosive bomb."

This governing class, said Wells, had not produced any politician capable of endowing Britain with fresh vision, for in his opinion Churchill was a wartime leader only. Lacking an objective, the British Empire would gradually fall to pieces; Britain would cease to play any decisive part in world policy, and that in a world where danger would still be acute, problems still alarming.

He looked back over the development of aggressive nationalism in Japan, wondering what had become of all those apparently liberal-minded Japanese who had betrayed the confidence of the West. What had happened to the rational element in those who had succumbed? The Japanese rulers in this war were Nazis with no Hitler, Fascists with no Mussolini; and as he pointed out, a headless monster is more difficult to tame or kill than one that has a head. For him, China was the reality, of the first importance, from the mental as well as the military viewpoint. It was not only the largest but also the most malleable mass of humanity in the world. China had withstood modernization for half a century after the awakening of Japan. It was only under pressure of Japan's intolerable outrages that a nationalistic spirit had tragically affirmed itself in China. The collective Chinese mind, said Wells, was a *tabula rasa* on which any constructive idea whatever could be inscribed. The notion that seemed most forcefully prepared to imprint itself upon this virgin awareness was a sort of communism, not the Russian article, but something that he describes as a para-communism of peasant stamp. In this year, 1942, Wells already foresaw the consolidation of the Chinese Red Army, with its partisan methods, so peculiarly suitable to conditions in the country, and the victory of para-communism over Chiang Kai-shek's para-fascism.

He had strangely alert perceptions, this old man who was tracing the picture of postwar conditions while the conflict still raged. He even foretold that Germany, after utterly collapsing, would achieve economic and social recovery with extreme rapidity. The militaristic tradition might hold its own for another generation or two; or Germany might be quicker than the other nations in attaining a liberal socialistic regime. It would all depend on a common, constructive policy among the allies. He stressed the dangerous agitation conducted in Canada by Otto Strasser, one of the earliest Nazis, a man whose hands were stained with blood, yet who was proposing to raise an army to protect Germany against the Bolsheviks and occupy Berlin with "Free German" forces. Wells charged the British Foreign Office with tolerating the activities of such an adventurer and even allowing it to be supposed that he enjoyed the protection of high circles. He also accused the British leaders of having been too hasty in committing themselves to support de Gaulle. He acknowledged that the General had been more clear sighted than his military colleagues as to the value of the Maginot Line and the importance of tanks and airplanes, and that he was animated by strong and sincere patriotism. "But the France that he loves is the France before the great Revolution, the pious and believing France of twenty wealthy families."

Influenced by certain anti-Gaullist French exiles in London, Wells became more and more hostile to the General. In the sequel to his memoirs, which covers the years 1942 to 1944, he gives de Gaulle a whole chapter, entitled "A Sample Adventurer." People, he says, are only just beginning to realize that British foreign policy is dangerously vague and opportunist, and that a more definite statement of its aims might avert costly misunderstandings in the crucial months lying ahead. "We fight to preserve the fruits of two great international revolutions, the great French Revolution which offered mankind liberty, equality and fraternity, and the still mightier effort of Russia to reorganize society upon a basis that would abolish the economic enslavement of the masses of humanity." But he feared that the reactionary elements entrenched in the War Office and the Foreign Office were involving the country in pledges and associations which, in these days of swift retribution, might nullify the sacrifices that the masses were making in their struggle for liberation. With a pen dipped in the gall that he reserved for his particular bugbears, the irascible veteran sketched a savage portrait of the man whom France, occupied yet still united, looked upon as the incarnation of her hopes. He made fun of the simplified pictures of himself that this "artlessly sincere megalomaniac" was handing around. "There is a certain parallelism," he wrote, "between the careers of de Gaulle and Hitler. Both are cases of a reactionary tool getting out of hand through sheer cerebral inflation." He believed that de Gaulle's day was over, that the road to obscurity lay before him, wide and imperative. But even if he disappeared as an individual, he would remain as a type and a warning of the dangers of political confusion.

It was with ever increasing anxiety that Wells looked toward the future. The end of the war, he said, would merely be "a prelude to further conflict"; an undeclared war would succeed the declared one. Russia was dangerously ignorant of the Western world. Western communist propaganda had been an obstacle to reconciliation, a yapping interruption instead of a help toward understanding. The Communists were now hoodwinked by their own short-sighted ideology, which was steadily losing its hold over the imagination. Wells, as he said himself, wrote about communism with prejudice, but not with prejudice in its favor.

He foresaw that there would be irrational and perhaps disastrous friction among the allies. Stalin took his precautions while the war was still going on. In 1942 he told General Sikorki, whom Wells had looked upon as a man of real constructive quality, that he hoped to see Germany completely beaten and disarmed and Poland free, strong, and united with Eastern Europe as a barrier between Russia and the unreliable West. Beneath apparent unity in action, there were already signs of a split into two blocks. The respective zones of influence had been settled in advance. Wells's gaze lingered, heavy with gloom, on the troubles that lay in wait for the world. And his anger was directed with vehemence against the forces that he accused of preparing a further conflict: three incalculable forces, toward which Stalin, too, might adopt an incalculable attitude.

Wells's most ferocious attacks were launched against the Roman Catholic Church. His indignation at its betrayal of a universal mission was strengthened by the terror and repulsion he had felt in childhood. When he wrote *The Conquest of Time,* he was still thinking of that sermon on the torments of the damned which he had heard in Portsmouth cathedral when he was fourteen years old. It was this fear of punishment, of death, that had delayed the maturity of man. "The crucifix, that pitiful, hideous symbol of torture, death, and human abasement, commemorating Paul's triumph over the Nazarene misrepresented and betrayed, fights to sustain our waning fear and abjection in the light of that dawn."

Wells had returned to the virulent anticlericalism of his youth. In *The Happy Turning,* he discusses with Jesus, whom he calls the most famous failure in the world, the reasons for his defeat. "They crucify me every day," says Jesus, "they" being the priests. Wells included the Church of Rome among the forces opposing the world's survival. He published a violent pamphlet, *Crux Ansata,* a rumble of accumulated anger. In *The Outlook for Homo Sapiens,* he speaks of Roman Catholicism as a clumsy system of frustrations, a strange jumble of old traditions and methods, still closely interwoven with the intellectual life of the Western world, and exerting its sway over millions of human beings, and thus the most formidable antagonist of human adjustment to the dangers that lurked in the future.

His resentment was whetted by the wartime political activity of the

Vatican. It was to this influence that he ascribed the injudicious behavior of the Foreign Office in supporting Franco, "the murderous little Christian gentleman"; and he accused Rome of having fostered political hostility between Russia and the Western world. He declared that the number of Catholics who would follow "the pro-German amateur statecraft" of the Pope was one of the Three Incalculables, another of which was the evolution of Great Britain and of the United States. The latter he regarded as even more incalculable and enigmatic. America, he said, was suffering from mental anemia, because her citizens never read books and only glanced at the headlines of their newspapers, thanks to which, the spirit of the country was as lively, inquisitive, and unstable as a monkey's. The war years confirmed this conviction. In the memoirs he brought out in 1944 he defines the English-speaking peoples as "conscious of a quite imaginary superiority, vain and sensitive, capable of enormous mischief, liable to hysteria to an extent unknown to the stabler populations of the eastern hemisphere," and he refers to America as "the great problem-child of humanity."

While his apprehensions were being substantiated by the course of events in this war, his own horizon was darkening. He had been arguing too vehemently, working too hard, giving himself too freely, and now his strength suddenly failed. His illness, diabetes, had taken firm hold of him before he would agree to consult a doctor. But at the back of his mind he knew that the health factor played only a very small part in his sudden breakdown. In 1942 he wrote that he had been almost shattered by the sight of the evil things that had been going on for the past six years—the wanton destruction of homes, the merciless hunting down of human beings, the bombardment of defenseless cities, the cold-blooded massacre and mutilation of children and harmless people, the raping and shameful humiliation, and above all the return of a deliberate, organized torture, mental torment, and terror that men had hoped were gone forever from the world. He could not manage to revive his optimism, that power of forgetfulness common to British and Americans, which leaves the dead to bury their dead. "The dead past is dead," he wrote, "but not for us. We have been too near it and we are splashed with blood."

It was this fellowship with suffering and horror that preyed upon the last years of his life. The allied victory was close at hand. A breath of liberation passed over the tortured human race. But what lay in store at the end of conflict and bloodshed, when the nightmare would be over? He felt no share in the great hopes that were finding expression all over the world. The Atlantic Charter was only a vague diplomatic promise, it might mean everything or nothing. "The occupation and disarmament of Germany will end nothing; it will only inaugurate a scramble of such egocentric 'liberators' as de Gaulle and his like, of the Roman Catholic Church, of the Communist Party, of the romantic Polish nationalists in exile, of every silly little intractable patriotism, and of the Big Business and banking systems, with their immense and stupid cunning," he repeated in 1944, with the same insistence as in 1942.

What chance remained for humanity to escape its destined doom? Wells had given its broad outline in *The Outlook for Homo Sapiens*. He details certain of its points in *Phoenix,* but adds: "This is the statement of hope and not of faith." A world revolution still seemed to him to offer the only possible way out of chaos. This revolution would have to include a world-wide socialist system, scientifically planned and directed, a legislation based on a declaration of human rights, and entire liberty of expression.

It was to the declaration of the universal rights of man that Wells gave the greater part of his time during the war, for he considered these rights to be a primary necessity, the fundamental law of a unified world. Since the very beginning of the struggle, far-sighted people had been asking, "What are we fighting for?" Wells was one of those who supplied the answer: for the rights of man. A circular was sent to a number of eminent personages, and the general public was asked for its opinion. A committee was formed to sort out the replies and to draft a Declaration of the Rights of Man. This committee consisted of ten members, including Wells, and had as its Chairman Lord Sankey, whose name remains associated with this first attempt at a charter for humanity. "These ten people," writes Wells, "had embarked upon the most important job human beings have ever attempted."

Unimagined difficulties arose during the discussions. But what chiefly exasperated Wells was the fact that his colleagues did not share his almost religious zeal. They arrived late, glanced often at their watches, and bolted off as early as possible on the plea of pressing engagements. The sense of urgency seemed to him to be absent from their meetings, as though they felt the Declaration were something not quite practicable, not quite real. He got impatient. He accused himself of lacking the subtlety of mind and the tact which were required for such difficult negotiations. He began a veritable crusade to promote this fundamental law of world unity. He gave lectures whenever a favorable opportunity seemed to present itself; he started violent arguments, denounced adversaries, assembled fervent believers. He tested the document on which the committee had reached final agreement, by having it translated into Chinese and Hindustani and submitting it for the approval of the School of Oriental and African Studies in London. He concerned himself over its dissemination, and was delighted with the help given by microfilm experts, who could photograph the document after translation into all the languages of the world.

He admitted later that he overtaxed his limited store of energy "by screwing myself up to the job more and more, the more complex it became." He gradually perceived, particularly during his enforced rest, that the document drafted by the Sankey Committee was too localized, too personal, and too parliamentary. He set to work to revise it. At the same time he was still going on with his plan for the world revolution. Ill-health hampered him greatly, he said he felt like a motorist whose clutch begins to slip at every hill.

His great dream was haunting him again. Was this Western revolution an Open Conspiracy too? Among the primary necessities of universal peace he had always included freedom of speech. The first duty of the world citizen was to fight for that freedom, not merely to resist all attempts to suppress it, but to find his own way through the fog. Wells emphasized that the chief reproach brought by the Atlantic world against the Soviet regime was that it had suppressed freedom of thought, freedom of the individual, for the sake of the community. But, he said, "We do not deplore the Russian Revolution as a Revolution. We complain that it was not a good enough Revolution and we want a better one." He blamed the Communists for their wildly irrational propaganda, which weighed like a tremendous threat over the West, and added: "It is difficult to overestimate the harm the dogmatism of the Communist party has done to human emancipation." But his personal quarrel with certain of Russia's representatives, and his anger, which often found expression in violent objurgations, did not make him swerve from his course. The end of the war would not be the peace, he reminded his readers when the conflict was at its height. Everything could be destroyed without remedying the principal evils.

How to get rid of the frontiers dividing the sovereign states, that was still the crucial problem. The only force capable of abolishing the rival sovereignties was that third factor of man's survival, world socialism. This was the hope to which Wells clung with the most persistent faith. There was something almost mystical in the obstinacy with which he proclaimed the inevitability of a great social change. "You may murder world socialism now and hide it in the cellar, and when you go upstairs again you will find it astraddle your hearth," he wrote in his souvenirs of 1942 to 1944.

The last of war made London skies an inferno once again. But the danger seemed to revive Wells's fighting spirit. He passed unharmed through the V1 and V2 raids, a sick old man, but with an aggressive spirit that no trial had sufficed to damp. In December, 1944 he wrote to me, giving a brief account of his life during the years when no news had filtered through the walls that cut off our gagged and bound country from the outside world. "I stick here," he wrote, "amidst my books, and say what I like, and every doodle-bug, or missile of any sort, misses me until I find it hard not to develop a conceit of invulnerability. I am angry with the Anglo-American Royalist tones, almost beyond measure, and the expression of this anger in effective terms is my principal activity."

He was rather surprised at finding himself still alive when the war ended. During his illness, a doctor had told him that he had the same weakness of the heart which had caused the sudden deaths of his father and his eldest brother, and warned him that he could not outlast the year. Was this a respite? Or a new lease of life? But his display of pugnacity, the defiance that he flourished like a banner in battle, served in reality to conceal a profound distress. In 1945 he brought out a little book with the characteristic title, *Mind at the End of Its Tether*. A very little book indeed, only thirty-four pages. He had never before been, or wanted to be, so brief. But these few pages set forth the conclusions of his whole life's activity. They summarize long compilations, verbose expositions, accurate prophecies, errors, optimistic forecasts that had not come true, battles lost or won and since forgotten. He himself described the book as a conclusive end, and asserted that its author, so far as fundamental things were concerned, had no more to say and never would have. Most of the assembled material, he added, could now be thrown away, like the scraps left behind in a laboratory sink after the termination of some piece of research.

These are the conclusions of a man exasperated by the folly of the world and the vanity of his own work, conclusions reflecting a despair that nothing can now lighten. "The end of everything we call life is close at hand and cannot be evaded."

Wells was thinking chiefly of the autobiographical notes that he had brought together during 1942 to 1944, and which had been published in a limited, expensive edition because he wanted to confine them to a small public. He compares this book, written during a period of physical discomfort and moral indignation, with the cries of angry people in a train which has rushed past once and for all. Now that he has recovered his lucidity, nothing remains of his old illusions, his hopes in a world revolution. Final disaster confronts the human species. He explains the reasons which have led him to this conclusion, a conclusion which is staggering to our habit of carrying on a normal existence in relation to past experience but not in relation to coming events, inevitable as they may be. In reality, he says, even quite unobservant people are beginning to notice that something very strange has come into life, that it will never again be what it was in the past. This element of "frightful queerness" comes in the first place from the sudden revelation that there is "an upward limit to quantitive material adjustability." Wells reviews his whole body of work. He had always believed in the natural sequence of life, the convergence of all changes that took place, like a rising spiral. He had believed that events were linked in a certain coherence, rather like the golden cord of gravitation that holds the heavenly bodies in place. But now the cord seemed to be broken. Chaos, incredible chaos, reigned throughout the world. Facts could no longer be marshaled in accordance with a predictable model, the pattern of things to come. At the beginning of Wells's conscious life there had been the discovery of the future; toward the end of his life he knew that no further trust could be placed in any kind of logical evolution. And knowing this, he saw no more meaning in life. What was the use of denouncing an inefficient general, a stupid diplomat, a brutal exploiter or the Catholic Church itself; what was the use of bursting one's lungs in justifiable rage? It was only a sleep-walking fury. "There are thousands of mean, perverted, malicious, heedless and cruel individuals coming into daylight every day, resolute to frustrate the kindlier purposes of man."

Wells's faith in humanity was dead. A cycle of his life had closed. Man was the enemy of man. Cruelty had submerged the world. Cruelty had become law. A force was governing the universe—a force hostile to survival, a cosmic process which must lead to final destruction. He sought to define this force, this still unknown quantity which had something of the inevitability of Greek tragedy. He called it the Antagonist.

For a long time, a very long time as men reckon time, the Antagonist had tolerated life. Now he had turned against it, decided to wipe it out. *Our* universe, the one into which even our own generation was born, had not only collapsed but completely vanished, without leaving so much as a trace of its ruins. "The human story has already come to an end . . . and Homo Sapiens in his present form played out. . . . The stars in their courses have turned against him and he has to give place to some other animal better adapted to face the fate that closes in more and more swiftly upon mankind."

This was Wells's final message. He was seventy-nine years old. Looking back over his personal career, he could say he had warmed both hands before the fire of life; and, condemned now to the subdued existence of an invalid, he felt that he was ready to depart. Not without emotion, he remembered the optimism of his early years, so different from his present stoically cynical frame of mind. But however thoroughly, in his thoughts, he had torn up all hope by the roots, he could not strip off his own nature, where a shred of dream still lingered. All his lucidity told him that there was no way out, no side road to avoid the deathtrap. "This is the end," he repeated. But before he closed his book, with its terribly negative summary of man's chances of survival, something stirred again to life in him, an irrational impulse or an inveterate habit. As though against his own will, a final sentence slips in: "But my own temperament makes it unavoidable for me to doubt . . . that there will not be that small minority which will succeed in living life out to its inevitable end."

He died, August 13, 1946, in London.

Mind at the End of Its Tether stands as his last will and testament. With this book, his life came to its real conclusion. Long months of illness, of suffering, of enfeebled existence carried him beyond this true departure, his true end. His private life, full and passionate, tempestuous and contradictory, had been subordinated to his work, had been simply a function of the task he had taken up. Sincerely and without false modesty he believed himself to be the possessor of an average brain, a typical representative of the human mass. He did not think his writings would outlive him, for he regarded them merely as milestones along his path, a clear path toward a definite goal. But the very intensity with which he responded to every summons of contemporary events, the passionate eagerness with which he flung himself into every struggle, made him the confluent of all the currents of his time, of all its hopes, of its distress, of its victories, and of its defeats. He defined himself one day, in passing, summing up the significance of his life and his creative activity: "The trace of the flow of thought during the past half-century."

BIBLIOGRAPHY

PRINCIPAL WORKS OF H. G. WELLS

1895   Select Conversations of an Uncle
       The Stolen Bacillus and Other Stories
       The Time Machine: An Invention
       The Wonderful Visit
1896   The Island of Dr. Moreau
       The Wheels of Chance
1897   Certain Personalities
       The Invisible Man
       The Plattner Story and Other Stories
1898   The War of the Worlds
1899   Tales of Space and Time
       When the Sleeper Wakes
1900   Love and Mr. Lewisham
1901   Anticipations
       The First Men on the Moon
1902   The Sea Lady
1903   Mankind in the Making
       Twelve Stories and a Dream
1904   The Food of the Gods and How It Came to Earth
1905   Kipps: The Story of a Simple Soul
       A Modern Utopia
1906   In the Days of the Comet
       The Future in America
1907   The Misery of Boots
1908   First and Last Things
       New Worlds for Old
       Socialism and the Family
       The War in the Air
1909   Ann Veronica
       Tono-Bungay

1910 The History of Mr. Polly
1911 Floor Games for Children
     The New Machiavelli
1912 Marriage
1913 Little Wars: A Floor Game Book
     The Passionate Friends
1914 An Englishman Looks at the World (in America: Social Forces in England and America)
     The Wife of Sir Isaac Harman
     The World Set Free
1915 Bealby: A Holiday
     Boon: The Mind of the Race, The Wild Asses of the Devil, and The Last Trump (as Reginald Bliss)
     The Research Magnificent
1916 The Elements of Reconstruction (as D.P.)
     Mr. Britling Sees It Through
     What Is Coming?
1917 God: The Invisible King
     Italy, France, and Britain at War
     The Soul of a Bishop
     War and the Future
1918 In the Fourth Year: Anticipation of a World Peace
     Joan and Peter: The Story of an Education
1919 The Undying Fire
1920 Frank Swinnerton (with A. Bennett & G. M. Overton)
     The Outline of History
     Russia in the Shadows
1921 The Salvaging of Civilization
1922 The Secret Places of the Heart
     A Short History of the World
     Washington and the Riddle of Peace
1923 Men Like Gods
1924 The Dream
     The Story of a Great Schoolmaster (F. W. Sanderson)
     A Year of Prophesying
1925 Christina Alberta's Father
1926 Mr. Belloc Objects to the Outline of History
     The World of William Clissold
1927 Democracy Under Revision
     Meanwhile (The Picture of a Lady)
1928 The Book of Catherine Wells
     Mr. Blettsworthy on Rampole Island

The Open Conspiracy (as What Are We To Do With Our Lives?
    1931)
The Way the World Is Going
1929 The King Who Was a King (novel from film)
The Science of Life (with J. S. Huxley & G. P. Wells) (parts pub-
    lished separately, 1937)
1930 The Autocracy of Mr. Parham
1932 The Work, Wealth and Happiness of Mankind
1933 The Bulpington of Blup
The Shape of Things to Come (as film, Things to Come, 1935)
1934 Experiment in Autobiography: Discoveries and Conclusions of a
    Very Ordinary Brain
1935 The New America, the New World
1936 The Anatomy of Frustration: A Modern Synthesis
The Croquet Player
The Man Who Could Work Miracles (film)
Treasure in the Forest
1937 The Brothers
Brynhild: or, The Show of Things
The Camford Visitation
Star-Begotten: A Biological Fantasia
1938 Apropos of Dolores
World Brain
1939 The Adventures of Tommy (illustrated by the author)
The Dictator
The Fate of Homo Sapiens (in America: The Fate of Man)
The Holy Terror
1940 All Aboard for Ararat
Babes in the Darkling Wood
The New World Order
1941 Guide to the New World
You Can't Be Too Careful
1942 The Conquest of Time (written to replace First and Last Things)
The Outlook for Homo Sapiens (amalgamation of The Fate of
    Homo Sapiens and The New World Order)
Phoenix
Science and the World-Mind
1944 Crux Ansata: An Indictment of the Roman Catholic Church
'42 to '44: A Contemporary Memoir Upon Human Behaviour Dur-
    ing the Crisis of the World Revolution
1945 The Happy Turning: A Dream of Life
1946 Mind at the End of Its Tether

INDEX

Index 335

Sheridan, Clare, 191

Sikorski, General, 319

Simmons, A. T., 65, 72, 80, 83, 86

"Slip under the Microscope, A," 37, 38, 41, 73

Snowden, Philip, 212

Social Forces in England and America, 230

Socialism, 47 ff., 145, 238, 241
world, 323

Socialist Party, The Educational Aims of the, 238

Sokols, 257

Soul of a Bishop, The, 203 ff.

Spencer, Herbert, 102

Stalin, 286, 319
pact with Germany, 311

Stead, W. T., 107

"Stolen Bacillus, The," 105, 106

"Story of Tommy and the Elephant, The," 130

Strasser, Otto, 317

Submarines, German, 182

Suffragette movement, 175-176

Sweden, in 1939, 301

Tanks, article on, 190

Teleferic scheme of Wells, 192

"Thesis on the Quality of Illusion in the Continuity of the Individual Life in the Higher Metazoa, . . .," 314

Time Machine, The, 78, 105-106, 108, 109, 126, 131, 232, 254, 299

Tolstoy, Count Alexis, 285

Tono-Bungay, 1, 6, 7, 20, 29, 60, 63, 81, 90, 155 ff., 174, 205, 264

Trotsky, Leon, 7

Undying Fire, The, 15, 204-205

UNESCO, inquiry into totalitarianism, 297

United States:
visits to, 283, 292, 311
Wells's attitude toward, 140, 230-235, 320

"Universe Rigid, The," 88, 89, 98

University Correspondence College, 84, 87, 92, 98

University Correspondent, The, 93

Up Park, 6, 7, 17, 22, 24, 29, 42, 69 ff., 84, 156

Up Park Alarmist, The, 56

Utopians, in *Men Like Gods*, 236-237

Verne, Jules, 107, 108

Victoria, Queen, 6, 13

Wales, school in, 66-68

War and the Future, 197

Ward, Mrs. Humphrey, 162, 164

War in the Air, The, 143-145, 152, 282

War of the Worlds, The, 120 ff.

War That Will End War, The, 190

Webb, Beatrice, 140-141, 171

Webb, Sidney, 140-141, 171

Welles, Orson, 121

Wells, Catherine Robbins, 93 ff.
appearance of, 94-95, 126
attitude toward free love, 166
death of, 252
in France, 250-251
meeting with Wells, 93-94
sense of humor of, 212-213, 214
visits Wells, 97
Wells's life with, 110, 116, 125, 165-166, 210-214, 243-244, 251-253
with Wells in London, 100-101, 103 ff.
writings of, 211, 213

Wells, Frank (brother of H. G. Wells), 6, 20, 28, 73, 89, 153